7th Edition

LEGAL OFFICE PROCEDURES

Joyce Morton, Ed.D.
Saddleback College

PEARSON
Prentice Hall

Upper Saddle River, New Jersey 07458

Library of Congress Cataloging-in-Publication Data

Morton, Joyce.
   Legal office procedures   /   Joyce Morton.— 7th ed.
     p. cm.
   Includes index.
   ISBN 0-13-220956-X
1. Legal secretaries—United States—Handbooks, manuals, etc.   I.   Title.
   KF319.M67 2007
   340.068—dc22   2005030582

Editor-in-Chief: Vernon R. Anthony
Director of Production and Manufacturing: Bruce Johnson
Senior Acquisitions Editor: Gary Bauer
Editorial Assistant: Jacqueline Knapke
Development Editor: Deborah Hoffman
Marketing Manager: Leigh Ann Sims
Marketing Coordinator: Alicia Dysert
Managing Editor—Production: Mary Carnis
Manufacturing Buyer: Ilene Sanford
Production Liaison: Denise Brown
Full-Service Production and Composition: Heather Willison/Carlisle Publishing Services
Manager of Media Production: Amy Peltier
Media Production Project Manager: Lisa Rinaldi
Senior Design Coordinator: Christopher Weigand
Cover Design: Eva Ruutopold
Printer/Binder: King Printing Co., Inc.
Cover Printer: Phoenix Color

Pearson Prentice Hall™ is a trademark of Pearson Education, Inc.
Pearson® is a registered trademark of Pearson plc.
Prentice Hall® is a registered trademark of Pearson Education, Inc.

Pearson Education Ltd.
Pearson Education Singapore, Pte. Ltd
Pearson Education, Canada, Ltd
Pearson Education—Japan

Pearson Education Australia PTY, Limited
Pearson Education North Asia Ltd
Pearson Educación de Mexico, S.A. de C.V.
Pearson Education Malaysia, Pte. Ltd
Pearson Education Upper Saddle River, New Jersey

8 9 10   V0CR   13 12 11
ISBN 0-13-220956-X

Dedication

This book is dedicated to my husband, Gordon Wyatt Wiles,
whose understanding, patience, support, and love have made this edition possible.

CONTENTS

PREFACE

The material in this book has been organized in a logical, step-by-step manner to provide the terminology, background, and knowledge of the legal procedures required to work in a law office. Overall, the text is simple and concise, designed to assist students who have little or no background in the legal field. For practical applications, the Student Assignments at the end of each chapter provide relevant and interesting projects to complete that deal with various areas of the law.

ORGANIZATION OF EACH CHAPTER

The text follows a logical organization, with chapters building on each other and on prior chapters. Each chapter provides an excellent learning experience and is organized as follows:

1. Objectives
2. Chapter text
3. Summary
4. Vocabulary
5. Student Assessment
6. Student Assignments

Objectives are listed at the beginning of each chapter that identify the material to be covered in that chapter. The chapter text reflects this organization and presents the material in an orderly manner. The Summary reviews the material presented in the chapter, and the Vocabulary section provides definitions for the words highlighted in the chapter. The Student Assessment provides questions that evaluate the learning process and reinforce understanding of the topic covered. The Student Assignments provide relevant and interesting learning activities that have been taken from a sample law office.

ORGANIZATION OF THE TEXT

The fifteen chapters are organized into six main parts:

Part 1 The Law Office

Chapter 1 provides a background of the law office and those persons involved in its operation. Chapter 2 provides an overview of the duties required of the legal support staff. Chapter 3 provides information on the dramatic changes that have occurred in the law office as a result of advances in technology, software, and telecommunications. Chapter 4 discusses the preparation and formatting of legal correspondence.

Part 2 Court Structure

Chapter 5 discusses the court structure and its influence on the legal environment.

Part 3 Litigation Procedures

Chapters 6, 7, and 8 deal with preparing legal documents and the procedures involved in the litigation process. This section covers the preparation of pleadings and other court papers used in civil matters, from the initial filing of a lawsuit through discovery, trial, and the appellate procedures.

Part 4 Substantive Law

Part 4 (Chapters 9 through 13) describes the other areas of the law, such as family; wills, trusts, and probate; business organizations; real estate; and criminal law. These chapters focus on increasing your knowledge of the law while providing activities that improve document processing skills and understanding of the procedural sequence. Actual legal cases that have been adapted into practice sets provide realistic training in these areas of the law.

Part 5 Legal Research

Chapter 14 provides information on the U.S. legal system and the sources for doing legal research. Activities provided at the end of the chapter make use of Internet search procedures that relate to the legal field.

Part 6 Getting a Job

Chapter 15 helps those seeking employment as a legal administrative assistant in a law office to assess their strengths and weaknesses and outlines a guide to prepare for employment and develop a job search plan to achieve that goal. This chapter discusses sources for employment, suggestions for preparing a résumé, the letter of application, and follow-up procedures.

FEATURES OF THE BOOK

This book contains many features that provide excellent information and training for the law office staff.

CD-ROM

Documents have been recorded on the CD-ROM that is located in the pocket in the back of the book. Since this is a "read-only" CD, you will have to save your completed documents to your disk or hard drive. This CD includes legal documents that you use for the completion of the various projects. These documents have been created in Microsoft Word and can be easily converted to other software programs used by most schools.

As you complete the projects, you are instructed to key changes to the documents, save a copy to your disk or hard drive, and print a hard copy for your instructor. Simulation activities are presented for most chapters, which enable you to prepare documents in a "real life" office scenario using the legal skills for the document preparation outlined in the chapter.

Practice Sets

The practice sets at the end of selected chapters are prepared in conjunction with the text and provide you with practical experience in performing the actual work involved in preparing a client's case. These projects provide you with information relating to various areas of the law, as well as the manner and sequence in which these papers are prepared. The areas covered include:

1. Personal Injury
2. Probate (Testate)

3. Corporation
4. Unlawful Detainer (Eviction of a Tenant)
5. Criminal Law

The practice sets are actual court cases in which the names, dates, and circumstances of the case have been changed somewhat to make them suitable for student use. Cases have been selected from areas of the law that would most frequently occur in the law office and with which the legal office support staff would most often come into contact.

Internet Legal Research

The legal research chapter contains end-of-chapter projects that require you to use the search engines of the Internet to find information relating to the law. With the many advances taking place in technology, this is an interesting and relevant exercise.

Illustrations

The book contains illustrations of legal forms relating to each section of the law. They are presented in the sequence in which they would be used in the preparation of the case. Though it is impossible to include all the forms, a good sample has been selected to represent the various areas of the law and the procedures each chapter covers.

Photographs

Many of the law office pictures included in this book were taken at the Office of Jackson, DeMarco, Tidus, and Peckenpaugh law firm in Irvine, California, and the law firm of Graham & James in Costa Mesa, California. The models in the pictures are attorneys, legal office administrators, and legal support staff. Some of the models are former students of the author who have pursued a career in the legal field.

Instructor's Support

Instructor's Manual. The instructor's website provides an *Instructor's Manual* with teaching suggestions as well as the answers to the Student Assessments (*chapter tests*) and the final exam. Samples of the hands-on Student Assignments (*projects*) are also included.

Instructor's PowerPoint Presentation. A PowerPoint presentation with slides for each chapter is also available for instructors using this book.

Instructors can obtain these materials, with an access code, at www.prenhall.com.

RELEVANT LEARNING EXPERIENCES

This book has been designed to prepare you to perform office skills in today's rapidly changing legal environment, and to help you take the necessary steps to plan your career goals. Understand, however, that legal procedures, filing fees, and the format of documents and their captions and headings will vary from state to state and jurisdiction to jurisdiction. You should be able to adapt to the procedures used and preferred by your particular office. Also, legal procedures and laws change regularly, and it is important that you and your attorney stay abreast of these constant changes.

Though this book will give you the necessary background to work as a law office professional, each area of the law is vast and complex. It is impossible to cover every case or procedure that you may encounter in a law office, and it is this variety that makes legal work so interesting. After completing this book, you may find that certain areas of the law are particularly attractive to you, and these may be the areas in which you will want to specialize. You may obtain this specialization through employment and experience, or you may want to obtain additional training and education.

SUMMARY

This book introduces you to the career of a legal professional. It presents basic legal concepts and the various fields of law and outlines the preparation of documents commonly used in these fields. After completing this book, you should be able to select documents appropriate for a particular situation, identify the information necessary to complete the documents, and prepare the documents correctly.

ACKNOWLEDGMENTS

Thanks should go to *David Thorne* and staff at Jackson, DeMarco, Tidus, and Peckenpaugh for their cooperation in allowing us to take pictures of their legal office, staff, and equipment. Thanks should also go to *Sharon A. Owen*, Office Administrator at Gibson, Dunn & Crutcher, LLP, for her help in allowing us to take pictures of her law firm, and the help and access she has provided to us in the legal community.

Thanks should go to *Caterina Tuminello*, with Gibson, Dunn & Crutcher, Irvine, California. Her knowledge, law office experience, and contributions have been important in the preparation and organization of this book.

My grateful thanks to the following reviewers whose excellent suggestions have been invaluable in the revision of the 7th Edition of *Legal Office Procedures*.

Cheryl Canty, Esq., Field Sales Representative, Thomson-West
Nancy Commerdinger, Gibson, Dunn & Crutcher, LLP
Kathleen Constance, Application Specialist II, Saddleback College
Lynn Jahnke, EA, Larson and Risley
Chandra Moss, Attorney at Law, Violet Woodhouse
Jason B. Seleno, I.T. Manager, Jackson, DeMarco, Tidus, and Peckenpaugh
Sherman Winnick, Professor, South Coast College

Special thanks to the reviewers of this text: Dora Dye, City College of San Francisco, San Francisco, CA and Laura Barnard, Lakeland Community College, Kirtland, OH.

Part 1

THE LAW OFFICE

Chapter 1

THE LAW OFFICE

OBJECTIVES

Upon completion of this chapter, you should be able to:

1. Briefly describe how law offices may vary in size
2. Discuss the different types of law that may be practiced
3. Describe how technology has changed the law office
4. Discuss desirable personal qualities of the law office staff
5. Describe the different professions and careers represented in the law office
6. State desirable ethical and human relations qualities required of support staff
7. Discuss the associations that support law office professionals
8. Demonstrate an understanding of law office terminology

Law offices vary in size from a single office with one attorney and one full- or part-time **support person** to a suite of offices with many attorneys and support personnel. Also, two attorneys with their own private practices often share a reception room and the services of one support person or secretary between them.

When a law firm is organized as a **partnership**, generally it does a larger volume of business than a one-attorney office. This type of practice may consist of the partners, associates, law clerks, legal assistants or paralegals, legal secretaries, support personnel, bookkeepers, file clerks, and a receptionist.

Some law firms may have both senior and junior partners, associates (attorneys who are not partners), senior law students (sometimes called law clerks) who usually do library research or assist with the preparation of the briefs, the support staff (which may include legal assistants, legal secretaries, and a receptionist), a bookkeeper or accountant, and a law office manager. In smaller offices, a secretary or support person, in cooperation with the attorney, may be responsible for all the duties performed by a larger staff.

Law firms vary in size and organization. They may be organized as a sole proprietorship, partnership, **limited liability company (LLC)**, or **professional corporation**. An LLC is a combination of the partnership and the corporation. The main advantage of the LLC is that it allows for limited personal liability for company debts (just as a corporation does), but it is treated like a partnership for income tax purposes. An incorporated law firm may be a single individual or have a large staff and facilities. An incorporated law firm is patterned more like a corporation, while a partnership operates on the basis of the agreement signed by the partners.

Law offices also may be classified according to the type of law practiced by the firm. For example, a law office specializing in probate work may require a different staff than an office that specializes in criminal work. Much of the probate work can be done by a qualified support person, legal secretary, or legal assistant, whereas a criminal practice requires more time and preparation on the part of the attorney in court appearances and trial work. There are many special areas of the law, for example, personal injury, domestic and family, corporate, wills and probate, estate management, patent, maritime, and international. Each area of law has different personnel requirements.

As a prospective support person, you may want to ask yourself these questions:

- Do I want to work for a large or small firm?
- In what areas of the law do I want to specialize?
- What responsibilities in a legal office would I like to have, and what duties am I qualified to perform?

TECHNOLOGY IN THE LAW OFFICE

Today's legal office employees work in an environment that has seen many changes as a result of the use of technology. The use of computers, the Internet, and electronic equipment has changed the nature of the operation of the legal office and the manner in which attorneys and legal professionals perform their jobs. The basic office tasks of placing and answering telephone calls, keyboarding documents, greeting clients, arranging meetings, filing, and performing numerous other jobs related to the office are no longer the responsibility of the legal administrative assistant.

These duties are performed by all the staff, regardless of the degree of responsibility, from an entry-level position to someone at the management level. Knowledge of the use of computers and the Internet has become a requirement for all employees at all levels. Though understanding the use of technology is important, it is also important to be a team player and to be able to interact with others on a day-to-day basis in a cordial and effective way.

As technology has affected the way we function in the office, it has also changed the appearance of the office. It is not unusual to see notebook computers and cell phones being used, and they can be taken with you anywhere you might go. Your home, car, and hotel room can also serve as an office, as new technology allows employees to access, send, and receive information wherever they might be. Technology has revolutionized the traditional law office and transformed it into a computer-based administrative center.

HUMAN RELATIONS IN THE LAW OFFICE

Human relations is not just getting along with people—it is much more than that. Legal professionals never know what situations they may encounter until they answer the phone, access their e-mail, listen to their voice mail, or greet clients. It is important to respond in a manner that will create a positive attitude for the firm. Your performance on the job is closely linked to your ability to communicate and get along with others, and this will depend on your understanding of human relations (see Figure 1-1).

The relationships among the attorney, client, and legal professionals are very special. Because law is a profession concerned with helping others to solve their problems, most people who come to a law office need assistance. The welfare of the client is of primary concern to the attorney and other members of the legal staff. Law is a helping profession, and the client—be it an individual, business, or corporation—is seeking the help, advice, and counsel of the attorney.

Human relations is:

- Building and maintaining relationships with many different people, such as coworkers of different cultural backgrounds

- Knowing how to handle difficult situations when they arise
- Understanding yourself and others (personality, behavior, and attitudes)
- Being a team player, and taking responsibility for your part of the workload and for the problems that arise within the scope of your job

Reception

Clients usually are referred to a law practice by other clients or friends. Typically, the first person a prospective client meets in the law office is the receptionist or legal professional. The manner in which clients are greeted is a reflection of the attorney and the professional atmosphere of the law office. Support staff should be pleasant, dignified, and courteous in their relationships with clients and outside visitors (see Figure 1-2).

CONFIDENTIAL RELATIONSHIPS

Legal professionals must use discretion in their relationships with clients. They can listen sympathetically to clients' problems and concerns, but they are not authorized to give opinions or legal advice. Oral and written communications between the attorney and client in the course of working in a law office should be kept in the strictest confidence. The attorney's representation of a client is confidential in nature and should not be discussed socially or outside the law office (see Figure 1-3).

Privileged Communications

Privileged communication exists between the client and the attorney. Privileged communication also exists between the attorney and support staff. Information relating to the client received through the performance of a job in the law office is also considered privileged communication. Law office support staff cannot be called on to testify in court concerning information learned about clients (see Figure 1-4).

FIGURE 1-1 *First impressions can be very important to prospective clients.*

FIGURE 1-2   *Law office reception areas can be very attractive.*

FIGURE 1-3   *Information relating to the client's case needs to be discussed.*

THE ATTORNEY

The words **attorney** and **lawyer** commonly are used to designate those who practice law. The attorney has probably spent four years in college as a prelaw major and then three years in a public or private law school. In order to receive a license to practice law in a given state, prospective lawyers must pass the state bar exam. To practice in another state they must also pass the bar exam in that state. When they pass the exam and receive their licenses, they are admitted to the bar. (The term **bar** comes from the phrase *bar of justice*, and **barrister** is the term used in England to denote someone who has passed the bar.)

Some attorneys take the bar in more than one state so that they can practice in states other than the one in which they live. Many attorneys continue their

FIGURE 1-4 *Information relating to the client is confidential and should not be discussed outside the office.*

education and specialize in a particular field or area of law (see Figure 1-5). After passing the bar, an attorney may want to become an accountant in order to specialize in tax law. Another attorney might decide to go on to medical school and specialize in medical malpractice or personal injury. While it is not required that attorneys practicing in these specialized areas attend other professional schools, many feel that the knowledge acquired as a result of this education will improve their skills in the practice of law (see Figure 1-6).

In general, the larger the law firm, the more titles the attorneys may have. For example, a large law firm may have titles for senior partners, partners, junior partners, senior associates, associates, and junior associates.

Government law offices have different titles for their attorneys, such as district attorney, prosecutor, public defender, advocate, and so on. Corporate legal departments also have different titles for their attorneys, such as general counsel, general attorney, or some other title depending on the nature of the company. In order to use these titles, each individual must have passed the bar in the state in which they are practicing.

The actual owners of the firm are the partners, and they receive a percentage of the profits. The founders of the law firm are generally the senior partners, and they have a greater ownership interest than the other partners. Associates are paid a salary. They are not allocated an ownership interest in the firms and do not share in the profits.

Because laws are changing constantly, attorneys need to keep informed of these changes. They may do this by attending legal seminars, professional meetings, and conferences; through subscriptions to legal newspapers and journals; and by keeping their law libraries current with the addition of legal supplements.

Some states may mandate that an attorney keep current on the law, and this may be done through a subgroup called **Continuing Legal Education** or **CLE**. These subgroups offer information on the law provided in a variety of forms, from the traditional seminars, books, and videotapes to the latest forms of communications, such as videoconferencing, teleconferences, and webcasting. Attorneys also can gain professional information and association by belonging to organizations that relate to the legal profession, such as the **American Bar Association (ABA)** or their own state or local bar association.

FIGURE 1-5 *Preparing cases for trial is an important responsibility of the attorney.*

FIGURE 1-6 *Attorneys spend a good part of their time on the telephone.*

THE LAW CLERK

Law students wishing to get practical experience in a law office on a part-time basis will often seek employment with a law firm or work for judges in the court system. These students have usually completed at least two years of law school. Their duties, of course, vary with the size of the firm, but include legal document preparation, drafting pleadings, case investigation, legal research, as well as miscellaneous duties that assist the attorney. This practical experience familiarizes the student with the day-to-day operation of the law firm, and in some instances may help the student obtain a full-time position when law school is completed and the bar is passed.

Professional Associations

While many local and state bar associations are available to the attorney, the national bar association is the ABA:

American Bar Association
321 North Clark Street
Chicago, IL 60610
(312) 988-5000
www.abanet.org

THE LEGAL ADMINISTRATOR

While the managing attorneys are responsible for the daily *legal* operation of the law firm, and dividing the caseload among the attorneys, most large law firms employ someone to handle the business and administrative operation of the firm. Many law offices now have full- or part-time office administrators. The responsibilities of the job depend on the size and complexity of the law office. The duties of the job may include one or more of the following categories: personnel, finance, facilities, and equipment.

Personnel

The **legal administrator** usually is important in the selection, evaluation, and termination of nonlawyer personnel. Administrators are responsible for assigning work and maximizing the resources of the support staff. Administrators implement standard operating procedures and usually mediate employee conflicts. The administrator also manages employee benefit matters, such as tax savings plans and health benefits.

Finance

An administrator may also be responsible for overseeing the firm's day-to-day billing, collections, and other financial operations. An administrator may supervise or prepare budgets and financial and accounting statements.

Facilities and Equipment

The law office administrator usually is responsible for determining office space requirements, furniture, computer systems, communications equipment, and library resources. The job of the administrator is to make recommendations to the decision makers and then handle the details of purchasing, leasing, and disposing of office systems and equipment.

Professional Associations

The professional association for legal administrators is the **Association of Legal Administrators (ALA)**:

Association of Legal Administrators (ALA)
75 Tri-State International, Suite 222
Lincolnshire, IL 60069-4435
www.alanet.org

The goal of the ALA is to enhance the competence of the legal administrator and the legal management team.

FIGURE 1-7   *Delegation of responsibility is important.*

THE PARALEGAL/LEGAL ASSISTANT

Law firms often employ nonlawyer assistants, called **paralegals** or **legal assistants**, whose duties can include interviewing, legal research, case preparation, interrogatories (written questions), probate (proving a will), and office management. Most of the larger law firms have two different positions, with the paralegal having additional responsibilities. In a smaller firm, however, the paralegal may have both paralegal and administrative duties.

This is a comparatively new field, and training programs vary. Day and evening courses have been developed, along with the requirements for licensing and certification of legal assistants. Anyone interested in pursuing a career as a legal assistant can check with local community colleges, universities, and private schools concerning programs and courses available. Training programs may vary considerably from nine months to one year, two years, and four years.

Paralegals and legal assistants work under the supervision of the attorney and are not authorized to give legal advice (see Figure 1-7). A survey of job possibilities in the intended area may be desirable prior to taking the specialized courses needed to become certified. Knowledge of software applications is important, as much of the preparation of documents is done using a computer.

Professional Associations

There are local professional paralegal associations as well as two national professional organizations for paralegals:

National Federation of Paralegal Associations
P.O. Box 33108
Kansas City, MO 64114
(816) 941-4000
www.paralegals.org

National Association of Legal Assistants, Inc.
1516 South Boston Avenue, Suite 200
Tulsa, OK 74119-4013
(918) 587-6828
www.nala.org

FIGURE 1-8 *Good working relationships are essential.*

THE LEGAL ADMINISTRATIVE ASSISTANT, LAWYER'S ASSISTANT, AND LEGAL PROFESSIONAL

The functions of the **legal administrative assistant**, legal assistant, or **legal professional** are many and varied. The terms describing this function are used interchangeably in the legal profession, but all describe the person who assists the attorney and provides administrative support in the exacting work of the law office (see Figure 1-8). For all practical purposes, in this book, this person shall be referred to as the "legal administrative assistant," "lawyer's assistant," or "legal professional."

The first person to greet the client entering a law office may be the receptionist or the legal administrative assistant. Because first impressions are often lasting impressions, it is important that this person be professional, thoughtful, considerate, and courteous. The legal professional should exercise tact in contacts with clients and treat them with courtesy and consideration.

Duties of the Legal Professional

Although the duties of the legal professional vary according to the size and type of law that is practiced in the law office, this person should have the following skills and be able to perform the following functions:

1. Understand legal terminology and legal office procedures
2. Maintain office records and files
3. Prioritize office tasks
4. Maintain the law library and keep books current
5. Order and maintain office supplies
6. Sort, organize, and prioritize mail
7. When necessary, transcribe dictation accurately
8. Assist the attorney in the smooth operation of the law office

This person should also be familiar with the use of technology and have the following skills to assist in the smooth operation of the office:

1. Knowledge of the computer and software applications
2. Compose and send e-mail messages
3. Ability to distribute documents electronically
4. Receive and place telephone calls
5. Send and receive faxes
6. Using an intelligent copier to send documents electronically
7. Electronically arrange meetings and conferences
8. Prepare clients' fees and statements
9. Maintain office and court calendars
10. Research information on the Internet

The level of skill and responsibility required of the legal professional has changed considerably, and this person is expected to handle people as deftly as he or she handles computers (see Figure 1-9). In fact, many legal professionals are now required to do jobs that a decade ago would have been considered managerial responsibilities. In the office of the future, keying letters and paper filing may be the least of the tasks that the legal professional performs (see Figure 1-10).

Working hours have also become more flexible. The concept of working 9 a.m. to 5 p.m. Monday to Friday is disappearing. With computer networking, many legal office professionals perform some of their responsibilities from a home computer. Flextime is a growing trend that saves both the employer and office professional time and money.

Flextime   Flextime allows employees to decide on their own starting and ending time. The office usually establishes a two- or three-hour time frame in which employees may select the start or end of their workday. There are generally core hours when all employees must be present in the office. When flextime has been an option, absenteeism and tardiness are usually reduced, and employee morale is improved. Flextime allows the employee greater flexibility in meeting their personal needs, such as child care, elder care, and scheduling medical appointments.

FIGURE 1-9 *Competent law office professionals provide valuable support for the attorney.*

FIGURE 1-10 *Scheduling appointments and calendaring are important duties of the legal support staff.*

FIGURE 1-11 *Consideration for others is important.*

Personal Qualifications

In addition to performing the preceding functions, a good legal administrative assistant or legal professional should be willing to assume responsibility and get along well with others (see Figure 1-11). This person also should have the personal qualities described in the following paragraphs.

Attitude

The role the legal professional plays in the attorney-client relationship is an important one. **Empathy** with and understanding of clients and their problems can do much to improve the client's relationship with the law office. Even though the staff may not give legal advice, the ability to listen can contribute to the human relations of the office and the success of the attorney. Good legal office staff get along well with the attorneys and the other members of the office. They are considerate of others, courteous, and thoughtful in their relationships.

The ability to get along with others, neatness in personal appearance and work habits, willingness to learn and grow on the job, and a friendly smile for clients are all important **attributes** of the legal staff.

Discretion

The ability to exercise good judgment and discretion is another important quality of law office staff. Because of the confidential nature of the attorney-client relationship, all business matters in the law office must be considered confidential. As a general rule, the only person who should discuss a case with a client is the attorney.

Loyalty

A sense of dedication to the position and a desire to do the best job possible are important attributes of the legal staff. Loyalty to the employer and the employer's clients is equally important. If excessive demands are made, the responsible person should be able to communicate his or her feelings to the attorney and keep the lines of communication open. The legal staff should be helpful in assisting the attorney in identifying problems, as well as in identifying solutions to problems.

Accuracy

A good legal professional is a perfectionist, particularly in the preparation of court papers and legal documents, proofreading all work carefully and paying minute attention to detail. It is important to make accurate entries in the calendar, to watch all deadlines, and to file documents on time. A wrong date on a calendar could result in a case being lost. Being systematic in work and being organized in keeping records, meeting deadlines, and keeping court dates are also necessary for the smooth operation of the office.

Appearance

The law office is a professional office, and those working in the office should look professional (see Figure 1-12). The legal staff should wear conservative clothing that reflects the professionalism of the law office. If there is uncertainty as to what is appropriate, new employees should take their cue from the dress worn by other office staff. Of course, each person will want to express her or his own style and taste, but this is an indication of what is considered to be appropriate dress for the office.

Desire to Learn

An inquisitive mind and the desire to learn are important attributes of good legal professional. Choosing the legal profession is an excellent career for anyone eager to learn, as the law and legal procedures are changing constantly (see Figure 1-13). These changes alone result in a stimulating and challenging job.

Legal Ethics, Responsibility, and Confidentiality

Ethics is an important topic, not only because a law office or attorney can be disciplined for violating ethical rules, but because it also determines whether quality legal

FIGURE 1-12 *Neatness in appearance and good work habits are important in the office environment.*

FIGURE 1-13 *Accurately transcribing and proofreading legal documents are necessary skills.*

services are provided to clients. The American Bar Association's *Model Rules of Professional Conduct* states that

> "a lawyer having direct supervisory authority over the nonlawyer shall make reasonable efforts to ensure that the person's conduct is compatible with the professional obligations of the lawyer . . ."

The following items suggest how the law office staff may avoid confidentiality problems.

- Do not talk to people outside the law office about what goes on in the law office, whether or not it is client related.

- Only talk to other members of the office staff on a "need-to-know" basis. Do not go around the office talking about a client's case to employees who do not have a reason to know about it.
- Do not discuss the specific facts or circumstances of a client's case to anyone—not even friends or relatives.
- Always clear your desk of other case files when meeting with clients. If a case file is left open, other clients can read the files and have access to confidential information.
- Do not take phone calls from other clients when meeting with a client. Be aware of who is in your office when talking about confidential matters on the phone.
- Managers must create policies and systems to ensure confidentiality. Under legal malpractice theory, a law office that reveals client confidences through its employees may be legally liable to the client for damages that result.

CODE OF ETHICS FOR ATTORNEYS, LEGAL ASSISTANTS, AND LEGAL PROFESSIONALS

Codes of ethics have been adopted in the field of law. In 1969, the American Bar Association adopted *The Code of Professional Responsibility*. The code is divided into three sections: canons, ethical considerations, and disciplinary rules and has been amended regularly since that date. See Figure 1-14 for some of the canons.

FIGURE 1-14 *An excerpt from the American Bar Association's* Canons of Professional Responsibility. *(Courtesy of the American Bar Association)*

AMERICAN BAR ASSOCIATION
CANONS OF PROFESSIONAL RESPONSIBILITY

1. A lawyer should assist in maintaining the integrity and competence of the legal profession.
2. A lawyer should assist the legal profession in fulfilling its duty to make counsel available.
3. A lawyer should assist in preventing the unauthorized practice of law.
4. A lawyer should preserve the confidences and secrets of a client.
5. A lawyer should exercise independent professional judgment on behalf of a client.
6. A lawyer should represent a client competently.
7. A lawyer should represent a client zealously within the bounds of the law.
8. A lawyer should assist in improving the legal system.
9. A lawyer should avoid even the appearance of professional impropriety.

The *Code of Ethics* from the National Association of Legal Assistants is given in Figure 1-15.

Professional Associations

It is important that the legal professionals support the profession by participating in professional associations. Professional associations for legal support staff can be found in almost all cities. These organizations provide opportunities for legal professionals to interact with one another and grow professionally. Some associations provide educational opportunities to help members develop a high standard of performance. These organizations have developed a code of ethics for members and publish reference materials and handbooks to assist those working in the profession.

NALS (The Association for Legal Professionals) NALS originally was formed to enhance the careers of legal secretaries. As the profession evolved, so did

FIGURE 1-15 *National Association of Legal Assistants Code of Ethics and Professional Responsibility, Canons 1–5. (Courtesy of the National Association of Legal Assistants)*

The National Association of Legal Assistants

Code of Ethics and Professional Responsibility

In **2001**, NALA members also adopted the ABA definition of a legal assistant/paralegal, as follows:

A legal assistant or paralegal is a person qualified by education, training or work experience who is employed or retained by a lawyer, law office, corporation, governmental agency or other entity who performs specifically delegated substantive legal work for which a lawyer is responsible. (Adopted by the ABA in 1997)

Canon 1.
A legal assistant must not perform any of the duties that attorneys only may perform nor take any actions that attorneys may not take.

Canon 2.
A legal assistant may perform any task which is properly delegated and supervised by an attorney, as long as the attorney is ultimately responsible to the client, maintains a direct relationship with the client, and assumes professional responsibility for the work product.

Canon 3.
A legal assistant must not: (a) engage in, encourage, or contribute to any act which could constitute the unauthorized practice of law; and (b) establish attorney-client relationships, set fees, give legal opinions or advice or represent a client before a court or agency unless so authorized by that court or agency; and (c) engage in conduct or take any action which would assist or involve the attorney in a violation of professional ethics or give the appearance of professional impropriety.

Canon 4.
A legal assistant must use discretion and professional judgment commensurate with knowledge and experience but must not render independent legal judgment in place of an attorney. The services of an attorney are essential in the public interest whenever such legal judgment is required.

Canon 5.
A legal assistant must disclose his or her status as a legal assistant at the outset of any professional relationship with a client, attorney, a court or administrative agency or personnel thereof, or a member of the general public. A legal assistant must act prudently in determining the extent to which a client may be assisted without the presence of an attorney.

NALS. The information needed by legal secretaries was changing along with their job descriptions, and the information provided by NALS paralleled this shift. Diversity of membership reflected a changing legal services industry.

After several years of discussion on the topic of a name change to better reflect the nature and membership of NALS, it was determined that NALS would no longer be used as an acronym but rather as a name. This was determined because it was evident that something needed to change but the rich history could not be abandoned. NALS determined to go with the new name along with the tag line "The Association for Legal Professionals" in 1999.

Today NALS remains a leader in the legal services industry, offering professionals development by providing continuing legal education, certifications, information, and training to those choosing the legal services industry as a career (see Figure 1-16). NALS members represent every area of this industry from paralegals and legal assistants to legal administrators and office managers (see Figure 1-17). Because of this diversity and an openness to welcome all members of the industry, NALS offers a broad spectrum of expertise to make the programs offered valuable to all members of the legal services industry. This allows NALS members to learn about other areas of the industry, making career enhancement as well as advancement easily attainable.

Information about NALS and its education and certification programs can be obtained from:

NALS, The Association for Legal Professionals
314 East 3rd Street, Suite 210
Tulsa, OK 74120
Phone (918) 582-5188
E-Mail: Info@nals.org
Fax: (918) 582-5907

FIGURE 1-16   *NALS Code of Ethics. (Courtesy of NALS)*

NALS *Code of Ethics and Professional Responsibility*

Members of NALS are bound by the objectives of this association and the standards of conduct required of the legal profession.

Every member shall

- Encourage respect for the law and the administration of justice;
- Observe rules governing privileged communications and confidential information;
- Promote and exemplify high standards of loyalty, cooperation, and courtesy;
- Perform all duties of the profession with integrity and competence; and
- Pursue a high order of professional attainment.

Integrity and high standards of conduct are fundamental to the success of our professional association. This Code is promulgated by the NALS and accepted by its members to accomplish these ends.

SUMMARY

Law offices may vary in size from a single practitioner with part-time staff to a partnership or large corporation. The law office may also vary in the type of law that is practiced, which may include personal injury, domestic and family, criminal, corporate, or wills and probate.

Technology has had a dramatic impact on the traditional law office and has changed the responsibilities and duties of the office staff. The use of the computer, the Internet, and electronic equipment has redesigned and modified the nature of office work.

Relationships in the law office and with clients are very important. Legal matters and communications should be courteous, confidential, and professional. In addition to the attorney, members of the staff may include a legal administrator, legal assistants, legal administrative assistants, support staff, and a receptionist.

Desirable professional and ethical qualities are important requirements for those working in the legal profession. Professional associations are available in almost all cities and provide opportunities for interaction, education, certification programs, and professional growth.

FIGURE 1-17 *Desirable professional requirements are important in the legal office.*

VOCABULARY

American Bar Association (ABA)   The professional association that represents attorneys in the United States and to which most attorneys belong.

Association of Legal Administrators (ALA)   A professional association for legal administrators.

attorney   One legally appointed by another to transact legal business.

attribute   An inherent characteristic.

bar   Lawyers as a group are sometimes referred to as *the bar*. This term is derived from English courts; the bar is the place where the accused stands in a court.

barrister   In England, a counsel admitted to plead at the bar and undertake the public trial of causes in the superior court, as compared with the English solicitor, who advises clients and represents them in the lower courts. The American attorney-at-law may try cases in either the higher or lower courts.

Continuing Legal Education (CLE)   State organization dedicated to providing attorneys with an ongoing education.

empathy   The capacity to understand the feelings or ideas of another.

ethics   Principles of conduct governing an individual or profession.

lawyer   An attorney; a legal counselor.

legal   Permitted or established by law; lawful.

legal administrator   A person responsible for the efficient operation of the law office.

legal assistant   A person qualified to perform substantive legal work that requires knowledge of the law. May research cases but is not authorized to render legal advice. Activities are always carried out under the supervision and direction of the attorney.

legal administrative assistant   An employee in a law office or legal department who performs tasks necessary for the smooth functioning of the office and the procedural aspects of legal matters.

legal professional   Employee in the legal field.

limited liability company (LLC)   A hybrid form of legal structure that combines the corporate and partnership form.

paralegal   See *legal assistant*.

partnership   An association of two or more individuals to carry on a business, the profits and losses of which are to be shared in a prescribed manner.

personal injury   A personal wrong; an injury to one's person; bodily injury.

privileged communication   Communication that is not subject to disclosure in a court of law.

professional corporation   In a professional corporation, the founding attorney or attorneys receive shares in the business.

support person or staff   The person or staff in the law office assisting the attorney in the performance of duties.

STUDENT ASSIGNMENTS

PROJECT

1. Visit a local law office.

    a. Discuss with your instructor the possibility of visiting a local law office.

    b. Contact the local law office; ask for someone in charge of the support staff, and identify yourself as a student in a legal office procedures class.

    c. Set up an appointment to interview someone on the support staff about ten responsibilities of his or her position and five reasons why this career opportunity was selected.

2. While visiting a local law firm, observe the type of attire worn by the staff. Write down ten apparel items you would consider appropriate to wear.

3. Observe the professional interactions among the office staff. What did you notice about those interactions?

4. Analyze the *Canons of Responsibility* for the American Bar Association and the *Code of Ethics and Professional Responsibility* for NALA and NALS. How do they vary, and what similarities did you find?

2

OFFICE DUTIES

OBJECTIVES

Upon completion of this chapter, you should be able to:

1. Explain the changes taking place in workplace telecommunications
2. Describe new features available in telecommunications and how they can assist legal professionals in becoming more efficient in communicating
3. Explain the changes taking place in voice mail
4. Explain the advantages of VoIP (Voice over Internet Protocol) and cell phones
5. Discuss the skills necessary for the proper use of the telephone
6. Explain the use of e-mail
7. Discuss the advantages of faxing information
8. Describe calendaring procedures
9. Explain different billing procedures
10. Describe the different attorney fees
11. Discuss the features available on office photocopiers
12. Explain the elements of a filing system
13. Discuss the duties of a notary public
14. List the different postal services available and why they are used
15. Discuss the resources for travel arrangements

WORKPLACE TELECOMMUNICATIONS

As a result of rapid advances in technology, many different telephone systems and features are available to improve **telecommunications** (see Figure 2-1). It is important to be familiar with these new telephone systems and their capabilities. Many offices may respond to a call with a voice message or number selection for contacting their party.

The following features may be available on your telephone system:

- *Conference call.* allows you to speak to a number of people at once
- *Call forwarding.* allows calls to be forwarded to another number or destination
- *Preferred call forwarding.* calls from specific telephone numbers to be forwarded
- *Hold features.* delay your current conversation with privacy
- *Speaker options.* allow hands-free use of the telephone
- *Privacy features.* allow screening of incoming calls
- *Caller ID.* displays the telephone number of incoming calls
- *Call coverage.* allows for certain telephones in pickup groups to answer telephones that may be unattended
- *Cost allocation feature.* captures information for billing charges to clients

Current telephone systems have many capabilities that can save time and effort. Learn about these features and apply them, when available, to make efficient use of time (see Figure 2-2).

Voice Mail

Voice mail is an answering system recording a caller's voice for later playback. Instead of having an answering machine for each office telephone, most large law offices have a voice answering system for the entire office. Your office will train you on how to set up your voice mailbox, and your messages can be retrieved at the office, at home, or from a cell phone. Your mailbox can be opened by keying in an individual access code or password, and after the voice message has been heard, it can be deleted, forwarded, stored, or you can respond to it by dialing the caller who sent you the message. Your office will train you on how to set up your voice mailbox and record a greeting. You can use a standard greeting or personalize your greeting.

VoIP (Voice over Internet Protocol) Telephones

VoIP phones operate similar to standard phones except the voice message is converted into a computerized sound file and processed using Internet Protocol procedures. This phone service uses the integration of digital technology and the Internet and can store and display information about the length of calls and the lists of calls sent and received. An office using VoIP makes and receives calls in the same way as those using a standard phone, and the VoIP technology is transparent to both the caller and the receiver. If full VoIP is implemented in an office, it is possible to make long distance calls at almost no charge because there is no Internet charge for the amount of voice or data that is sent.

Cell Phones

Cell phones have become a standard means of communication in our society. These are small, wireless phones that can send and receive information. Most cities and rural areas in the United States offer cell phone service. Today's cell phones use digital technology and come with many attractive features. They can be connected to the Internet and fax machines, can receive e-mails, and can be used to receive pictures, music, and short video clips. Cell phones even come with built-in cameras, which is causing security and personal privacy concerns.

Though the cell phones being built in the United States do not work overseas, there are companies that now sell or rent cell phone systems to travelers to foreign countries.

TELEPHONE SKILLS

Answering the telephone in a law office requires skill, experience, tact, and understanding. In many instances, the client communicates with the attorney primarily by means of the telephone. The telephone manner of the legal professional indicates to the caller how efficient the office is. It is important to be cheerful on the telephone and to speak clearly and slowly. Attitudes do travel by telephone.

Here are some pointers to assist in developing good telephone techniques:

1. Answer all calls promptly, within a certain number of rings. There is nothing more annoying to a caller than having to wait for the telephone to be answered.
2. Determine how the attorney wants the telephone answered. For example, "Good morning, law offices"; "555–1183"; "Mr. Morgan's office, Miss Burns speaking"; or "Mr. Morgan's office, Mr. Morgan's assistant speaking."
3. Be friendly, courteous, and professional; give the caller your full attention.

FIGURE 2-1 *Organized files help in placing phone calls.*

FIGURE 2-2 *Telephone equipment is becoming more sophisticated. This is an example of a digital phone with many options. (Courtesy of Jackson, DeMarco, Tidus, Peckenpaugh, A Law Corporation)*

4. If you do not recognize the caller, ask for the caller's name and try to determine the nature of the call. This provides an opportunity to obtain information about the case for the attorney.

5. Do not give a caller any information about clients, cases, or law office business unless permission has been given to do so.

6. When taking a message, be sure to get the correct spelling of the caller's name, the telephone number including area code (see Figure 2-3), and the time of the call. (Repeat the telephone number to be sure it is correct.) If there is a different area code, write it down (see Figure 2-4). If the message is lengthy, write it on a longer piece of paper than those used for message pads.

FIGURE 2-3 *Support staff should be careful in recording telephone messages.*

FIGURE 2-4 *Sample telephone messages.*

TELEPHONE MESSAGE

TO: *Mr. Morgan*   DATE: *6/10*

FROM: *Mr. John Lewis* TIME: *2:15 p.m.*

OF *Superior Court*

PHONE NO: *(714) 832-4430*

☒ URGENT!   TIME DEADLINE *by 5:00 p.m. today*

☒ TELEPHONED   ☒ PLEASE CALL
☐ RETURNED CALL   ☐ WILL CALL AGAIN
☐ WAS IN   ☐ WILL RETURN

MESSAGE: *Wants to discuss filing on Jones and Wilson P.I. Case #38620 Wants to hear from you by 5:00 p.m today.*

RECEIVED BY *Betty*

TELEPHONE MESSAGE

TO: *Mr. Morgan*   DATE: *6/8*

FROM: *Mr. Walt Pray* TIME: *10:30 a.m.*

OF *Fullerton Savings and Loan*

PHONE NO: *(714) 870-3660*

☐ URGENT!   TIME DEADLINE

☒ TELEPHONED   ☒ PLEASE CALL
☐ RETURNED CALL   ☐ WILL CALL AGAIN
☐ WAS IN   ☐ WILL RETURN

MESSAGE: *Wants to discuss Sales contract on Smith property in Fullerton*

RECEIVED BY *Betty*

7. Some offices prefer to have telephone messages noted on a log or in the client's file. Find out what procedures are followed at your office.

8. Some offices bill their clients for incoming calls that require legal information. Check with the attorney to determine preferences.

9. Encourage law office staff to advise someone on the support staff when they leave the office and how they may be reached. Systems for noting the location and availability of staff save office time and avoid unnecessary telephone calls.

10. Be sure to understand where the attorney would like the messages placed, and deliver all messages promptly.

A telephone directory for the office, as well as for the attorney, should be kept. Support staff may also want to have personal directories at their work stations.

Telephone Tag

Many of us spend a considerable amount of time playing "telephone tag." You call a person and receive her voice mail—she calls you back and receives your voice mail—you call that person, again. This may continue for some time and become very frustrating to both the caller and the receiver. One way to handle this problem is to establish a specific time of day to return the call. If that person is not available at that time, leave a message as to when you will be calling back, or you might leave one of the following messages on your voice mail:

I will be out of the office tomorrow morning, but I will be available to receive and return calls tomorrow from 1 p.m. to 5 p.m.

Or,

I will be in my office tomorrow between 9 a.m. and 12 noon, and I will be accepting and returning calls between 3 p.m. and 5 p.m.

Telephone Directories

There are several types of telephone directories that may be helpful to establish.

Rotary Files   A rotary file where rotary file cards are manually inserted and deleted can be created by using computer software templates and printing out the cards on a laser printer.

Computerized Directories   Depending on the computer software, computerized telephone and address directories may also be created. These directories may take the form of a database where data can be sorted, searched, cross-referenced, and prioritized. The data from this file can also be used to generate office documents, letters, statements, and labels. This list may include numbers for the courthouse, other attorneys, the local bar association, legal stationery suppliers, and other places contacted on a regular basis.

Long Distance Calls

Time Zones   When making a long distance call, take into consideration the time zone of the destination called (see Figure 2-5). For example, calling Hawaii at 1:00 p.m., California time is noon Hawaii time, which may be the lunch hour of the person called. If you call Los Angeles, California, from Chicago, Illinois, at 9:00 a.m., there may be no one in the office, since it is 7:00 a.m. in California. Keep the time zones in mind when making long distance calls. A time zone map usually is included in most telephone directories.

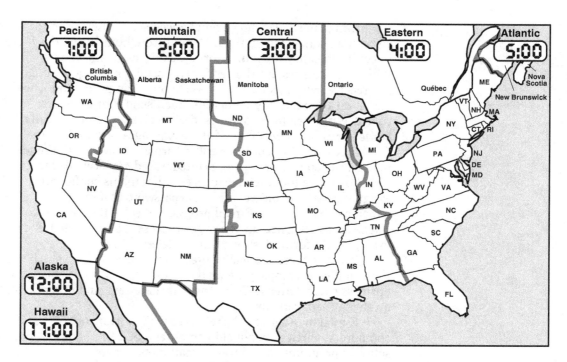

FIGURE 2-5   *Time zone map of the United States.*

If you need to make a long distance call and you do not know the number, call long distance information at 1-(desired area code)-555-1212.

If you are unsure as to the time of the location you are calling, you can use the following websites on the Internet to check the current time in over 500 cities. These websites will assist you in determining the time at your call destination.

Time and Date Information:

www.timeanddate.com/worldclock
www.worldtimeserver.com
www.worldtimezone.com

E-Mail (Electronic Mail)

E-mail can be defined as the transmission of messages by computer from one person to another. It involves using the computer, a modem, and communications software and is an electronic system for sending and receiving messages that is quick and easy to use.

Each user has an E-mail mailbox that must be accessed through a special code or password. Electronic mail is rapidly replacing telephone calls and business letters because it eliminates frustrating phone tag, saves on expensive delivery charges, makes it easy for clients to receive information and immediate support, and provides a printed record.

E-mail is popular because of the speed at which information can be transmitted and the fact that it can be sent and stored in an electronic form when the recipient is ready to receive it. The cost does not depend on the size of the document or the distance traveled, and a person can send an electronic message and attach to it a report, picture, spreadsheet, or graphic. While picture and sound quality depend on the equipment used, video messaging, and audio and video files can be sent with e-mail.

E-mail messages can be sent between computers in the same office or between computers connected on the Internet throughout the world. It is a convenient way to communicate with your attorney, team members, clients, and other businesses. With an e-mail system the sender will send a message through the computer and the receiver will receive the message on a computer, and it will automatically be stored on the receiving computer. Each sender or computer needs to have an assigned e-mail address, as does the receiver, which typically takes this format: *name@business.com*. One of the advantages of e-mail is that the recipients can quickly respond to a message and return an answer to the sender. Messages can be read on the computer screen, printed, saved, or forwarded to another receiver.

To ensure that each person's e-mail remains confidential, each user should be assigned a mailbox and a confidential password that must be entered before the user's e-mail can be accessed. E-mail programs display the list of incoming messages that can be accessed. Once the message is accessed and selected, the user can do the following: reply, forward, save, print, or delete.

Because there are few printed e-mail directories, you should make your personal and your company's e-mail addresses readily available by including them on business cards, letterheads, in the body of letters, and in marketing brochures, and by giving them verbally.

E-mail messages can be retrieved while you are out of the office using notebook computers, wireless handheld computers, or cell phones. Sophisticated computer software programs can convert e-mail messages into words so that the receiver can listen to e-mail messages by telephone.

There are also disadvantages to using e-mail. Messages can be lost or delayed if there is a computer malfunction. There is also a tendency to electronically share jokes on the Internet, which can be time consuming. Companys have a legal right to monitor employee e-mails to make sure employees are using company equipment and time appropriately. Be sure you are familiar with your company's policy regarding the use of company equipment and e-mail.

E-Mail Guidelines

Carefully check that you have keyed in the correct e-mail address. Most companies use the first letter of the first name with the last name as an individual's e-mail address. Therefore, John Smith who works at Law Offices would probably use JSmith@LawOffices.com as his e-mail address.

- Check your e-mail messages regularly throughout the day, just as you would traditional incoming mail. You may want to set a certain time aside each day for checking messages and responding to them.
- Keep your messages as concise as possible. With the advent of electronic mail, legal professionals receive many messages each day, and most people do not have the time to read lengthy e-mails.
- Delete messages regularly so that you do not have to read through old ones. If you want to keep your messages, you can save them to electronic folders or a diskette.
- Be sure to use an appropriate subject line—the decision to read or not read an e-mail in a busy office is often based upon the subject line.
- E-mail messages travel to many readers, so never send anything through e-mail that you do not want to be made public.
- If someone sends you an e-mail message, always get that person's permission before forwarding it on to others, as the writer may have assumed that the message was confidential. Also, be careful what you write as it may be passed on to others.
- When you are out of town, use the Automatic Reply feature to notify the sender that you will be out of town for a certain period.

- Use discretion in using the Reply All or Copy features unless the recipients will benefit from the e-mail. Office staff frequently complain about the unnecessary and redundant e-mails that are received.
- Use your spellchecker and reread messages before sending them. Check the facts and figures, as sending out incorrect information can create delays and legal complications.
- E-mail can be sent at all hours, and communication with a person in a foreign country or another time zone is not restricted by your local time.
- When sending e-mails internationally, be aware of cultural differences, and do not use slang, as it can be mistaken or offend someone of another culture.
- Do not open questionable e-mails. If the subject line is strange and you do not know the sender, the e-mail may contain a virus.
- Under United States law (the Controlling the Assault of Non-Solicited Pornography and Marketing Act of 2003, also known as CAN-SPAM Act of 2003), it is illegal to send commercial e-mail (1) that uses a false address, header, or subject line to mislead the recipient regarding the subject of the e-mail, (2) that does not provide the recipient with the opportunity to request not to receive future e-mails from the sender, or (3) that the recipient has indicated an objection to receiving.

Some offices use encryption software to protect e-mail messages; if your office provides this service, use it when appropriate.

Format

Heading   Most e-mail recipients scan the subject line to determine the nature of the e-mail. Therefore, for best results:

- Keep each message to one topic.
- Be concise in the subject line.
- Send yourself a blind copy (bcc) of important messages for your files.

Body   Use the first few sentences to explain what you want and who you are.

- Keep your message concise.
- Focus on the topic and use correct grammar, and if you are unsure of your spelling, spell check your message.

Signature   Closing statements are no longer required in e-mails.

- Most electronic programs include signature footers that will include your name, company, department, address, telephone, and fax numbers. These are automatically created and attached to all the messages you send.

FAXES

A fax machine (**facsimile** machine) is a standard piece of equipment in most offices and is used to send exact copies of reports, letters, graphics, and so on over a telephone line. A laser scans a page and converts images, text, or graphics into an electronic signal. The document is converted to electronic signals and is sent to a receiving fax machine. The copy is printed when the fax is received. Remember, a fax sent via a modem is only a *picture* of the document—not the document itself—so it cannot be edited. However, some machines send the electronic signals to a computer instead of a fax machine, and the document is stored on the disk of the computer as a regular document and can be edited. If no computer is involved, only the hard copy is received and the document cannot be edited.

Most fax machines conform to international standards and can send a document to a foreign country for the cost of a phone call. Fax machines that are connected to their own telephone line can answer the telephone and automatically receive the information transmitted.

The advantages of fax machines are similar to e-mail, and especially useful when you need an exact copy of a document displaying the signature. Be careful when you are entering the fax number because if it is sent to the wrong number, it may be sent to the trash. Some fax machines keep a transmission log so that you can check to see that the fax was sent to the correct number. Other fax machines may print the first page of the document to confirm the number and that the document has been sent.

A cover sheet is usually sent with the faxed documents, and law offices usually have templates (stored documents) that have been set up on the computer for faxing purposes. You can also fax to groups or address lists. This is known as a *broadcast fax* or *blast fax*. This is an efficient and low-cost method of sending many faxes to groups of people or overseas at low-cost rates.

CALENDARING

The practice of law is filled with appointments, deadlines, court dates, deposition dates, and other commitments. It is important for any law office and the support staff to track this information (see Figure 2-6). Law offices control these events by calendaring. Individual lawyers, paralegals, and staff usually maintain personal calendars.

A **calendar** is a daily record of appointments and future meetings. Most law offices maintain two calendars, an office calendar and a court calendar.

Accurate and dependable calendaring is very important in the operation of the law office. Deadlines play an important part in the activities of the law office, and law offices should have calendaring systems for recording these significant dates to ensure that all deadlines are met.

FIGURE 2-6 *It is important to calendar all court dates and appointments.*

Computer Software

Many firms are expanding their calendaring systems through the use of computer software. These programs remind the user of tasks that need to be accomplished by beeping and flashing a message on the computer screen.

Office Calendar

The **office calendar** is used to record office appointments; deadlines for the payment of bills, taxes, and insurance; and other office business. It also serves as a personal reminder for birthdays, anniversaries, and special occasions. The legal professional should keep the attorney informed of these dates, and the attorney also may want the legal professional's to keep a similar record on his or her desk or pocket calendar.

Keeping track of deadlines and appointments is a very important part of the legal professional's responsibilities. Though many law offices have computers with the capability of performing this function, someone has to record the correct information such as dates, times, and names.

Correspondence coming into the law office should be read and logged into a mail log and the appropriate action indicated. This action can be recorded manually or in the computer. Some offices prefer using a computer system and others prefer doing it manually. For those who prefer the manual system, many manual systems are available, and a desk calendar, card index, or diary may be used. It is important that this action is accurately done to avoid missed deadlines and the possibility of a malpractice suit against the attorney.

One method of keeping the attorney aware of appointments is a daily schedule that is prepared each morning with the appointments and upcoming court dates. This can be given to the attorney with the morning mail to assist in scheduling.

Court Calendar

Most legal offices also maintain a **court calendar** on which the important dates of pending cases are recorded (see Figure 2-7). This is an important responsibility of the legal staff. Accurate, dependable calendaring is vital to the proper operation of the law office.

Hearing and court dates are formal proceedings before a court. It is extremely important that these dates be tracked carefully. Most courts have little tolerance for attorneys who fail to show up for court. In some instances, the attorney can be fined or disciplined for missing court dates.

Incoming mail should be checked on receipt for any dates noted, and those dates should be entered onto the calendar. Each entry on the calendar should be noted on the actual date, and a notation should be made two or three days in advance of that date to allow enough time for preparation of the case. Deadlines for filing complaints, responses, and special proceedings should be recorded on the calendar, as well as the dates and times for court appearances, depositions, or other legal proceedings.

If a trial date is set, a notation should be made on the calendar two or three weeks before this date. The time provided by law by which any act is to be done is computed by *excluding the first day and including the last day*, unless the last day is a holiday, in which case the period is extended to the next day that is not a holiday.

> If any city, county, state, or public office, other than a branch office, is closed for the whole of any day, insofar as the business of that office is concerned, that day shall be considered as a holiday for the purpose of computing time under Sections 12 and 12a. (*Code of Civil Procedure*)

A record of cases awaiting action in a court is called a **docket**. As cases are filed with the court, they are assigned a number and placed on the court docket.

FIGURE 2-7 *A sample court calendar on a computer screen. (Courtesy of Jackson, DeMarco, Tidus, Peckenpaugh, A Law Corporation)*

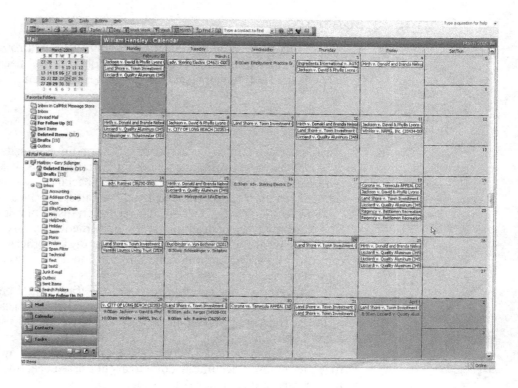

Court days are counted on the court calendar. Weekends and holidays are included in the number of days allowed by the courts. County courts may take holidays that do not appear on other calendars. Each date should be entered on the exact day, as well as a few days before; thus, the attorney and support staff will have advance notice for the preparation of pending matters.

It is essential that the legal professional keep these calendars current and make certain that conflicts do not occur and deadlines are met.

Tickler Systems

Many offices use a **tickler card file** calendaring system. Its purpose is to remind office staff of important dates and pending deadlines. Important dates are recorded on multipart cards called tickler cards. Information from the cards is recorded in the computer, thereby generating a master calendar on a weekly basis. The cards are stored in a file by date so that a copy of the card can be given to the interested party as a reminder before that date.

BILLING PROCEDURES

Depending on the size of the office and the practice, billing procedures vary somewhat from law firm to law firm. Large legal firms may have their own accounting departments; medium-sized offices may have one person responsible for paying the bills and maintaining client charges. In a one- or two-attorney office, the support staff may be responsible for keeping clients' charges and, under the direction of the attorney, preparing and mailing statements to the clients.

The person responsible for timekeeping must keep a complete, detailed, and accurate record of the time the attorney spends on each client's project, often called a **charge record**. Most systems keep time in fractions of an hour, and the most commonly used increments of time are six minutes (one-tenth of an hour) and fifteen minutes (a quarter-hour). Some firms have adopted standard time allotments for certain activities, and many firms bill for travel time to or from a court appearance or meeting. Most law firms set a specific billable hours goal for each attorney. If an attorney fails to meet the billable hours set for her or him, projected income may fall short of expected expenses.

A common method of recording time is to keep an informal running tally of how attorneys spend their time (see Figure 2-8). It is important that the timesheet be completed each day because it is difficult to remember details after a few days have passed.

TIME RECORD
ALL-STATE® LEGAL ▲
A Division of ALL-STATE International, Inc.
800-222-0510 • NJ 908-272-0800

Codes for Services Performed

C - Conference With	LF - Letter From	P - Preparation Of
CT - Court Hearing	LR - Legal Research	PC - Phone Conference With
D - Dictation Of	LT - Letter To	R - Review Of
DP - Deposition OF	NC - Non-Chargeable Time	RV - Revision Of
©1973 ALL-STATE International, Inc.		SA - Sum Advanced For

Conversion of Time Into Decimals

6 Minutes - .1 Hour	24 Minutes - .4 Hour	45 Minutes - .75 Hour
12 Minutes - .2 Hour	30 Minutes - .5 Hour	48 Minutes - .8 Hour
15 Minutes - .25 Hour	36 Minutes - .6 Hour	54 Minutes - .9 Hour
18 Minutes - .3 Hour	42 Minutes - .7 Hour	60 Minutes - 1.0 Hour

To reorder specify Form TR100

Date	Client/Case	File No.	Services Performed	Attorney	Time Hours & Tenths	
3/10	Samuel Smith Probate	PRO3201	C Discussed Probate Procedures	RM	2	.5
"	"	"	LT Samuel Smith	"		.25
"	Juan Gomez P.I.	PI2108	C Discussed PI Complaint	"	1	.1
"	"	"	P Drafted PI Documents	"	2	.3

FIGURE 2-8 *Sample timesheet for recording billable hours.*
(Courtesy of All-State Legal)

Computerized Timekeeping

Many law firms now have computerized timekeeping systems in which the attorney or support staff enters information. At the end of the billing period, the time indicated on the timesheet is totaled and the fee is calculated. Then a detailed statement is prepared for each client. Client-related costs can include such in-house services as photocopying and word processing, as well as court filing fees and fees charged for other services, such as messengers and investigators. A benefit of computerized accounting systems is its ability to generate reports for management.

Attorney's Fees

Client statements are usually mailed monthly, and the amount of the statement is determined by how much time the attorney has spent on behalf of the client. This record of the client's account is usually kept on a billing sheet, which lists the client's name, charges, payments received, and the balance of the account. Some attorneys charge for phone conferences and initial visits, whereas others include these services as part of the total billing. Determine what the attorney or office manager prefers. Clients billed on a monthly basis usually are those clients who are billed by the hour. Some new clients may be required to pay a deposit or retainer, which is placed in the firm's trust account and is withdrawn from the account as services are provided. Depending on the client's credit history, fees may be collected in advance or after the legal service has been rendered.

Project Fees

Project fees are attorney's fees that are charged for a project or on a flat-fee basis. Preparing a simple will, living trust, or setting up a corporation may be charged on a flat- or project-fee basis.

Retainer Fees

Some clients may require the services of the attorney on a regular basis and may want to hire the attorney on a retainer. This arrangement allows clients to receive professional advice whenever it is needed. Of course, if extraordinary or unusual services are rendered, these are usually charged against the client.

Retainer fees are paid at the outset of the case and may be in addition to other fees and charges. They are used to reserve the attorney's time and may be deposited into the client's trust account and drawn on as needed. For example, if a client is charged a $5,000 retainer fee, and the attorney performs $2,000 worth of work, the $2,000 would be withdrawn from the client's trust account, leaving a balance of $3,000 for future work. When all the monies in the retainer account are used up, the attorney would charge the client on an hourly basis.

Statutory Fees

In probate and worker's compensation cases, some attorney's fees are determined by state statute, and are called **statutory fees**. These fees are based on the size of the estate and represent a percentage of its assets. In probate cases that require an extraordinary amount of the attorney's time, the attorney may petition the court for "extraordinary fees," or those fees greater than the ones set by statute in probate cases.

Contingency Fees

Contingency fees are usually used for personal injury/property damage cases, and the attorney's fee is a percentage of the award that the client receives from the defendant. In contingency cases, normally, the attorney charges the client a contingency of 40% of what is awarded. Therefore, if the client were awarded $100,000 in damages, the attorney would receive $40,000 of that award. If there is a contingency fee agreement, the contingency fees usually are deducted from the amount collected at the end of the lawsuit. If clients are remiss in paying their bills, law firms may be required to take legal action to collect fees. If the client is not awarded any damages, and the attorney fees are contingent on the client receiving a monetary award, the attorney would not receive any fees. In divorce, dissolution, or criminal cases, contingency fees are not allowed.

PHOTOCOPYING

The most frequently used method of copying a document is **photocopying**. However, a support person should be aware of other methods of copying and the unique advantages of each. The manner of making copies and the extent of the legal professional's involvement vary from office to office.

In the small or decentralized office, the legal professional may be responsible for preparing all the copies, whereas in a larger office there may be a reprographics center with specially trained personnel. **Reprographics** refers to all means of copying and duplicating a document (see Figure 2-9).

The number of copies to be made depends on the office and the type of document being prepared. Support staff should find out what the preferences are for preparing multiple copies and the number of copies that should be prepared. Always be sure to make a file copy of every document prepared in the law office.

Most law offices have some form of photocopy process. The equipment may be very simple or complicated, depending on the size of the office and the equipment used. The equipment may consist of a small desktop unit, or a whole center may be

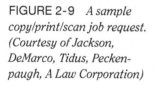

FIGURE 2-9 *A sample copy/print/scan job request. (Courtesy of Jackson, DeMarco, Tidus, Peckenpaugh, A Law Corporation)*

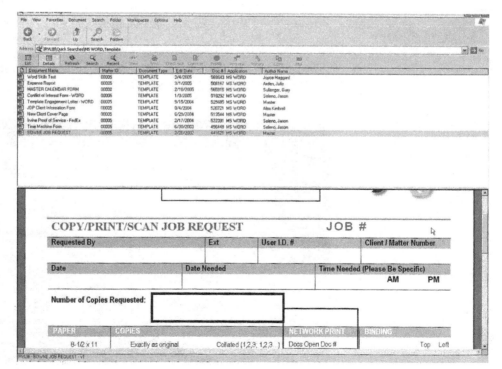

designed for reproduction. Small desktop units are ideal for small reproduction jobs and keep the copy center free from being overloaded with small jobs that can be done faster and more efficiently in the work area, whereas the larger equipment is designed for large production jobs (see Figure 2-10). Depending on the sophistication of the copy equipment, copies can be made the same size as the original or reduced or enlarged. Two-sided copying, called duplexing, and automatic feeding, sorting, collating, and stapling can also be done on the more advanced photocopiers.

Today's photocopiers have a wide range of features and capabilities depending on the sophistication of the equipment (see Figure 2-11). Some of these features include the following:

1. *Copier counters.* Some copy machines make it possible for the user to enter a client identification number, which then tracks the number of copies to be billed to each client. The issue of tracking and billing clients for copies should be considered when buying a copier.
2. *Improve the print quality.* Some copiers can analyze the original copy and improve and enhance the print quality.
3. *Built-in messages.* Some copiers have built-in microprocessors that let you know when you are out of paper, when the paper jams, or when the toner in the copier is running low.
4. *Reduce and enlarge copies and graphics.* Some copiers can control the size of the copy and reduce or enlarge the page. This is a useful feature when using charts, graphics, or images that are to be included in a document.
5. *Automatic paper feed.* Another popular feature is the ability of the copier to automatically pull the original from a stack and feed it through the copier. This frees the office worker from standing over the copier to feed each page by hand.
6. *Collate.* Copiers can automatically **collate** materials by photocopying and then automatically separating and stacking pages into bins. This saves the operator a lot of time that can be used to perform other tasks.
7. *Duplex.* Duplexing, or two-sided copying, can be an automatic feature of the photocopier and saves both the cost of paper and the operator's time.
8. *Staple.* Photocopiers can collate and also staple stacks of materials automatically, which saves the operator's time.
9. *Color print.* Colored paper and colored toners can be used on some copiers. Some machines can also make high-quality color copies from colored copy, color transparencies, and color slides.

FIGURE 2-10   *The Xerox Personal Copier offers reduction and enlargement of original size. (Courtesy of Xerox Corporation)*

FIGURE 2-11 *Large photocopiers can collate, duplex, and staple. (Courtesy of Xerox Corporation)*

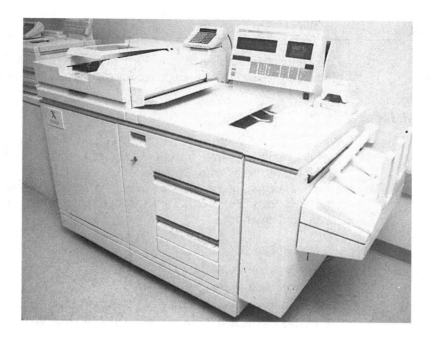

A key advantage to the photocopying process is that no master is required, and copies of text, drawings, photographs, or printing can be made. Misuse of the copy machine in some offices may be a problem—a chargeback system or copy counter may be installed to protect against misuse of the equipment by the staff.

Some companies lease equipment instead of purchasing the equipment. A lease contract may or may not include maintenance of the equipment, so it is important to know the terms of the lease before requesting repairs.

Digital technology has transformed the standard photocopier into a flexible piece of equipment that can perform many functions. Older, nondigital machines copied regular correspondence and documents very well. They could copy at least two sizes of paper, reduce and enlarge the size of the copy, collate and staple multiple copies, duplex, and diagnose machine problems.

Today's digital copier scans a page and stores that page in memory, these pages can then be enlarged, and images can be scanned and files stored to computers on local area networks. When used with OCR (optical character recognition) software, images can be brought into a word processor or other software and can then be edited. A digital copier can also be connected to a telephone line and serve as a fax machine. A digital copier can combine the functions of a printer, photocopier, scanner, and fax machine into one unit, and can be connected to an office computer network and to other computers via phone lines or the internet. Color copiers are also becoming more popular in offices because of their reduced costs and the increased use of colored graphics, pictures, and images.

MICROGRAPHICS

Micrographics is the process of storing permanent records on film in a miniaturized form and refers to the microfilming of documents into microforms, the equipment used, and the procedures followed. The manner in which micrographic records are stored is called microforms, and the most common types of film storage are microfilm, microfiche, and aperture cards. Because records stored on microforms are considered legal documentation, the field of micrographics is used in many areas of the legal field and particularly by the courts.

FILING SYSTEMS

Every office has established some form of filing system. A file is opened for each new client, and separate files are opened for each project for that client.

Client Records

When an attorney agrees to represent a client, a **new case memo** or **new matter report** is usually prepared for that client (see Figure 2-12). Stationery supply houses usually have these forms available for use in the law office, or the support staff and attorney may want to develop their own system. Although the information included on the client record varies from office to office, it usually includes the following information:

1. Name of client
2. Names of other parties to the action
3. Type of legal action
4. Service performed by attorney or law office
5. Payments made by firm in conjunction with account

FIGURE 2-12 *New client record form. (Courtesy of Jackson, DeMarco, Tidus, Peckenpaugh, A Law Corporation)*

New Client Record Form

CHECK HERE IF NEW CLIENT: ☐

CLIENT NAME:			CLIENT NUMBER:
MATTER CONTACT NAME:		TITLE:	
TELEPHONE:	FAX:		EMAIL:

BILLING ADDRESS:
(Only insert if new address)

ADDITIONAL PARTIES REPRESENTED IN THIS MATTER:

MATTER TITLE:

DESCRIPTION OF MATTER:

	Attorney Name	Personnel #	Secretary Name
PARTNER APPROVING ENGAGEMENT:			
BILLING PARTNER:			
PARTNER IN CHARGE:			
Other Attorneys Who Will Work On the Matter:			

NAMES OF ALL PARTIES WHO ARE ADVERSE TO CLIENT IN THIS MATTER:

NAMES OF ALL COUNSEL REPRESENTING PARTIES WHO ARE ADVERSE TO CLIENT IN THIS MATTER:

Attention:		Phone:	
Address:		Fax:	

OTHER PARTIES WHO HAVE AN INTEREST IN THE MATTER:

FROM: _____   PHONE: _____   DATE: _____

NewClientRecord.doc
Rev. 06/17/2005

In a law firm, the clients' records are usually filed in manila folders and stored in a file cabinet in the attorney's offices (see Figure 2-13). (Files can also be scanned to disk or microfilmed.) Folders containing clients' records are called **case files**. Individual files are identified by name and number (see Figure 2-14). The file's name usually identifies the client and the type of legal action. A file numbering system may be used in which the number of the case will indicate when the file was opened, the type of action, and the responsible attorney. If they are arranged by number, a case-file index of the numbers must be maintained together with a name cross reference. The case file must bear the names of the parties to the litigation, client versus the adverse party, or, if office numbers are used, the office-designated case number. This must be maintained as changes occur.

Case files contain correspondence, pleadings, and exhibits relating to the case. All elements in the file are kept in place by metal brackets called **Acco fasteners** or similar devices. The correspondence relating to the case usually is attached to the left of the file folder, while legal documents and exhibits are secured by Acco fasteners to the right side of the folder. In large cases, multiple folders must be created, and documents must be placed in boxes. The documents are filed in chronological order, with the most recent date appearing on the top.

FIGURE 2-13 *Lateral filing cabinets are useful in providing additional storage. (Courtesy of Jackson, DeMarco, Tidus, Peckenpaugh, A Law Corporation)*

FIGURE 2-14 *Work trays are helpful in filing records and providing additional workspace.*

FIGURE 2-15 *Client records require proper methods of indexing and storage.*

FIGURE 2-16 *Records maintenance is important in a law office. (Courtesy of Jackson, DeMarco, Tidus, Peckenpaugh, A Law Corporation)*

Color Coding

It is important to keep the filing up to date and to not allow papers to accumulate (see Figure 2-15). Be sure to file all the notes made by the attorney in the appropriate file. Colored cards and colored file labels can play an important part in filing by indicating a specific legal area or field, or colors may be used in a large law office where there are a number of attorneys to denote the attorney representing the case. Plain-colored, 3-by-5-inch reference cards can be color coded to represent certain areas, for example, red for personal injury, blue for dissolution of marriage, and green for corporation. The file labels can be selected in the same manner. This system makes it easy for anyone using the files to quickly identify a specific area, and it also serves as a means of determining when cards or files are out of order (see Figure 2-16).

NOTARIZING LEGAL CORRESPONDENCE AND FORMS

Notary Public

Many law offices require the services of a notary public, and typically someone on the legal staff will serve in this capacity. In order to qualify as a **notary public**, an individual must be licensed by the state to perform certain specific functions. Any U.S. citizen over the age of 18, of good moral character, who has resided in a state for a certain period of time, may apply to the state for a license. After July 1, 2005, most states require that the applicant pursue a course of study and complete a written examination.

An application to become a notary must be sent to a state official (usually the secretary of state), along with a fee. Upon receiving the commission, the notary may purchase a notary kit, which includes a notary seal. While the wording on the seal may vary from state to state, it usually includes the number of the notary's license and may include the expiration date or the name of the county granting the license. The seal may be one that makes an impression on the paper or a stamp that stamps the seal on the paper.

The most important duty of a notary is to obtain proper and complete identification for the person whose signature is being notarized. Driver's license, credit card, or a passport are acceptable to establish the individual's identity. The notary does not verify as to the contents of the document(s), but instead, the notary:

1. Attests to the authenticity of the signature
2. Administers oaths
3. Attests to the fact that the signer swears in the presence of the notary that the statements in the documents are true

In addition to the notary's signature, the document must indicate when the notary's commission expires (for example, in California the notary's commission is valid for a four-year period). After all the documents have been notarized, all transactions should be recorded in the notary's journal. (Some states require that the person signing the document sign the entry in the notary's journal as well.)

Notaries are legally responsible for what they notarize and cannot be forced to perform an illegal notarization. A notary does not need to read the document that is being notarized, but the acknowledgment should be carefully read, and all the blanks in the document and acknowledgment should be carefully checked and completed (see Figure 2-17).

Because the official acts of the notary may become somewhat repetitive, there is an inclination to become careless about details. However, the responsibility of a

FIGURE 2-17 *A notary's acknowledgment.*

```
 7                                          Samuel Smith
                                            SAMUEL SMITH
 8     State of California   )
 9     County of Orange      )  ss.

10              I, NANCY JAMES, a notary public, DO HEREBY CERTIFY

11     that SAMUEL SMITH, who is personally known to me to be the

12     same person whose name is subscribed to the foregoing instru-

13     ment, appeared before me this day in person, and acknowledged

14     that he signed, sealed and delivered said instrument as a

15     free and voluntary act, for the uses and purposes therein set

16     forth.

17              GIVEN under my hand and notarial seal this 5th day

18     of May, 20--.

19
                            Nancy James
20                          Notary Public

21     My commission expires March 30, 20--.
```

notary is considerable and is secured by a bond in most states. Bonding is similar to taking out an insurance policy to protect people from being injured in case the notary does not carry out the duties properly. It is important that a notary adhere to the rules of procedure governing notaries under the statutes of a given state.

MAIL PROCEDURES

The orderly processing of mail is an important duty in the law office. Incoming mail may be delivered by a letter carrier or picked up from a post office box. In large law firms, mail may be processed by a separate department, whereas in a small law firm, it may be processed by legal support staff.

Incoming correspondence must be dated, given a file notation, and presented in prioritized order to the attorney. Be sure to check for enclosures and return addresses on the incoming mail.

Care also should be taken with outgoing mail. It is important to check for correct spelling of names, accurate addresses and zip codes, and correct postage. The **zip (Zone Improvement Plan) code** should be included in the address so that correspondence can be sorted electronically by the United States Postal Service (USPS) using **OCR (optical character reader)** devices that can automatically sort correspondence by zip code. Sectional centers use OCR devices to sort mail by zip code. They read the last two lines of the address and print a bar code on the envelope for more efficient handling.

ZIP CODES

The USPS has divided the United States into ten zones representing the digits 0 through 9 (see Figure 2-18). The first digit in the zip code is the zone. The first three digits represent a large city or sectional center. The last two digits represent the individual post office. For example, the zip code 92834 represents

9   Western part of United States
2   Area for California
8   Section center in Fullerton, California
34 Post office in Fullerton, California

FIGURE 2-18 *Division of the United States into postal zones.*

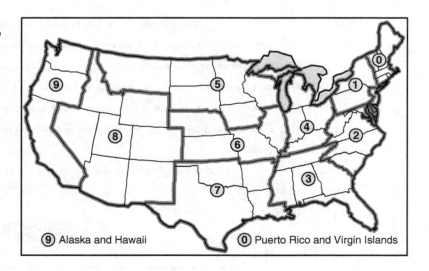

Nine-Digit Zip Code

By using the nine-digit zip code, you can reduce mailing costs. An example of a nine-digit zip code is 92834-1509. The 15 indicates the specific area or sector, which may be several blocks, and the 09 represents a segment of that area—one side of the street or certain floors in a building. This nine-digit number will reduce mailing costs and help to maintain postal charges by automating services.

If you do not know the zip codes of your clients, check with your local post office or find them on the Internet at www.usps.com. Postal employees are willing to explain the advantages of presorting your mail and how this can reduce your postal charges.

USPS (UNITED STATES POSTAL SERVICE) MAIL CLASSES AND SERVICES

It is important for the legal staff to be familiar with the various USPS services because speed of delivery of legal forms and correspondence is important. Excessive and unnecessary postal expenditures also can be avoided by a support staff that understands the different services offered and when each type of service should be used.

Domestic mail services apply to letters and parcels transmitted within the United States, its territories, and possessions. Domestic mail is categorized as follows:

Postal Services

First-Class Mail.
First-class mail includes all personal correspondence, all bills, and statements of accounts, all matter sealed or otherwise closed against inspection, and matter wholly or partly in writing or typewriting (see Figure 2-19). Any mailable items may be sent as first-class mail. Each piece must weigh 13 ounces or less. Pieces over 13 ounces can be sent by priority mail.

FIGURE 2-19   *Postal charges can be determined in the office with the use of postal meters.*

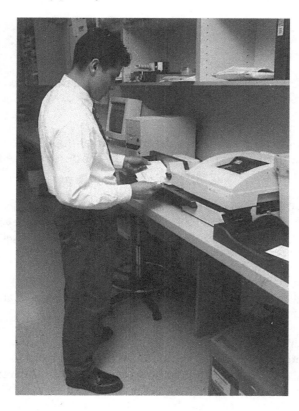

Priority Mail.
Priority mail offers one- to three-day service to most domestic destinations. Items must weigh 70 pounds or less and measure 108 inches or less in combined length and girth. Priority mail envelopes, label, and boxes are available at no additional charge at post offices.

Express Mail.
Express mail is the fastest service, with next-day delivery by noon available for most destinations. Express mail is delivered 365 days a year—no extra charge for Saturday, Sunday, or holiday delivery. All packages must use an Express mail label. Features include merchandise and document reconstruction, tracking and tracing, delivery to post office boxes and rural addresses, domestic rates for APO and FPO address, money-back guarantee, **collect on delivery (COD)**, return receipt service, and waiver of signature.

Media Mail.
Small and large packages, thick envelopes, and tubes can be sent using **media mail.** Contents are limited to books, film, manuscripts, sound recordings, videotapes, and computer media (such as CDs, DVDs, and diskettes). Sometimes called "book rate," media mail cannot contain advertising. Media mail is less expensive than parcel post.

Parcel Post.
Small and large packages, thick envelopes, and tubes containing gifts and merchandise can be sent using **parcel post.**

Bound Printed Matter.
Small and large packages and thick envelopes can be sent using this service. Contents are limited to permanently bound sheets of directory, advertising, or editorial matter, such as catalogs or phone books. **Bound printed matter** rates are less expensive than Parcel Post.

Supplemental Services

Forms and labels for supplemental services are available from the post office lobby or from the local rural letter carrier.

Certificate of Mailing.
A **certificate of mailing** provides proof of mailing. The receipt must be purchased at the time of mailing; no record is kept by the post office. A fee is charged in addition to the postage.

Certified Mail.
Certified mail provides proof of mailing at time of mailing and the date and time of delivery or attempted delivery. Delivery information is available by hard copy or online (see Figures 2-20 and 2-21).

Insured Mail.
Insured mail provides coverage against loss or damage and the fee is based on the value of the item.

Registered Mail.
Registered mail provides maximum security, and includes proof of mailing at time of mailing and the date and time of delivery or attempted delivery. Insurance can be added and the fee is based on the value of the item. The delivery information is available by hard copy and return receipt can be added to confirm delivery for an extra charge.

SENDER: *COMPLETE THIS SECTION*	*COMPLETE THIS SECTION ON DELIVERY*	
■ Complete items 1, 2, and 3. Also complete item 4 if Restricted Delivery is desired. ■ Print your name and address on the reverse so that we can return the card to you. ■ Attach this card to the back of the mailpiece, or on the front if space permits.	A. Received by *(Please Print Clearly)*	B. Date of Delivery
	C. Signature X	☐ Agent ☐ Addressee
1. Article Addressed to: *Julie Crisp* *2206 Arrowhead Lane* *Naperville, IL 60564*	D. Is delivery address different from item 1? ☐ Yes If YES, enter delivery address below: ☐ No	
	3. Service Type ☒ Certified Mail ☐ Express Mail ☐ Registered ☐ Return Receipt for Merchandise ☐ Insured Mail ☐ C.O.D.	
	4. Restricted Delivery? *(Extra Fee)* ☒ Yes	
2. Article Number *(Copy from service label)* *P120-631-247*		
PS Form **3811**, July 1999	Domestic Return Receipt	102595-99-M-1789

FIGURE 2-20   *Receipt for certified mail.*

SENDER: *COMPLETE THIS SECTION*	*COMPLETE THIS SECTION ON DELIVERY*	
■ Complete items 1, 2, and 3. Also complete item 4 if Restricted Delivery is desired. ■ Print your name and address on the reverse so that we can return the card to you. ■ Attach this card to the back of the mailpiece, or on the front if space permits.	A. Received by *(Please Print Clearly)* *Julie Crisp*	B. Date of Delivery 4/6/00
	C. Signature X *Julie Crisp*	☐ Agent ☐ Addressee
1. Article Addressed to: *Julie Crisp* *2206 Arrowhead Lane* *Naperville, IL 60564*	D. Is delivery address different from item 1? ☐ Yes If YES, enter delivery address below: ☐ No	
	3. Service Type ☒ Certified Mail ☐ Express Mail ☐ Registered ☐ Return Receipt for Merchandise ☐ Insured Mail ☐ C.O.D.	
	4. Restricted Delivery? *(Extra Fee)* ☒ Yes	
2. Article Number *(Copy from service label)* *P120-631-247*		
PS Form **3811**, July 1999	Domestic Return Receipt	102595-99-M-1789

FIGURE 2-21   *Signed return receipt for certified mail.*

Delivery Confirmation.

Delivery confirmation provides the date and time of delivery or attempted delivery. This service is free when you buy Priority Mail labels with prepaid postage from www.usps.com.

Signature of Confirmation.
Signature confirmation provides the date and time of delivery or attempted delivery and the name of the person who signed for the item. You can request a hard copy of the signature, and delivery information is available by hard copy, online, or by calling the USPS.

Return Receipt.
Provides a postcard with the date and time of delivery and the recipient's signature.

Restricted Delivery.
This service ensures that only a specified person (or the person's authorized agent) will receive a piece of mail. There is a charge for this service, and it is only available if certified mail, insured mail, or registered mail is used.

International Mail

Letters, large envelopes, and packages from the United States can be mailed through international mail. As with domestic mail, you need to choose the best service based on speed, cost, and extra services.

Other Delivery Services

FedEx.
FedEx provides the fastest same-day delivery service within the United States for packages not exceeding 70 pounds and not larger the 48 inches. Next-day delivery is available with early morning, mid-morning, or mid-afternoon delivery options at additional costs, and FedEx offers second-day and third-day delivery service. International delivery service to more than 220 countries and is also available for packages up to 150 pounds, with delivery choices from one to five days. FedEx also delivers to the home and offers a ground delivery service (www.fedex.com).

UPS (United Parcel Service).
UPS provides same-day service and pick-up at the customer's location. There are three levels of next-day service: by 8 a.m., by 10:30 a.m., or by 3:30 p.m. UPS provides worldwide express delivery service to many cities in Europe and Canada, and is known in the United States by its network of brown vans (www.ups.com).

Courier and Air Courier Service.
Courier services in many large metropolitan areas will pick up and deliver a package or document within a matter of hours. Just place a phone call for the courier service, and a messenger picks up the package for immediate delivery. In congested areas, the courier may use a bicycle to speed the delivery through crowded city streets.

Same-day service is also available from several airlines that will place a letter or small package to the destination city on the next flight, and may require that the package be picked up by the receiving party or specialized services may complete the delivery to the recipient's address. Delta Airlines provides such a service.

Postage Machines

Most legal offices use postage meters to print postage on mailings. There is also computerized equipment available that addresses the envelope, weighs the envelope, and determines the postage and seals the envelope. This equipment is very useful in large legal offices that create a lot of mailings.

TRAVEL ARRANGEMENTS

Making travel arrangements is an important part of today's legal office. Your office may have a travel company that is used for making travel arrangements or the travel arrangements may be done in-house by the staff. Either way, the Internet is a useful source for making travel arrangements as well as obtaining maps for local travel.

When making travel arrangements, it is important to be aware of your office's travel policies, and the second requirement is to know the personal preferences of the traveler. Personal preferences may include the method of transportation, particular airline, the auto-rental company, choice of hotels, and food preferences. It is also a good idea to check the weather forecasts for the destination area.

The Internet can be very helpful in providing information on airline, auto, rail, and weather information. You can even order airline tickets and make hotel and dinner reservations directly from your computer. The Internet can also provide you with city maps, hotels, restaurants, and special events in the area you are researching.

Local Travel

When you are making reservations locally, a number of Internet sites can provide you with maps to assist in finding your destination. All you need to do is to indicate the starting location and your destination location and select the driving icon and you will receive a detailed map with driving directions, estimated mileage, and driving time. Be aware, however, that this driving time does not always consider traffic conditions, so adjust the time accordingly.

The following sites will provide you with maps and directions for both local and long distance destinations:

http://www.travelocity.com
http://www.mapquest.com
http://www.mapblast.com

These services also provide information on hotels, restaurants, and points of interest. These sites can change often, so it is a good idea to always be on the lookout for new and useful websites. When you find an interesting website, be sure to "bookmark" it on your Internet browser so that you do not have to search for it again.

Long Distance Travel

When it is necessary for the attorney or legal professional to travel to remote locations, the Internet can be very useful in providing maps, travel reservations, and information about weather, hotels, and cities. Most airlines have their own websites where e-tickets can be purchased. E-tickets are e-mails that include confirmation numbers, flight date and time, and flight number, and they avoid the necessity of the traveler obtaining the actual tickets. If an e-ticket is lost, it can be reissued without a penalty, whereas if a paper ticket is lost, the price of the ticket may or may not be refunded. Although airline tickets may be paid for by cash, credit card, or check, most tickets are ordered over the phone or the Internet and a credit card is the usual form of payment.

Though airline tickets are often discounted, it is important to be aware of the restrictions on discounted fares. Most business travelers, however, require immediate purchase of airline tickets and are not in a position to order the tickets seven to thirty days in advance to take advantage of these discounts. Be sure to give the airline the traveler's home, office, and cell phone numbers in case there is a change in the schedule or a flight cancellation. Reservations should be confirmed several days prior to traveling and again on the day of the departure. To avoid last-minute problems, it is always best to confirm flight times.

Frequent Flyer Programs Airlines encourage travelers to use their airline by offering them bonus programs in which the traveler earns extra points and can

JACKSON, DeMARCO, TIDUS & PECKENPAUGH
REQUEST FOR REIMBURSEMENT OF EXPENSES

Instructions:

If an expense involves an existing client please include the existing client matter number in the description of expense, i.e. "Dinner with John Doe (matter number)." If the expense is to be charged to a client, put the matter number in the "Bill Matter No." column. Each expense must be accompanied by a receipt or other evidence of payment or the request will be returned. Please leave the accounting (Acctg) column blank.

Date of Expense	Bill Matter No.	Firm Chg.	Expense Description/Attendees	Amount	Acctg	R
			TOTAL	0		
			LESS CASH ADVANCED			
			NET			

Dated: _____

_____
<Insert Name Here>

APPROVED: _____
President or CEO

FIGURE 2-22 *Attorney's expense form. (Courtesy of Jackson, DeMarco, Tidus, Peckenpaugh, A Law Corporation)*

use those points for earning a free trip or upgrade. Some firms will allow the traveler to use these bonus points for personal use, while other firms may require that these points be used for only business purposes.

Airport Security　Many changes in airport security occured following the terrorist attacks of September 11, 2001. These changes affect every airline traveler. All persons and items carried on an airplane must pass through a security inspection system operated by the Transportation Security Administration (TSA) under the authority of the federal government, and all travelers need to display a boarding pass and photo ID.

Travel Abroad　The State Department's home page (http://www.state.gov/index.html) provides information on obtaining passports. The State Department also provides information on countries that have travel warnings. These warnings are issued when it has been determined that these countries are dangerous for Americans traveling abroad to visit. Terrorist threats, bomb threats to airlines, coups, and other conditions suggesting significant risk to the security of American travelers are posted on the website http://www.travel.state.gov/travel_warnings.html.

Expense Accounts　Some offices may advance cash or traveler's checks to staff to cover the cost of the trip, and others may have their staff submit an expense statement at the end of the trip. Legal offices usually pay only for approved travel expenses for such items as transportation, food, and lodging. Some offices allow staff a **per diem** allowance, which is a fixed amount for traveling expenses per day. The per diem allowance may not require the traveler to submit receipts, and the cost of the trip is covered by the per diem allowance.

If the travel expenses are not advanced or are on a per diem basis, it is important for the traveler to keep track of the traveling expenses so that at the conclusion of the trip, that individual can be reimbursed for the expenses. For that reason, the business traveler should make a daily listing of the expenses while traveling. Figure 2-22 is an example of a form submitted to request reimbursement costs for traveling expenses.

SUMMARY

Dramatic changes are taking place in today's legal office as a result of the advances in technology. New features and advances have been made in the use of the traditional telephone, and VoIP phones can convert voice into sound files that can be transmitted over the Internet. The use of personal cell phones has become a standard form of communication, and the use of digital technology has added many features to the everyday cell phone.

Though these changes in telecommunications have occurred, common courtesy, accurate message taking, and speaking clearly are skills that are still required when using the telephone.

E-mail has become a popular method of communication in the legal office because information can be sent and stored in an electronic form and is available when the recipient is ready to receive it. Depending on the quality of the equipment, advances have been made so that video messaging and audio and video files can be sent with the e-mail.

Fax machines are also a very popular item in today's offices. The advantages of a fax machine are similar to the use of e-mail, and are especially useful when you need an exact copy of a document displaying a signature.

An understanding of the requirement and features of mail delivery services is important to those responsible for the delivery and shipment of documents and packages. Planning and organizing travel arrangements is another important duty of the legal professional. The use of the Internet has simplified a lot of the planning, but it is important for the legal professional to become familiar with available websites that can assist in making these arrangements.

Answering the phone, using e-mail, calendaring important events, billing, filing, and making travel arrangements are all important tasks that need to be done by the legal staff for the smooth operation of the law office.

VOCABULARY

Acco fastener   A two-pronged fastener used to secure legal papers to a file folder.

bound printed matter   Small and large packages with contents limited to permanently bound sheets of directory such as catalogs or phone books.

calendar   Record of time; schedule.

case files   Files containing records of clients' actions.

cell phones   Telephones that operate over a wireless network. Cell phones can also offer Internet access and text messaging.

certificate of mailing   Provides proof of mailing.

certified mail   Provides proof of mailing at time of mailing and the date and time of delivery or attempted delivery. Delivery information is available online or by hard copy.

charge record   A client record showing services rendered, time spent on client matter, and money expended on client's behalf.

collate   To assemble in order for binding.

collect on delivery (COD)   Mail that is delivered to an addressee who pays for the postage as well as the contents of the letter or parcel.

contingency fee   A percentage of the award received in a civil case that is paid as the attorney's fee.

court calendar   Calendars on which dates of cases and their actions pending in court are recorded and kept by law offices.

delivery confirmation   Provides sender with the date and time of delivery or attempted delivery.

docket   A digest of court cases; a record of court proceedings.

electronic mail (e-mail)   The transmission of messages by computer from one person to another.

express mail   Mail delivered within a one- or two-day period by the U.S. Postal Service.

facsimile (FAX)   The transmission of text and graphic matter by telecommunications.

Federal Express (FedEx)   A private shipping company that expedites the delivery of mail.

first-class mail   Mail that is given the fastest transportation possible. Correspondence, postcards, bills, statements of account, and checks are sent first-class mail.

insured mail   Provides coverage of loss up to a certain amount.

media mail   Contents are limited to books and media—sometimes called "book rate."

micrographics   The production of graphic material in microform.

new case memo   (Also **new matter report**) Contains client information necessary to set up a new file.

notary public   A bonded public officer who administers oaths or certifies to the authenticity of certain documents.

office calendar   A record of office appointments, meetings, and important reminders.

optical character reader (OCR)   The process of scanning a document with a beam of light and detecting individual characters.

parcel post   U.S. Postal classification for mailing certain items such as books, circulars, and catalogs weighing less than 70 pounds.

per diem   A daily allowance as determined for travel expenses.

photocopy   To make a photographic reproduction of printed, written, or graphic material.

priority mail   Mail weighing between 12 ounces and 70 pounds sent the fastest way possible.

project fee   Attorney's fees that are based on the work performed, such as setting up a corporation or drafting a will.

registered mail   Mail that is locked in a special mailbag that must be signed for by postal employees as it goes from one area to another. Registered mail provides the most secure mail for items sent by first-class or priority mail.

reprographics   The entire process of copying and duplicating documents.

retainer fees   Fees paid to an attorney or law firm who serves a client on a continuing basis, usually billed monthly.

rotary file   A rotating file on a stand in which cards containing information can easily be inserted or deleted.

signature confirmation   Provides the date and time of delivery (or attempted delivery) and the name of the person who signed for the item.

statutory fees   Attorney's fees set by statute, such as probating an estate.

telecommunications   Transmission of information over telephone lines.

tickler card file   A method of reminding personnel of work to be done daily by using a card system showing each day of the month.

United Parcel Service (UPS)   A private service that provides for the domestic and foreign delivery of mail.

voice mail   A telephone answering system that records a caller's voice for later playback.

voice over IP (VoIP)   The transmission of a phone call over the same data lines and networks that make up the Internet.

zip code (Zone Improvement Plan code)   A code developed by the postal service and assigned to each post office for identification and for more efficient processing of mail.

STUDENT ASSESSMENT 1

Instructions: Circle T if the statement is true or F if the statement is false.

T   F   1.   The way the secretary answers the telephone and talks to the caller is a reflection of the law office.

T   F   2.   If the attorney is not available, it is permissible to give the caller information regarding the case if the caller is related to the client.

T   F   3.   When taking telephone messages, it is important to record the correct spelling of the caller's name and the time of the call.

T   F   4.   In calendaring, the time is calculated by including the first day and excluding the last day.

T   F   5.   Rules for calendaring are determined by the *Code of Civil Procedure*.

T   F   6.   Color coding can be very helpful in organizing filing systems.

T   F   7.   It is necessary for notaries to read each document that they notarize.

T   F   8.   Changing postal rates and services require the legal office assistant to keep informed on current mailing procedures.

T   F   9.   The responsibilities performed by a notary are important and need to be secured by a bond.

T   F   10.   Attorneys can be fined or disciplined for missing court dates.

STUDENT ASSESSMENT 2

Instructions: Fill in the word(s) that best complete(s) the statement.

1.   Most law offices maintain two calendars: the _____ and the _____.

2.   A suspense or reminder card calendaring system is referred to as a(n) _____ system.

3.   _____ mail includes letters, post cards, and greeting cards.

4.   Books, film, and manuscripts are sent by _____ mail.

5.   A _____ machine sends exact copies of reports, letters, and graphics over telephone lines.

6.   COD is the abbreviation for _____.

7.   _____ is the most secure way to send mail and includes proof of mailing at the time of mailing.

8.   _____ is traceable, and the fastest service available from the U.S. Postal Service.

9.   _____ converts voice messages to a sound file that can be transmitted over the Internet.

10.   The _____ contains the client information that is necessary to establish a new file.

STUDENT ASSIGNMENTS

PROJECT 1: RECORD PHONE MESSAGES

You have been asked to answer the phone and take messages. Prepare three forms similar to the ones shown on page 23 of your textbook. Complete these forms with the information from the following phone calls:

A.   The call is for Henry Morgan, received on June 7 at 11:00 a.m. Mr. John Lewis of the Superior Court called and wants Mr. Morgan to call him back immediately. He needs to discuss the court charges on the *Jones vs. Smith*, Case No. 1648, and he needs to talk with Mr. Morgan before 4:30 this afternoon. His number is (714) 555-4430, extension 21.

B.   The call is for Henry Morgan. Mr. Lee Nguyen of Computer Systems, Case No. 16178, wants Mr. Morgan to call him back about the lease on the relocation of his facilities. He called June 8 at 4:00 p.m. Phone Mr. Nguyen at (714) 555-1811, extension 34.

C.   Mr. Jose Mendoza, of Landscape Architects, Case No. 1530, called from the emergency room at Hope Hospital regarding injuries he had suffered working on Merrill Butler's yard. Mendoza wanted to speak to Paul Jones; he called June 9 at 10:00 p.m. Ask Mr. Jones to discuss the situation with you first, and then call Mendoza immediately. Mr. Mendoza's phone number is (714) 555-1804.

(continued)

PROJECT 2: KEYING AND SORTING A PERSONAL DIRECTORY

Your attorney has just asked you to key and sort the directory in the following table. Use your word processor to key and sort this information in Arial 10-point type. Be sure to clear tabs and key new tabs as indicated between the columns. Make three sorts by (A) last name, (B) zip code, and (C) phone number.

Follow the instructions for sorting suggested by your specific word-processing software package. Save your documents as ch2 - PJ2A, ch2 – PJ2B, and ch2 – PJ2C; respectively. Print each sort and submit it to your instructor.

Personal Directory

Name	Address	ZIP	Phone
Scholtz, Dan	116 Von Karman, Anaheim, CA	92667	555-3526
Eddy, Arnold	12 Seashore, Anaheim, CA	98740	555-7860
Blake, Robert	13546 Red Hill Avenue, Fullerton, CA	93645	555-7843
Nichol, Karen	1454 Cypress Lane, Buena Park, CA	92660	555-8234
Alexander, Alex	155 Loma Lane, Fullerton, CA	92634	555-4589
Jackson, Susan	223 Belcourt Lane, Anaheim, CA	97134	555-8900
Burns, Ed	23 Sea Lane, Buena Park, CA	93450	555-3428
Duncan, Merrill	235 Coyotes Drive, Buena Park, CA	97320	555-9087
Burnham, John	2435 Bayshore Drive, Fullerton, CA	92630	555-7897
Johnson, Diane	2668 North Hill Drive, Fullerton, CA	94523	555-6570
LaFollette, Marian	2711 Harbor Drive, Buena Park, CA	94520	555-7626
Lundholm, Margie	2783 Harbor Drive, Buena Park, CA	93420	555-2080
Casey, Thomas	3425 Sequoia Lane, Fullerton, CA	93540	555-3478
Yahn, Michelle	45 Sunflower, Buena Park, CA	92599	555-3462
Van Fleet, Fran	56 Leslie Lane, Fullerton, CA	92772	555-4536

PROJECT 3: TRAVEL ARRANGEMENTS

Compare the travel time and prices from your home to a city of your choice by calling three airlines and compiling this information. Prepare this information in a report and submit it.

PROJECT 4: OBTAIN A PASSPORT

Use the Internet to find out how to obtain a valid passport form, and print out this information. If you do not have a valid passport, use this information to apply for one.

3

COMPUTERS AND OFFICE SYSTEMS

OBJECTIVES

Upon completion of this chapter, you should be able to:

1. Describe how new technologies have changed the legal office
2. Define a computer and discuss the four basic computer operations
3. Describe the types of computers available today
4. Discuss the main components of the computer and their importance
5. Understand the different types of storage devices and their application
6. Describe the difference between system and application software
7. Explain the different kinds of application software and how they are used
8. Understand the way computer communications and networks operate
9. Describe how computers and advances in technology have changed the way we work

THE USE OF COMPUTERS IN THE LAW OFFICE

Computers can be used to perform many tasks in the practice of law. Today's law firms use computers to draft and word process documents, do legal research, perform accounting functions, facilitate case management, organize evidence, and prepare control and calendaring procedures (see Figure 3-1). The courts use computers to keep track of cases and prepare court dockets.

Sophisticated electronic law offices are using the new technologies available to create integrated office systems. Software such as Microsoft Office has integrated basic software applications—such as word processing, spreadsheets, database, and presentations—with telecommunications, e-mail, scanning, reprographics, file

FIGURE 3-1 *Many attorneys do their own keyboarding. (Courtesy of Jackson, DeMarco, Tidus, Peckenpaugh, A Law Corporation)*

transfer, and voice processing. Some or all of these technologies may be integrated in today's law office.

Voice processing is used in integrated services for voice mail, and messaging that can take and store messages.

Through telecommunications networks, law office professionals can transmit and receive information from computers, telephone systems, and satellites. This technology provides direct access to file sharing and databases.

Law office professionals can reproduce visual and graphic images such as spreadsheets and business presentations at their work stations through image processing. Some integrated systems have direct links to scanning and reprographics equipment, which allows the system to copy final documents from the work station without going to another location or duplicating service.

DEFINITION OF A COMPUTER

A **computer** is an electronic device that operates under the control of **binary** instructions that are specific to the processor (CPU) installed. Once the instructions are stored in memory, data is entered and the CPU processes the data (arithmetically and/or logically), produces new data (output) from the process, and stores the results for future use.

Computers perform four tasks that comprise the information-processing cycle: **input, process, output,** and **storage** (see Figure 3-2). These operations generally describe what a computer does to process data into information and store it for future use.

The processing of information requires data. Data may include text, numbers, images, and sounds given to a computer during the input operation. The result of the data processing is information that is meaningful and useful. The output of the information can be put in a form, such as a letter, report, or financial statement, that people can use. The information can also be stored for some future use.

TYPES OF COMPUTERS

As technology has become more advanced and electronics have become smaller and less expensive, a number of computer-like devices have evolved to assist businesses and legal professionals. In addition to the standard desktop computer, other alternatives are available to perform certain functions and assist the user in job performance. Categories for computers include the following: network computers, notebook computers, and handheld computers.

Network Computers

In most large law offices, **network computers** are designed to work on a LAN (local area network) that connects all the computers in the office together. The network may reside on a single computer or may be controlled by a central network that will limit, manage, or monitor the performance of each computer. The network may or may not allow each computer to share printing devices, access to a central database, file share, e-mail, or internet use. The central network computer can back up and save information to a central location, thereby increasing the reliability of the network and the cost of maintaining the system.

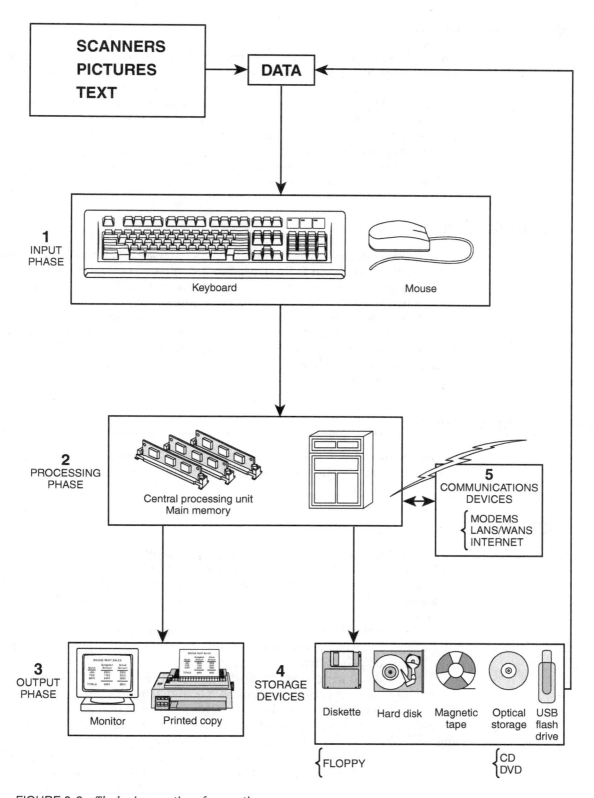

FIGURE 3-2   *The basic operation of computing.*

Notebook Computers

Notebook **computers** have the same configuration as the standard computer, but are usually miniaturized so that they can be carried from place to place in a briefcase or computer case. They usually weigh less than 10 pounds and are battery operated so that they can be used anywhere and do not need access to an electrical connection. They are very helpful for the staff needing to travel. The same software used on a desktop computer can be used on a notebook computer, e-mails can be transmitted and received, and files can be shared with standard office computers. Many hotels have installed high-speed internet connections to accommodate those who travel and are in need of such support services.

Handheld Computers

Computers small enough to fit into a person's hand are called **handheld computers, personal digital assistants (PDAs), personal information managers (PIMs)**, and electronic organizers. These computers are sometimes as small as $6 \times 4^{1}/_{4}$ inches. They are so small and light that they can fit into a purse or coat pocket and can be carried easily by the user. Handheld and pocket computers originally served as a pocket calendar, scheduler, address book, or memo pad. However, as technology has improved, these miniature systems can now be used to download information through the internet from a desktop computer in another location in the form of schedules, documents, spreadsheets, graphics, and databases.

COMPONENTS OF A COMPUTER

There are many forms of input devices, but the most common ways to input information into the computer are through the keyboard or mouse.

Input Devices

The Keyboard   The keyboard is the most common way to input information and usually looks similar to the illustration in Figure 3-3. All keyboards have a standard set of alpha and numeric keys that you use when typing. There are other keys on a keyboard that have special functions, and knowing how to use these will help you increase your efficiency.

The **function keys** appear across the top of the keyboard. Each key performs a single function and may be used to save additional keystrokes, depending on the purpose designed by the different software packages.

The **alphanumeric keys** are in the center of the keyboard and the **numeric keypad** is to the right of the keyboard and is activated by pressing the Num Lock key. The insert key on the numeric keypad is a toggle key and changes its function each time you touch it: When toggled on, the Insert key inserts new text in the line of writing, and when toggled off, it replaces or overwrites existing characters with new characters as you type. The Num Lock and the Caps Lock keys are also toggle keys.

The **cursor control keys** or **arrow keys**, located between the alphanumeric and numeric keypad keys, allow the user to move the cursor around on the computer screen. There are two sets of these keys on the right of the keyboard. The first one is always active; the second resides in the numeric keypad and is only activated when the Num Locks is off.

The Shift keys at the base of the keyboard allow the user to type capital letters and the symbols that are on the top of the number and symbol keys. The Caps Lock

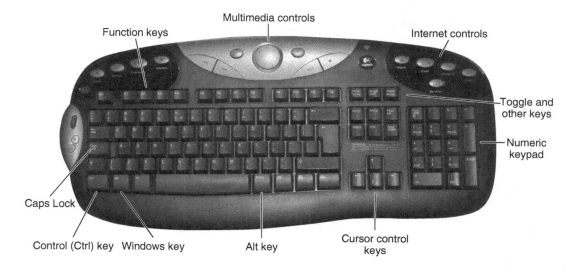

Function keys

Multimedia controls

Internet controls

Toggle and other keys

Numeric keypad

Caps Lock

Control (Ctrl) key   Windows key   Alt key   Cursor control keys

FIGURE 3-3   *Desktop keyboards have a variety of keys that help you work more efficiently. (Courtesy of Jackson, DeMarco, Tidus, Peckenpaugh, A Law Corporation)*

key sets the stage of the keyboard. When it is turned on, all input is in uppercase, and when it is turned off, all input is in lowercase.

Some keyboards, as shown in Figure 3-3, include internet keys or buttons that allow you to open a Web browser, view e-mail, or use the search feature, and unlike the other keys on a standard keyboard, they are not always in the same location on every keyboard.

Because laptop keyboards need to be more compact than standard keyboards, they have fewer keys. Most laptop keyboards, however, have alternate functions so that you get the same capabilities from the limited keys as you would from a standard keyboard.

PDA (Personal Digital Assistants)   Small, handheld computers called personal digital assistants use a stylus, a pen-shaped device that you use by tapping or writing on the touch-sensitive screen of the PDA. Some PDAs, however, have built-in keyboards that allow you to type in text just as you would with a normal keyboard.

Wireless Keyboard   A wireless keyboard does not use cables to connect to a computer but is powered by batteries, and sends data to the computer using a form of wireless technology. Using infrared light waves, wireless keyboards communicate with the computer (similar to how a remote control communicates with the TV).

The Mouse   The mouse (Figure 3-4) is a pointing device that allows the user to select menu options, open and close files, select commands, manipulate graphics, and perform other functions. By moving the mouse across the surface of a pad, the traction activates a rolling ball on the bottom of the mouse and sends information to the computer, thereby moving the cursor on the screen. Most operating systems and applications use both the left and right mouse button. Generally the left mouse button is used to select or activate icons or buttons, while the right mouse button is used to activate context-sensitive menus. These right-click menus normally allow changes to be made to the selected item(s).

A traditional mouse has a rollerball at the bottom of the mouse that moves when you drag the mouse across a mousepad. An **optical mouse** has an optical laser or sensor on the bottom that detects the movement of the mouse. The optical mouse doesn't use a mousepad, but instead uses an internal sensor or laser to detect the

FIGURE 3-4 *The computer mouse.*

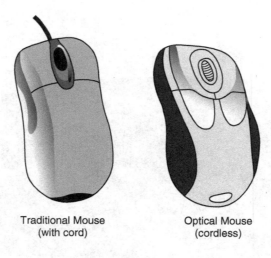

Traditional Mouse
(with cord)

Optical Mouse
(cordless)

FIGURE 3-5 *Scanners are used in some law offices. (Courtesy of Hewlett Packard)*

mouse's movement. The sensor sends signals to the computer, telling it where to move the pointer on the screen.

Just as there are wireless keyboards, there are wireless mice, both standard and optical. Similar to wireless keyboards, wireless mice use batteries to send data to the computer by radio or light waves.

Scanners Scanning (Figure 3-5) enables the user to scan hard-copy images of a picture, document, or text into a computer. Scanners reflect light on the document and translate the document into digital signals that are recognized by the computer. Through the use of **optical character recognition (OCR)** software, users can scan printed material into a computer so that the text of the document can be imported into a word processor and be edited or changed. It is possible to scan printed information into the computer much faster than to type it in. Large OCR scanners can scan thousands of pages of text into a computer. This operation can be very useful in a law office.

Imaging and optical character recognition are similar, but different. When scanners scan the entire image of the document into a computer, such as a photograph or microfilm image, this is called imaging. Imaging allows the user to see the document's image in the original form, but no text can be edited or changed, and no word search can be performed. Optical character recognition allows the user to see and use straight text, search for word patterns, and change and edit documents. Imaging allows the user to view the entire picture.

Voice Processing

Voice processing, or voice recognition, is the process that allows the computer to understand speech. The user speaks into a microphone that is connected to the computer. Through the use of sophisticated hardware and software, the computer interprets the speech and converts it to digital signals, and then it matches these signals with word "signatures" to provide typed words on the display. Voice recognition is becoming popular as a solution to transcription. Legal proceedings and medical case histories can be dictated into a microphone, and the computer then converts the spoken words into digital information that can be entered into a word processing package or other legal office software.

The Processor Unit

The central processing unit (CPU) (Figure 3-6) and main memory compose the **processor unit**. The **central processing unit (CPU)** organizes and processes information. The CPU is the brain of the computer. It performs logical operations (in accordance with the operating system software) and communicates with storage, input, output, and communications devices.

The heart of the CPU is the processor chip that performs the actual computations of the computer. The processor chip used in microcomputers is called a **microprocessor**. The microprocessor interprets instructions to the computer, performs the logical and arithmetic processing operations, and causes the input and output operations to occur; its speed is determined by the clock speed in cycles per second and is measured in **megahertz (MHz)** and now **gigahertz (GHz)**. As the CPU receives data from the input devices (keyboard or mouse) it carries out the various operations, and then sends out the results to the output devices (such as a computer monitor or printer).

Main Memory or Random Access Memory (RAM)   RAM is temporary memory that is utilized while the computer is operating; RAM is your workspace. If the computer is turned off and the data have not been saved, the information held in RAM will be lost. Data that are processed will be stored in **main memory** until saved

FIGURE 3-6   *The system unit.*

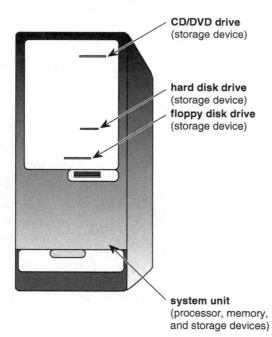

CD/DVD drive
(storage device)

hard disk drive
(storage device)

floppy disk drive
(storage device)

system unit
(processor, memory,
and storage devices)

to storage media (floppy disk, hard drive, network, etc.) RAM is measured in **megabytes (MB)**. A megabyte equals approximately 1 million bytes (a byte equals one character), that is, 1 million characters, or the equivalent of one book (500 pages of text).

Output Devices

Once the data has been processed, it is sent to an output device. The output device could be a printer or computer screen.

Printers   Printers are output devices that print a hardcopy of the data results onto paper. Printers are classified in two categories: impact and nonimpact.

An **impact printer** operates similarly to a typewriter; it uses a print head with many pins to strike the ribbon and produce output. Dot matrix printers are a type of impact printer and can be used with personal computers.

Nonimpact printers print data on paper without physically striking the paper, therefore, nonimpact printers are quieter than impact printers. They can also print graphics and fonts in varying type sizes and styles. Several different methods are used for doing this, including ink jet and laser printing.

Ink jet printers form a character by using a nozzle that sprays drops of ink onto the page. The print quality of ink jet printers has greatly improved and is now considered letter/high quality. Because of this, and the fact that they are quiet, they are used in many law offices.

Laser printers (Figure 3-7), the most common type of nonimpact printers used in law offices, uses a laser beam to form characters on a page. This process is similar to that of a copy machine. Laser printers convert data from the computer into a beam of light that is focused on a photoconductor drum, forming images to be printed. The photoconductor attracts particles of toner that are fused by heat and pressure onto paper to produce an image. Laser printers can produce high-quality output in the form of text and graphics. Laser printers are quiet and much faster than other printers, and some laser printers can print in color, as do many of the ink jet printers.

The Multifunction Print Device (Print, Fax, Scan, and Copy)   Legal offices and businesses have traditionally purchased separate machines to do printing, facsimile (fax), scanning, and copying (photocopying) (see Figure 3-8). With the advances in technology, manufacturers have been able to combine all of these

FIGURE 3-7 *Laser printers produce high-quality documents.*

FIGURE 3-8
Multifunction print device.
The machine can print, fax,
copy, scan, and capture
information. (Courtesy of
Jackson, DeMarco, Tidus,
Peckenpaugh, A Law
Corporation)

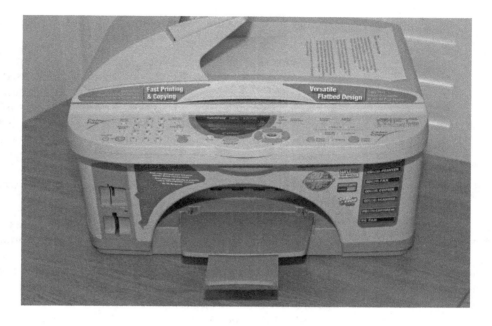

functions into a **multifunction print device** that performs all of these functions. These machines are popular in the small legal office or home environment where the volume of work or the speed of production is not a consideration. The laser multifunction device (printer, fax, scanner, and copier) is faster and more expensive than the ink jet multifunction device. The popularity of the multifunction device has exploded since the quality and speeds of these devices have improved, and it is possible to purchase just one machine that will perform four functions for the same cost as purchasing one or two separate machines.

Monitors and Displays   The **screen** on which text and images appear is called a **monitor** or **display**. A monitor is similar to a television set and uses a **cathode ray tube (CRT)** to display the text and graphics on the screen, while a display is usually referred to as a **liquid crystal display (LCD)**. A Display screen used for **graphics** is divided into dots called "**pixels**." The more pixels, the higher the screen resolution or clarity. Portable computers use a flat panel display with a liquid crystal display similar to those used in digital devices. Most organizations now purchase the flat panel displays as part of their computer systems instead of CRT monitors. These displays were first used in notebook and handheld computers, and they are now affordable for office and home use. Flat panels take up less desk space, are lighter than the CRT monitors, and use only a third of the electricity. As the price decreases, they will be used more extensively in offices.

Many affordable desktop systems include a 17-inch display, high-end systems often include 19-inch display, and 21-inch displays are desirable for intense graphics use.

Storage

Auxiliary Storage   When the computer is turned on, RAM (random access memory) stores data and the instructions to process data. Prior to shutting down the computer, any data or instructions located within RAM that are required for future processing must be stored on **auxiliary storage** or the information will be lost. Auxiliary storage devices and RAM are sometimes confused with one another. RAM is where information is stored temporarily. It is erased each time the computer is turned off. An auxiliary storage device, such as a diskette, is where information can be stored permanently. **Storage capacity** refers to the maximum amount of data that can be stored on a device. The two types of auxiliary storage most often used on personal computers are diskettes and hard disks. Writeable CD-ROM disk drives are also becoming common for personal data storage.

Diskettes   A floppy disk drive can store data on a nonrigid magnetic disk called a **diskette** or **floppy disk**. Diskettes are a widely used storage medium for the microcomputer and are available in various sizes and storage capacities. Most microcomputers today use floppy disks that are 3½ inches in diameter and have storage capacities between 720,000 bytes and 1.44 million bytes. Floppy disks can be obtained in different densities. Density refers to the amount of space available for storage on the floppy disk. The number of characters that can be stored on a floppy disk depends on the recording density of the bits on a track and the number of tracks on a floppy disk. Diskettes are not being used as often when hard disks and other storage devices are available.

Hard Disks   A hard disk drive (Figure 3-9) stores data on a rigid magnetic disk. **Hard disks** are very reliable and have faster access times than floppy disks. Hard disks are usually mounted inside the computer and have storage capacities ranging from 100 MB to hundreds of gigabytes. A **gigabyte (GB)** is 1 billion bytes and represents the data that would be included in 1,000 books or an entire library. Hard disk information should be periodically backed up or copied onto another source to protect critical information from being lost or damaged.

Hard disks are a must for most law offices because law offices usually work with large quantities of information, and they need the storage capacity that hard disks can provide. They also give users quick access to information. Today's sophisticated software programs, including those used in law offices, cannot run on a computer that does not have a hard disk.

CD-ROM   A CD-ROM (compact disk—read-only memory) uses optical technology, or laser beam(s), to store large quantities of information on a laser disk. CD-ROMs are a "write once/read many" technology that has a storage capacity running from 1 to 450 MB, and each CD-ROM disk can hold about 125 books. CD-ROM technology is very important to the law office. Libraries of information can now be placed on CD-ROM, and law offices are finding the use of CD-ROMs less expensive than purchasing stacks of reference libraries containing state and federal statutes and case law.

The CD-ROM disk drive has played an important role in PC storage. A CD-ROM disk drive is used to access information stored on CDs. You would have a difficult time

FIGURE 3-9 *Parts of a hard disk drive.*

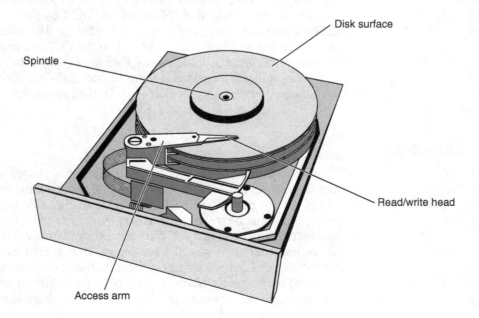

Disk surface

Spindle

Read/write head

Access arm

getting software loaded on your computer without it, because all software comes in the form of CD-ROM disks. Each CD holds more storage per disk than the floppy. A CD-ROM disk holds 650 MB per disk whereas a floppy holds 1.44 megabytes (MB) per disk.

A single CD-ROM disk has the capacity of 700 floppy disks or enough memory to store 300,000 pages of text. CD-ROM is read-only memory and cannot be written on like a floppy disk.

The **compact disk—recordable (CD-R)** has surfaced as the best media for the amount of data required to digitally record music, video, and large volumes of information. CD-Rs can be written to only one time and cannot be reused. CD-Rs are considered by some to be the best for archival storage purposes because the data cannot be modified or deleted.

The **compact disk—rewritable (CD-RW)** disks are more expensive than the CD-R disks, but the advantage of the CD-RW format is that you can write to it unlimited times, and this is very attractive as you have the option of writing files to this disk at a later time. The disadvantage is the cost.

Digital versatile disks (DVDs) store high-capacity multimedia on a single disk. These disks are attractive because of their huge storage capacity—a DVD can hold a full-length film or up to 133 minutes of high-quality video and audio.

Flash Memory Storage   **Flash memory** is a recordable computer chip that can store from 8 megabytes to 2 gigabytes of information on a very small physical space. This storage is available on very small cards that can be inserted in the appropriate slot in a desk computer, notebook computer, digital camera, handheld computer, or other digital device. Because these cards are reusable, they can be used for permanent or temporary storage.

USB Flash Drive   Another form of memory storage is an external device or portable mini-drive called a USB flash drive or "thumb drive" (because it is about the size of a thumb), and it can be easily connected to any personal computer via a USB (Universal Serial Bus) port. A USB port or connection is a primary standard for connecting peripheral devices to a personal computer. These **portable minidrives** are useful to quickly store and transfer large amounts of information from one computer to another.

Cartridge-Based Storage   **Cartridge-based storage** systems are commonly used for PC backup. The growth of computer disk storage, networks, and database applications has increased the demand for backup data storage to support these needs. The advantage of tape cartridges is that you can back up most hard drives on one tape, but the disadvantage is that they are slower than other removable storage devices.

COMPUTER SOFTWARE

The key to the productive use of computers is software. Software can be categorized into two types: operating system software and application software.

Operating System Software

The operation of the computer is controlled by the programs contained in the **system software**. An important part of the system software is a set of programs called the operating system. The operating system must be loaded into the computer's memory before the application software is loaded because the operating system tells the computer to run the application software program. The application program must be compatible with the operating system in order to function.

Application Software

Software programs include **operating system** and **application software**. An application software program is a set of instructions written for a special task such as word processing, spreadsheets, presentation graphics, database, desktop publishing, and communications. The most commonly used application software is Microsoft Office, which includes e-mail, word processing, spreadsheet, presentation graphics, database, and publishing software. This **integrated software** is referred to as an **office suite** because it combines several applications functions into one software package. Integrated software has many advantages, and one of the most important is that the command menu structure is the same for each program and information can be exchanged quickly between the modules. Another advantage is that integrated programs cost less than individual programs that perform the same applications.

Word Processing　The major activity in most law offices is the processing of documents, and one key advantage of using **word processing** is the ability to edit text without having to retype the entire document. Word processing software does more than assist in the preparation of letters and legal documents, it also contains features that include templates for letters, legal proceedings, reports, and faxes. Word processing programs provide various **font** styles and sizes and include linking features to other software applications, such as spreadsheet and database functions. Advanced features include automatic spell checking, thesaurus, centering, margin setting, footnote placement, and header functions. Though a word processing package is more oriented toward text, it can also include graphic and number functions in addition to page layout features. Microsoft Word® is a popular word processing software package.

Spreadsheets　Electronic spreadsheet software, sometimes called worksheet program, contain spreadsheets with columns and rows and can calculate and manipulate numbers. The advantage of spreadsheet software is that it allows the user to change a number and have that change reflected automatically in all the other numbers or formulas in the spreadsheet. Information within word processing documents can be exchanged or linked and incorporated with a spreadsheet document, such as a presentation or budget document. Spreadsheets can be used for many purposes in a law office, such as preparing budgets, statements, and calculating damages for a lawsuit. Without starting over, errors can be corrected quickly and easily. The most commonly used spreadsheet software program is Microsoft Excel®.

Database Software　Database software allows the user to enter, retrieve, and update related information in a timely manner. Database programs have the ability to create custom menus, screens, and reports. One of the most powerful aspects of database management systems is the ability to link the data from more than one file, and reports can be created from the new database files without having to reenter information into the computer. Law offices use databases to organize information or documents for a lawsuit, track legal briefs, and prepare information in a sequential order. Microsoft Access® is commonly used to create database files.

Presentation Graphics　Presentation graphics software allows the computer to produce professional-quality pie, bar, line, and area charts. Presentation graphics packages are used by speakers at conferences and meetings and are an effective way to inform listeners about a new idea or concept. A presentation can be given to an audience by linking a computer to a projection system, and sound and video can be added to the text or graphic material. Many law firms use presentation graphics because visual presentations in the courtroom hold the listener's attention and can be persuasive. This software provides a quick and inexpensive way of presenting information without hiring professional artists. Microsoft PowerPoint® is a commonly used presentation software package.

Communications software enables the computer to communicate. Enhanced communication has been brought about by the rapid changes taking place in technology and the capability of the computer to store more information. Communications software allows the user to transmit data and information from one computer to another. The need to transfer and exchange information between computers within and outside the law office has become very important to the practice of law. In addition to the required software, work stations need to be equipped with a communications hardware device such as a modem or a network adapter.

A **modem** enables computers to communicate with each other and at different locations by using some form of communications carrier (such as a telephone line, coaxial cable, fiber optics, microwave, or satellite transmission). The term *modem* stands for *mo*dulate *dem*odulate. The modem (Figure 3-10) converts the **digital** signals (electrical impulses representing characters) produced by the computer to **analog** (electronic signals of varying voltage), or vice versa, so that information can be both sent and received. A modem is necessary for both the sending and receiving ends of the communication. The modem may be connected to the computer either externally or internally. Most new computers have internal modems already installed. With a modem and some form of communications software, users can transfer information from one location to another and access legal databases such as LEXIS and WESTLAW (Figure 3-11).

Another form of computer communication software used in law offices is **e-mail (electronic mail)**. When e-mail software is used in conjunction with some communications device, it is possible for users to send and receive messages from one location to another either within or outside the office.

Some modems may also include **fax (facsimile)** capability, which allows the user to prepare a document on the computer and fax it directly to the recipient. While this may be advantageous in terms of saving time, it does not allow the user to transmit hard copies as a standalone fax machine does. Standalone fax machines

FIGURE 3-10 *Basic model of a communications system.*

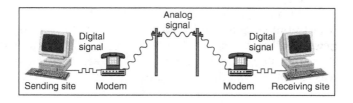

FIGURE 3-11 *Internal modems are useful for retrieving information. (Courtesy of Jackson, DeMarco, Tidus, Peckenpaugh, A Law Corporation)*

FIGURE 3-12 *Fax machines provide quick communications to clients.*

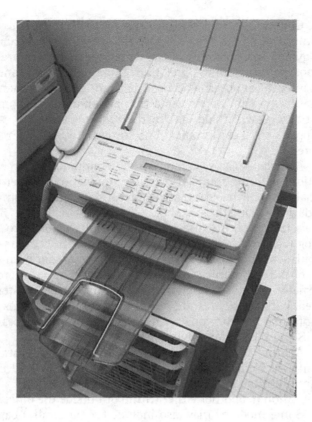

(Figure 3-12) enable the user to use telephone lines to transfer hard-copy documents to other fax machines. Fax machines use a photocell or laser beam to scan a printed page from the office sending the communication. It converts that image into an analog symbol that can be sent over telephone lines to the office receiving the information.

With the proper communications software and hardware, it is possible to connect to online communications services or the Internet, which offer the latest in news, weather, and sports. These online services also provide such features as e-mail, shopping, stock quotes, and information searches. Most law offices find these services useful in obtaining information and in researching cases and the law.

COMMUNICATION NETWORKS

Networking is essentially linking a number of personal computers together, enabling users to share files, programs, printers, and information, as well as to communicate through electronic mail. Each computer acts as a standalone unit as well as a terminal able to access, manipulate, and store information on the system. The type of network that is self-contained within a department, business, or organization is called a **local area network (LAN)**.

The center of the network is called the **file server** (Figure 3-13). A file server is a dedicated computer (usually a powerful microcomputer or a minicomputer) that contains a CD, floppy disk drive, and multiple hard disks with some sort of backup system. The file server may be dedicated or nondedicated. A dedicated server is one in which the computer is used only for a specific task, while a nondedicated server is one that is used as the center of the network as well as handling another task, such as a printer or e-mail server or as an individual workstation. File servers are

FIGURE 3-13 *File servers support the office computer network. (Courtesy of Jackson, DeMarco, Tidus, Peckenpaugh, A Law Corporation)*

responsible for managing the file sharing and the system security; they also control station-to-station communications, licensing, and peripheral equipment (printers, scanners, and others). Software application programs can be loaded on the file server, and users can access these programs without needing to have them on their individual workstations.

An individual computer linked to a network is called a **work station.** Network users can create, edit, save, and retrieve network files using these computers. Individual work stations in a LAN allow users to communicate with one another, the file server, and other work stations connected to the system. Users can communicate with each other through electronic mail, which allows users to send messages without having to worry about whether the receiver is available.

LANs typically connect computers in the same area. The connection may be done by fiber optic or coaxial cable or simple telephone cable or as a Windows system. The distance separating devices in a local area network may vary from a few feet to a few thousand feet. As few as two and as many as several hundred computers can be linked on a single LAN. Most law offices are linked to a LAN to share valuable resources.

The **MAN,** or **metropolitan area network,** is a network designed for a large structure or a city. MANS are more encompassing than LANs, but are smaller than wide area networks.

A **WAN (wide area network)** provides networking in the same way as a LAN, only over a wider area, connecting two or more LANs by long distance communication lines.

Networks allow the law office professional to communicate with other staff through the use of e-mail, sending draft copies to others for revision and correction, co-editing large documents, and electronically routing documents for approval.

The person in charge of the operation of the network is called the **network administrator,** or **manager.** This person oversees the operation of the network, provides user access, maintains the equipment and software, and provides for network security.

The advantages of a network in the legal office are many and include information sharing, software control, greater use of storage, backup control, and better security. The disadvantages of a network include the initial cost, and responsibility for network maintenance and control.

FIGURE 3-14 *Digital cameras have many uses in the legal environment. (Courtesy of Jackson, DeMarco, Tidus, Peckenpaugh, A Law Corporation)*

DIGITAL CAMERAS

The **digital camera** is a tool that can be used to capture still and video images (see Figure 3-14). The digital camera has become a popular consumer item and records images digitally rather than on traditional film. Unlike traditional cameras, digital cameras also allow you to see your images the instant you shoot them. When a digital camera takes a photo, it stores the images on a flash memory card inside the camera.

Flash memory cards are very small and powerful and allow you to transfer digital information between your camera and your computer or printer. Personal computing and the internet have made it possible to share these images and videos with friends and offices throughout the world. Modern digital cameras have a form of flash memory that can store hundreds of images. Information can be uploaded and downloaded when a digital camera is connected to a PC via a USB port, and its memory stick is treated as another disk. This is a convenient way to transfer files between PCs.

These cameras are not only used for personal enjoyment, but to document people and places in the legal environment.

SUMMARY

Computers are electronic devices that perform four operations: input, processing, output, and storage. The components of the computer include input devices (the keyboard and the mouse); the CPU and main memory (RAM); output devices (printers and the computer screen); and some form of storage, such as diskettes, hard drives, tape, CDs, flash memory, or portable minidrives.

Computers cannot operate without software. Software can be categorized into two kinds: operating system software and application software. System software includes UNIX and **Microsoft Windows**. Application software may include word processing, electronic spreadsheet, database, presentation graphics, office suites, and communications programs. Communications software requires that work stations be equipped with a modem and use some form of communications carrier to convert digital signals into analog. Some modems may include the capability to fax documents, similar to the way standalone fax machines operate. With the proper communications software and hardware, you can connect to the Internet or with on-line services.

Communications networks link together individual work stations, allowing these work stations to share files, programs, printers, and electronic mail. The center of the network is called the file server.

Technology has brought about dramatic changes in today's law office. Though there has been much change as the result of advances in technology, the demand for qualified legal professionals has continued to grow despite all the changes. No matter how automated law offices become, attorneys always need people to operate the equipment and make the decisions that process information (see Figure 3-15).

The changes brought about as a result of the technology are not eliminating jobs, but the changes certainly are changing the nature of the way we work. Successful employees will have to accept change as an opportunity to work more efficiently. Changes brought about by technology will require that support staff increase their own value and skill by becoming more competent using computers and new technologies (see Figure 3-16).

FIGURE 3-15 *An organized work station is important for quality work.*

FIGURE 3-16 *The use of technology is important for law offices.*

VOCABULARY

alphanumeric keys The keys found in the center of the keyboard and on most typewriter keyboards.

analog Electronic signals that transverse ordinary telephone lines.

application software Software programs that assist in the performance of specific tasks.

arrow keys Keys that allow the user to move the cursor around on the computer screen.

auxiliary storage Devices that store information to be retrieved for later use after the computer has been turned off.

binary A numbering system using zeros and ones to describe numerical values.

booting The process of starting the computer.

cartridge-based storage A means of storage on a magnetic tape—usually used for backing up files.

cathode ray tube (CRT) See *display*.

CD-R (compact disk—recordable) A portable, optical storage device that can be written to once and can be used with either a CD-R drive or a CD-RW drive.

CD-ROM (compact disk—read only memory) A storage device that uses laser beams (optical technology) to store large quantities of data on a laser disk.

CD-RW (compact disk—rewritable) A modification of CD-ROM that provides for recording and erasing of data.

central processing unit (CPU) The logical component of the computer system that interprets and executes programs. The brain of the computer.

communications software A software package that enables computers to communicate and share data.

computer An electronic device that can accept and process data, produce output, and store the results for future use.

cursor control keys See *arrow keys*.

database software Allows users to search, sort, select, delete, and update files.

digital An electronic signal represented by discrete pulses representing zeros and ones.

digital camera (digicam) A camera that records images digitally rather than on film.

DVD (digital versatile disk). Can store up to 9.4 GB of data, depending on whether data is stored on one or two sides of the disk, and how many layers of data each side contains.

diskette A circular piece of plastic with a magnetic coating enclosed in a case that is used for storing data.

display A TV-like electronic device that shows information on a screen in visual form.

electronic spreadsheet software Application software that allows users to perform calculations with numbers arranged in a grid of rows and columns.

e-mail (electronic mail) Allows users to send and receive messages on networked computers.

ergonomic The relationship between people and machines.

fax (facsimile) A device that enables users to send and receive hardcopies of files through the telephone lines.

file server The main computer in some network configurations that contains the programs and data to be accessed by the work stations on the network.

flash memory A type of nonvolatile memory that can be altered easily by the user.

floppy disk See *diskette*.

font An assortment or set of type faces of one style or size.

function keys Special keys on a computer keyboard that reduce often-used commands to a single keystroke.

gigabyte (GB) A byte measurement indicating approximately 1 billion bytes.

gigahertz (GHz) The clock speed of the computer measured in billions of cycles per second.

graphical user interface (GUI) A user interface that operates with pictures, allowing the users to utilize icons to represent data and applications.

handheld computer Any personal computer than can be held comfortably in a person's hand (usually weighs less than a pound).

hard disk Rotating magnetic-coated platters that are sealed inside a case and used for storage inside the computer.

icon A picture that represents a program, disk, or file.

imaging The process of scanning a document into the computer so that the user can see the exact image of the document on the computer screen.

impact printer A device that prints data on paper by physically striking the paper, similarly to how a typewriter functions. A dot matrix printer is an impact printer.

ink jet printer A printer that sprays drops of ink on paper to create text and images.

input Any information that is entered into the computer from one or many input devices.

integrated software An application suite that combines several applications functions (such as word processing, spreadsheet, and database functions) into one program.

keyboard A device used for entering data.

laser printer A nonimpact printer that uses a beam of light to create text and images.

liquid crystal display (LCD) A flat panel display technology used in notebook computers.

local area network (LAN) A network used to connect a number of microcomputers to share data or peripheral devices.

main memory The computer's primary memory pool; holds the programs and data used for processing.

megabytes (MB) The measure of computer memory representing approximately 1 million bytes.

megahertz (MHz) The clock speed of the computer measured in millions of cycles per second.

metropolitan area network (MAN) A data network designed for use within the confines of a town or city.

microprocessor The central processing unit, or brain, of the minicomputer.

Microsoft Windows Software that provides a GUI to the user and DOS, enhancing the computer's usability.

modem   An acronym for *modulate/dem*odulate; a device that converts digital computer signals to analog signals (audible sounds that can be sent over telephone lines), and vice versa.

monitor   See *display*.

mouse   A handheld device that electronically signals the computer to move the cursor on the display.

multifunction print device   A device that combines the functions of a printer, scanner, fax machine, and copier into one machine.

network administrator or manager   Someone who manages a computer system that uses communications equipment and software to connect two or more computers and their resources.

network computers   A group of two or more computers that are configured to share information and resources such as printers, files, and databases.

nonimpact printer   A device that prints data on paper without physically striking the paper.

notebook computers   A notebook-sized computer sometimes referred to as a "laptop."

numeric keypad   The keys on a computer keyboard that are used to enter numeric information.

office suites   Several software application packages that are combined into one product.

operating system   Provides the essential internal activities of the computer and interface to the user.

optical character recognition (OCR)   Using OCR software with a scanner, users can scan text into the computer to be edited or changed.

optical mouse   A mouse that uses an internal sensor or laser to control the mouse's movement. The sensor sends signals to the computer, telling it where to move the pointer on the screen.

output   Results of processing data.

personal digital assistant (PDA)   A handheld computer or small device that enables a user to carry digital information.

personal information managers (PIMs)   Similar to a personal digital assistant.

pixels   Individual dots on the computer screen that, together, constitute text or graphics.

portable minidrive (USB flash drive)   Small minidrive that can be connected to any computer with a Universal serial bus port.

presentation graphics software   A software package that allows users to create presentations with illustrations, graphs, and charts.

process   A series of actions that brings about a result.

processor unit   The part of the CPU that performs the actual computations of the computer.

random access memory (RAM)   Temporary memory that stores data and program instructions.

scanning   The process of scanning hard-copy text or images into a computer.

screen   See *display*.

storage   The keeping of data.

storage capacity   The maximum amount of data that can be stored on a device.

system software   Programs that run the fundamentals of the computer.

voice processing or voice recognition   The ability of the computer to convert spoken words into digital information.

wide area network (WAN)   A computer network that connects work stations in a wide geographic area.

Windows   An operating system produced by Microsoft that uses a graphical user interface.

wireless keyboard   A keyboard that is battery operated or uses radio waves instead of wires or cable as its transmission medium.

word processing   Software that enables users to create, edit, format, and print documents.

work station   An individual computer that is cabled to a local area network or communications system.

STUDENT ASSESSMENT 1

Instructions: Circle T if the statement is true or F if the statement is false.

T F 1. Word processing is useful in producing repetitive legal documents.

T F 2. Diskettes come in different densities.

T F 3. A gigabyte is bigger than a megabyte.

T F 4. Hard disks usually are mounted within the computer.

T F 5. Laser printers are the most common printers used in law offices.

T F 6. CD-ROMs typically store more data than diskettes.

T F 7. A mouse is a communication device used to convert between analog and digital signals so that telephone lines can carry data.

T F 8. The central processing unit contains the processor unit and main memory.

T F 9. A laser printer provides high-quality output.

T F 10. A floppy disk is considered to be a form of main memory.

STUDENT ASSESSMENT 2

Instructions: Circle the letter that indicates the most correct answer.

1. Which of the following is an impact printer?
    a. laser
    b. dot matrix
    c. ink jet
    d. none of these

2. The four operations performed by a computer include
    a. input, control, output, and storage
    b. interface, processing, output, and memory
    c. input, output, processing, and storage
    d. input, logical/rational, arithmetic, and output

3. A handheld input device that controls the cursor location is
    a. the cursor control keyboard
    b. a mouse
    c. a modem
    d. the CRT

4. A printer that forms images without striking the paper is
    a. an impact printer
    b. a nonimpact printer
    c. a laser printer
    d. both b and c

5. The amount of storage provided by a floppy disk is a function of
    a. the thickness of the floppy disk
    b. the recording density
    c. the number of recording tracks on the floppy disk
    d. both b and c

6. Portable computers use a flat-panel screen called
    a. a multichrome monitor
    b. a cathode ray tube
    c. a liquid crystal display
    d. a monochrome monitor

7. CD-ROM is a type of
    a. main memory
    b. auxiliary storage
    c. communications equipment
    d. system software

8. An operating system is considered part of
    a. word processing software
    b. database software
    c. system software
    d. spreadsheet software

9. The type of application software most commonly used to create and print documents is
    a. word processing
    b. electronic spreadsheet
    c. presentation graphics
    d. none of these

10. The type of application software most commonly used to send messages to and receive messages from other computer users is
    a. e-mail
    b. database
    c. presentation graphics
    d. none of these

11. Data may include
    a. text
    b. numbers
    c. images
    d. all of these

12. Which of the following is *not* an advantage of having a LAN?
    a. software control
    b. network maintenance
    c. information sharing
    d. greater storage
    e. none of these

STUDENT ASSESSMENT 3

Instructions: Fill in the word(s) that best complete(s) the statement.

1. The acronym _____ is an abbreviation for local area network.
2. A _____ is a pointing device that allows you to select menu options and open and close files.
3. The computer keyboard is a(n) _____ device.
4. The four basic computer operations are: _____, _____, _____, and _____.
5. The _____ is the brain of the computer.
6. The surface of the computer screen is made up of individual dots called _____.
7. A(n) _____ allows two computers to communicate with each other over phone lines.
8. A(n) _____ is equal to approximately 1 million bytes.
9. Telephones send _____ signals, whereas computers send _____ signals.
10. The _____ is the center of a computer network.

STUDENT ASSIGNMENTS

PROJECT 1: ANALYZE PERSONAL COMPUTER SYSTEMS

Instructions: Describe the personal computer that you use at school, work, or home. Give details about any input, processing and memory, output, secondary storage, and communications components that are part of that system. If you could spend your own money to improve this system, what would you spend it on and why? Would it be more cost effective to buy a new computer system instead?

PROJECT 2: COMPARE PERSONAL COMPUTER ADVERTISEMENTS

Instructions: Obtain a copy of a recent computer magazine and review the advertisements for desktop personal computer systems. Compare the ads for the most and least expensive computer systems that you can find. Discuss the differences between the two.

PROJECT 3: VISIT LOCAL COMPUTER RETAIL STORES

Instructions: Compare the various types of computers and support equipment that are available at your local computer retail store. Ask the staff about warranties, hardware setup, installing software, and repair services. Describe the knowledge of the sales staff and their willingness to answer your questions. Would you feel confident buying a computer system from this store? Why or why not?

Chapter 4

PREPARING LEGAL CORRESPONDENCE

OBJECTIVES

Upon completion of this chapter, you should be able to:

1. Format legal correspondence
2. Describe the guidelines for preparing legal correspondence
3. Discuss the guidelines for envelope creation
4. Create a legal letterhead using word processing software
5. Use word processing software to prepare an envelope
6. Discuss the guidelines for creating a standard office memo
7. Create an office memo using a template
8. Explain dictation and transcription procedures

PREPARING LEGAL CORRESPONDENCE

The preparation of legal correspondence is a very important function of the law office staff. Almost all the information in the law office is recorded in the form of letters, memorandums, agreements, contracts, and court pleadings. Original documents may be dictated, written in longhand, or typed into the computer by the attorney. In the past, a legal secretary or support person assisted each attorney in the preparation of correspondence, legal documents, and other office duties. Because of all the changes in technology and the use of word processing software, many attorneys may now share support staff and type their own documents. Often, the support staff will be responsible for cleaning up the documents and preparing the final copy. These changes also have affected the job requirements and responsibilities of the office support staff and the tasks they are required to perform.

Word Processing

Word processing is the method by which information is assembled into a document. Word processing includes the use of computers, software, and printers to convert information to printed documents. The true value of word processing, however, is the ability to change or rewrite text without retyping an entire page, a series of pages, or an entire book.

The basic features of word processing include **word wrap**, **text insertion**, and **editing** features such as cut, copy, and paste. Word processing may also include many user-friendly features, such as **spell checking**, **thesaurus**, formatting, **templates**, and a wide selection of font types, sizes, effects, and styles.

FIGURE 4-1 *Accuracy is important in document production.*

LEGAL CORRESPONDENCE STYLES

A letter represents the writer and reflects the law firm. A thoughtfully written letter attractively arranged on high-quality paper adds to the prestige of the law office (see Figure 4-1). The stationery used by law offices generally is quality bond paper. The letterhead on the stationery is conservative in nature and reflects the tastes of the office. The letterhead usually includes the name of the attorney or firm, the address, the telephone number, and e-mail address. This information is printed or embossed on the stationery.

Letters

The following guidelines provide information on setting up legal correspondence. These guidelines are illustrated in Figure 4-2. While there are many variations from office to office, this style generally is acceptable for preparing correspondence. Check the files to see what the preferred style is for your office, or ask your supervisor.

1. *Letterhead or return address.* The **letterhead** or **return address** includes the attorney or firm name and address, along with other information, such as a telephone number, fax number, or e-mail address. Some firms may list all the attorneys in the firm, whereas others may list only the partners. State bar associations have indicated that paralegals may be listed on the letterhead, but if paralegals are listed, their title must appear so that clients will not mistake them for attorneys.

2. *Date.* On letterhead paper with a mailing address, place the **date line** a double space below the last line in the letterhead or allocate a 2-inch margin from the top edge of the paper. The date may be centered, begin at the center of the page, or even be positioned at the right margin. Be sure to check the accuracy of the date.

3. *Inside address.* The **inside address** contains some or all of the following: courtesy title (Mr., Mrs., Ms., Dr.), name, professional title, company name or institution, street or mailing address, city, two-letter state abbreviation in caps (postal usage), and zip code.

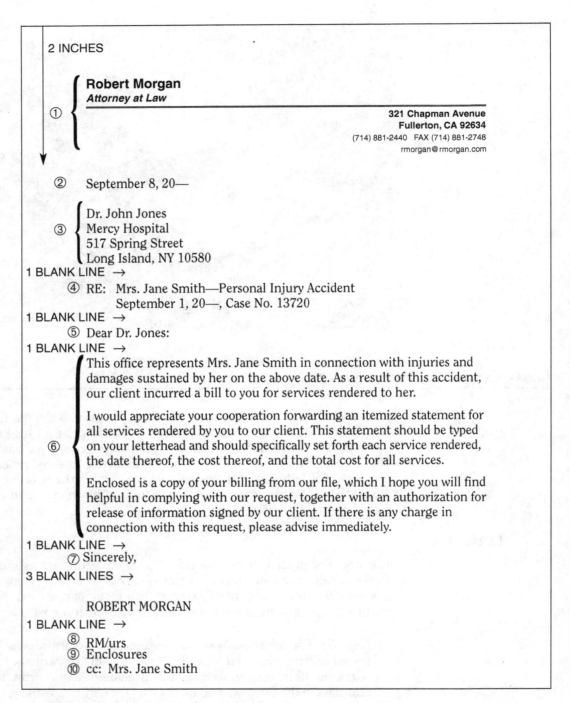

FIGURE 4-2 *Sample legal correspondence.*

4. *Subject line.* RE means "regarding." Use it to begin the **subject line.** RE is placed in caps two lines above the salutation, followed by a colon. If a case number has been assigned, giving that number in the subject line is useful. (Some offices underscore the subject line.)

5. *Salutation.* Place the **salutation** two lines below the RE: line. The salutation is followed by a colon.

6. *Body.* For the majority of business letters, single space paragraphs within the **body of the letter** and double space between each paragraph. The first line of each paragraph may be flush with the left margin or indented.

7. *Complimentary closing.* The **complimentary closing** goes two lines below the last line of the body of the letter and is followed by a comma. Some legal firms include the name of the firm in the signature lines. The name of the firm is placed in all capital letters two lines below the complimentary close. Space down four lines for the handwritten signature.

   Combinations of names and titles should be typed so that balance is achieved in the signature lines. Ordinarily, type the writer's name in all caps or upper- and lowercase on the fourth line below the complimentary closing, or firm name, if used. The name and title may appear on the same line or on separate lines, depending on the length of each item.

   If a letter is signed by a person other than the one whose name appears in the typed signature line, the initials of the person signing the letter usually follow the signature.

8. *Reference initials.* **Reference initials** are used to show the writer and who keyed the letter. They are created in lowercase letters a double space below the last line of the signature block at the left margin. In large firms, the correspondent's initials are used, and the typist's initials are usually typed in lowercase letters next to the uppercase letters of the dictator, for example, RM:urs. The initials can be separated by a slash or colon.

9. *Enclosures.* If any enclosures are to be included in the envelope, an **enclosure notation** is typed at the left margin a single space below the reference initials.

10. *Copy notation.* When a courtesy copy of the correspondence is sent to a third party, the name is noted in the **copy notation** after *cc:* at the bottom of the letter a single space below the enclosure notation, if used; otherwise, it should be placed a single space below reference initials.

11. *Blind copy notation:* If sending a copy of the letter to other individuals is unnecessary or inappropriate for an addressee to know, use a **blind copy notation**. The blind copy notation appears only on copies of the letter, not the original.

    The blind copy notation may be placed (1) one inch from the top edge of the page at the left margin or (2) where the regular copy notation normally appears. Examples of blind copy notation follow:

    bcc: **Donald R. Douglas**

    bcc: **Ms. Rose Grammer**

12. *Postscripts.* A **postscript** is used if you want to add an idea or emphasize a message. The postscript is written in the last position of the letter and may be typed or handwritten. A blank line should be left between the last line and the postscript.

13. *File numbers.* Some firms require that a coded file number appear after the signature line at the bottom of the letter on each piece of correspondence. This code helps to identify the writer, client, and file number. It also helps to locate correspondence stored on the system.

14. *Second-page headings.* **Headers** for second and succeeding pages should be prepared on plain paper. Use a 1-inch top margin and the same side margins that appear on the first page. The continuation-page heading should include the name of the addressee, the page number, and the date. Either a horizontal or vertical format may be used.

Sample Horizontal Format

Mercy Hospital   2   October 1, 20–

Sample Vertical Format

Mercy Hospital
Page 2
October 1, 20–

Folding and Inserting Letters   Figure 4-3 illustrates how to fold and insert letters into No. 10 and No. 6¾ envelopes.

Envelopes   Most law offices use stationery measuring 8½ by 11 inches and use a No. 10 (9½ by 4⅛ inches) or a No. 6¾ (6½ by 3⅝ inches) envelope.

The return address usually is printed in the upper-left corner of the envelope. In large offices the writer's or sender's initials or name are typed above the company name and return address.

1. On No. 10 envelopes, allow a 2-inch top margin and begin the address 4¼ inches from the left edge of the envelope. Single space and block the address line. See Figure 4-4 for the return and inside address placement on a 6¾ envelope.
2. Capitalize the first letter of each word, except prepositions, conjunctions, and articles.
3. Type the city, state, and zip code on the last line. One space is typed between the state name and the zip code. The state may be a two-letter abbreviation (postal usage) or spelled out in full.

Word Processing Software Envelope Printing Feature   Word processing software has automated the process of printing an envelope. The envelope printing feature uses the address from the existing document to print an envelope, with or without the return address. Envelopes can be printed separately or attached to the respective document. Envelopes also can be printed using the bar code to assist in mail sorting and accuracy of delivery.

Formatting Considerations   With the extensive use of word processing software programs in today's law offices, modifications are being made to letter and envelope formatting to accommodate the use of these software programs. While it has been acceptable in the past to have the **attention line** on manual-typed letters placed at the left margin two lines below the inside address, this is not possible when using the envelope function in word processing software packages.

FIGURE 4-3 *Letter folding.*

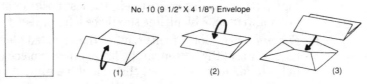

No. 10 (9 1/2" X 4 1/8") Envelope

(1)   (2)   (3)

Fold the letter into thirds from bottom to top and insert in the envelope with the first creased edge into the envelope first.

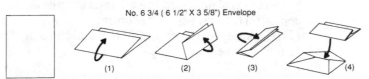

No. 6 3/4 (6 1/2" X 3 5/8") Envelope

(1)   (2)   (3)   (4)

Fold the letter in half and then fold in thirds from right to left. Insert left creased edge of letter into the envelope first.

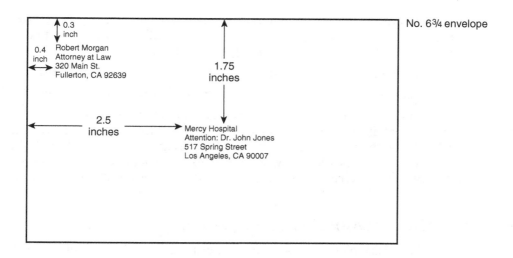

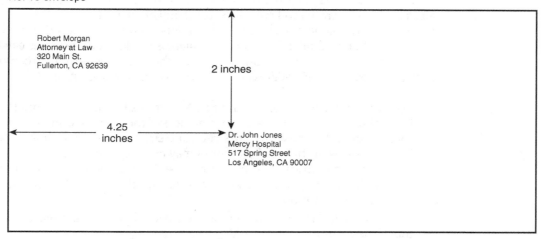

FIGURE 4-4 *Suggested envelope formatting style.*

It is suggested that, when using word processing software in creating letters with envelopes, the attention line be typed on the second line of the inside address below the company name. The attention line then will appear in the envelope address generated by the software without requiring further keyboarding adjustments by the operator.

Computer-generated address labels   Word processing programs as well as database programs can easily generate mailing labels from a database merge file or a database file. Addresses are compiled and formatted for printing on predefined label forms prepared commercially by companies such as Avery or 3M. The following example is a printout of labels prepared on a word processor using a label form:

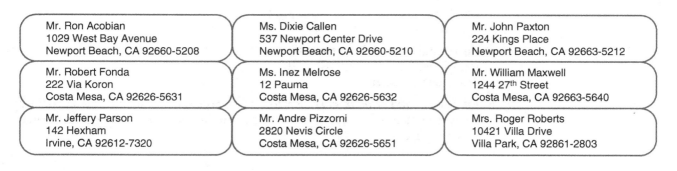

To process mail faster and more economically, the U.S. Postal Service has assigned four additional digits to the zip codes of mailing addresses that do not have their own separate zip code with a hyphen. For example:

Sacramento, CA 92450-0001   Metairie, Louisiana 70003-4217
Hingham, MA 02403-9123   Santa Clarita, California 91380-9047

The use of zip + 4 is recommended by the U.S. Postal Service and bulk mailers may obtain reduced rates for the use of zip + four. Zip + 4 codes may be located through various media available for purchase from the U.S. Postal Service and from various private software companies. Zip + 4 for specific addresses may be retrieved free of charge at the U.S. Postal Service website at www.usps.com/zip4/.

Memos (Interoffice Memos, Memorandums)

Most large legal offices use some form of printed memo to send information within the organization. Usually this is done by using a word processing template or a custom template prepared for the specific needs of the law office (see Figure 4-5). E-mail also is used as a way to send messages inside and outside the office. Imprinted on the form is the firm name, the fact that it is a memorandum, and DATE, TO, FROM, RE or SUBJECT, and CC lines. If no such template is available, these words can be typed in all caps, followed by a colon, similar to the sample interoffice memorandum shown in Figure 4-6. No address is used because the message stays within the firm.

1. *TO and FROM lines.* The TO and FROM sections include the names (and sometimes the titles and the department names) of the addressee and the writer. Personal titles such as Miss, Ms., Mrs., Mr., and Dr. are not used. In smaller and more informal firms, initials or first names may be used. If the memo is sent to more than one person in another area, it is possible to fit more than one name in the space following TO, or the names can be listed below the body of the memo indicating the distribution.

2. *Date line.* The date of the memo can be typed following the subject line or at the top of the memo.

3. *Subject or RE line.* Usually the subject line is the title under which the correspondence will be filed. It should be brief and yet include enough information to inform the reader of the subject of the communication.

4. *Body.* The body of the message usually begins several lines below the last line of the heading, and the style is single spaced with double spacing between paragraphs, with either block or indented paragraphs.

5. *Second page.* If there is a second page or succeeding pages, a horizontal or blocked **second-page heading** is keyboarded 1 inch from the top of each succeeding page. Starting at the left margin, indicate the addressee's name and department, page number, and date.

Vertical Second Page
John Jones
Probate Department
August 1, 20–

Horizontal Second-Page Heading
John Jones   2   August 1, 20–
Probate Department

6. *Enclosures and attachments.* Enclosures or attachments are indicated two lines below the memo at the left margin. The number of enclosures or attachments may be indicated.

INTEROFFICE MEMORANDUM

TO: [CLICK **HERE** AND TYPE NAME]

FROM: [CLICK **HERE** AND TYPE NAME]

SUBJECT: [CLICK **HERE** AND TYPE SUBJECT]

DATE: 1/19/20--

CC: [CLICK **HERE** AND TYPE NAME]

HOW TO USE THIS MEMO TEMPLATE

Select text you would like to replace, and type your memo. Use styles such as Heading 1-3 and Body Text in the Style control on the Formatting toolbar. To save changes to this template for future use, on the File menu, click **Save As.** In the **Save As Type** box, choose **Document Template** (the filename extensions should change from *.doc* to *.dot*) and save the template. Next time you want to use the updated template, on the **File** menu, click **New.** In the **New Document** task pane, under **Templates,** click **On my computer.** In the **Templates** dialog, your updated template will appear on the General tab.

FIGURE 4-5   *Sample memo (memorandum) template.*

INTEROFFICE MEMORANDUM

TO: JOHN JONES

FROM: ROBERT MORGAN

SUBJECT: IMPLEMENTATION OF NEW EQUIPMENT

DATE: 1/19/20--

CC: BOB WILSON, ANN NGUYEN, SAM GONZALEZ, BOB FREDMAN

There will be a meeting on Tuesday, January 25, 20--, at 10:00 a.m. in the conference room to discuss the attached proposal on computer-related equipment. This proposal and the implementation of this equipment will provide our staff with better administrative support and improve the quality and production of our legal documents and correspondence.

Please plan to attend this meeting. You will want to read the attached proposal as you will find it helpful in understanding the new procedures.

Refreshments will be available; please reply to Sally Sloan at ext. 36 if you will be attending.

Attachments

FIGURE 4-6   *Sample memo (memorandum) form.*

Word Processing Templates, Macros, and Wizards

Word processing software programs include time-saving features called templates, macros, and wizards. A template is a stored document pattern that can be used to create new documents. The document pattern for a specific document has already been formatted and created. With templates, you can easily create a variety of documents, such as letters, memos, faxes, brochures, reports, awards, and manuals.

Templates include **default settings** that can be changed or modified to meet the user's specifications or needs. You can select the template from the template list, type in the information you want included, and save to a disk as a new document.

Word processing software also includes another time-saving feature called a macro. A **macro** is a document containing recorded commands that can accomplish a task automatically and save time. The word *macro* was coined by computer programmers for a collection of commands used to make a large programming job easier and save time. Creating a macro is referred to as *recording*. As a macro is being recorded, all the keys pressed and the menus and dialog boxes accessed are recorded and become part of the macro. For example, you can record a macro for the letterhead and signature of a letter that can be used over and over again. You can also record a macro to change the left or right margins or insert page numbering in a document. This process will save keyboarding time by automating the task.

Along with templates and macros, word processing programs also include wizards. **Wizards** are programs that provide on-screen guidance as you create a new document. Wizards do most of the work for you in creating a document. There are wizards for calendars, agendas, faxes, letters, memos, newsletters, pleadings, résumés, and tables. For example, if you choose the fax wizard, you are guided through the entire process of creating a fax cover sheet, step by step. All you need to do is follow the instructions in the dialog boxes as they appear on the screen. A series of buttons along the bottom of the wizard dialog boxes enables you to move from one dialog box to the next.

DICTATION AND TRANSCRIPTION

Machine Dictation

While shorthand dictation once was a qualification for employment in the law office, this is no longer true. **Machine dictation** is still used, however, in many law offices. Machine dictation involves the use of a machine into which the dictator has dictated information on some form of media from which the support staff transcribes. This process can be in the form of a handheld portable unit (see Figure 4-7), desktop recording unit, or centralized dictation unit. Many suppliers use the same type of equipment for both the dictator and transcriber, but the transcriber's unit usually involves earphone attachments. The earphone is either a lightweight ear clip that covers one ear or a heavier, over-the-head headset (see Figure 4-8).

Transcription

Successful **transcription** is an art and the result of good procedures. When transcribing, if there is a word, a meaning, or the spelling of a name about which there is a question, check with the attorney. The changing of a letter or legal paper may

FIGURE 4-7 *Attorney using a handheld dictation unit. (Courtesy of Jackson, DeMarco, Tidus, Peckenpaugh, A Law Corporation)*

FIGURE 4-8 *The headset or the earphone can be used by the legal professional in the transcription process. (Courtesy of Jackson, DeMarco, Tidus, Peckenpaugh, A Law Corporation)*

result in unnecessary problems for the attorney and client. Some guidelines for effective transcription procedures include the following:

1. Prepare a clear space in which to work.
2. Prioritize the importance of the documents to be transcribed. (A trained dictator can indicate the importance of dictated materials through the use of cues from electronic devices.)
3. Keep dictionaries and reference and procedure manuals available for ready use.
4. Use effective listening techniques during the transcription. Strive for continuous flow of information.
5. Use care with sound-alike words, spelling, punctuation, capitalization, numbers, and word division.
6. Proofread carefully. Carefully record and store media for future reference.
7. Assemble necessary copies, along with envelopes, for the author's signature and approval.

Some of the features available on today's transcribers include the ability to automatically replay a few words each time the dictation unit starts, telephone recording dictation from an outside phone, and conference recording for recording of voices of several individuals in a meeting.

Scanning Devices

Devices used to scan dictation are called **scanning devices** and can be either manual or electronic. These devices indicate the length of documents and any corrections or special notations. **Electronic cueing devices** provide the same kind of information on an electronic display.

Voice Recognition

Voice recognition is the machine's capacity to receive spoken words and print them on a screen. This technology is the direction of the future in dictation equipment, and it is being used in some environments today. With improved technology in this area, the lawyer's assistant may change from keying a completely dictated document to formatting and editing the voice-dictated draft.

SUMMARY

The preparation of legal correspondence is a very important function of the law office support staff. Original documents may be dictated, handwritten, or typed into the computer by the attorney. Because the price of technology is dropping and support staff salaries are rising, many attorneys are typing in their own information and using the support staff to prepare the final finished copies.

The use of computers and word processing software applications has automated and simplified the processing of information. Basic editing features, word wrap, and text insertion have made it easier for the user to process information. User-friendly features such as spell check, thesaurus, formatting, and templates simplify the document production.

There are many legal correspondence styles for preparing business letters. Guidelines have been developed for the creation of legal correspondence, envelopes, and letters, and they need to be followed in the preparation of these documents. The use of macros, templates, and built-in word processing features simplifies these operations.

Dictation and transcription still are used by many offices, and skilled transcribers are useful in producing legal correspondence. Good procedures and personal skills are necessary to produce successful transcripts and legal correspondence. Scanning devices also are helpful in transcription by indicating to the transcriber the length of documents, revisions to be made, or special notations from the dictator. Voice recognition is the direction of the future in dictation equipment.

Maximizing the talents of support staff is important to the successful operation of the law office. New computer software programs have become more user-friendly and adapt to the user's work style and environment. Word processing software is being updated continually, and it is important in the production of legal correspondence in the law office.

VOCABULARY

attention line   The line that is used for directing correspondence within a company. Usually it appears below the inside address.

blind copy notation   Used when a copy of the letter to other individuals is unnecessary or inappropriate for an addressee to know.

body of the letter   The single-spaced paragraphs that represent the content of the letter.

complimentary closing   The salutation that appears below the body of the letter.

copy notation The notation on the letter that indicates when copies of the correspondence are directed to individuals other than the addressee and the distribution of these copies.

date line The date of the letter. Usually this line is placed below the letterhead.

default settings Settings that are preestablished in software packages.

edit The process of changing or modifying text from its original state.

electronic cueing device A device used in transcription that allows the user to determine the length of the transcribed document. It also may include special instructions for the transcriber.

enclosure notation A notation on the letter placed below the reference initials that indicates that additional information is included or enclosed with the letter.

header Text that appears at the top of each page.

inside address The addressee, the one to whom the letter is being sent. Usually the inside address includes the courtesy title, full name, professional title, department name, company name, street or mailing address, city, state, and zip code of the recipient.

letterhead The letterhead includes the attorney or firm's name along with the address, phone number, fax number, and e-mail address. It also may include some form of graphic design.

machine dictation Use of machine into which someone dictates information to be recorded on some form of media. The transcriber then can transcribe this information at some future time.

macro A previously saved series of stored keystrokes or commands that, when invoked, replays those commands or keystrokes.

postscript A notation in the last position of a letter that may be used to emphasize or add an idea that was unintentionally omitted from the body of the letter.

reference initials The initials on the letter that are used to show who typed the letter. The initials of both the writer and preparer may be included in the reference initial notation.

return address The address of the person or office mailing the letter.

salutation The personal greeting at the beginning of the letter.

scanning devices Devices used with transcription equipment that indicate the length of the documents and special notations for the transcriber.

second-page headings Headings that appear on second and succeeding pages of a letter that may include the name of the addressee, the page number, and the date.

spell checking A word processing feature that checks the correct spelling of every word in a document against the word processor's dictionary.

subject line The line in the letter below the salutation that indicates what kind of information is included in the letter.

templates A stored document pattern used to create word processed documents.

text insertion The ability to insert text into previously keyed information and have that information accommodate and adjust to the insertion.

thesaurus A word processing feature that gives the user synonyms for words.

transcription The act or process of transcribing previously recorded information.

wizards A time-saving software feature that provides on-screen guidance in the creation of a document.

word processing A software program that is used to edit, manipulate, and revise text to create documents.

word wrap A feature in word processing and other types of programs that automatically ends each line of text and wraps the remaining text down to the next line.

STUDENT ASSESSMENT 1

Instructions: Circle T if the statement is true or F if the statement is false.

T F   1. Some firms require that a coded file number appear after the signature line on each piece of correspondence.

T F   2. It is not yet possible to telephone record on dictation equipment from an outside phone.

T F   3. The base of the letterhead on the return address on plain papers should be no lower than 2 inches from the top of the paper.

T F   4. The salutation on a letter usually appears four lines below the inside address.

T F   5. When a courtesy copy of the letter is sent to a third party, the "bc:" notation usually appears at the bottom of the letter.

T F   6. Most law offices use a No. 9 size envelope for most of their correspondence.

T F   7. Templates are stored document patterns created in word processing software programs.

T F   8. Wizards are word processing programs that provide on-screen guidance as a new document is created.

T F   9. Voice recognition is not being used in today's law offices.

T F 10. The body of most business letters is double spaced, with a single space between the paragraphs.

STUDENT ASSESSMENT 2

Instructions: Circle the letter that indicates the most correct answer.

1. What is keyed directly under the reference initials?
    a. copy notation
    b. enclosure notation
    c. file notation
    d. mailing notation

2. A block letter has
    a. an indented date and indented closing lines
    b. an indented date and indented paragraphs
    c. everything flush at right margin
    d. none of these

3. Macros are used to
    a. make something larger
    b. put together two documents
    c. quote information
    d. store keystrokes

4. Word processing features include
    a. word wrap
    b. editing and text insertion
    c. spell checking
    d. all of these

5. Which of the following may be included in the letterhead?
    a. attorney's name and address
    b. attorney's phone number
    c. attorney's fax and e-mail address
    d. all of these

6. Courtesy copies are indicated with the following abbreviation:
    a. C:
    b. bc:
    c. cc:
    d. c:

7. Use a _____ inch top margin on second and succeeding pages of a letter.
    a. 1/2
    b. 1
    c. 2
    d. 3

8. Allow a _____ inch top margin on No. 10 envelopes.
    a. 1/2
    b. 1
    c. 2
    d. 3

9. Memo forms usually do not include the following:
    a. date line
    b. signature block
    c. TO and FROM lines
    d. subject line

10. Word processing programs provide wizards for which of the following?
    a. agendas
    b. faxes
    c. résumés
    d. all of these

STUDENT ASSIGNMENT

PROJECT 1: CREATE A LEGAL LETTERHEAD USING WORD PROCESSING SOFTWARE

Using your word processing software, create the following letterhead for a document.

Creating a Legal Letterhead (California)

Robert Morgan
Attorney at Law

---

320 Main Street
Fullerton, CA 92634
(714) 555-2440 FAX (714) 555-2748

(continued)

Instructions

1. Open a new document and use the default margin settings.

2. Select Arial, bold, font size 14, left alignment, key in **ROBERT MORGAN**, and press Enter.

3. Select font size 12, italic, key in *Attorney at Law*, and press Enter twice.

4. Reposition the cursor in front of the "A" in Attorney at Law, and choose the bottom border button and the 3/4-point double underline, and insert a line across the page.

5. Position the pointer below the line; be sure the bottom border button is turned off. Select right alignment, font size 10, and key in the address, and city and state lines. Press Enter after each line.

6. Select font size 8, and key in the phone and FAX number.

7. Print preview your document.

8. Save your document on your data disk as **ch4_lthd.doc**, and print one copy for your instructor.

9. Be sure to close the file.

Notes: (1) This letterhead was created using Microsoft Word® software. If you are using another software package, there may be variations in the font sizes and spacing in the projects in this book. You may want to make adjustments or check with your instructor for preferences. (2) If you prefer, you may want to create this letterhead as a macro instead of a stored document. Check with your instructor for specific instructions.

This project has been developed for California. If you live in Texas or New York, you may want to create the same style letterhead using the following addresses. If you live in a state other than these three, you may want to make up your own addresses. Refer to the above instructions for creating a legal letterhead to create the letterhead.

TEXAS

Greg Bailey
Attorney at Law
460 Main Street
Austin, TX 77418
(409) 555-5912 FAX (409) 555-5906

NEW YORK

Ken Kvitka
Attorney at Law
460 Harbor View
Long Island, NY 10580
(603) 555-5912 FAX (603) 555-5906

PROJECT 2: PREPARE A NO. 10 SIZE ENVELOPE

Open document **ch4fg4_**. Using the envelope feature of your word processing program, create an envelope for the letter. Print the envelope. Close your document.

PROJECT 3: CREATE AN OFFICE MEMO USING A TEMPLATE

Using the template feature of your word processing program, create a **sample** memo similar to Figure 4–6.
Save it as **ch4_memo** and print one copy for your instructor. Close your document.

Part 2

COURT STRUCTURE

Chapter 5
The Court Structure

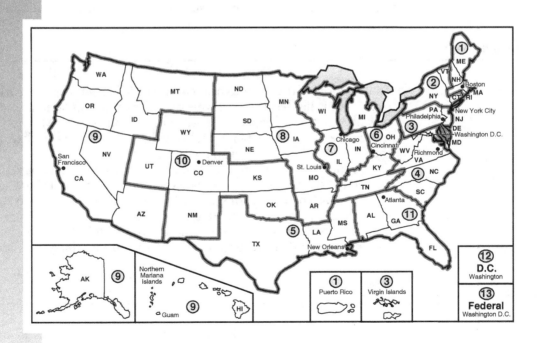

THE COURT STRUCTURE

OBJECTIVES

Upon completion of this chapter, you should be able to:

1. Define the terminology used with court systems and procedures
2. Discuss the difference between original and appellate jurisdiction
3. Explain the definition of venue
4. Describe the roles of the officers of the court
5. Discuss the organization and jurisdiction of the federal court system
6. Discuss the organization and jurisdiction of the state court systems
7. Explain the statutes of limitations
8. Describe court filing procedures, forms, and fees

The court system is that part of the government established to apply the law and administer justice. For every wrong, it has been said, there is a remedy, and for every remedy, there is a court to review the evidence and render a verdict. There are fifty-one separate court systems in the United States, the federal court system and the 50 state court systems. The fifty state court systems are similar in design to the federal court and usually include a supreme court, **appellate court**, and **trial court**.

JURISDICTION

The authority of the court to hear cases is called its **jurisdiction**. Jurisdiction is fixed by law and is limited as to territory, type of case, and amount of controversy. Courts may have original or appellate jurisdiction, or both. Courts with **original jurisdiction** hear a case when it is first brought into court. Courts with **appellate jurisdiction** have the power to review cases of an inferior court.

Courts frequently are classified according to the nature of their jurisdiction. A civil court is authorized to hear and decide cases involving private rights and duties, such as breach of contract or slander. A criminal court is one that tries cases involving offenses against society or the state, such as homicide, embezzlement, or theft. Courts also are classified as juvenile, domestic, or probate. It is the responsibility of the attorney and support staff to determine the proper court for filing the initial legal papers.

VENUE

In addition to knowing at what level or jurisdiction legal papers are to be filed, the attorney must also determine in which geographic area the papers are to be filed. The geographic area is known as the **venue**, and it includes the name of the county and the state in which a document is to be notarized. *Venue* is the geographical location; it indicates where the trial will be held, whereas *jurisdiction* is the authority of a court to hear and decide the case. The format for specifying the venue is established by the laws of the state and varies considerably from state to state, county to county, and court to court. It is important to check with the court clerk to find out where the legal papers should be filed and how the papers are to be prepared.

OFFICERS OF THE COURT

The **judge** or **justice** is the primary officer of the court, and judges either are elected or appointed (federal judges are appointed). The judge presides over the trial and hearings and instructs the jury on the law in jury trials. The term *court* is sometimes used instead of *judge*.

Clerks of the court sometimes are appointed in higher courts, but usually they are elected to office in the lower courts. Their main duties are to supervise the deputies who enter cases on the court calendar, keep accurate records of the proceedings, approve bail bonds, and compute the costs involved.

The **court reporter** is the official stenographer of the court who records and transcribes a verbatim record of the proceedings at a hearing or trial, either by shorthand or by machine shorthand. The transcript is called a *court of record*.

The **bailiff** is responsible for maintaining order in the courtroom and may also be responsible for moving the jury to and from the jury room.

Depending on the type of jurisdiction in which they serve, **marshals**, **sheriffs**, and **constables** serve the summons, take charge of the jury, and execute judgments.

THE JURY

The **jury** is a body of citizens sworn by a court to try to determine a verdict from the issues of fact submitted to them. A trial jury in most state courts consists of twelve persons who listen to the facts and present their decision, termed a **verdict**. In civil actions, most states require a three-fourths majority, while in criminal actions a unanimous vote of the jurors is necessary. In civil cases tried without a jury, the judge applies the law to the facts and announces his or her **judgment**. In criminal cases, the judge reviews the case and the jury's verdict and then pronounces the **sentence**.

FEDERAL COURTS

The federal court system (see Figure 5-1) includes the following:

1. *Supreme Court of the United States.* The Supreme Court is the only federal court established by the Constitution in Article III. It consists of nine justices appointed for *life* by the president of the United States, with the approval of Congress. Although a person, through an attorney, may request the Supreme Court to review a case, it is not required to review all cases. The Supreme Court has the right to hear or not hear a case presented to it on appeal. If it refuses to hear the case, the decision of the lower court remains in force. The Supreme Court is the only court that can hear a case between two states, and the Supreme Court only will hear a case from a state court when a question of constitutional or federal law

FIGURE 5-1 *The federal court system.*

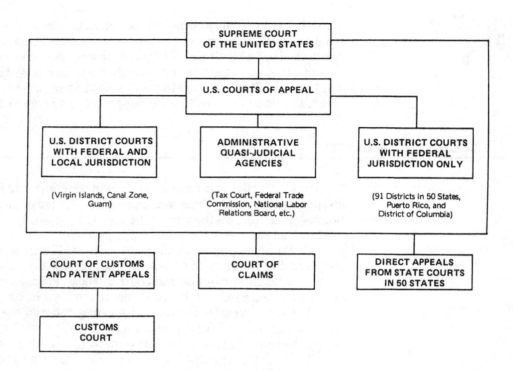

is involved. Because the decisions of the Supreme Court have such a far-reaching effect, usually they include both a majority and a minority opinion.

2. *United States Court of Appeal (Circuit).* The United States, including the District of Columbia, is divided into judicial circuits, and each of these circuits has a **court of appeals.** Appeals from district courts are made to the courts of appeals. Presently there are thirteen different circuits. The **circuit courts** review all final decisions and certain interlocutory decisions of district courts within the circuit. For example, appeals from district courts located in New York would be heard in the Second Circuit, while appeals heard in California would be heard in the Ninth Circuit, and appeals in Texas would be heard in the Fifth Circuit. Each of these courts is presided over by three federal judges. The three judges review cases tried in state courts on the basis of written information, and there are no witnesses or juries. A significant part of our law is made from the decisions of the U.S. courts of appeal and the precedents that they set.

3. *United States District Court.* The United States, including the District of Columbia, is divided into a number of judicial districts (see Figure 5-2). Some states form a single district, while others are divided into two or more districts. The district courts have original jurisdiction in almost all cases that may be heard in federal courts; that is, they try cases having to do with federal laws. Both civil and criminal cases are tried in district courts. Civil cases that may be brought in district courts are (a) civil suits brought by the United States; (b) actions brought by citizens of different states claiming land under grants by different states; (c) bankruptcy, internal revenue, postal, copyright, and patent law proceedings; (d) civil cases affecting admiralty and maritime jurisdiction; (e) proceedings against national banking associations; and (f) civil matters involving citizens of different states.

4. *Other federal courts.* In addition to the preceding courts, the following tribunals have been created by Congress to act on matters indicated by their titles: Customs Court, Court of Customs and Patent Appeals, Court of Claims, Tax Court, Court of Military Appeals, bankruptcy courts, and territorial courts.

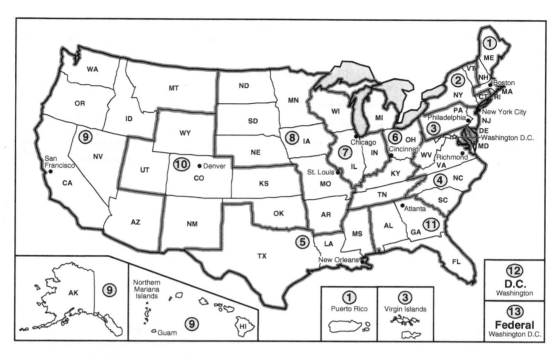

FIGURE 5-2   *The thirteen federal judicial districts.*

STATE COURTS

The system of courts in the various states is similar to the federal court system, although it may differ somewhat in the number, name, and jurisdiction of the courts (see Figure 5-3 through Figure 5-7).

1. *State supreme courts.* The highest court in most states is called the **supreme court.** In some states it may have a different name. For example, it is called a Court of Appeals in New York. The jurisdiction is original in a few instances, although it is ordinarily appellate in nature. With the exception of matters involving the U.S. Constitution, the decision of the state supreme court is final in most cases.

2. *Intermediate courts.* In some states, intermediate courts have original jurisdiction in a few cases, but generally they have appellate jurisdiction for cases that were moved for review from the county or district courts. These courts are known by various names, such as court of appeals, district court of appeals, district court, appellate court, court of civil appeals, and court of criminal appeals.

3. *County and district courts (Figure 5-7).* Most of the work of attorneys and their support staff is done in courts of original or general jurisdiction. These courts have broad general jurisdiction involving disputes between two or more parties, as well as criminal offenses against the state. They are called **courts of original jurisdiction** because it is in them that the case is first instituted. These courts are known by various names in different states: **superior courts,** circuit courts, district courts, or county courts. On occasion these courts hear appeals from inferior courts, but the bulk of their work is composed of the more serious criminal cases and civil cases in which the amount in controversy exceeds a specified amount set by the state legislature.

FIGURE 5-3 *Jurisdiction of California appellate courts.*

SUPREME COURT—Jurisdiction	COURTS OF APPEAL—Jurisdiction

ORIGINAL JURISDICTION: Habeas corpus and extraordinary relief in the nature of mandamus, certiorari and prohibition.

APPELLATE JURISDICTION: When judgment of death has been pronounced.

TRANSFER OF CAUSES: The Supreme Court may, before decision becomes final, transfer to itself a cause in a court of appeal. It may, before decision, transfer a cause from itself to a court of appeal or from one court of appeal or division to another.

ORIGINAL JURISDICTION: Power to issue writs as original matter is equal to and concurrent with Supreme Court.

APPELLATE JURISDICTION: Except when judgment of death has been pronounced, all cases in which superior courts have original jurisdiction and in other causes prescribed by statute.

TRANSFERRED CASES: All cases, matters, and proceedings pending before the Supreme Court ordered transferred by the Supreme Court to a Court of Appeal for hearing and decision; cases on appeal within original jurisdiction of a municipal or justice court which a Court of Appeal orders transferred to it when the Superior Court certifies or the Court of Appeals on its own motion determines from an opinion of the appellate department published or to be published in Advance California Appellate Reports that such transfer appears necessary to secure uniformity of decision or to settle important questions of law.

FIGURE 5-4 *California court structure.*

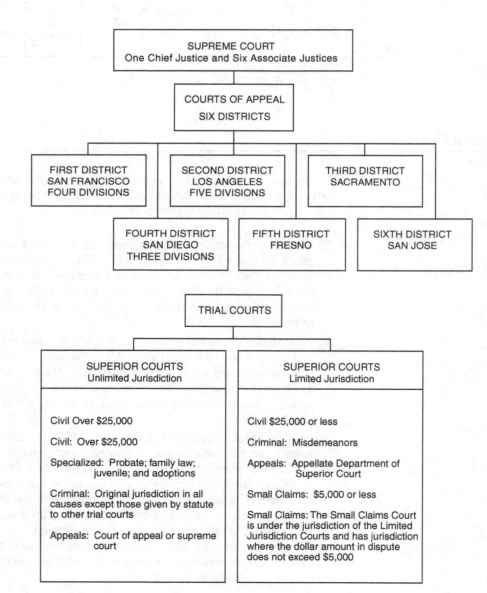

FIGURE 5-5 *New York court system.*

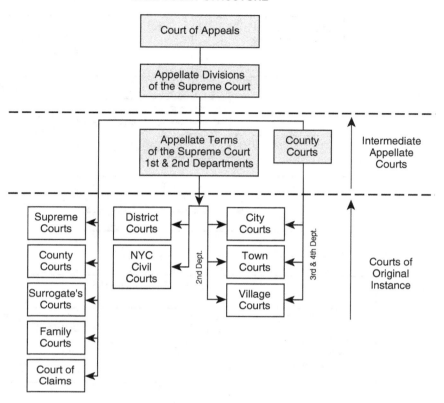

CIVIL COURT STRUCTURE

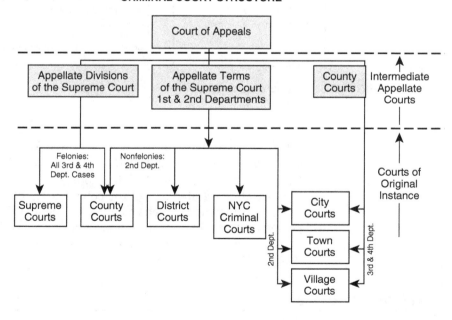

CRIMINAL COURT STRUCTURE

4. *Other state courts.* In addition to the preceding, the following courts usually have jurisdiction as indicated by their titles: city or municipal, police, traffic, and justice of the peace. Their jurisdiction varies according to the size of the community and the authority granted to them by their state constitution. In New York City, cases are heard either in the New York City Criminal Court or the New York

TEXAS COURT SYSTEM

| SUPREME COURT
Civil Jurisdiction Only
9 Justices | | COURT OF
CRIMINAL APPEALS
Criminal Jurisdiction Only
9 Judges | State
highest
appellate
courts |

COURT OF APPEALS
Intermediate Appellate Jurisdiction
14 Courts

Civil Appeals   Criminal Appeals

State intermediate appellate courts

DISTRICT COURTS
Trial Courts of General Civil and Criminal Jurisdiction
(Some Courts Specialize by Subject Matter)

State trial courts of general and special jurisdiction

COUNTY-LEVEL COURTS

| CONSTITUTIONAL
COUNTY COURTS
Limited Civil and Criminal
Jurisdiction
(1 in each County) | COUNTY COURTS
AT LAW
Limited Civil and/or Criminal
Jurisdiction | STATUTORY PROBATE
COURTS
Limited to probate
matters. |

County trial courts of limited jurisdiction

MUNICIPAL COURTS
Limited Criminal Jurisdiction

JUSTICE OF PEACE
COURTS
(Small Claims Courts)
Limited Civil and Criminal Jurisdiction

Local trial courts of limited jurisdiction

FIGURE 5-6   *Texas court system.*

City Civil Court, whereas in the State of New York, outside New York City, these courts are known by various names, depending on the population of the area.

5. *Small claims courts.* **Small claims courts** are not a separate system, but usually they are an integrated part of the court system of most states. These are informal courts in which citizens may go for relief in minor matters. In these courts, persons represent themselves, and there is no jury. The judge makes a decision on the basis of the information supplied by the parties. The amount of money involved is limited by law.

AUTHORITY OF THE COURT

Courts vary in their degree of authority, from the limited jurisdictions of the small claims court to the appellate power of the Supreme Court of the United States. The authority of the court is defined by law, and no court has authority except within its jurisdictional and geographical boundaries as prescribed by law.

FIGURE 5-7 *California superior court.*

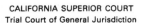

CALIFORNIA SUPERIOR COURT
Trial Court of General Jurisdiction

ORIGINAL JURISDICTON: In all causes except those given by statute to other trial courts.

ONE SUPERIOR COURT WITH AT LEAST ONE JUDGE IN EACH COUNTY. Most counties have more than one judge, each of whom presides over his or her own department.

RULES OF COURT—State rules for the operation of the superior court are adopted by the Judicial Council of the State of California. Local rules for the internal organization of the superior court of each county are adopted by its judges. An appeal from the superior court is generally on a court reporter's transcript of testimony, the clerk's transcript of filed documents, and briefs and oral argument by attorneys.

CIVIL

Jurisdiction includes civil suits over $25,000, and those below $25,000 (i.e., probate matters and actions affecting title to real property). Jury costs are paid by the litigants.
A jury verdict requires votes by at least 9 of the 12 jurors.
Procedure generally similar to that shown for municipal court.

EQUITY

Special matters, such as declaratory relief, injunction proceedings, administration of trusts, foreclosure of mortgages.

PREROGATIVE WRITS

Habeas corpus and extraordinary relief in nature of mandamus, certiorari, and prohibition.

SPECIALIZED

Appeals—from municipal and justice courts. Normally the last word except for review (rare) by the U.S. Supreme Court. Cases may be transferred to the court of appeals for hearing and decision, however, on its order or on certificate of the superior court where necessary to secure uniformity of decision or to decide important questions of law under California Rules of Court Nos. 61-69.

Probate—(wills and administration) guardianships; conservatorships.

Domestic Relations—includes dissolution and nullity of marriage, legal separation, reciprocal enforcement of support, and paternity actions, as well as Conciliation Court in some counties. Final judgment of dissolution sets forth the date that the parties' marital state terminates, which cannot be any sooner than six months from the date the court acquired jurisdiction of respondent. Residence requirement: six months in state, three months in county.

Juvenile—correction and protection of delinquent and uncared-for minors.

Adoptions—of minors and adults. Petition must be filed in county in which petitioners reside.

Psychiatric—protection and custody of the mentally ill.

CRIMINAL

Misdemeanors—not otherwise provided for.

Felonies—criminal offenses punishable by death or by imprisonment in the state prison.
a.   Must ordinarily be brought to trial within sixty days after signing of an indictment or filing of the information unless good cause is shown.
b.   Grand jury indictments are brought directly to the superior court; informations are filed with the court by the district attorney after a preliminary hearing has been held in the municipal court and the defendant has been bound over to the superior court for arraignment.
c.   The right of trial by jury is provided by the California Constitution, which also allows a waiver of the right to trial by jury in criminal cases by consent of both parties, expressed in open court by defendant and his or her counsel. Jury costs are paid by the county.
d.   Verdict of jurors must be unanimous.
e.   Matter of sentencing falls on the judge. Following a felony conviction of a defendant eligible for probation, the judge must, and in other cases the judge may, refer to probation officer for report prior to sentencing. The judge may send the defendant to state prison for the term prescribed by law, may suspend a state prison sentence, place the defendant on probation under certain conditions, or may place the defendant on probation providing that the defendant serves a sentence in the county jail.

In respecting these jurisdictional and geographical boundaries, courts must follow specific rules that specify exactly how legal documents are to be prepared and the procedures that are to be followed. These **rules of the court** are prescribed by law, and it is important for the personnel of a law office to become familiar with the procedures that must be followed to prepare legal papers correctly. Clerks of the court usually are responsible for seeing that the legal documents filed within their authority follow the rules of the court. It is important for the legal support staff to develop a good working relationship with the office of the court clerk and become familiar with the procedures and format required for the preparation of court documents and legal papers.

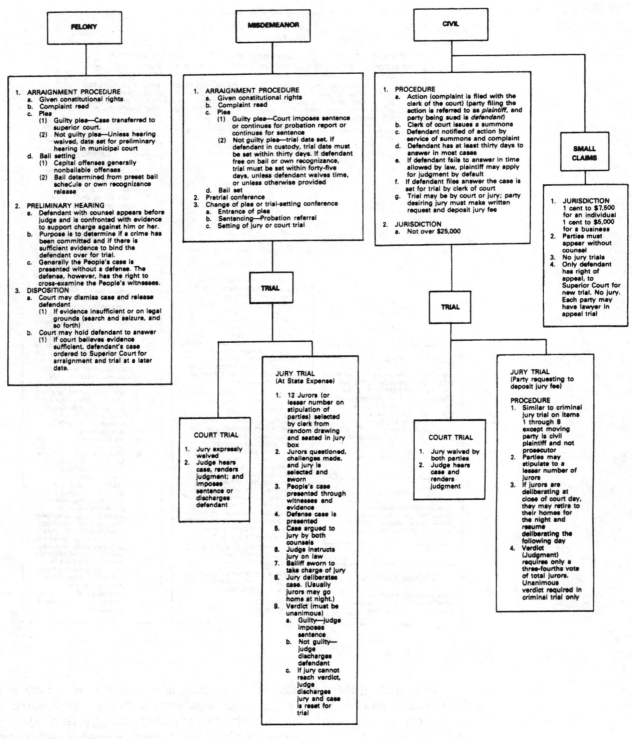

FIGURE 5-7 *Continued*

STATUTE OF LIMITATIONS

The law provides a time limit covering the period in which certain actions must be filed in the court. These time limits are called **statutes of limitations,** and failure to comply with these legal deadlines can result in the client being prohibited from filing suit. It is important that the attorney and support staff note these legal deadlines so that the client's interest or case is not jeopardized. In order to ensure that the statute of limitations is not overlooked, the expiration date should be calendared five, ten, thirty, sixty, and ninety days before it expires.

FILING PROCEDURES

A legal action is commenced by filing the appropriate pleading with the court clerk. The court clerk, or clerk of the court, usually has a number of assistants, often called *deputy clerks*, and other clerical staff who work under the clerk's direction. The staff of the court clerk can be very helpful in providing advice and information for the attorney and legal support staff on questions regarding the preparation and filing of court papers, but they cannot give legal advice. The court clerk also is responsible for maintaining a master calendar and setting cases for trial by recording the date, time, and courtroom in which the case is to be heard. If the support staff or attorney should find it necessary to change a hearing date or time, in most cases they would contact the court clerk to make these changes.

When an action is filed with the court clerk, the clerk assigns a case or docket number to the case and collects a filing fee. In most states, the original copy of all documents is filed with the court, so it is important that a file copy be retained for law office files. The original case number is used on all subsequent papers relating to the case.

Many clerks microfilm or scan the documents filed with them for easy reference and compact storage. By standardizing the size and form of the documents filed, this system has streamlined the maintenance of court records.

COURT FORMS

Every law office should have a supply of court forms. Each federal and state court has specific forms required by that particular court. These forms are available from the various federal and state agencies. Some court forms may be used throughout all state courts, whereas others may be required in a specific court only.

The ability to access court forms quickly in a law office is very important, and the forms relating to a specific court must be easy to identify. Court forms change often, and a current library of court forms must be kept in the office.

Court forms usually are stored in three ways:

1. Manually
2. Photocopied from masters
3. Computer generated

The forms that are stored manually are stored in a filing cabinet, and they are rarely filed alphabetically by title. They are usually organized alphabetically by subject matter, such as civil litigation, corporations, and probate. All forms relating to a particular subject then can be found in one place. Some law firms store court forms in a numerical filing system. Each form is given a number, and each number provides the information regarding the form that may include the subject and applicable court. File folders and labels may be color coded in a numerical system to further identify the form.

Photocopy-created forms may be stored in three-ring binders to save space. The binders are indexed and divided by subject. As the form is needed, it is photocopied. It is important that the staff photocopying the form return the original to the binder when they have finished photocopying it.

Computer-generated software programs contain court forms that can be printed after the information is filled in and completed. These forms are convenient and save storage space.

All forms need to be current and updated to accommodate the changes made by the courts. Though some courts take responsibility for distributing new forms, most courts delegate this responsibility to a printing company or a forms service. There are many court form services that distribute and provide law offices with updated forms. Without this service, law firms constantly must be kept aware of the changes in court forms and order the new ones as they become effective.

FILING FEES

The filing fees required by the court vary from state to state and from county to county. All legal offices should keep an up-to-date schedule of filing fees for easy reference.

Some law offices mail the papers to be filed directly to the court clerk with a cover letter, others employ an attorney service to do the actual paperwork. An **attorney service** usually provides an instruction sheet for the documents so that directions for filing and special instructions can be noted (see Figure 5-8). It is important for the support staff to understand which procedures the law firm wants to use in filing the court papers.

LEGAL SUPPORT SERVICES
1262½ West 2nd Street
Los Angeles, California 90026
Phone (213) 555-0228 FAX (213) 555-1921

FOR COURT SERVICE ONLY. NOT FOR SERVICE OF PROCESS
Instructions to Sender:
1. Pink Copy is your file copy; remove and retain.
2. Send Original Copy to Legal Support Services.

Date 1/24/20 No. 768864 Court Superior District Central County Orange

Title ESCOBAR v. ESCOBAR

Document NOTICE OF EVALUATION CONFERENCE

Attached is Attorney's: ☐ Check $ ☐ Cash $ **Appearance fee was paid** ☐ YES ☐ NO

INSTRUCTIONS: ☒ File ☒ Conform ☐ Record ☐ Obtain ☐ (Plain) or ☐ (Certified) Copy(s)

☐ Serve Pursuant to Attached Inst. ☐ Have Signed By: Dept.

☐ Must Be Filed By (Date) (Time) in Dept. or,

☐ At Main Filing Window. ☐ **Statute Date** ☐ Other

PLEASE FILE, CONFORM AND RETURN

REPORT: **HEARING DATE:** March 3, 199- At 9:00 A.M. In Dept. 27

☐ L.S.S. Advanced: $ By:

☐ Original Delivered to Dept.: ☐ Copy to follow:

☐ Return In Court days to complete order ☐ Clerk will mail
(Please provide Stamped, self-addressed envelope)

☐ Order Completed on

☐ **SEE REPORT REVERSE SIDE**

Attorney: Address: *KENNETH A. ROBERTS & ASSOCIATES*
BRINDERSON TOWER II
19900 MAC ARTHUR BLVD.
SUITE 1180
IRVINE, CA 92715

Phone No.: (714) 555-1019

Attn: Anne File No.: 782

FIGURE 5-8 *Sample of filing instructions to an attorneys' service. (Courtesy of Legal Support Services)*

SUMMARY

It is important for staff in the law office to have an understanding of the court structure and procedures used in our legal system. Each court serves a certain purpose, and it is important to know what the jurisdictions are and the venue or geographic area where papers are to be filed.

The officers of the court primarily are represented by the judge or justice, the clerk of the court, the court reporter, the bailiff, and, depending on the jurisdiction, the marshal, sheriff, or constable. The jury is a body of citizens who listen to the facts of the case and present their decision or verdict. In civil actions, most states require a three-fourths majority, while in criminal matters a unanimous vote of the jurors is required.

The federal court system includes the Supreme Court of the United States, United States Court of Appeal (Circuit), United States District Courts, and other federal courts. The state court system consists of the state supreme court, intermediate courts, county and district courts, municipal or other courts, and small claims courts.

Courts have specific rules that determine how legal documents are prepared and the procedures that need to be followed. These rules and procedures are called *rules of the court*. It is important for the law office support staff to become familiar with these rules and procedures to facilitate the preparation of court documents and legal papers.

The law provides a time limit for filing certain actions, called a *statute of limitations*. The court also requires court forms that need to be completed for the processing of legal matters. These forms can be obtained from the court, photocopied from a master copy, or generated by computer software. Filing fees for processing court forms are required, and these fees vary from state to state.

It is important for support staff to become familiar with the manner in which legal documents are prepared and filed. Legal document preparation and filing are very important functions of law office staff and are essential to the practice of law.

VOCABULARY

appellate court   The court that has the authority to review a case that has already been heard in a lower court.

appellate jurisdiction   The authority of a court to review the decision of a lower court.

attorney service   A service provided for a fee to assist the legal office in filing court papers and obtaining court forms.

bailiff   A deputy, sheriff, or marshal, frequently serving as a courtroom attendant, who is responsible for keeping order.

circuit court   A court presided over by a judge or judges at different locations.

clerk of the court   An officer of the court having custody of its records, with the power to certify transcripts from the records and to perform ministerial duties.

constable   A public officer of a town or township responsible for keeping the peace and performing minor judicial duties.

court of appeals   A state court in which appeals from a lower court are heard and decided.

court of original jurisdiction   A court where a case is to be originally tried.

court reporter   A person skilled in taking dictation and certified to take verbatim testimony during court proceedings.

judge   A public officer who is charged with and performs judicial functions. Principal officer of a court.

judgment   The decision of the judge after hearing the evidence or reviewing the verdict of the jury.

jurisdiction   The authority of the court to hear and decide cases.

jury   A body of citizens sworn to give a verdict on a matter submitted to them.

justice   See *judge*.

marshal   A court officer who performs duties similar to those of a sheriff; a city law officer with special duties.

original jurisdiction   Jurisdiction in the first instance; not appellate.

rules of the court   Specific rules determined by the court for the preparation and arrangement of legal papers.

sentence   The punishment given to a person found guilty in a criminal trial.

sheriff   The chief law enforcement officer in a county.

small claims court   A court to which individuals may go for relief in minor legal matters.

statute of limitations   The time set by law to bring action after the right of action has been established.

superior court   State courts of original jurisdiction.

supreme court   The highest court in most states.

Supreme Court of the United States   The highest court in the United States.

trial court   The court having original jurisdiction over a case.

United States District Court   The United States is divided into judicial districts, in each of which is established a district court.

venue   The geographical place at which a case is to be tried.

verdict   Decision of a jury in a trial.

STUDENT ASSESSMENT 1

Instructions: Circle T if the statement is true or F if the statement is false.

T   F   1.   Jurisdiction is the authority of the court to hear a lawsuit brought before it.

T   F   2.   Venue refers to the geographic location of the court.

T   F   3.   Some state laws are made by the state government, and some laws are made by the federal government. Bankruptcy laws are an example of federal laws.

T   F   4.   There are fifty separate court systems in the United States.

T   F   5.   Courts are classified by the nature of their jurisdiction. Civil courts try cases that involve private rights and responsibilities.

T   F   6.   The clerk of the court is usually an appointed official.

T   F   7.   It is necessary to have all jurors agree on their verdict in a civil action.

T   F   8.   It is necessary to have complete agreement of the jury on cases that are tried in the U.S. Circuit Court of Appeal.

T   F   9.   The structure of the state Court System is somewhat similar to that of the federal court system.

T   F   10.   The decisions of the U.S. Courts of Appeal, and the precedents they set, make up a significant part of our law.

T   F   11.   The U.S. Supreme Court is required to review all cases brought to it by the U.S. Court of Appeals.

T   F   12.   The Customs Court operates under our federal court structure.

T   F   13.   The originals of all documents are generally filed with the clerk of the court.

T   F   14.   Many court clerks have found it necessary to use microfilm for the storage and reference of court documents.

T   F   15.   The assistants to the clerk of the court are usually referred to as *deputy clerks*.

T   F   16.   The court clerk's office is usually an elected position.

T   F   17.   A marshal is a federal court officer who performs duties similar to those performed by the sheriff.

T   F   18.   Ten justices sit on the United States Supreme Court.

T   F   19.   Although a trial jury may vary in the terms of the number of citizens selected, the number who serve on the jury is usually twelve.

T   F   20.   The terms *judgment* and *sentence* have the same meaning.

STUDENT ASSESSMENT 2

Instructions: Fill in the word that best completes the statement.

1.   The _____ is responsible for maintaining order in the courtroom.

2.   The judge pronounces a(n) _____ in a criminal matter based on the verdict of a jury.

3.   There are _____ justices serving on the U.S. Supreme Court. (fill in number)

4.   In the U.S. Circuit Court of Appeals, _____ judges review the cases on the basis of the written information.

5.   Most small claims courts are limited to matters involving an amount not in excess of _____.

STUDENT ASSESSMENT 3

Instructions: Match the most correct letter to the number.

_____ 1. Supreme Court justice	A. no jury necessary
_____ 2. appellate jurisdiction	B. needs approval of Congress
_____ 3. marshal	C. authority to review the decisions of lower courts
_____ 4. judge	D. maintains order in the courtroom
_____ 5. bailiff	E. sets forth procedures for filing documents
_____ 6. sheriff	F. time limit for filing documents
_____ 7. superior court	G. courts of original jurisdiction
_____ 8. small claims court	H. chief law enforcement officer in the county
_____ 9. rules of the court	I. federal court officer
_____ 10. statute of limitations	J. principal officer of the court

STUDENT ASSESSMENT 4

Instructions: Fill in the word that best completes the statement.

California:

1. Cases are first initiated in the courts of _____ _____.

2. Civil actions are filed in the _____.

3. There are _____ associate justices who serve on the California Supreme Court.

4. California is under the jurisdiction of the _____ U.S. Circuit Court of Appeals.

5. In California, probate matters are handled in the _____ Court.

STUDENT ASSIGNMENTS

PROJECT 1: VISIT A TRIAL COURT

Make arrangements through your instructor, your local court clerk, or court administrator's office to visit a trial court in your geographic area. Write a report of 500 or more words about your observations. Include the following information:

1. Write down the name of the judge, court reporter, court clerk, and bailiff.

2. Write down the name of the plaintiff and defendant.

3. What was the defendant accused of doing?

4. What allegations was the plaintiff making?

5. What defense was the defendant making?

6. How attentive were the members of the jury?

7. How effective were the attorneys in presenting their cases and representing their clients?

8. Was the judge attentive and objective to the issues being presented?

9. Did you think the defendant was guilty or innocent?

10. What was the final outcome of the case?

PROJECT 2: OBTAIN A FILING FEE SCHEDULE AND COURT FORMS

Go to your local courthouse and obtain the court forms required for a civil litigation lawsuit and a list of the filing fees for filing court documents.

Part 3

LITIGATION PROCEDURES

6

PREPARING LEGAL DOCUMENTS

OBJECTIVES

Upon completion of this chapter, you should be able to:

1. Use the correct format for preparing legal documents
2. Explain the guidelines for preparing legal documents
3. Describe the formatting style for legal documents
4. Explain how legal documents are organized
5. Use the correct legal format to indicate when lines and sections have been omitted
6. Explain the correct form for preparing signature blocks on legal documents
7. Discuss the proper punctuation on legal documents
8. Describe the correct form for capitalization
9. Explain the guidelines for preparing a court pleading
10. Describe supporting court documents such as affidavits, acknowledgments, and verifications
11. Prepare a complaint

GENERAL PREPARATION

The various state and court rules designate the form of papers presented for filing. *Papers* means all documents, except exhibits or copies of documents, that are offered for filing, not including printed court forms, briefs, or records of appeal.

Court rules designate that all papers must be typewritten, printed, or prepared by photocopying or other duplication process producing clear and permanent copies. Only one side of the paper should be used, and the lines on each page should be one-and-one-half spaced or double spaced and consecutively numbered. However, real property descriptions, footnotes, and quotations may be single spaced.

The pages of documents must be numbered consecutively at the bottom, consist entirely of original pages without rider, and be firmly bound at the top.

In addition to statewide rules, local courts designate their own rules for the preparation of documents. Become familiar with the rules adopted by the courts in the counties or jurisdictions where you file pleadings. For example, California now requires the use of recycled paper.

Advances in Computer Technology

Computers and word processing software are affecting the way work in a legal office is performed. Many of the repetitive and manual tasks have been computerized, and almost every law office uses some form of word processing to create legal documents. Templates, macros, and wizards that are included in software packages automate many of the repetitive tasks. Forms previously obtained from the court now are available for a fee on disk. Therefore, much of the time required by legal support staff in obtaining these forms no longer is required, as these services provide the correct forms and current updates.

GUIDELINES FOR PREPARING LEGAL DOCUMENTS

The following guidelines are used in Figure 6-1:

1. *Paper.* Legal ruled or legal cap paper that measures $8\frac{1}{2}$ by 11 inches is used for legal papers and pleadings.

2. *Attorney's name.* The attorney's name, address, telephone number, and bar number must appear on the first page of each document or legal paper that is filed. The attorney's name and address begin on line 1 and are single spaced. The state can be abbreviated or spelled out in full. If it is abbreviated, the two-letter postal abbreviation without punctuation is recommended. The attorney's phone number and area code should follow below the address. The fax number also may be included.

3. *Attorney's representation.* The name of the **party** represented by the attorney usually follows two lines below the attorney's name and address: "Attorney for Plaintiff."

4. *Court title* (line 8). In California, the title of the court must be placed no higher than line 8 of the first page of attorney-prepared documents. The title of the court is centered on the page, typed in capital letters, and double spaced if two or more lines are used.

5. *Caption* (lines 8 to 16). Court procedures require that every **pleading** contain a **caption** setting forth (1) the name of the court and county, and in municipal and justice courts the name of the judicial district in which the action is brought; and (2) the title of the action.

6. *Case title* (lines 11 to 16). The title of a case consists of the names of the plaintiffs and the names of the defendants separated by the abbreviation *v.* or *vs.* for versus. All the names of the parties must be included in the title of the action. First names and middle initials are customarily stated, if known. If the party's name is common, his or her full middle name may be given. In subsequent papers, only the name of the first party on each side needs to be stated, followed by an appropriate indication of the other parties, such as *et al.*, or *et als.*, or *and others.*

7. *Case or docket number.* The number of the case is placed to the right of the title of the case. On the first paper presented for filing, only *No.* is typed on the paper, and a blank space is left for the clerk to stamp or write the number assigned to the case. This number then is typed on all subsequent documents.

8. *Document title.* The nature of the paper must be set forth in the space immediately below the number of the case. It is customary to type these words in capital letters. If the title is long, it must be single spaced and separated into sections; each section should be centered or neatly blocked on the page.

9. *Signature.* The usual practice is to have the client or attorney sign his or her name on a line under which the name has been typed.

SIGNATURE VARIATIONS

Legal documents may be signed in different ways. However, at least two lines of the last paragraph must appear on the last page, and signature lines go below them.

If the document requires the signature of both the client and the attorney, the client signs on the right and the attorney usually signs on the left.

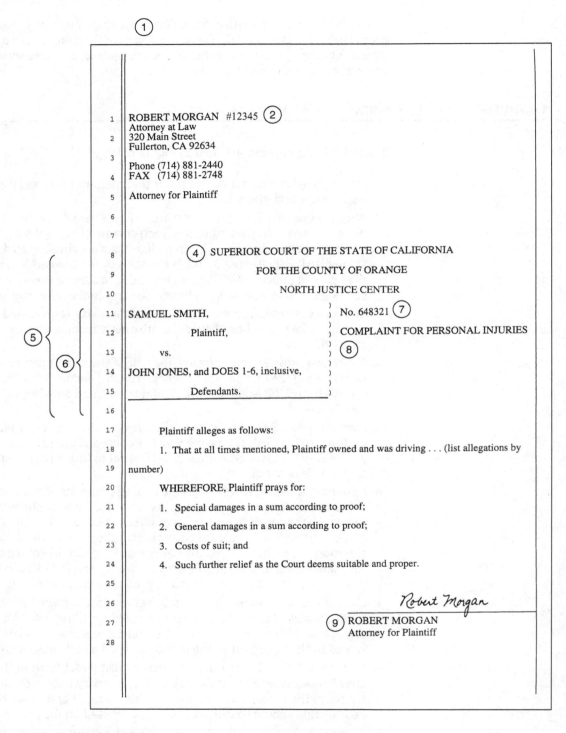

FIGURE 6-1 *A complaint.*

Signature lines begin at the center of the page and extend to the right margin to allow adequate space for signing. Some examples of variations in signature lines follow: When the date appears with the signature:

DATED: January 20, 20—

ROBERT MORGAN
Attorney for Plaintiff

When the attorney is a member of a law firm:

as the Court may deem proper.

JOHNSON, MILLER & SMITH

BY_____

ROBERT MORGAN

Attorney for Plaintiff

When the client and the attorney both sign the document:

_____

SALLY SMITH, PLAINTIFF

_____

ROBERT MORGAN,

Attorney for Plaintiff

LEGAL CAP DOCUMENTS

Legal cap is paper with ruled left and right margins that can be numbered, and measures 8½ by 11 inches, 8½ by 14 inches, or 8 by 13 inches. Some states have discontinued using legal cap, and some states are using letter-sized paper for legal documents.

Formatting

Indentation   Traditionally, paragraphs have been indented ten spaces in the body of the pleading. However, many counties and other localities have adopted rules that state that paragraphs should be indented five spaces, and this appears to be the future for the indentation rule. Subparagraphs, legal descriptions, and quoted material should be indented five more spaces than the body of the document.

Numbering Paragraphs   All primary paragraphs should be designated by an Arabic numeral indented on the left side of the page. Primary paragraphs should be consecutively numbered throughout a pleading. Roman numerals should be avoided. Subparagraphs should be designated by the letters of the alphabet, that is, (a), (b), and so on, and indented from the subparagraph in generally accepted outline form.

Each cause of action should be separately numbered and specifically identified by written designation in words typed in capital letters, two spaces below the preceding paragraph, and centered.

Blank Lines   If any lines within a document need to be left blank, some form of notation must be filled in on the blank areas so the blank areas of the document cannot be altered. It is recommended that three diagonals (slashes) be typed at the left margin for each numbered line left blank or at each margin for each numbered line left blank, as shown in Figure 6-2.

Z-Rule   A z-rule may be used to fill up an incomplete page in a wholly typed document or to fill unused space on a printed form in order to prevent the material filled in from being altered. Neatly draw in pen a z-rule as shown in Figure 6-3.

Signatures   Be certain that the document bears all the required signatures. It is recommended that you type the name in all caps under the signature line. The designation of the party can be typed in upper- and lowercase.

Signature lines begin in the center of the page and extend to the right margin. However, when the attorney and client both sign the document, usually the client's signature appears to the right of the center of the page, while the attorney's signature appears two lines below the client's signature and to the left of the center of the page.

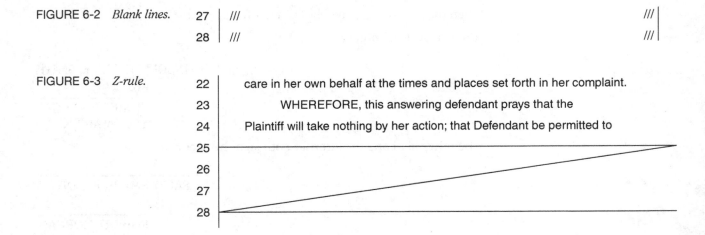

FIGURE 6-2 *Blank lines.*

FIGURE 6-3 *Z-rule.*

At least two lines of typed material should appear on any page containing signatures of parties or witnesses.

Conforming Documents   All copies of legal documents must be made identical to the original document. This means that before any documents are sent out of the office, they must be **conformed**.

The symbol S/, /S/, or s/ indicates that the document has been signed. Signatures can be indicated on copies of the original documents in the following manner:

S/JOHN Q. SMITH
JOHN Q. SMITH, PLAINTIFF

/S/JOHN Q. SMITH
JOHN Q. SMITH, PLAINTIFF

When a document is prepared, blank lines are used for dates and signatures. When the document is signed and dated on the original, these dates and signatures and any other notations are handwritten on the original. The legal office support staff are responsible for indicating this information on the conformed office copies.

Organization

Backing   Some jurisdictions require that original pleadings be stapled to a heavy backing paper, often colored, called **blueback**. This paper is $3/4$ to 1 inch longer than the paper on which the document is typed, and the extra length of the backing paper is folded over the top of the document and secured with staples so the document is secure within the fold of the back sheet.

On one of the folds of the backing sheet, information regarding the case will be typed, indicating the name of the law firm, parties to the action, and the date signed. This information is referred to as the **endorsement**.

Hole Punch   Some jurisdictions require that all documents presented for filing must contain two prepunched normal-sized holes, centered $2^1/_2$ inches apart and $1^1/_8$ inches from the top of the paper.

Number of Copies   The original copy is filed with the court unless specified otherwise. Copies should be made as follows: one copy to be conformed by the court and one office copy to be held until the conformed copy is returned from the court, one copy to be served on each opposing party, and one copy for the client, if applicable. Sometimes, support staff will keep a copy of the document in their personal files and use it to make notations about specific legal and formatting rules for future reference.

Punctuation

In legal documents, it is customary to introduce a series of related paragraphs with a short, introductory paragraph closing with a colon. The paragraphs that follow may be numbered, but their relationship to each other and to the introductory statement is indicated by punctuation at the end of each section.

Semicolons   Semicolons often are used in enumerated lists after consecutive paragraphs or after items in a list. Type a semicolon after each item in the list except the last item, which ends with a period. If the word "and" appears before the last item in a list, place the semicolon before the word "and."

Example

WHEREFORE, the plaintiff prays for judgment against defendants, and each of them for:

1. General damages in the amount of Ten Thousand Dollars ($10,000);
2. All medical expenses according to proof;
3. All costs of suit; and
4. Such other and further relief as this Court may deem proper.

Periods   Use a period after *paragraphs* beginning with the word "That" when they occur after an introductory statement that serves as the subject. If the last paragraph is preceded by the word "and," a semicolon is used after each paragraph except the last paragraph, which ends with a period.

Example

The plaintiff will show:

1. That on or about April 21, (year), the defendant was the registered owner of a Chevrolet truck bearing California License No. LAW123.
2. That on or about April 21, (year), the plaintiff, Carolyn Shultz, was driving her Lexis automobile in a westerly direction on Harbor Boulevard.
3. That defendant John Smith struck plaintiff's vehicle.

Capitalization

The use of capitalization varies from office to office, so check with your firm to determine the preferences. The name of a specific document usually is written with an initial capital letter when it is referred to in a legal document or letter. Such terms as Complaint, Answer, Demurrer, Petition, and Pleading usually are capitalized. Do not capitalize short prepositions, conjunctions, or articles (a, an, the) such as Complaint *for* Damages.

Names   Capitalize all proper nouns; that is, capitalize the name of specific persons, places, or things. Many law firms use full caps on names of parties, attorneys, and judges in legal documents, while others use only initial caps. It is important that you check to find out the preferences in your office. Within a document, however, always be consistent with one method or the other.

Example

Plaintiff, **ROBERT S. WILSON**, is a resident of the County of Orange, State of California.

or

Plaintiff, **Robert S. Wilson**, is a resident of the County of Orange, State of California.

Capitalize "Attorney for Plaintiff" and "Attorney for Defendant" when it is part of an address. The term *attorney* is not capitalized when it is used alone as a common noun.

COMES NOW the Plaintiff, JOHN J. JONES, through his *attorney* and presents the following allegations:

Capitalize the word "Court" when it is used in a sentence as a substitute for *judge*. Also, capitalize Court when used with the official name of a tribunal.

Capitalize the first letter of the party designation (Plaintiff or Defendant) in legal documents. Some firms choose to use lowercase letters. Whichever method you choose, it is important that you be consistent.

Example

On March 28, (year), the **Defendant** JONES TRUCKING, INC., was traveling south on Main Street.
On March 28, (year), the **defendant** JONES TRUCKING, INC., was traveling south on Main Street.

Geographic Terms   Capitalize *city*, *county*, and *state* when they appear, for example, before or after a geographic location as in *City of Fullerton, County of Orange, State of California*. Always capitalize the name of the county and state as in *Orange County, California*.

Words and Phrases in All Caps   Certain words and phrases are usually capitalized. The following expressions are customarily typed in all capital letters.

PLEASE TAKE NOTICE, which begins a prepared document called a Notice.
IT IS HEREBY ORDERED, which usually begins an order prepared for signature by the court.
WHEREFORE, which begins the last paragraph of a complaint or answer.
WHEREAS, which begins paragraphs of an agreement.
COME the Plaintiffs, by and through their attorneys.
COMES NOW your Plaintiff and pursuant to Rule 36.

Numbers

Expressing Numbers   Numbers that begin a sentence *must* be expressed in word form. It is recommended that numbers one through ten be spelled out and numbers above ten be written in figures.

In legal documents, numbers other than dollar amounts are written in words and figures. The written amount is expressed in lowercase letters. For example,

Defendant requests an extension of *thirty* (30) days.

Dollar Amounts   Because of the importance of sums of money in legal papers, dollar amounts are written in words and figures. The first letter of each word is capitalized, while the second term in a hyphenated number is keyed in lowercase letters. Type parentheses around the numeric figures, which express exactly what is written in words. Note the use of "and" between dollars and cents.

Five Hundred Thousand Dollars ($500,000). The .00 is not included because it is not referred to in the spelled-out version.
Five Hundred Thousand and no/100 Dollars ($500,000.00)
Twenty-five Thousand and 00/100 (25,000.00) Dollars. The $ is not included in the parentheses because the words before the parentheses do not refer to dollars.
Fifty-five and 25/100 Dollars ($55.25)
Fifty-five Dollars and Twenty-five Cents ($55.25)

Doe Clause   In many instances the plaintiff does not know the names of the parties to sue. When the names of one or more of the defendants are unknown, a **Doe** clause is used in the original complaint. This allows the plaintiff's attorney to amend his or her complaint when the true names and capacities of all the defendants are known, and they can be added at a later date. The procedure in New York in such a situation varies—defendants are named later in a third-party complaint or are added to the complaint at a later date with the permission of the court (see Figure 6-1, line 14).

Supporting Documents

Affidavits   An affidavit is a written statement of fact made voluntarily under oath in which the affiant swears to the truth of the statements made in the affidavit. The **affiant** is the person who swears to the truth of the document, and the notary public is the person who administers the **oath**. Affidavits are documents in themselves, and they are required in many legal situations. Affidavits may be very long or very short, and they are used in a variety of ways. They may be used in real estate transactions; applications for licenses; and affirmations of birth, citizenship, or age. An affidavit is a complete instrument within itself and is different from an *acknowledgment*, which is part of or an appendage to another instrument.

The format for an affidavit begins with a statement of venue, indicating the state and county in which the acknowledgment is made (see Figure 6-4). The venue is boxed by closing parentheses or brackets and may be followed by ss., the abbreviation for **scilicet** (a Latin word meaning "to wit; namely") typed in capital or small letters and followed by a period. The statement of venue is followed by the name of the affiant and a statement that the affiant appeared before a notary and swore under oath to the statements contained in the document. The statements of fact are followed by the affiant's signature.

The notary public also signs the document and imprints on the paper the official seal. The section of the document bearing the notary's signature and seal and the statement that the document was signed in his or her presence and sworn to under oath is known as the **jurat**. The jurat is essential to the affidavit and may be stamped or typed on the document.

Acknowledgments   An acknowledgment is a statement attached to the document stating, in effect, that the person who signed the document is the person mentioned in that document and did in fact sign the document (see Figure 6-5). The person making the acknowledgment signs the document involved; the notary public or other official signs the acknowledgment itself. The difference between an acknowledgment and an affidavit is that an affidavit is a complete instrument within itself, but an acknowledgment is *always part of another instrument*. The purpose of an affidavit is to prove a fact, whereas the purpose of an acknowledgment is to declare that the person in question did in fact sign the document to which the acknowledgment is attached. An acknowledgment is used on deeds, satisfactions of judgment, and papers in business transactions. Printed forms of acknowledgment may be obtained from a stationery supplier.

Verification   A verification is a sworn statement made by the plaintiff, defendant, or one of the parties stating that the allegations in the pleadings are true. Statements of fact relating to the court case often need to be verified, or signed, by the client, stating that the client has read the document and believes the statements as contained in the document to be true. Some firms use printed forms for verifications and attach them to the last page of the document. Other offices type the verification on the documents themselves, usually four lines below the signature block. These verifications are of two types: verification by declaration and verification by attorney.

1. *Verification by declaration*, or a *declaration*, is a simple statement made in writing under penalty of perjury in which the party signing the document declares the facts contained in the document to be true. Such a verification has the same legal effect as an affidavit, but *it is not* signed before a notary public. In some states this may be all that is required for the document, but other states require

FIGURE 6-4 *An affidavit.*

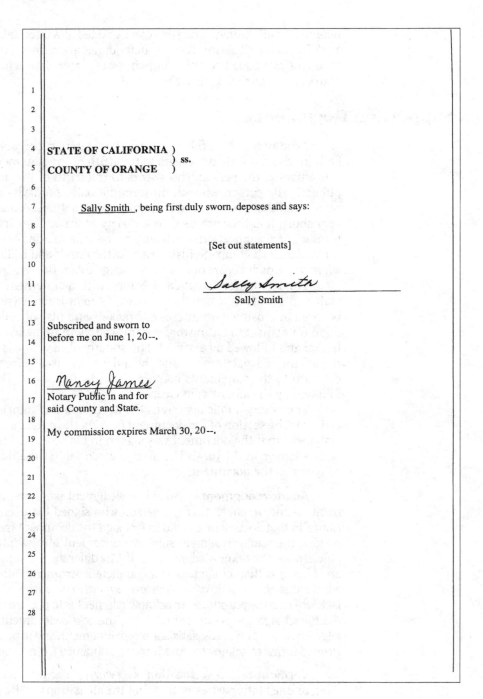

that the verification be signed before a notary public. Figure 6-6 is a sample of a verification by declaration.

2. *A verification by affidavit* is generally what is meant by the term *verification*, whereas a verification by declaration is usually referred to as a *declaration*. Whereas the verification needs to be notarized (see p. 38), the declaration does not. Verifications are used in many circumstances. A typical case is when a document needs to be signed by the attorney because the client is not available to sign it (see Figure 6-7). Another example is when a person signing a verification is an officer of a corporation and signs in that capacity, stating that he or she has read the contents of the document and believes, under penalty of perjury, that they are true.

FIGURE 6-5 *An acknowledgment (always part of another document).*

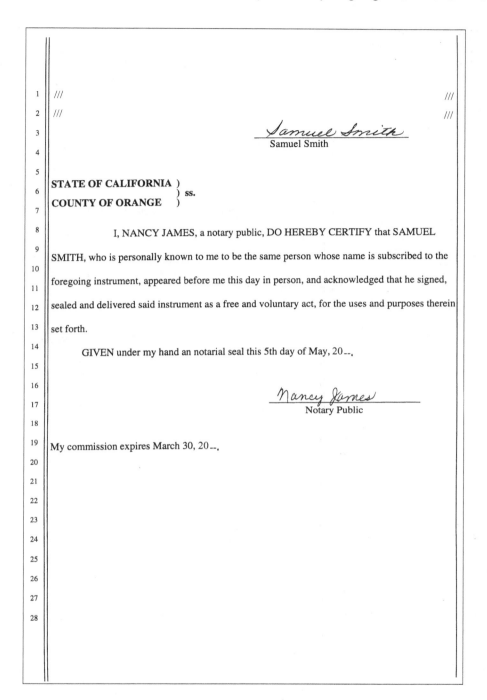

```
 1   ///                                                              ///
 2   ///                                                              ///
 3                        Samuel Smith
                          Samuel Smith
 4
 5
 6   STATE OF CALIFORNIA  )
                          ) ss.
 7   COUNTY OF ORANGE     )
 8            I, NANCY JAMES, a notary public, DO HEREBY CERTIFY that SAMUEL
 9   SMITH, who is personally known to me to be the same person whose name is subscribed to the
10   foregoing instrument, appeared before me this day in person, and acknowledged that he signed,
11
12   sealed and delivered said instrument as a free and voluntary act, for the uses and purposes therein
13   set forth.
14            GIVEN under my hand an notarial seal this 5th day of May, 20--.
15
16
17                        Nancy James
                          Notary Public
18
19   My commission expires March 30, 20--.
20
21
22
23
24
25
26
27
28
```

Proofreading

It is essential that the material typed in legal documents be accurate. *Do not rely on word processing spellcheckers.* Property descriptions and technical data such as numbers may be read aloud to another person in the office while the other person checks the draft copy in order to verify the accuracy of the typed information.

FIGURE 6-6 *A verification by declaration (not signed by a notary public).*

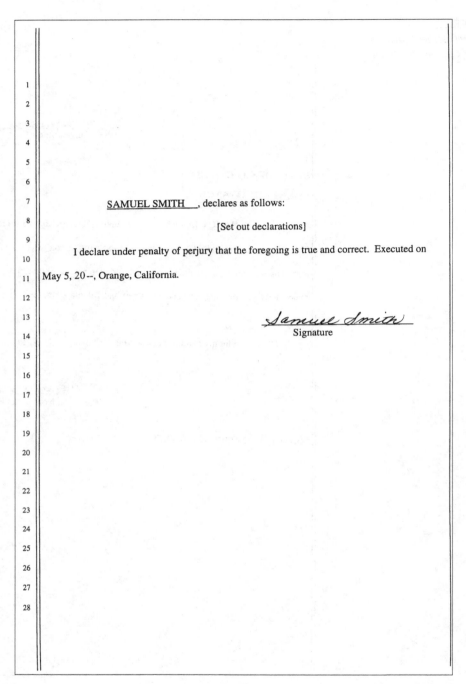

```
  1
  2
  3
  4
  5
  6
  7                SAMUEL SMITH    , declares as follows:
  8                          [Set out declarations]
  9
            I declare under penalty of perjury that the foregoing is true and correct.  Executed on
 10
 11    May 5, 20--, Orange, California.
 12
 13                                          Samuel Smith
 14                                             Signature
 15
 16
 17
 18
 19
 20
 21
 22
 23
 24
 25
 26
 27
 28
```

Manuscripts

Attorneys often are asked to prepare papers for the court or legal journal or to give testimony or talks to various legal or political organizations. The ability to outline can be very useful in organizing these materials. The outlining of materials can easily be done using word processing software outline features. See Figure 6-8 for an example of the outline styles available.

FIGURE 6-7 *A verification by attorney (signed before a notary public).*

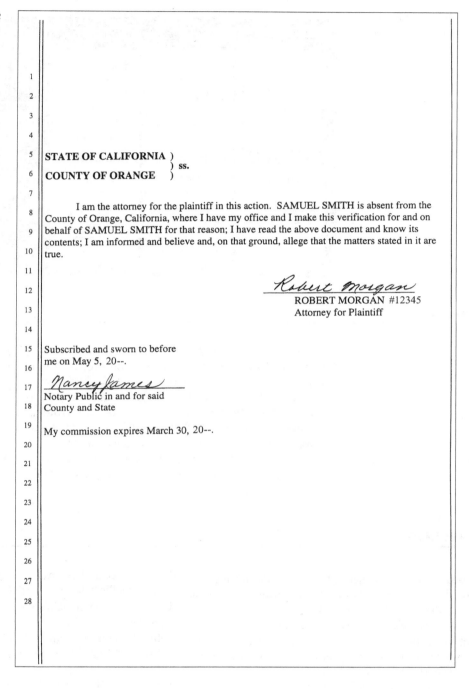

STATE OF CALIFORNIA)
) **ss.**
COUNTY OF ORANGE)

    I am the attorney for the plaintiff in this action. SAMUEL SMITH is absent from the County of Orange, California, where I have my office and I make this verification for and on behalf of SAMUEL SMITH for that reason; I have read the above document and know its contents; I am informed and believe and, on that ground, allege that the matters stated in it are true.

ROBERT MORGAN #12345
Attorney for Plaintiff

Subscribed and sworn to before
me on May 5, 20--.

Notary Public in and for said
County and State

My commission expires March 30, 20--.

FIGURE 6-8 *An example of word processing outline features.*

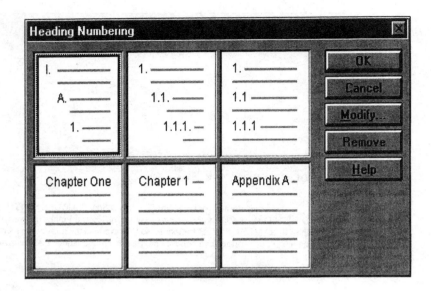

SUMMARY

It is important for the legal professional to understand how to prepare legal office documents. The correct formatting and preparation of these documents are essential in the processing of legal papers. Standards for capitalization and punctuation should be followed, and the consistent accuracy in the preparation of court documents is a reflection of the office and its staff. Guidelines for preparing legal pleadings have been established by the different states, and these guidelines need to be followed in the preparation of court documents.

It is also essential for the legal professional to know how to prepare supporting documents, such as affidavits, acknowledgments, and verifications.

VOCABULARY

acknowledgment A statement attached to a document declaring that the person who signed the document is the person mentioned in the document and did sign the document.

affiant The person who makes and signs an affidavit.

affidavit A written statement of fact made voluntarily under oath in which the person taking the oath swears to the truth of the statements made in the affidavit.

blueback Legal backing used to protect documents.

caption The term referring to the following data required on a court document: jurisdiction, venue, document title, court number, and the parties to the action.

conform To make a copy identical to that of the original.

docket number The case number assigned by the clerk's office.

Doe clause A clause used in the initial pleading to indicate parties to the action when their true names and capacities are unknown.

endorsement (also *indorsement*) Identifying information typed on the outside of the legal backing; usually includes document title, parties, name of law firm, and date.

jurat The clause written at the foot of an affidavit; it states when, where, and the notary before whom the affidavit was sworn.

legal cap Paper containing vertical ruled lines at the left and right edges.

oath A solemn attestation of truth by which a person signifies being bound by conscience to perform an act faithfully and truthfully.

party In legal context, refers to a person or entity (such as a corporation) involved in a legal matter.

pleadings Documents filed in a legal action.

prayer clause The last paragraph of the complaint or petition in which the plaintiff demands judgment against the defendants.

scilicet (ss.) A Latin word meaning "to wit; namely."

verification A signed statement at the end of a document alleging that the statements of fact in the document are true.

z-rule A mark designed to fill in an unused area of a legal document to preclude changes or alterations.

STUDENT ASSESSMENT 1

Instructions: Circle T if the statement is true or F if the statement is false.

T   F   1.   In legal documents, paragraphs are always indented five spaces.

T   F   2.   Z rulings are used to prevent any alteration of the document.

T   F   3.   Real property descriptions may be single spaced in legal documents.

T   F   4.   In legal documents, capitalize the words City, County, State, and similar terms when they appear before or after the name of the geographic location.

T   F   5.   It is not important to make copies of legal documents identical to the original.

T   F   6.   Legal cap paper is always numbered.

T   F   7.   All primary paragraphs of a legal document should be designated by Roman numerals.

T   F   8.   Court rules are all the same.

T   F   9.   *Et al.* is an abbreviated title that stands for "and others."

T   F   10.   When a document requires the signature of both the attorney and the client, the attorney's signature usually appears to the right of the center of the page.

STUDENT ASSESSMENT 2

Instructions: Fill in the word that best completes the statement.

1.   When expressing numbers in legal documents, it is recommended that numbers one through _____ be spelled out in full.

2.   The person making the affidavit is referred to as the _____.

3.   When the client and the attorney both sign a document, the client's signature usually appears to the _____ of the center of the page.

4.   To _____ means to make identical.

5.   The information regarding the case that is typed on the fold of the backing sheet is called the _____.

6.   At least _____ line(s) of the last paragraph must be typed on the top of the last page with signature lines below them.

7.   _____ is a written statement under oath signed in the presence of a notary.

8.   It is recommended that an _____ space indentation be used for the beginning of paragraphs in legal documents.

9.   The _____ clause is used in legal documents when the plaintiff does not know the names of the parties to sue.

10.   The abbreviation for *scilicet* is _____.

STUDENT ASSIGNMENTS

PREPARING LEGAL DOCUMENTS

Captions for the Different States

At this point, you should check with your instructor for the correct format that you will use for preparing your legal documents. Examples of the different captions for Texas and New York are shown on pp. 119–120. The reference section of your book has a more extensive listing of the state captions that you may want to use. You may want to check with the local court clerk or a local law office to provide you with the rules of the court and guidelines for the preparation of legal documents in your area.

(continued)

Variations Within the Same State

If you decide to use the Robert Morgan format for California, please be aware that when you are on the job you may have to adjust to the jurisdiction or even the law office in which you work, even within the same law firm, different attorneys may prefer different formats for their legal documents. It is important that you remain flexible. When you find employment in a law firm, you must adapt to the requirements of your firm.

Creating Document Templates

The projects that follow this chapter will require many repetitive keystrokes. In order to save valuable keystrokes, it is recommended that word processed templates (stored documents) be created for selected projects. These documents, which can be reused, will vary with the kind of word processing software being used. When instructions to create a template are given, they are to create a stored document that may use the template, wizard, or other features of a word processing package for creating this document. The document then is saved to disk, reused, edited, and saved again with a new filename. Check with your instructor as to preference in preparing templates.

Assigning Names to Files

To be consistent in naming and working with the word processed files, the data files on the disk that accompany this book begin with ch0, the number of the chapter, an underline, and the name or abbreviation of the file. When you edit or change these files and save them to your data disk, you use the ch (without the 0), the number of the chapter, an underline, and the name of the file. This will help you to distinguish the difference between the files that were stored originally on the data disk and the files that you have created, changed, or edited. Exceptions to this procedure are the variable files used in Chapter 12 that are listed by a name, and the caption template file **chx6_tmp** in Chapter 6.

PROJECT 1: CREATE A CAPTION TEMPLATE

Instructions: Using your word processor, create a caption template for Sample 6.1 (p. 121), or use file **chx6_tmp** on your data disk. This file will be used again in future documents to save you from using repetitive keystrokes. If you create your own template, save your document as **ch06_tmp**, and print one copy for your instructor. If you use the file on your data disk, retrieve it, save it as **ch07_tmp**, and print one copy for your instructor.

PROJECT 2: CREATE A COMPLAINT

Instructions: Prepare a complaint similar to the one shown on p. 106. Before you begin, go over the instructions in the text for placement, spacing, and punctuation. (If your word processing software has a template or wizard feature for pleadings, you may want to follow the instructions from your instructor or the software package for using it.) Save your document as **ch6_com**, and print one copy for your instructor.

PROJECT 3: CREATE SUPPORTING DOCUMENTS

Instructions: Prepare the following.

A.   affidavit— (see Figure 6-4).
B.   acknowledgment— (see Figure 6-5).
C.   verification by declaration— (see Figure 6-6).
D.   verification by attorney— (see Figure 6-7).

Save your documents as ch6_pj3a, ch6_pj3b, ch6_pj3c, and ch6_pj3d, respectively, and print one copy for your instructor.

Sample Court Caption--Texas

IN THE UNITED STATES DISTRICT COURT
SOUTHERN DISTRICT OF TEXAS
HOUSTON DIVISION

SAMUEL SMITH	§	
	§	
Plaintiff	§	CIVIL ACTION NO.
	§	
v.	§	_____
	§	
CROWN MANUFACTURING, INC.,	§	JURY
a California corporation, and DOE ONE	§	
and DOE TWO	§	
	§	
Defendants	§	

COMPLAINT

[Identity of parties, allegation of jurisdiction, causes of action, prayer.)

Greg Bailey, 09876
Attorney at Law
460 Main Street
Austin, TX 77418
Phone: (409) 555-5912   FAX: (409) 555-5906
Attorney in Charge for Plaintiff

Sample Court Caption--New York

Ken Kvitka #54321
Attorney at Law
460 Harbor View
Long Island, NY 10580

Telephone: (603) 555-5912
Fax: (603) 555-5906

Attorney for Plaintiff, SAMUEL SMITH

SUPREME COURT OF THE STATE OF NEW YORK
COUNTY OF SCHENECTADY

SAMUEL SMITH,
 	
                Plaintiff,
 	
     against
 	
CROWN MANUFACTURING, INC.,
a California corporation, and DOE ONE
and DOE TWO,
 	
               Defendants,
	Complaint
	Index No. _____
	
	Assigned to
	Justice _____

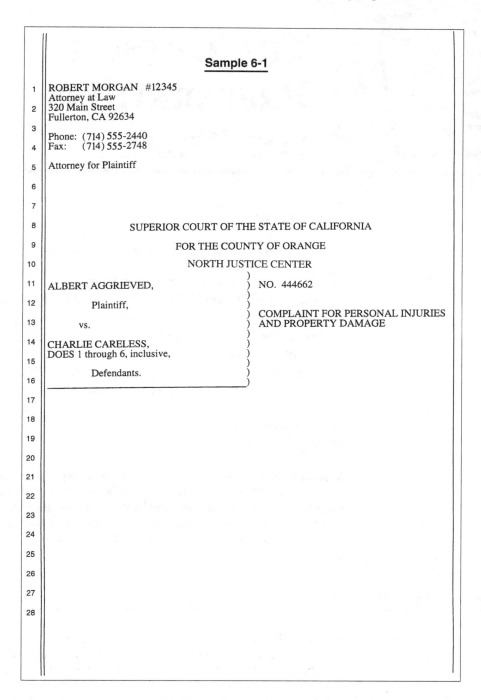

Sample 6-1

1   ROBERT MORGAN #12345
    Attorney at Law
2   320 Main Street
    Fullerton, CA 92634

3
    Phone: (714) 555-2440
4   Fax: (714) 555-2748

5   Attorney for Plaintiff

6

7

8   SUPERIOR COURT OF THE STATE OF CALIFORNIA

9   FOR THE COUNTY OF ORANGE

10   NORTH JUSTICE CENTER

11   ALBERT AGGRIEVED,   ) NO. 444662
)
12   Plaintiff,   )
) COMPLAINT FOR PERSONAL INJURIES
13   vs.   ) AND PROPERTY DAMAGE
)
14   CHARLIE CARELESS,   )
     DOES 1 through 6, inclusive,)
15   )
          Defendants.   )
16   )

17

18

19

20

21

22

23

24

25

26

27

28

7

THE LAWSUIT: PREPARATIONS FOR TRIAL

OBJECTIVES

Upon completion of this chapter, you should be able to:

1. Discuss the initial paperwork required to prepare for a lawsuit
2. Describe the different kinds of attorney-client fee arrangements
3. Describe the phases involved in a lawsuit
4. Discuss the stages of a jury trial
5. Describe how the jury reaches a verdict
6. Explain how documents are filed with the clerk of the court
7. Discuss how a summons is prepared and served on the defendant
8. Prepare a complaint
9. List the different responses a defendant can make
10. Describe the procedure for preparing a cross-complaint

A **lawsuit**, or **litigation**, is commenced when one party sues another in a court of law. This can be either a criminal or a civil action. Some of the documents will be the same for both cases, such as complaints, motions, and orders. Criminal cases occur, however, when someone has broken the law, such as having committed a burglary or murder, and the case goes to court. In this instance, a governmental body is the prosecution for the plaintiff.

GENERAL LITIGATION INFORMATION

Litigation is the act of litigating or processing a suit in a court of law or equity. Legal actions follow similar patterns and procedures, and the papers in a lawsuit consist of office-typed pleadings and printed court forms. All these papers must be typed. The court file or record consists of all original office-typed pleadings and printed court forms. Copies of these pleadings must be served on the adverse party, and proof of service may be accomplished by mail or by personal delivery. A copy of all papers relating to the case should be made and retained in the attorney's file.

Complaint

A **complaint** is the initial pleading filed with the court by the plaintiff that begins the lawsuit. The complaint is filed in the court having the jurisdiction and venue over the parties and the subject matter of the lawsuit. Because the number of the case will be assigned by the clerk of the court when the case is filed, initially the case number is left blank. Once the clerk assigns the case number, all subsequent documents filed with the court by either party must contain this case number.

Each **allegation** in the complaint is set forth in a separate paragraph and numbered consecutively throughout the documen. The complaint ends with a **prayer** or **prayer for relief** and requests that the court grant the palintiff's demands, states the relief sought, and is signed by the attorney.

Motions

A **motion** may be in the form of an oral request of the court made by the attorney in the courtroom or a typewritten document prepared according to the rules of the court. A motion usually precedes a court order, which is an official instruction by the judge.

Orders

A court **order** is prepared by the petitioning attorney, and, if approved, it is signed by the judge. Usually the attorney will instruct the legal staff to type the order at the same time the petition or motion is prepared. After the judge studies the legal papers and approves them, he or she will sign the order.

Stipulations

A **stipulation** is an agreement between opposing attorneys that is legally binding on their clients. A stipulation may be used for an extension of time, to amend a complaint, or to take a deposition. The stipulation is signed by the attorney, but not necessarily by the parties to the action (see Figure 7-1). If the stipulation is made in open court, it may be an oral agreement.

If the legal staff is responsible for preparing the stipulation, the attorney should sign the original and conform (make identical) the other copies. The original then is sent to the opposing attorney along with the file copy. When the original is returned, the office copies should be conformed. If the stipulation is to be filed with the court, the original copy is filed, and a copy is retained for law office files.

In a civil case involving a dispute between two or more parties, the parties to the action could be individuals, businesses, or governmental bodies. This usually occurs when someone has been injured or wronged and the parties cannot agree on a solution to the matter. To sue a person, there must be a cause of action. A **cause of action** is the wrong or injury. A cause of action might be an injury in an automobile accident, falling or slipping on someone's property, or someone's tree falling on your property.

LAWYER-CLIENT RELATIONS

When a client decides to be represented in a civil case, some important considerations need to be discussed. Usually the attorney will interview the client, a client information form will be completed, and the background of the legal dispute will be discussed.

The client and the attorney also need to determine the kind of fee arrangements that will be used. Fee arrangements usually include the following:

1. *Contingency fee contract.* The **contingency fee** contract is based on the amount of money the attorney is able to collect for the client. The client usually pays the costs of the lawsuit, but the attorney's fee is based on a percentage of what is collected as a result of the lawsuit. In most states contingent fees are inherently illegal in criminal and domestic relations cases because there is no restitution or recovery.

2. *Retainer.* The **retainer** form of payment means that the client will pay the attorney an established amount of money per month or by the year to use the attorney's services. Usually these services are spelled out in the retainer and listed in the

FIGURE 7-1 *Stipulation.*

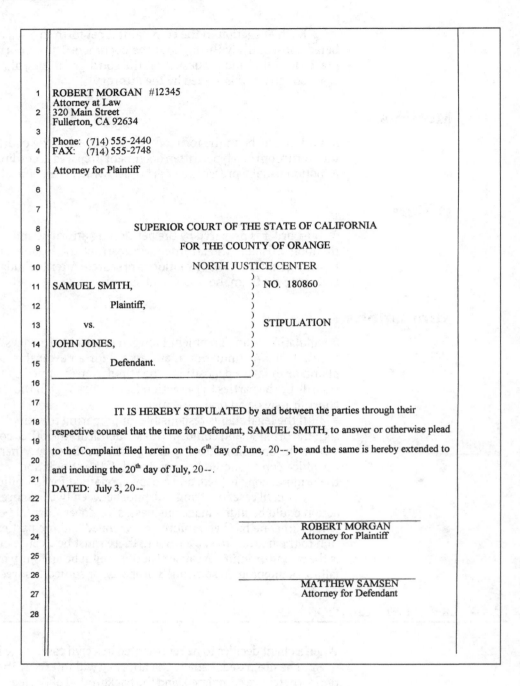

1 | ROBERT MORGAN #12345
Attorney at Law
2 | 320 Main Street
Fullerton, CA 92634
3 |
Phone: (714) 555-2440
4 | FAX: (714) 555-2748
5 | Attorney for Plaintiff

SUPERIOR COURT OF THE STATE OF CALIFORNIA

FOR THE COUNTY OF ORANGE

NORTH JUSTICE CENTER

SAMUEL SMITH,   ) NO. 180860
)
          Plaintiff,   )
)
     vs.   ) STIPULATION
)
JOHN JONES,   )
)
          Defendant.   )

IT IS HEREBY STIPULATED by and between the parties through their respective counsel that the time for Defendant, SAMUEL SMITH, to answer or otherwise plead to the Complaint filed herein on the 6th day of June, 20--, be and the same is hereby extended to and including the 20th day of July, 20--.

DATED: July 3, 20--

_____
ROBERT MORGAN
Attorney for Plaintiff

_____
MATTHEW SAMSEN
Attorney for Defendant

agreement. Any services that are not listed in the agreement are paid for separately. This form of agreement is used by professional organizations, businesses, and schools.

3. *Fixed or flat fees.* A flat fee may be established at the beginning of a case and usually includes such cases as uncomplicated dissolutions, bankruptcies, or adoptions.

4. *Hourly fees.* There are many cases where it is difficult to determine the amount of time required of the attorney or the legal staff. This fee is determined by the amount of time (in hours) spent on the case.

5. *Statutory fees.* **Statutory fees** are determined by the state statutes and regulate the amount that can be charged for a particular service. Legal services for probate often are determined by statutory fees.

FIGURE 7-2 *Client talking to attorney.*

DEFINITION OF A LAWSUIT

A lawsuit is an action or proceeding in a civil court that takes the form of a judicial contest. The term *lawsuit* is a popular word meaning litigation, or legal action; the **litigants** are the parties to the suit. A claim, or grievance, is filed with the court with the hope that the court will resolve the differences. The injured party who initiates the suit is called the **plaintiff**, and the accused party is called the **defendant**. Either party to the suit may consist of more than one person.

The parties to the action may be represented by an attorney or they may represent themselves. If they represent themselves, they are said to be appearing in a *propria persona*, or *pro per*. The Latin term used to indicate that there is litigation in process is *pendente lite,* and *lis pendens* or *notice of lis pendens* is a latin term used for the purpose of notifying all persons that the title to certain property is under litigation.

Phases of a Lawsuit

Usually there are certain phases to a lawsuit. Initially, the attorney has to define and analyze the problem to determine if it can be settled out of court. If, after attempts at negotiation and settlement, the problem cannot be resolved out of court, the attorney will probably recommend that the case be taken to trial (see Figure 7-2).

The Complaint   Once it is determined that a case will go to court, the plaintiff must file a complaint in the proper court. The complaint is a written declaration or petition setting forth the cause of action. A legal action is commenced by the filing of the original complaint, which is the first document filed by the plaintiff.

Summons   When a complaint is filed with the office of the court clerk, the clerk will **issue** a summons. The **summons** is a written legal order to the defendant to respond within a specified time to the plaintiff's complaint. In most states, the law requires that the defendant be served personally with a summons, although some states allow the substituted service (other than personal) of a summons. The defendant usually receives a copy of the plaintiff's complaint at the same time that he or she is served with a summons. The summons indicates what action is pending against the defendant and is the first official document issued by the court clerk in a legal action.

Pleadings   The plaintiff's complaint and the defendant's reply, prepared by their respective attorneys, constitute the **pleadings**; pleadings reduce the issues to definite terms. All court pleadings, printed court forms, and other papers filed in an action at law must be typed in compliance with the rules of the court. After the pleadings have been filed with the court clerk, a trial date is requested.

Judgment by Default   If the defendant fails to file an answer to the complaint within the specified time, the defendant is in **default**, and the plaintiff is entitled to a judgment against the defendant, which may include court costs and damages. If either party fails to appear in court on the day set for trial, the other party is entitled to a judgment by default.

Trial   In a civil action, the defendant may waive the right to a jury trial and let the judge decide the case; otherwise, a jury of eligible, impartial persons will decide the issues. A trial jury is not used in a **court of equity** (a court where the relief is not available to the petitioner through money damages or criminal punishment), but it is almost always used in criminal actions.

In a jury trial, the judge rules on points of law and the jury decides on the basis of the facts. After the jury has been sworn in, the trial usually follows this sequence:

1. *Opening statements* are given to the jurors by the plaintiff's lawyer. The defendant's lawyer then has an opportunity to make statements presenting his or her side of the case. In criminal cases, the defense has the option of waiting until the conclusion of the prosecution's case to make the opening statements.
2. After all the plaintiff's witnesses have been called, the defendant *presents the evidence*, which may include written documents, objects, pictures, or testimony of witnesses.
3. *Closing statements* are made, first by the plaintiff's lawyer and then by the defendant's lawyer. In these statements, each attorney summarizes the evidence and attempts to persuade the jury to bring in a favorable verdict for his or her client.
4. The jurors are *charged by the judge*, that is, the judge instructs the jury as to the rules of law relating to the case and provides guidance in reaching a verdict.

Verdict   After the judge's charge, the jury is taken to a private room where a foreman is selected; the foreman acts as the chairperson of the jury. The instructions are read and the evidence is studied, and a vote of the jury is taken in order to arrive at a decision. The failure of the jury to agree on the results of its charge by the court may require that a new trial be ordered.

Judgment of the Court   The judge enters the verdict of the jury in the court records, and the case is said to be decided. The party losing the case is required to pay the amount specified or to provide for specific performance of an act. In addition to the judgment, court costs, but not legal fees, usually are assessed against the party losing the case.

Execution of Judgment   A judgment for specific amounts of money serves as a **lien**, or claim against the loser's property, and if this judgment is not paid, the court will order the property to be sold. This court order is known as a **writ of execution**, and any excess of the sale must be returned to the losing party.

The **execution of judgment** also may be used against any income, wages, salaries, or dividends; such an execution is known as execution against income, or **garnishment**. Only a limited percentage of wages or salaries can be garnished (usually 10 percent), and bank checking accounts also can be included in this proceeding.

A **writ of attachment** is a special proceeding granted by the court if there is a suspicion that the defendant may try to conceal his or her assets or convert them into cash. This writ enables an officer of the court to hold the defendant's property until the case is decided.

Appeal   If a party is not satisfied with the judgment and believes that certain legal errors were made, the case may be **appealed** to a higher or appellate court and may require a new trial. If a new trial is scheduled, the same procedures are followed except that no new pleadings are required.

COMMENCING A LEGAL ACTION

Plaintiff's Pleadings

Since the legal action is commenced by the filing of an original complaint and the issuance of the original summons by the court clerk, these papers must be prepared by the attorney's office. All court pleadings, completed printed court forms, and other documents filed in an action at law must be typed and made to comply with the court rules.

Although the style of these papers may vary from office to office, and even within the same office, the examples in this book are intended as guidelines for the preparation of these pleadings and legal papers. It is important that you learn the style preferred by your employer for typing legal papers.

Preparing the Complaint   The attorney dictates the parties to the action (plaintiff versus defendant), the facts or allegations constituting the cause of action, and the **prayer**, or the closing statement. You will type the original complaint for filing and make sufficient copies for service upon each named defendant as well as an office copy. If a verification is attached, be sure to prepare sufficient copies for each copy of the complaint as well as for the office copy. The plaintiff's attorney will sign the original complaint, and the plaintiff will sign the original verification. As soon as all papers have been signed, be sure to conform the copies (make them identical by indicating signatures and dates signed).

Preparing the Summons   A *summons* is a printed court form, and it is the first official document issued by the clerk in a legal action. The summons is the official notice to a defendant advising that a civil complaint has been filed against him or her and informing the defendant of his or her legal rights. The summons usually is issued at the time that the complaint is filed with the appropriate clerk of the court.

Filing Court Documents with the Clerk of the Court

The complaint and summons usually are prepared for **filing** in the following order, with the Civil Case Cover Sheet (see Figure 7-3) on top:

1. Civil Case Cover Sheet
2. Summons
3. Complaint
4. Attachments or exhibits

982.2(b)(1)

ATTORNEY OR PARTY WITHOUT ATTORNEY *(Name, state bar number, and address):*	FOR COURT USE ONLY
ROBERT MORGAN #12345 Attorney at Law 320 Main Street Fullerton, CA 92634 TELEPHONE NO: (714) 555-2440 FAX NO: (714) 555-2748 ATTORNEY FOR *(Name):* Plaintiff	

INSERT NAME OF COURT, JUDICIAL DISTRICT, AND BRANCH COURT, IF ANY:
SUPERIOR COURT OF THE STATE OF CALIFORNIA
COUNTY OF ORANGE, CENTRAL JUSTICE CENTER

CASE NAME: JOHN JONES v. SAMUEL SMITH

CIVIL CASE COVER SHEET ☐ Limited ☒ Unlimited	Complex Case Designation ☐ Counter ☐ Joinder Filed with first appearance by defendant (Cal. Rules of Court, rule 1811)	CASE NUMBER: ASSIGNED JUDGE:

Please complete all five (5) items below:

1. Check **one** box below for the case type that best describes this case:

Auto Tort
☐ Auto (22)
Other PI/PD/WD (Personal Injury/Property Damage/Wrongful Death) Tort
☐ Asbestos (04)
☐ Product liability (24)
☐ Medical malpractice (45)
☐ Other PI/PD/WD (23)
Non-PI/PD/WD (Other) Tort
☐ Business tort/unfair business practice (07)
☐ Civil rights *(e.g., discrimination, False arrest)* (08)
☐ Defamation *(e.g., slander, libel)* (13)
☐ Fraud (16)
☐ Intellectual property (19)
☐ Professional negligence *(e.g., legal malpractice)* (25)
☐ Other non-PI/PD/WD tort (35)
Employment
☐ Wrongful termination (36)

Other employment (15)
Contract
☒ Breach of contract warranty (06)
☐ Collections *(e.g., money owed, open book accounts)* (09)
☐ Insurance coverage (18)
☐ Other contract (37)
Real Property
☐ Eminent domain/inverse condemnation (14)
☐ Wrongful eviction (33)
☐ Other real property *(e.g., quiet title)* (26)
Unlawful Detainer
☐ Commercial (31)
☐ Residential (32)
☐ Drugs (38)
Judicial Review
☐ Asset forfeiture (05)
☐ Petition re: arbitration award (11)
☐ Writ of mandate (02)

☐ Other judicial review (39)
Provisionally Complex Civil Litigation
(Cal. Rules of Court, rules 1800-1812)
☐ Antitrust/Trade regulation (03)
☐ Construction defect (10)
☐ Claims involving mass tort (40)
☐ Securities litigation (28)
☐ Toxic tort/Environmental (30)
☐ Insurance coverage claims arising from the above list provisionally complex case types (41)
Enforcement of Judgment
☐ Enforcement of judgment *(e.g., sister state, foreign, out-of-country abstracts)* (20)
Miscellaneous Civil Complaint
☐ RICO (27)
☐ Other complaint *(not specified above)* (42)
Miscellaneous Civil Petition
☐ Partnership and corporate governance (21)
☐ Other petition *(not specified above)* (43)

2. This case ☐ is ☒ is not complex under rule 1800 of the California Rules of Court. If case is complex, mark the factors requiring exceptional judicial management:
  a. ☐ Large number of separately represented parties
  b. ☐ Extensive motion practice raising difficult or novel issues that will be time-consuming to resolve
  c. ☐ Substantial amount of documentary evidence
  d. ☐ Large number of witnesses
  e. ☐ Coordination and related actions pending in one or more courts in other countries, states or countries, or in a federal court
  f. ☐ Substantial post-disposition judicial disposition
3. Type of remedies sought *(check all that apply):*
  a. ☒ monetary   b. ☐ nonmonetary; declaratory or injunctive relief   c. ☒ punitive
4. Number of causes of action *(specify):* 5
5. This case ☐ is ☒ is not a class action suit.
Date: August 5, 20--

ROBERT MORGAN   ▶
_____   _____
(TYPE OR PRINT NAME)   (SIGNATURE OF PARTY OR ATTORNEY FOR PARTY)

NOTICE
- Plaintiff must file this cover sheet with the first paper filed in the action or proceeding (except small claim cases or cases filed under the Probate, Family, or Welfare and Institutions Code). (Cal. Rules of Court, rule 982.2.)
- File this cover sheet in addition to any cover sheet required by local court rule.
- If this case is complex under rule 1800 et seq. of the California Rules of Court, you must serve a copy of this cover sheet on all other parties to the action or proceeding.
- Unless this is a complex case, this cover sheet shall be used for statistical purposes only.

Form Adopted for Mandatory Use Judicial Council of California 982.2(b)(1) [Rev. January 1, 2000]	**CIVIL CASE COVER SHEET**	Cal. Rules of Court, rules 982.2, 1800-1812· Standards of Judicial Administration, § 19 2001 © American LegalNet, Inc.

FIGURE 7-3 *Civil Case Cover Sheet.*

The first paper filed in a legal action or proceeding must be accompanied by a Civil Case Cover Sheet. The Cover Sheet is used for statistical purposes and may affect the assignment of a complex case.

These legal papers then are presented for filing with the clerk of the court.

The court clerk's office is supervised by the clerk of the court and staffed by deputy clerks. The clerks check to make sure that all the necessary papers have

CM-010

ATTORNEY OR PARTY WITHOUT ATTORNEY (Name, state bar number, and address):	FOR COURT USE ONLY
ROBERT MORGAN #12345 Attorney at Law 320 Main Street Fullerton, CA 92634 TELEPHONE NO.: (714) 555-2440 FAX NO.: (714) 555-2748 ATTORNEY FOR (Name): Plaintiff	

SUPERIOR COURT OF CALIFORNIA, COUNTY OF   ORANGE
STREET ADDRESS: 700 Civic Center Drive West
MAILING ADDRESS:
CITY AND ZIP CODE: Santa Ana, CA 92701
BRANCH NAME: CENTRAL JUSTICE CENTER

CASE NAME: JOHN JONES v. SAMUEL SMITH

CIVIL CASE COVER SHEET	**Complex Case Designation**	CASE NUMBER:
☒ **Unlimited** ☐ **Limited** (Amount (Amount demanded demanded is exceeds $25,000) $25,000 or less)	☐ **Counter** ☐ **Joinder** Filed with first appearance by defendant (Cal. Rules of Court, rule 1811)	JUDGE: DEPT:

All five (5) items below must be completed (see instructions on page 2).

1. Check **one** box below for the case type that best describes this case:

Auto Tort
☐ Auto (22)
☐ Uninsured motorist (46)
Other PI/PD/WD (Personal Injury/Property Damage/Wrongful Death) Tort
☐ Asbestos (04)
☐ Product liability (24)
☐ Medical malpractice (45)
☐ Other PI/PD/WD (23)
Non-PI/PD/WD (Other) Tort
☐ Business tort/unfair business practice (07)
☐ Civil rights (08)
☐ Defamation (13)
☐ Fraud (16)
☐ Intellectual property (19)
☐ Professional negligence (25)
☐ Other non-PI/PD/WD tort (35)
Employment
☐ Wrongful termination (36)
☐ Other employment (15)

Contract
☒ Breach of contract/warranty (06)
☐ Collections (09)
☐ Insurance coverage (18)
☐ Other contract (37)
Real Property
☐ Eminent domain/Inverse condemnation (14)
☐ Wrongful eviction (33)
☐ Other real property (26)
Unlawful Detainer
☐ Commercial (31)
☐ Residential (32)
☐ Drugs (38)
Judicial Review
☐ Asset forfeiture (05)
☐ Petition re: arbitration award (11)
☐ Writ of mandate (02)
☐ Other judicial review (39)

Provisionally Complex Civil Litigation (Cal. Rules of Court, rules 1800-1812)
☐ Antitrust/Trade regulation (03)
☐ Construction defect (10)
☐ Mass tort (40)
☐ Securities litigation (28)
☐ Environmental /Toxic tort (30)
☐ Insurance coverage claims arising from the above listed provisionally complex case types (41)
Enforcement of Judgment
☐ Enforcement of judgment (20)
Miscellaneous Civil Complaint
☐ RICO (27)
☐ Other complaint (not specified above) (42)
Miscellaneous Civil Petition
☐ Partnership and corporate governance (21)
☐ Other petition (not specified above) (43)

2. This case ☐ is   ☒ is not   complex under rule 1800 of the California Rules of Court. If the case is complex, mark the factors requiring exceptional judicial management:
   a. ☐ Large number of separately represented parties
   b. ☐ Extensive motion practice raising difficult or novel issues that will be time-consuming to resolve
   c. ☐ Substantial amount of documentary evidence
   d. ☐ Large number of witnesses
   e. ☐ Coordination with related actions pending in one or more courts
   f. ☐ Substantial post-judgment judicial supervision
3. Type of remedies sought (check all that apply):
   a. ☒ monetary   b. ☐ nonmonetary; declaratory or injunctive relief   c. ☒ punitive
4. Number of causes of action (specify):
5. This case ☐ is   ☒ is not   a class action suit.
Date: August 5, 20--
ROBERT MORGAN
_____   ►   _____
(TYPE OR PRINT NAME)   (SIGNATURE OF PARTY OR ATTORNEY FOR PARTY)

NOTICE
• Plaintiff must file this cover sheet with the first paper filed in the action or proceeding (except small claims cases or cases filed under the Probate, Family, or Welfare and Institutions Code). (Cal. Rules of Court, rule 201.8.) Failure to file may result in sanctions
• File this cover sheet in addition to any cover sheet required by local court rule.
• If this case is complex under rule 1800 et seq. of the California Rules of Court, you must serve a copy of this cover sheet on **all** other parties to the action or proceeding.
• Unless this is a complex case, this cover sheet will be used for statistical purposes only.

Page 1 of 2

| Form Adopted for Mandatory Use
Judicial Council of California
CM-010 [Rev. July 1, 2003] | **CIVIL CASE COVER SHEET** | American LegalNet, Inc.
www.USCourtForms.com | Cal. Rules of Court, rules 201.8, 1800-1812;
Standards of Judicial Administration, § 19
www.courtinfo.ca.gov |

FIGURE 7-4   *Summons.*

been submitted and all the forms have been completed correctly. If the papers submitted are incorrect or improperly completed, they will be returned to the attorney's office for correction. Therefore, it is important that the support staff prepare the legal papers and complete court forms correctly when first submitting them for filing.

SUM-100

SUMMONS
(CITACION JUDICIAL)

NOTICE TO DEFENDANT:
(AVISO AL DEMANDADO):
JOHN JONES

YOU ARE BEING SUED BY PLAINTIFF:
(LO ESTÁ DEMANDANDO EL DEMANDANTE):
SAMUEL SMITH

FOR COURT USE ONLY
(SOLO PARA USO DE LA CORTE)

You have 30 CALENDAR DAYS after this summons and legal papers are served on you to file a written response at this court and have a copy served on the plaintiff. A letter or phone call will not protect you. Your written response must be in proper legal form if you want the court to hear your case. There may be a court form that you can use for your response. You can find these court forms and more information at the California Courts Online Self-Help Center (www.courtinfo.ca.gov/selfhelp), your county law library, or the courthouse nearest you. If you cannot pay the filing fee, ask the court clerk for a fee waiver form. If you do not file your response on time, you may lose the case by default, and your wages, money, and property may be taken without further warning from the court.
There are other legal requirements. You may want to call an attorney right away. If you do not know an attorney, you may want to call an attorney referral service. If you cannot afford an attorney, you may be eligible for free legal services from a nonprofit legal services program. You can locate these nonprofit groups at the California Legal Services Web site (www.lawhelpcalifornia.org), the California Courts Online Self-Help Center (www.courtinfo.ca.gov/selfhelp), or by contacting your local court or county bar association.

Tiene 30 DÍAS DE CALENDARIO después de que le entreguen esta citación y papeles legales para presentar una respuesta por escrito en esta corte y hacer que se entregue una copia al demandante. Una carta o una llamada telefónica no lo protegen. Su respuesta por escrito tiene que estar en formato legal correcto si desea que procesen su caso en la corte. Es posible que haya un formulario que usted pueda usar para su respuesta. Puede encontrar estos formularios de la corte y más información en el Centro de Ayuda de las Cortes de California (www.courtinfo.ca.gov/selfhelp/espanol/), en la biblioteca de leyes de su condado o en la corte que le quede más cerca. Si no puede pagar la cuota de presentación, pida al secretario de la corte que le dé un formulario de exención de pago de cuotas. Si no presenta su respuesta a tiempo, puede perder el caso por incumplimiento y la corte le podrá quitar su sueldo, dinero y bienes sin más advertencia. Hay otros requisitos legales. Es recomendable que llame a un abogado inmediatamente. Si no conoce a un abogado, puede llamar a un servicio de remisión a abogados. Si no puede pagar a un abogado, es posible que cumpla con los requisitos para obtener servicios legales gratuitos de un programa de servicios legales sin fines de lucro. Puede encontrar estos grupos sin fines de lucro en el sitio web de California Legal Services, (www.lawhelpcalifornia.org), en el Centro de Ayuda de las Cortes de California, (www.courtinfo.ca.gov/selfhelp/espanol/) o poniéndose en contacto con la corte o el colegio de abogados locales.

The name and address of the court is:
(El nombre y dirección de la corte es):

CASE NUMBER:
(Número del Caso):
403782

SUPERIOR COURT FOR THE STATE OF CALIFORNIA
FOR THE COUNTY OF ORANGE
700 Civic Center Drive West
Santa Ana, CA 92701-4079
CENTRAL JUSTICE CENTER

The name, address, and telephone number of plaintiff's attorney, or plaintiff without an attorney, is:
(El nombre, la dirección y el número de teléfono del abogado del demandante, o del demandante que no tiene abogado, es):
ROBERT MORGAN   12345   (714) 555-2440
Attorney at Law
320 Main Street
Fullerton, CA 92634

DATE: January 2, 20--   Clerk, by _____, Deputy
(Fecha)   *(Secretario)*   *(Adjunto)*

(For proof of service of this summons, use Proof of Service of Summons (form POS-010).)
(Para prueba de entrega de esta citación use el formulario Proof of Service of Summons, (POS-010)).

NOTICE TO THE PERSON SERVED: You are served

[SEAL]

1. ☒ as an individual defendant.
2. ☐ as the person sued under the fictitious name of *(specify):*

3. ☐ on behalf of *(specify):*
   under: ☐ CCP 416.10 (corporation)   ☐ CCP 416.60 (minor)
          ☐ CCP 416.20 (defunct corporation)   ☐ CCP 416.70 (conservatee)
          ☐ CCP 416.40 (association or partnership) ☒ CCP 416.90 (authorized person)
          ☐ other *(specify):*
4. ☒ by personal delivery on *(date):*

Page 1 of 1

Form Adopted for Mandatory Use
Judicial Council of California
SUM-100 [Rev. January 1, 2004]

SUMMONS

Code of Civil Procedure §§ 412.20, 465

American LegalNet, Inc.
www.USCourtForms.com

FIGURE 7-4   *Continued*

If all the papers are correct, the clerk, or the clerk's designate, accepts them, assigns them a case number, and signs and dates them. These papers then become an official record of the court.

A legal action is commenced with the filing of the original complaint in the office of the clerk of the court, payment of the filing fee, and the issuance of the summons by the clerk. The summons is issued by the clerk when the clerk signs it and

POS-010

ATTORNEY OR PARTY WITHOUT ATTORNEY *(Name, State Bar number, and address):* ROBERT MORGAN #12345 Attorney at Law 320 Main Street Fullerton, CA 92634 TELEPHONE NO. *(Optional):* (714) 555-2440 FAX NO. *(Optional):* (714) 555-2748 E-MAIL ADDRESS *(Optional):* ATTORNEY FOR *(Name):* Plaintiff	*FOR COURT USE ONLY*

SUPERIOR COURT OF CALIFORNIA, COUNTY OF ORANGE
STREET ADDRESS: 700 Civic Center Drive West
MAILING ADDRESS:
CITY AND ZIP CODE: Santa Ana, CA 92701-4079
BRANCH NAME: CENTRAL JUSTICE CENTER

PLAINTIFF/PETITIONER: JOHN JONES DEFENDANT/RESPONDENT: SAMUEL SMITH	CASE NUMBER: 403782

PROOF OF SERVICE OF SUMMONS	Ref. No. or File No.:

(Separate proof of service is required for each party served.)

1. At the time of service I was at least 18 years of age and not a party to this action.
2. I served copies of:
   a. ☒ summons
   b. ☐ complaint
   c. ☐ Alternative Dispute Resolution (ADR) package
   d. ☐ Civil Case Cover Sheet *(served in complex cases only)*
   e. ☐ cross-complaint
   f. ☐ other *(specify documents):*
3. a. Party served *(specify name of party as shown on documents served):*
      JOHN JONES

   b. Person served: ☒ party in item 3a   ☐ other *(specify name and relationship to the party named in item 3a):*

4. Address where the party was served:
   208 Via Luna Place, Fullerton, CA 92634
5. I served the party *(check proper box)*
   a. ☒ **by personal service.** I personally delivered the documents listed in item 2 to the party or person authorized to receive service of process for the party (1) on *(date):* January 4, 20--   (2) at *(time):* 8:30 a.m.
   b. ☐ **by substituted service.** On *(date):*   at *(time):*   I left the documents listed in item 2 with or in the presence of *(name and title or relationship to person indicated in item 3b):*

      (1) ☐ **(business)** a person at least 18 years of age apparently in charge at the office or usual place of business of the person to be served. I informed him or her of the general nature of the papers.
      (2) ☐ **(home)** a competent member of the household (at least 18 years of age) at the dwelling house or usual place of abode of the party. I informed him or her of the general nature of the papers.
      (3) ☐ **(physical address unknown)** a person at least 18 years of age apparently in charge at the usual mailing address of the person to be served, other than a United States Postal Service post office box. I informed him or her of the general nature of the papers.
      (4) ☐ I thereafter mailed (by first-class, postage prepaid) copies of the documents to the person to be served at the place where the copies were left (Code Civ. Proc., § 415.20. I mailed the documents on
         (date):   from *(city):*   or ☐ a declaration of mailing is attached.
      (5) ☐ I attach a **declaration of diligence** stating actions taken first to attempt personal service.

Page 1 of 2

Form Adopted for Mandatory Use Judicial Council of California POS-010 [Rev. July 1, 2004]	**PROOF OF SERVICE OF SUMMONS**	Code of Civil Procedure, § 417.10 American LegalNet, Inc. www.USCourtForms.com

FIGURE 7-4   *Continued*

stamps the docket number, date, and court seal on it. The clerk or one of the deputy clerks will imprint the word *filed*, the date, and the **docket number** assigned by the clerk's office on the original complaint. The docket number is the official designation of the case, and this number is used on all subsequent legal papers relating to the case. All future court reference to the case is made to the docket number rather than the parties to the action.

PLAINTIFF/PETITIONER: JOHN JONES	CASE NUMBER:
DEFENDANT/RESPONDENT: SAMUEL SMITH	403782

c. ☐ **by mail and acknowledgment of receipt of service.** I mailed the documents listed in item 2 to the party, to the address shown in item 4, by first-class mail, postage prepaid,

    (1) on *(date):*   (2) from *(city):*

      (3) ☐ with two copies of the *Notice and Acknowledgment of Receipt* and a postage-paid return envelope addressed to me. *(Attach completed Notice and Acknowledgement of Receipt.)* (Code Civ. Proc., § 415.30.)

      (4) ☐ to an address outside California with return receipt requested. (Code Civ. Proc., § 415.40.)

d. ☐ **by other means** *(specify means of service and authorizing code section):*

    ☐ Additional page describing service is attached.

6. The "Notice to the Person Served" (on the summons) was completed as follows:
   a. ☒ as an individual defendant.
   b. ☐ as the person sued under the fictitious name of *(specify):*
   c. ☐ as occupant.
   d. ☐ On behalf of *(specify):*
       under the following Code of Civil Procedure section:

☐ 416.10 (corporation)	☐ 415.95 (business organization, form unknown)
☐ 416.20 (defunct corporation)	☐ 416.60 (minor)
☐ 416.30 (joint stock company/association)	☐ 416.70 (ward or conservatee)
☐ 416.40 (association or partnership)	☐ 416.90 (authorized person)
☐ 416.50 (public entity)	☐ 415.46 (occupant)
	☐ other:

7. **Person who served papers**
   a. Name: CAROLYN ELAINE MILLER
   b. Address: 928 Blue Ridge Drive, Placentia, CA 92670
   c. Telephone number: (881) 555-2943
   d. The fee for service was: $ 13.00
   e. I am:
       (1) ☒ not a registered California process server.
       (2) ☐ exempt from registration under Business and Professions Code section 22350(b).
       (3) ☐ registered California process server:
           (i) ☐ owner ☐ employee ☐ independent contractor.
           (ii) Registration No.:
           (iii) County:

8. ☒ **I declare** under penalty of perjury under the laws of the State of California that the foregoing is true and correct.

    or

9. ☐ **I am a California sheriff or marshal** and I certify that the foregoing is true and correct.

Date: January 4, 20--

▶

_____   _____
(NAME OF PERSON WHO SERVED PAPERS/SHERIFF OR MARSHAL)   (SIGNATURE)

POS-010 [Rev. July 1, 2004]   **PROOF OF SERVICE OF SUMMONS**   Page 2 of 2

American LegalNet, Inc.
www.USCourtForms.com

FIGURE 7-4 *Continued*

After the original complaint is filed, copies of the complaint, the issued original summons, and copies of the summons are returned to the attorney's office. When the law office receives these papers, they should be conformed, and copies of the complaint and summons served on each named defendant.

Filing by Mail   When pleadings are filed by mail with the court clerk, the original complaint, summons, and attachments, as well as a check for the filing fee and a stamped, self-addressed envelope, are mailed to the appropriate court clerk. When the papers are received, the clerk will file the original complaint, issue the original summons, conform the copies of the summons, and return the original summons and copies of the papers in the envelope provided by the attorney's office. It is then up to the attorney to serve the papers on the parties concerned. The support staff prepares the original summons with adequate copies to be attached to each copy of the complaint for service, as well as an office copy. Each named defendant must be served with a copy of the complaint and a summons.

Serving a Summons

Because the lawsuit is initiated by filing a complaint, it is mandatory that the defendant be notified that a complaint has been filed. This is done by serving the defendant with notice either in person or by publication that he or she is being sued. The defendant must respond to this notice within a certain period of time. This notice, known in most states as a summons (see Figure 7-4), must be served on the defendant with a copy of the complaint.

While the original summons must be served on the defendant, in actual practice, the person performing the service shows the original summons to the defendant and says, "You are being served with a summons." The delivery person gives the defendant a copy of the summons and complaint and returns the original summons to the person or law office initiating the suit.

The method of serving a copy of the summons and complaint may vary somewhat from state to state and jurisdiction to jurisdiction, but the procedures usually follow the pattern described here.

Personal Service   Personal delivery of a copy of the summons and complaint is referred to as **personal service**. This service is usually done by a person of legal age and not a party to the action, or by a constable, sheriff, or marshal. A fee is paid for having the document served.

Most documents, however, are served by a **process server**. Process servers can be employed by an attorney's service, or they may work independently. A fee is charged for this service. The support staff is responsible for having the fee ready and for preparing the necessary papers with detailed instructions on how the papers are to be served and the location of the party. Usually the support staff supplies the process server with the original and one copy of the summons, a copy of the complaint, and the defendant's address, location, or place of business.

After the service has been performed, all office copies should be conformed and the original summons indicating service has been accomplished should be filed with the court clerk, who will attach it to the complaint and keep it on file. After the original jurisdiction of the defendant has been established by the service of the original summons and complaint, and when other documents are served by mail, the office of the plaintiff's attorney also must provide some proof to the court that they were served on the respective parties.

A **proof of service** states that a certain document, or several documents, were mailed to certain persons at stated addresses on a specific date and in a specific city. Proof of service can be created and signed by any support staff in the office eighteen years of age or older. This proof of service generally is made on a separate sheet of paper and attached to the original document as the last page. Some offices use printed forms, whereas other offices may type these forms or have stamps made. The form of the proof of service may vary in different jurisdictions and states. Depending on how it is served, the proof of service may be either a verification or an affidavit. If it is an affidavit, it must include the wording and space for notarization as well as a statement of venue and jurat.

Substituted Service   Substituted service is used when a defendant cannot be served personally after reasonable diligence (according to the Code of Civil Procedure).

A copy of the summons and complaint may be left at the following places under the following circumstances: At a dwelling house, place of business, or the abode of the person to be served, in the presence of a competent member of the household or individual in charge (at least eighteen years of age) who shall be informed as to the nature of the papers. Immediately thereafter, a copy of the summons and complaint must be mailed first class by the support staff to the person served at the place where the papers were left. The original summons and certificate of service will be returned to the attorney's office. The support staff should note the date of service on the office calendar and indicate the date by which the defendant should answer.

Service by Mail and Acknowledgment of Receipt   Using proof of service by mail, a summons and complaint may be served by mail on a defendant; however, the validity of the service depends on the defendant executing an acknowledgment of receipt of the complaint and summons. This method of service usually is used to accomplish service on a corporation or large commercial enterprise. The acknowledgment of receipt indicates to the court that the summons and complaint have been received by the defendant. If the defendant does not execute and return the acknowledgment of receipt, it is then necessary for the plaintiff's attorney to serve the defendant by personal or substituted service in order to give the court jurisdiction over the defendant.

Service of Complaint and Summons Outside the State   If the defendant resides outside the state, methods of service may vary. However, the following methods of service are used most frequently.

1. Copies of the summons and complaint are mailed to the defendant by registered mail with a return receipt requested. After a specified number of days, the court will have jurisdiction over the defendant, and the attorney should file a proof of service with the court.
2. Personal service also may be made on the defendant in accordance with the laws of the state in which the defendant resides. After personal service has been completed, a proof of service by mail should be filed with the court.
3. Jurisdiction also may be obtained by having the defendant sign and return the notice and acknowledgment of receipt.

Service of Summons by Publication   When the whereabouts of the defendant are unknown and a diligent investigation has been made, the defendant may be served by publication. It is usually necessary to obtain a court order authorizing the publication of the summons in a newspaper of general circulation. Procedures vary from state to state, and it is important to learn how this is handled in your state.

Date of Service   Because of legal time limitations for specific court actions, the date of service of a document is very important. The day on which the adverse party is deemed served is the starting point for the time allowed for parties to respond to certain documents, and if this time limitation is not adhered to, it may lead to a default judgment for the opposing party.

DEFENDANT'S PLEADINGS

There are many ways in which the defendant can respond to the plaintiff's complaint. These pleadings will depend on the nature of the allegations in the complaint. The following are examples of how the defendant may respond to the complaint.

1. File a demurrer
2. Make a motion to strike

3. Simultaneously file a demurrer and motion to strike
4. File an answer
5. File an answer and cross-complaint

Filing a Demurrer

In California and other states, a **demurrer** raises an issue as to the legal sufficiency of the complaint (see Figure 7-5). This means that, in the opinion of the defendant's attorney, the complaint fails to state a cause of action. In states where demurrers are

FIGURE 7-5   *Demurrer.*

```
 1   MATTHEW SAMSEN  #67890
     Attorney at Law
 2   480 Lemon Street
     Fullerton, CA 92634
 3
     Phone:   (714) 555-3060
 4   FAX:     (714) 555-3063

 5   Attorney for Defendant

 6

 7

 8              SUPERIOR COURT OF THE STATE OF CALIFORNIA

 9                     FOR THE COUNTY OF ORANGE

10                       NORTH JUSTICE CENTER
                                            )
11   SAMUEL SMITH,                          )   NO.  403782
                                            )
12            Plaintiff,                    )
                                            )
13        vs.                               )   DEMURRER TO COMPLAINT
                                            )
14   JOHN JONES,                            )
                                            )
15            Defendant.                    )
                                            )
16

17          Defendant JOHN JONES demurs to Plaintiff's complaint upon the following
     grounds:
18
          1.     Plaintiff has no legal capacity to sue . . . . . .
19

20

21                                    _____
                                            MATTHEW SAMSEN
22                                          Attorney for Defendant

23
            I hereby certify that this demurrer is filed in good faith and is not filed for the
24
     purpose of delay, and in my opinion, the grounds are well taken.
25

26                                    _____
                                            MATTHEW SAMSEN
27                                          Attorney for Defendant

28                      (Points and Authorities must be attached)
```

not acceptable, a motion to make the complaint more definite and certain may be used instead. The attorney usually dictates the grounds for the demurrer and the points and authorities that support the demurrer. Points and authorities are arguments and citations using previous cases and authorities to support the attorney's contention that the complaint has legal errors.

The procedure for preparing a demurrer is as follows:

1. The attorney dictates the grounds for the demurrer and the points and authorities. The support staff types the original and makes the necessary number of copies of the demurrer and the points and authorities. The attorney signs these papers.
2. A copy of the papers is served on the plaintiff, and the original with the proof of service is filed with the court. A filing fee is paid.

The attorneys submit their points and authorities and arguments at the court hearing, and the court may rule that the demurrer be *sustained*. This means that the objections made by the defendant to the complaint are correct, and the plaintiff must amend or correct the complaint within a specified time. If the court rules that the demurrer is sustained in all respects without leave to amend, the plaintiff is not permitted to change or correct the complaint. This, in effect, means that the lawsuit is disposed of in favor of the defendant, and the case then may be dismissed.

The court may decide against the defendant's contentions by overruling the demurrer, and the defendant then must file an answer to the complaint within the time allowed by the court.

Motion to Strike   In some jurisdictions, a *motion to strike* eliminates specific legally objectionable allegations of the complaint that are not reached by the demurrer. If grounds exist for filing both a demurrer and motion to strike, the two must be filed simultaneously. The notice of the motion to strike sets forth the following:

1. The precise words of the complaint that are objectionable
2. The exact page, paragraph, and lines where these words are found
3. Points and authorities that must accompany the notice of motion to strike

See Figure 7-6 for an example of a motion to strike.

The Answer   The answer is the defendant's formal reply to the plaintiff's complaint (see Figure 7-7). It is the pleading that brings the lawsuit to a head and raises issues of fact. For each allegation in the complaint, the answering party must admit or deny the allegations or state that he or she is without knowledge or information sufficient to respond to the allegation. The answer may be in the form of a general or specific denial of the facts alleged in the complaint, and it also may allege affirmative defenses, which are the facts designed to defeat the plaintiff's claims.

The defendant also may assert claims against the plaintiff in a **cross-complaint**. If the claim arises out of a related transaction, the cross-complaint may be filed at the same time that the answer is filed, but as a separate pleading (see the following section for details).

The procedure for making an answer to a complaint is as follows:

1. The attorney dictates the answer. The support staff types the original answer to be filed with the court, with a copy for service on the defendant and one file copy. The attorney signs these papers.
2. If the complaint has been verified, the defendant must verify the answer.
3. The support staff prepares the proof of service and signs it, indicating that the answer has been mailed to the plaintiff or all parties concerned.
4. The answer is filed with the court and a copy served on the plaintiff.

FIGURE 7-6 *Motion to strike.*

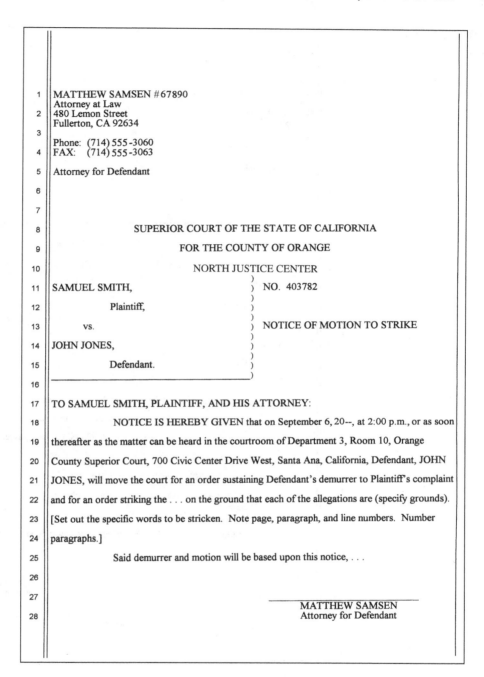

```
1   MATTHEW SAMSEN #67890
    Attorney at Law
2   480 Lemon Street
    Fullerton, CA 92634
3
    Phone:  (714) 555-3060
4   FAX:    (714) 555-3063

5   Attorney for Defendant

6

7

8                SUPERIOR COURT OF THE STATE OF CALIFORNIA

9                      FOR THE COUNTY OF ORANGE

10                        NORTH JUSTICE CENTER
                                             )
11  SAMUEL SMITH,                            )   NO.  403782
                                             )
12           Plaintiff,                      )
                                             )
13      vs.                                  )   NOTICE OF MOTION TO STRIKE
                                             )
14  JOHN JONES,                              )
                                             )
15           Defendant.                      )
                                             )
16

17  TO SAMUEL SMITH, PLAINTIFF, AND HIS ATTORNEY:

18           NOTICE IS HEREBY GIVEN that on September 6, 20--, at 2:00 p.m., or as soon

19  thereafter as the matter can be heard in the courtroom of Department 3, Room 10, Orange

20  County Superior Court, 700 Civic Center Drive West, Santa Ana, California, Defendant, JOHN

21  JONES, will move the court for an order sustaining Defendant's demurrer to Plaintiff's complaint

22  and for an order striking the . . . on the ground that each of the allegations are (specify grounds).

23  [Set out the specific words to be stricken.  Note page, paragraph, and line numbers.  Number

24  paragraphs.]

25           Said demurrer and motion will be based upon this notice, . . .

26

27                                            _____
                                                      MATTHEW SAMSEN
28                                                    Attorney for Defendant
```

The Cross-Complaint When a defendant has a claim against a plaintiff arising out of a related transaction to the cause of action in the complaint or arising out of a cause of action that is totally unrelated, the defendant has a right to assert the action in a cross-complaint (see Figure 7-8). If the defendant does not set forth the claim in a related action at this time, the defendant may not do so at a later date without the court's permission. If the action is *unrelated* to the alleged cause of action stated in the complaint, the defendant may file a separate action at a later date.

A cross-complaint is a pleading filed by the defendant in a pending action in which he or she alleges a related cause of action or claim against the plaintiff. When this happens, disputes arising out of the same transaction can be determined by the one case.

FIGURE 7-7 *Answer to complaint.*

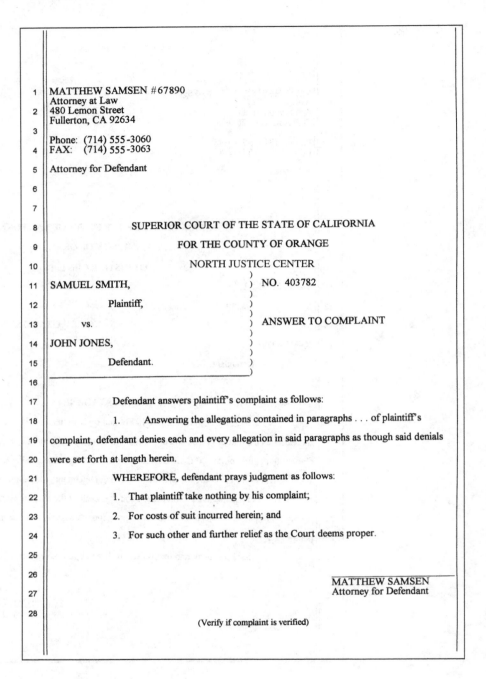

```
1   MATTHEW SAMSEN #67890
    Attorney at Law
2   480 Lemon Street
    Fullerton, CA 92634
3
    Phone:  (714) 555-3060
4   FAX:    (714) 555-3063

5   Attorney for Defendant

6

7

8                    SUPERIOR COURT OF THE STATE OF CALIFORNIA

9                        FOR THE COUNTY OF ORANGE

10                          NORTH JUSTICE CENTER
                                              )
11  SAMUEL SMITH,                             )    NO.  403782
                                              )
12            Plaintiff,                       )
                                              )
13       vs.                                  )    ANSWER TO COMPLAINT
                                              )
14  JOHN JONES,                               )
                                              )
15            Defendant.                       )
    ──────────────────────────────────────────)
16

17            Defendant answers plaintiff's complaint as follows:

18            1.    Answering the allegations contained in paragraphs . . . of plaintiff's

19  complaint, defendant denies each and every allegation in said paragraphs as though said denials

20  were set forth at length herein.

21            WHEREFORE, defendant prays judgment as follows:

22       1.  That plaintiff take nothing by his complaint;

23       2.  For costs of suit incurred herein; and

24       3.  For such other and further relief as the Court deems proper.

25

26                                              ─────────────────────────
                                                MATTHEW SAMSEN
27                                              Attorney for Defendant

28
                        (Verify if complaint is verified)
```

The cross-complaint is a separate pleading in which the defendant becomes the *cross-complainant* and the plaintiff becomes the *cross-defendant*. The cross-complaint may be filed at a later date by permission of the court or at the same time or before the answer is filed.

The procedure for preparing a cross-complaint is as follows:

1. The attorney dictates the answer, or answer and cross-complaint. The support staff types the original and makes the necessary number of copies. The attorney signs the papers, and if a verification is necessary, the defendant signs the verification.
2. The support staff files the pleadings with the court and has a copy served on the plaintiff. A filing fee is paid, if necessary.

FIGURE 7-8
Cross-complaint.

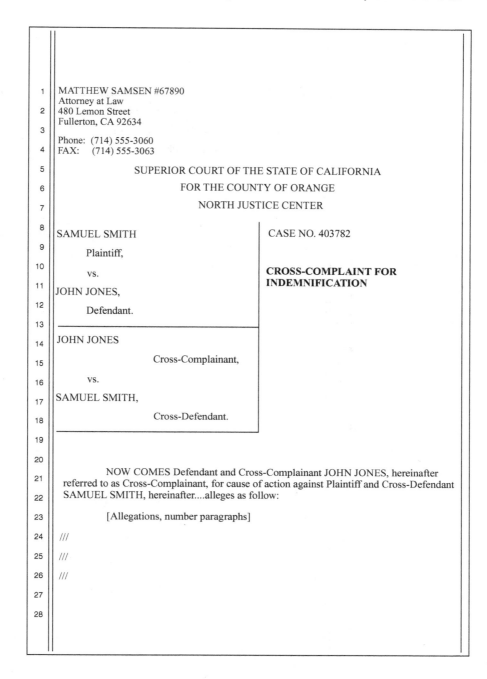

FIGURE 7-8
Continued

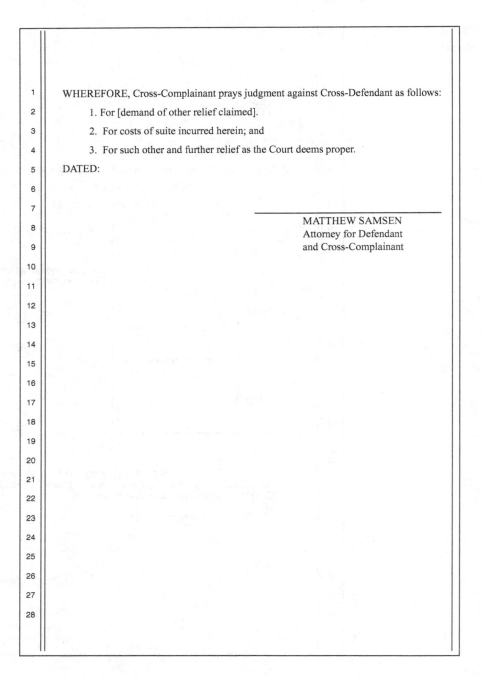

1	WHEREFORE, Cross-Complainant prays judgment against Cross-Defendant as follows:
2	1. For [demand of other relief claimed].
3	2. For costs of suite incurred herein; and
4	3. For such other and further relief as the Court deems proper.
5	DATED:

MATTHEW SAMSEN
Attorney for Defendant
and Cross-Complainant

SUMMARY

A lawsuit or litigation is commenced when one party sues another in a court of law. The lawsuit may be either criminal or civil. Criminal cases occur when someone has broken the law. Civil cases occur when someone has been injured or wronged and the parties cannot agree on a solution. The plaintiff is the party that sues, and the defendant is the party being sued.

The summons and complaint are the first documents prepared to begin a legal action. The complaint initiates the lawsuit and alleges what the plaintiff intends to prove, and the summons notifies the defendant that an action has been initiated.

Failure to respond to a summons and complaint can result in a judgment by default against the defendant. A summons can be served personally, by registered or certified mail with a return receipt, or by publication.

The answer is the defendant's formal reply to the complaint. The cross-complaint is a pleading filed by the defendant in a pending action in which the defendant alleges a related cause of action or claim against the plaintiff.

It is very important to serve legal papers carefully and within the time limitations to avoid a default judgment for the opposing party.

VOCABULARY

allegation   A fact that one side expects to prove.

answer   The pleading made in response to a complaint.

appeal   To bring a case from a lower court to a higher court for review.

cause of action   A legal claim that, if proved to the satisfaction of the court, is sufficient to justify the entry of judgment in favor of the plaintiff.

complaint   The initial pleading filed by the plaintiff in a civil matter.

contingency fee   A fee that is collected if an attorney successfully represents a client. The attorney is entitled to a percentage of the amount of money awarded the client.

cross-complaint   A pleading filed by the defendant asserting causes of action against the plaintiff as part of the same lawsuit.

court of equity   The name for a system of courts that originated in England to take care of problems where existing legal laws did not cover some situations in which a person's rights were violated by another person. In equity courts, relief is not available to the petitioner through monetary damages or criminal punishment.

deem   As if; treated as true unless proved otherwise.

default   The neglect or failure of a party to take a required step in a legal action. To take a default means to request the court for a judgment against the adverse party.

defendant   The party against whom a claim or charge is instituted; the party being sued.

demurrer   A formal objection attacking the legal sufficiency of the opponent's complaint.

docket number   The number assigned to the case by the court clerk.

execution of judgment   The process to carry into effect the decree of judgment of the court.

file   To deposit the original pleading or document with the appropriate office of the court clerk.

garnishment   A proceeding requiring one who holds money, usually wages or property belonging to another, not to deliver or dispose of it until the result of the suit is ascertained.

issue   To make a document an official document; to have the document stamped, dated, and signed by the clerk or one of the deputy clerks.

lawsuit   A legal proceeding.

lien   A claim against the loser's property in a judgment for specific amounts of money.

litigant   A party to a legal action or lawsuit.

litigation   A contest in court for the purpose of enforcing a right; a suit of law.

motion   A request to the court for an order or ruling by the judge.

notice of *lis pendens*   *Lis pendens* is a Latin term meaning "suit pending"; a notice that litigation or a lawsuit about property is pending.

order   A command issued by a judge that something be done.

pendente lite   A Latin term meaning "pending the suit"; litigation in process.

personal service   The personal delivery of pleadings or process upon a party to an action.

plaintiff   One who brings an action at law; the person suing.

pleadings   Documents filed in a legal action.

prayer or prayer for relief   The closing paragraph of a pleading in which is stated the relief or remedy sought.

process server   An individual who, for a fee, serves legal papers on those named in lawsuits.

proof of service   An affidavit or declaration attesting to the fact of the accomplishment of the service of pleadings or process.

proof of service by mail   An affidavit or declaration establishing the fact of mailing a pleading to the party named therein.

propria persona (pro per)   A Latin term meaning "in his or her own person"; not by representation of an attorney; "in *pro per*."

retainer   An agreement between a client and attorney for continuing legal services throughout the year.

statutory fee   The amount of money an attorney may charge for services based on statutes.

stipulation   An oral or written agreement between opposing counsel in a pending legal action.

substituted service   Service of pleadings or process other than personal.

summons   A writ or process served on a defendant in a court action for the purpose of securing the defendant's appearance in that action.

writ of attachment   A writ issued to a sheriff ordering the seizure of property identified in the case pending court action.

writ of execution   A writ issued by the clerk of the court to a designated enforcement officer authorizing the latter to take possession of and sell the property of the defendant and to apply the proceeds toward the satisfaction of judgment.

STUDENT ASSESSMENT 1

Instructions: Circle T if the statement is true or F if the statement is false.

T F 1. A plaintiff is the party who sues; a defendant is the party being sued.

T F 2. Failure to respond to a summons and complaint can result in a judgment by default against the defendant.

T F 3. Original pleadings are kept on file in the attorney's office.

T F 4. Personal service of a copy of the summons and complaint on the defendant in a civil suit is usually performed by one of the parties to the action who is over the legal age.

T F 5. All copies of the complaint should be conformed to match the original.

T F 6. A stipulation is an answer to a complaint.

T F 7. In civil actions, the defendant receives a copy of the plaintiff's complaint first and is served with the original summons a few days later.

T F 8. Pleadings are typewritten papers in a legal action that reduce the issues to definite terms.

T F 9. A default judgment is granted when the defendant does not respond to the plaintiff's complaint within a specified time.

T F 10. In a case involving a jury trial, the closing statements are given by the plaintiff's attorney, followed by the statements given by the defendant's attorney.

T F 11. In a jury trial, the foreman is selected by the judge.

T F 12. The losing party in a jury trial usually is required to pay court costs, the other party's legal fees, and a monetary judgment.

T F 13. In a civil case, the court clerk is responsible for serving a copy of the complaint and summons on the defendant.

T F 14. A complaint is the first legal document filed in a lawsuit.

T F 15. "Defendant" is spelled correctly.

T F 16. In a court trial, the opening statements are given to the jury by the defendant's attorney.

T F 17. A notice of *lis pendens* is similar to a proof of service.

T F 18. "Fee simple" is a legal term used to identify legal fees and charges.

T F 19. The service of the summons may be made only by a qualified, licensed process server.

T F 20. After the service of a summons, a defendant has a specified number of days within which to answer the complaint.

STUDENT ASSESSMENT 2

Instructions: Select the letter that indicates the most correct answer.

1. Extra copies of legal papers are provided to clients as
   A. a legal requirement
   B. the decision of the legal secretary
   C. a good public relations technique
   D. necessary

2. Original pleadings always must be
   A. kept in the attorney's office
   B. mailed to the adverse party
   C. sent directly to the judge
   D. filed with the court clerk

3. A demurrer is
   A. a pleading answering plaintiff's complaint
   B. a pleading stating that the facts in the complaint are insufficient to require an answer
   C. a pleading notifying the court that the defendant is represented by counsel
   D. a pleading between the two attorneys in the case

(continued)

4. The first document filed in a lawsuit is called
    A. an answer
    B. a complaint
    C. a judgment
    D. an order

5. A motion is a request for
    A. an affidavit
    B. an order
    C. a petition
    D. a summary

6. Which document would *not* be filed by a defendant?
    A. an answer
    B. a complaint
    C. a motion
    D. an order

7. If a contingency fee is established, the amount of money an attorney earns is based on which of the following factors?
    A. amount of money collected
    B. number of attorneys working on the case
    C. number of hours worked
    D. none of these

8. A written or oral application made to a court or judge for a ruling or an order is a
    A. reply
    B. motion
    C. counterclaim
    D. jurat

9. When the names of one or more defendants in a suit are not known, they are identified in the case title by a
    A. Doe clause
    B. venue
    C. service
    D. none of these

10. The delivery of a summons to the person named therein is called
    A. filed
    B. service
    C. venue
    D. jurisdiction

STUDENT ASSESSMENT 3

Instructions: For each section, match the most correct letter to the number.

Section I	*Section I*
_____ 1. demurrer	A. defendant's claim against plaintiff
_____ 2. stipulation	B. proceeding eliminating objectionable allegations of complaint
_____ 3. motion to strike	C. agreement between attorneys, binding on both parties
_____ 4. answer	D. issue of law as to legal sufficiency of complaint
_____ 5. cross-complaint	E. formal reply to plaintiff's complaint
Section II	*Section II*
_____ 1. complaint	A. designation of the source of a statement of law or statute
_____ 2. citation	B. order requiring property to be sold
_____ 3. writ of execution	C. the first document filed by plaintiff in legal proceeding
_____ 4. demur	D. file a pleading attacking the legal sufficiency of the complaint
_____ 5. *propria persona*	E. to represent oneself

STUDENT ASSIGNMENTS

Note: See the instructions for preparing these documents in Chapter 6, or check with your instructor.

PRACTICE SET 1: PERSONAL INJURY

The following practice set in a personal injury action is designed to assist in developing the following skills:

1. An *understanding of legal terminology*: correct usage and spelling.

2. An understanding of legal documents and how they are used.

3. The *ability to produce these legal documents* and the necessary *correspondence* used in a law office.

After completing the legal papers and correspondence in this practice set, you should be prepared to handle a similar case of this nature in a law office.

Directions

Assume that you have just obtained a position with *Mr. Robert Morgan,* attorney at law, who has his office at 320 Main Street, Fullerton, CA 92634. Mr. Morgan is presently working on a personal injury action and is representing *Mr. Albert Aggrieved. Mr. Charlie Careless* is the defendant in the action, and he is represented by Matthew Mediator, attorney at law.

The accident occurred at 10:15 P.M. on September 29, 20—, at Dale Street near the Orangewood Avenue intersection in Garden Grove, California.

You are required to prepare some of the legal documents and correspondence in this case, as well as keep a file on the proceedings.

Case Particulars

Plaintiff:	Albert Aggrieved, 200 Bell Avenue, Cypress, CA 92630
Attorney:	Robert Morgan, #12345, Attorney at Law
	320 Main Street
	Fullerton, CA 92634
	Telephone (714) 555-2440
	FAX (714) 555-2748
Witness:	Mary Martin, 10892 Allen Drive, Garden Grove, CA 92626
Defendant:	Charlie Careless, 404 Pico Place, Huntington Beach, CA 92646
Attorney:	Matthew Mediator #12354, Attorney at Law
	1212 Valley View Street
	Garden Grove, CA 92645
	Telephone (714) 555-1111
	FAX (714) 555-1222
Accident:	Date: September 29, 20—
Time:	10:15 P.M.
Place:	Dale Street near Orangewood Avenue intersection in Garden Grove, California

PREPARING THE CASE FILE

Project 1: Contingency Fee Contract

Instructions: Using your word processor, open file **ch07_FEE** (Contingency Fee Contract) on your data disk in the back pocket of your book and fill in the required information using today's date. Run a spell check, save your document as **ch7_FEE,** and print one copy for your instructor.

Project 2: Authorization

Instructions: Open file **ch07_AUT** (Authorization). Follow the same instructions as indicated in Project 1. Save your document as **ch7_AUT,** and print one copy for your instructor.

(continued)

Project 3: Create a Complaint

Note: When retrieving stored template documents from the student diskette, be sure to check in the All Files selection for any files stored as a template.

Instructions: Retrieve your template file **ch06_TMP** and prepare the complaint as illustrated in Sample 7-1. Save your document as **ch7_COM**, and print one copy for your instructor.

Project 4: PI Standard Letter Request

Instructions: Using your word processor, retrieve **ch07_LET** (PI Standard Letter Request file), change the date to today's date and type in the address, salutation, and the second paragraph requesting information on the case. (Be sure to indicate the enclosure notation when appropriate.)

Letters should be sent to the following addresses with the appropriate second and succeeding paragraphs as follows:

1. Ingal's Investigators
    54 Tremont Avenue
    Garden Grove, CA 92640
    Gentlemen:
    (succeeding paragraphs)
    It is our understanding that some adult education students witnessed this accident. We understand that the defendant was driving at night without lights. We would like to obtain any witnesses who can verify this.
    Please forward your report at your earliest convenience together with your statement.
    Save as **ch7_LET1**, and print one copy for your instructor.

2. Garden Grove Police Department
    11391 Acacia Parkway
    Garden Grove, CA 92640
    Gentlemen:
    (succeeding paragraphs)
    Please furnish us with a copy of the police report regarding this accident. Our check is enclosed.
    Thank you for your cooperation.
    Save as **ch7_LET2**, and print one copy for your instructor.

3. Garden Grove Memorial Hospital
    555 Main Street
    Garden Grove, CA 92640
    Gentlemen:
    (succeeding paragraphs)
    Please furnish us with a copy of your hospital record, together with a statement of service rendered as a result of the accident. Mr. Aggrieved's authorization is enclosed.
    Save as **ch7_LET3**, and print one copy for your instructor.

4. Ms. Minerva Mender
    Physical Therapist
    One Valley Place
    Garden Grove, CA 92641
    Dear Ms. Mender:
    (succeeding paragraphs)
    We would appreciate receiving a statement of services rendered to date. Mr. Aggrieved's authorization is enclosed.
    Save as **ch7_LET4**, and print one copy for your instructor.

Sample 7-1

1	ROBERT MORGAN #12345 Attorney at Law
2	320 Main Street Fullerton, CA 92634
3	
	Phone: (714) 555-2440
4	Fax: (714) 555-2748
5	Attorney for Plaintiff

SUPERIOR COURT OF THE STATE OF CALIFORNIA

FOR THE COUNTY OF ORANGE

NORTH JUSTICE CENTER

ALBERT AGGRIEVED,	NO. 444662
Plaintiff,	
vs.	COMPLAINT FOR PERSONAL INJURIES AND PROPERTY DAMAGE
CHARLIE CARELESS, DOES 1 through 6, inclusive,	
Defendants.	

Plaintiff alleges:

1. The true names and capacities, whether individual, corporate, associate, or otherwise, of Defendants, DOES 1 through 6, are unknown to Plaintiff, who, therefore, sues said Defendants by such fictitious names. Plaintiff is informed and believes, and therefore alleges, that each of the Defendants designated herein as a DOE is negligently responsible in some manner for the events and happenings herein referred to, and negligently caused injury and damages proximately thereby to Plaintiff as herein alleged, and leave of court will be asked to amend this Complaint to show their true names and capacities when the same have been ascertained.

2. At all times herein mentioned, Defendants, and each of them, were the residents of the County of Orange, State of California.

Sample 7-1

1   3.   Plaintiff has no information as to the nature of the entities sued and served herein as

2   DOES 1 through 6, or either of them, whether corporations, partnerships, sole proprietorships, or

3   unincorporated associations; the same is well known to said named Defendants, however.

4   Plaintiff will pray for leave to amend this Complaint when the nature of said entities has been

5   ascertained.

6   4.   At all times herein mentioned, Defendants CHARLIE CARELESS and DOES 1

7   through 3 were the owners of a certain motor vehicle referred to in this Complaint, and generally

8   described as a 1994 Chevrolet.

9   5.   At all times herein mentioned, Defendants CHARLIE CARELESS and DOES 4

10   through 6 were operating the aforementioned motor vehicle at or near the intersection of Dale

11   Street and Orangewood Avenue, the City of Garden Grove, County of Orange, State of

12   California.

13   6.   On or about September 29, 20--, this Plaintiff was operating his 20-- Chevrolet.

14   License No. 123 ABC, at or near the intersection of Dale Street and Orangewood Avenue,

15   Garden Grove, County of Orange, State of California.

16   7.   At all times mentioned herein, Dale Street and Orangewood Avenue were public

17   streets and highways in the City of Garden Grove, County of Orange, State of California.

18   8.   At all times mentioned herein, Defendants, and each of them, were the agents and

19   employees of each of the remaining Defendants, and were acting within the course and scope of

20   said agency and employment.

21   9.   At said time and place, Defendants, and each of them, so negligently entrusted,

22   managed, maintained, drove, and operated their motor vehicle as to proximately cause it to

23   collide with Plaintiff's automobile and so as proximately thereby cause the hereinafter described

24   injuries and damages to Plaintiff.

25   10. As a proximate result of the negligence of the Defendants, and each of them, Plaintiff

26   was hurt and injured in his health, strength, and activities, sustaining injuries to his body, and

27   shock and injuries to his nervous system and person, all of which said injuries have caused, and

28   continue to cause, Plaintiff great mental, physical, and nervous pain and suffering. Plaintiff is

Sample 7-1

1 informed and believes, and on that basis alleges, that these injuries will result in some permanent
2 disability to Plaintiff and to his general damage in an amount as yet unknown.

3   11. As a further proximate result of the negligence of the Defendants, and each of them,
4 Plaintiff was required to, and did, employ physicians and surgeons to examine, treat, and care for
5 him, and incurred medical and incidental expenses. The exact amount of such expense is
6 unknown to Plaintiff, and Plaintiff will ask leave of court to amend this Complaint to show the
7 true amount of such expense when the same has been ascertained.

8   12. As a further proximate result of the negligence of the Defendants, and each of them,
9 Plaintiff suffered property damage to his automobile and loss of use of said automobile in an
10 unknown amount. Plaintiff will ask leave of court to amend this Complaint to show the true
11 amount of such expense when the same has been ascertained.

12   13. As a further proximate result of the negligence of the Defendants, and each of them,
13 Plaintiff was, and will be, prevented from attending to his usual occupation, and thereby lost
14 earnings, and in the future will lose earnings. The amount of these lost earnings is not yet fully
15 known to Plaintiff, and Plaintiff will amend this Complaint to state these amounts when the same
16 have been ascertained.

17   WHEREFORE, Plaintiff prays for judgment against the Defendants, and each of them, as
18 follows:

19   1. For general damages in an unknown amount;

20   2. For medical and incidental expenses according to proof;

21   3. For loss of earnings according to proof;

22   4. For property damage and loss of use according to proof;

23   5. For costs of suit herein; and

24   6. For such other and further relief as the Court may deem just and proper.

25 DATED: October 4, 20--

26   S/ROBERT MORGAN

27   ROBERT MORGAN
                   Attorney for Plaintiff

28

Chapter 6

THE LAWSUIT: LITIGATION AND DISCOVERY PROCEDURES

OBJECTIVES

Upon completion of this chapter, you should be able to:

1. Discuss why some cases never go to trial
2. Prepare an answer to a complaint
3. List four kinds of discovery devices
4. Describe the difference between interrogatories and a deposition
5. Prepare a set of interrogatories
6. Prepare answers to interrogatories
7. Prepare a notice to take deposition
8. Explain the use of a subpena and when it is used in a court proceeding
9. Discuss the different kinds of subpenas
10. Describe the difference between a judge's verdict and a jury trial
11. Explain the jury selection process
12. Discuss the procedures at the conclusion of a trial
13. Explain appellate procedures
14. Discuss the purpose of a brief
15. Prepare a verdict court form

Many procedures are involved in the process of the lawsuit after the initial complaint has been filed. Some cases, however, may never go to trial because the defendant does not respond to the initial complaint filed by the plaintiff. The defendant thus places himself or herself in the position of permitting the plaintiff to obtain a *judgment* by default. The latter may be granted the amount asked for in the complaint without the necessity of going to trial.

THE DEFAULT

A **default** occurs when the defendant does not make an appearance or take the correct legal steps to respond to a properly served complaint and summons. An **appearance** means the defendant has filed a legal pleading or taken some appropriate legal action in response to a complaint or summons.

When the plaintiff files a request to enter default, he or she thus prevents the defendant from making a valid late appearance. When the default entry has been signed by the court, the litigation is terminated. It is important that the support staff watch the time limitations and advise the attorney when the default proceedings should be initiated.

DISCONTINUANCE AND DISMISSAL

A civil action can be stopped or discontinued at any time. If the parties agree out of court, it is **voluntary abatement**, which means that both parties agree to it. There are instances, however, where the court may require that the case be discontinued. This may be because the plaintiff does not meet certain legal requirements. This type of discontinuance is called **involuntary dismissal**.

An action may be dismissed by the plaintiff at any time, provided no cross-complaint has been filed. A dismissal may be *with prejudice*, which means that the action has been terminated, which prevents the plaintiff from filing at a later date on the same matter. A dismissal *without prejudice* means that at some later date the plaintiff may bring another legal action based on the same facts.

Summary Judgment   Occasionally it is advantageous for a party to a legal action to use a legal procedure that will obtain a judgment on the case without the necessity of a trial. This procedure is used by either party to claim that there is no genuine issue of material fact, and the court can rule as a matter of law. The **motion for summary judgment** must be supported by a declaration together with points and authorities.

The procedure for preparing a motion for summary judgment is as follows:

1. The attorney determines the grounds on which the motion will be made and dictates the motion, points and authorities, and declaration.
2. The support staff types the papers and makes adequate copies.
3. The attorney signs the papers, and the declarant signs the declaration.
4. The support staff prepares a declaration of service and serves the papers on the adverse party by mail.
5. The support staff files the original papers with the proof of service with the court.
6. After hearing on the motion (if the motion is granted), the support staff types the *order for entry of summary judgment* and files it with the appropriate court.

See Figure 8-1 for an example of a motion for summary judgment.

DISCOVERY PROCEEDINGS

The process of uncovering evidence and learning as much as possible about the issues of a case is called **discovery**. After the pleadings have been filed and before the trial of the case, each litigant has the right to demand and obtain information pertaining to the claims, defenses, and evidence of the adverse party. The **adverse party** is the party on the opposing side of an action. **Witnesses** are people who have information pertinent to the case, but who are neither plaintiffs nor defendants. The oral testimony, records, and documents are considered **evidence**. Federal and state laws govern the manner in which information and evidence can be developed to support the attorney's case. Since the enactment of the Federal Rules of Civil Procedure in 1938, discovery proceedings are no longer treated as a part of the pleadings. Instead, they constitute a separate phase of litigation, and special rules govern the way that discovery is conducted. Most of the states follow the procedure governed by this enactment.

FIGURE 8-1   *Motion for summary judgment.*

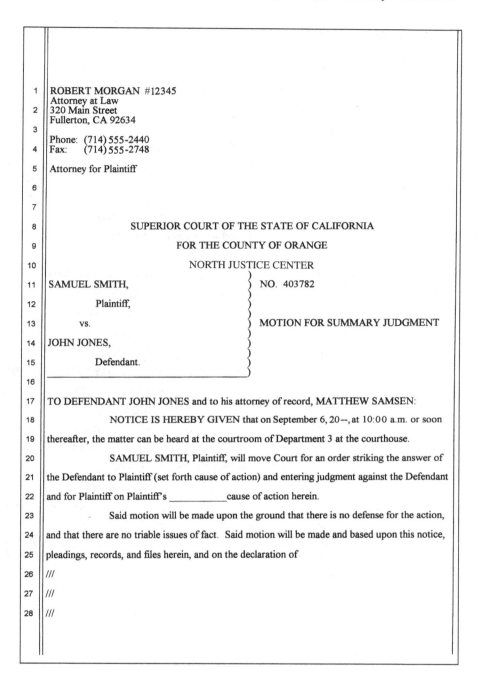

```
 1  ROBERT MORGAN  #12345
    Attorney at Law
 2  320 Main Street
    Fullerton, CA 92634
 3
    Phone:  (714) 555-2440
 4  Fax:    (714) 555-2748

 5  Attorney for Plaintiff

 6

 7

 8              SUPERIOR COURT OF THE STATE OF CALIFORNIA

 9                    FOR THE COUNTY OF ORANGE

10                      NORTH JUSTICE CENTER
                                          )
11  SAMUEL SMITH,                         )   NO.  403782
                                          )
12          Plaintiff,                    )
                                          )
13          vs.                           )   MOTION FOR SUMMARY JUDGMENT
                                          )
14  JOHN JONES,                           )
                                          )
15          Defendant.                    )
                                          )
16

17  TO DEFENDANT JOHN JONES and to his attorney of record, MATTHEW SAMSEN:

18          NOTICE IS HEREBY GIVEN that on September 6, 20--, at 10:00 a.m. or soon

19  thereafter, the matter can be heard at the courtroom of Department 3 at the courthouse.

20          SAMUEL SMITH, Plaintiff, will move Court for an order striking the answer of

21  the Defendant to Plaintiff (set forth cause of action) and entering judgment against the Defendant

22  and for Plaintiff on Plaintiff's _____ cause of action herein.

23          Said motion will be made upon the ground that there is no defense for the action,

24  and that there are no triable issues of fact.  Said motion will be made and based upon this notice,

25  pleadings, records, and files herein, and on the declaration of

26  ///

27  ///

28  ///
```

DISCOVERY DEVICES

There are many ways in which an attorney can gather information relevant to the case. The information or discovery may be obtained by:

1. Written interrogatories
2. Depositions or oral interrogatories
3. Bills of particulars
4. Other devices

FIGURE 8-1   *Continued*

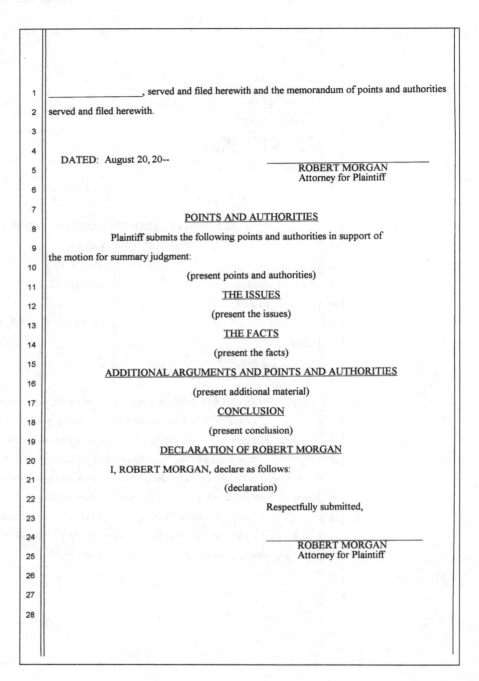

1 _____, served and filed herewith and the memorandum of points and authorities

2 served and filed herewith.

3

4

5 DATED: August 20, 20--   _____
                                                  ROBERT MORGAN
6   Attorney for Plaintiff

7   POINTS AND AUTHORITIES

8   Plaintiff submits the following points and authorities in support of

9 the motion for summary judgment:

10   (present points and authorities)

11   THE ISSUES

12   (present the issues)

13   THE FACTS

14   (present the facts)

15   ADDITIONAL ARGUMENTS AND POINTS AND AUTHORITIES

16   (present additional material)

17   CONCLUSION

18   (present conclusion)

19   DECLARATION OF ROBERT MORGAN

20   I, ROBERT MORGAN, declare as follows:

21   (declaration)

22   Respectfully submitted,

23

24   _____
                                                  ROBERT MORGAN
25   Attorney for Plaintiff

26

27

28

Written Interrogatories   Written interrogatories are a series of questions directed to an adverse party with a demand that they be answered within a specified date from the date of service (see Figure 8-2). The attorney dictates the questions. The adverse parties are required to respond by means of written answers within thirty days from the effective date of service. It is important for the legal staff to meet time deadlines.

Depositions or Oral Interrogatories   A deposition or oral interrogatories, is testimony taken under oath as oral questions requiring answers. The procedure to obtain such information is known as taking a deposition or oral interrogatories. The

FIGURE 8- 2
Interrogatories.

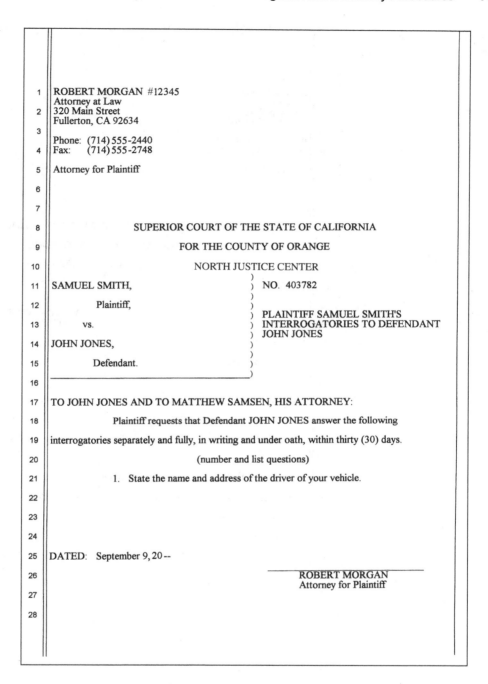

procedure for taking a deposition is spelled out by law (see Figure 8-3). The questions are asked by the attorney requesting the deposition. The questions and answers are taken down by a reporter, transcribed, and fastened into a booklet. The party questioned must read the transcript, make corrections, and sign it. After the corrections are made, however, the party questioned may be cross-examined at the time of the trial regarding the corrections. The original deposition transcript is lodged with the clerk at the time of trial. The party taking the deposition is charged the cost of the original and receives a copy of the deposition. The adverse party may purchase a copy of the deposition.

Bill of Particulars   When litigation is commenced, it is not necessary to set forth all the items of the litigation, but only a statement in general terms. However,

FIGURE 8-3 *Notice of intention to take deposition.*

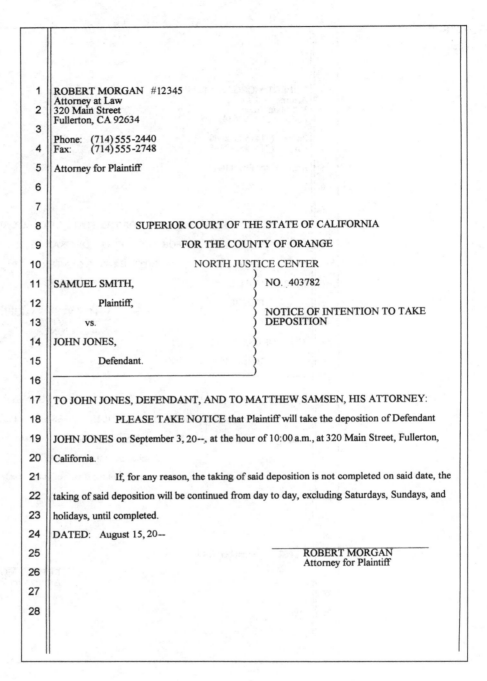

1   ROBERT MORGAN   #12345
     Attorney at Law
2   320 Main Street
     Fullerton, CA 92634
3
     Phone: (714) 555-2440
4   Fax: (714) 555-2748

5   Attorney for Plaintiff

6

7

8   SUPERIOR COURT OF THE STATE OF CALIFORNIA

9   FOR THE COUNTY OF ORANGE

10   NORTH JUSTICE CENTER
)
11   SAMUEL SMITH,   )   NO. 403782
)
12   Plaintiff,   )
)   NOTICE OF INTENTION TO TAKE
13   vs.   )   DEPOSITION
)
14   JOHN JONES,   )
)
15   Defendant.   )
)
16   _____

17   TO JOHN JONES, DEFENDANT, AND TO MATTHEW SAMSEN, HIS ATTORNEY:

18   PLEASE TAKE NOTICE that Plaintiff will take the deposition of Defendant

19   JOHN JONES on September 3, 20--, at the hour of 10:00 a.m., at 320 Main Street, Fullerton,

20   California.

21   If, for any reason, the taking of said deposition is not completed on said date, the

22   taking of said deposition will be continued from day to day, excluding Saturdays, Sundays, and

23   holidays, until completed.

24   DATED: August 15, 20--

25   _____
                                                ROBERT MORGAN
26   Attorney for Plaintiff

27

28

as a protection against any surprise that may result from this general pleading, the defendant and his or her counsel have the right to demand a copy of the account. This demand is known as a demand for a **bill of particulars** (see Figure 8-4). This pleading demands a detailed account of the plaintiff's claim, which was not fully itemized or alleged in the complaint. The demand for a bill of particulars not only furnishes full information to the defendant of the individual items, but it also gives the defendant actual notice of all the plaintiff's claims so the defendant can prepare for the trial.

Other Devices   If the attorney wants additional evidence regarding the case, the attorney may want to petition the court for the right to inspect evidence or other documents. The attorney also may petition the court for the right to order a physical or mental examination of the involved party. These types of proceedings probably will require motions, notices of hearing and motions, and orders.

FIGURE 8-4   *Bill of particulars.*

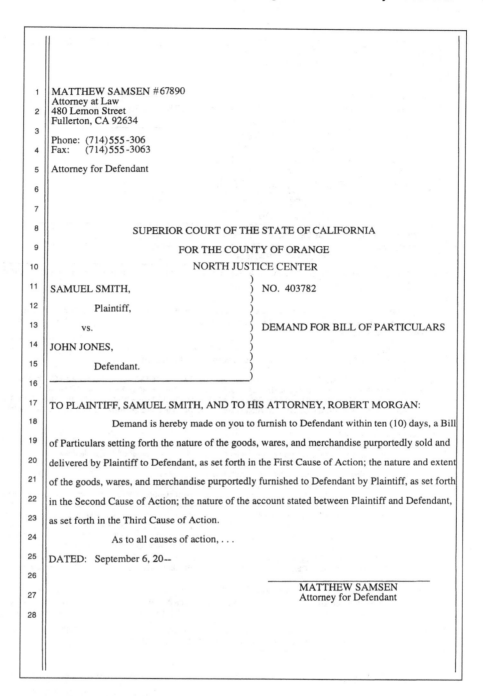

1   MATTHEW SAMSEN #67890
    Attorney at Law
2   480 Lemon Street
    Fullerton, CA 92634
3
    Phone: (714) 555 -306
4   Fax: (714) 555 -3063
5   Attorney for Defendant
6
7
8   SUPERIOR COURT OF THE STATE OF CALIFORNIA
9   FOR THE COUNTY OF ORANGE
10   NORTH JUSTICE CENTER
)
11 SAMUEL SMITH,   )   NO. 403782
)
12   Plaintiff,   )
)
13   vs.   )   DEMAND FOR BILL OF PARTICULARS
)
14 JOHN JONES,   )
)
15   Defendant.   )
)
16
17 TO PLAINTIFF, SAMUEL SMITH, AND TO HIS ATTORNEY, ROBERT MORGAN:
18   Demand is hereby made on you to furnish to Defendant within ten (10) days, a Bill
19 of Particulars setting forth the nature of the goods, wares, and merchandise purportedly sold and
20 delivered by Plaintiff to Defendant, as set forth in the First Cause of Action; the nature and extent
21 of the goods, wares, and merchandise purportedly furnished to Defendant by Plaintiff, as set forth
22 in the Second Cause of Action; the nature of the account stated between Plaintiff and Defendant,
23 as set forth in the Third Cause of Action.
24   As to all causes of action, . . .
25 DATED: September 6, 20--
26
27   _____
                                            MATTHEW SAMSEN
                                            Attorney for Defendant
28

NOTIFYING WITNESSES AND ADVERSE PARTIES

When depositions need to be taken from witnesses or adverse parties, these people must be notified as to the time, date, and place for the appearance. It is also essential to notify the attorney of record and arrange for a reporter to take and transcribe the depositions. Documents served on witnesses requiring that they appear and give testimony are called *subpenas*.

Subpena

A **subpena** (subpoena) is a writ, signed and dated by an officer of the court, requiring a person to appear in person at a trial or deposition as a witness and to testify on the

982(a)(15.1)

ATTORNEY OR PARTY WITHOUT ATTORNEY *(Name, state bar number, and address):*	FOR COURT USE ONLY
ROBERT MORGAN #12345 Attorney at Law 320 Main Street Fullerton, CA 92634 TELEPHONE NO: (714) 555-2440 FAX NO: (714) 555-2748 ATTORNEY FOR *(Name):* MARILYN MENDEZ	

NAME OF COURT: SUPERIOR COURT, STATE OF CALIFORNIA
STREET ADDRESS: 700 Civic Center Drive West
MAILING ADDRESS: 700 Civic Center Drive West
CITY AND ZIP CODE: Santa Ana, CA 92701
BRANCH NAME: CENTRAL JUSTICE CENTER

PLAINTIFF/PETITIONER: MARILYN MENDEZ
DEFENDANT/RESPONDENT: CHARLES HERNANDEZ

CIVIL SUBPOENA (DUCES TECUM) for Personal Appearance and Production of Documents and Things at Trial or Hearing AND DECLARATION	CASE NUMBER: 58932

THE PEOPLE OF THE STATE OF CALIFORNIA, TO *(name, address, and telephone number of witness, if known):*
The Custodian of Records of Thriftway Foods, Inc.

1. **YOU ARE ORDERED TO APPEAR AS A WITNESS** in this action at the date, time, and place shown in the box below UNLESS your appearance is excused as indicated in box 3b below or you make a special agreement with the person named in item 3 below:

   a. Date: September 5, 20-- Time: 9:00 a.m. ☐ Dept.: 5 ☐ Div.: ☐ Room:
   b. Address: 700 Civic Center Drive West, Santa Ana, California 92701

2. **IF YOU HAVE BEEN SERVED WITH THIS SUBPOENA AS A CUSTODIAN OF CONSUMER OR EMPLOYEE RECORDS UNDER CODE OF CIVIL PROCEDURE SECTION 1985.3 OR 1985.6 AND A MOTION TO QUASH OR AN OBJECTION HAS BEEN SERVED ON YOU, A COURT ORDER OR AGREEMENT OF THE PARTIES, WITNESSES, *AND* CONSUMER OR EMPLOYEE AFFECTED MUST BE OBTAINED BEFORE YOU ARE REQUIRED TO PRODUCE CONSUMER OR EMPLOYEE RECORDS.**

3. YOU ARE *(item a or b must be checked):*
   a. ☐ Ordered to appear in person and to produce the records described in the declaration on page two or the attached declaration or affidavit. The personal attendance of the custodian or other qualified witness and the production of the original records are required by this subpoena. The procedure authorized by Evidence Code sections 1560(b), 1561, and 1562 will not be deemed sufficient compliance with this subpoena.
   b. ☒ Not required to appear in person if you produce (i) the records described in the declaration on page two or the attached declaration or affidavit and (ii) a completed declaration of custodian of records in compliance with Evidence Code sections 1560, 1561, 1562, and 1271. (1) Place a copy of the records in an envelope (or other wrapper). Enclose the original declaration of the custodian with the records. Seal the envelope. (2) Attach a copy of the subpoena to the envelope or write on the envelope the case name and number; your name; and the date, time, and place from item 1 in the box above. (3) Place this first envelope in an outer envelope, seal it, and mail it to the clerk of the court at the address in item 1. (4) Mail a copy of your declaration to the attorney or party listed at the top of this form.

4. **IF YOU HAVE ANY QUESTIONS ABOUT THE TIME OR DATE YOU ARE TO APPEAR, OR IF YOU WANT TO BE CERTAIN THAT YOUR PRESENCE IS REQUIRED, CONTACT THE FOLLOWING PERSON BEFORE THE DATE ON WHICH YOU ARE TO APPEAR:**
   a. Name of subpoenaing party or attorney: Robert Morgan   B. Telephone number: (714) 555-2440

5. **Witness Fees:** You are entitled to witness fees and mileage actually traveled both ways, as provided by law, if you request them at the time of service. You may request them before your scheduled appearance from the person named in item 4.

DISOBEDIENCE OF THIS SUBPOENA MAY BE PUNISHED AS CONTEMPT BY THIS COURT. YOU WILL ALSO BE LIABLE FOR THE SUM OF FIVE HUNDRED DOLLARS AND ALL DAMAGES RESULTING FROM YOUR FAILURE TO OBEY.

Date issued: August 28, 20--
Alan Slater
(TYPE OR PRINT NAME) ▶ (SIGNATURE OF PERSON ISSUING SUBPOENA)
Clerk of the Superior Court
(Declaration in support of subpoena on reverse)   (TITLE)   Page one of three

Form Adopted for Mandatory Use Judicial Council of California 982(a)(15.1) [Rev. January 1, 2000]	CIVIL SUBPOENA (DUCES TECUM) FOR PERSONAL APPEARANCE AND PRODUCTION OF DOCUMENTS AND THINGS AT TRIAL OR HEARING AND DECLARATION	Code of Civil Procedure, §1985 et seq. 2001 © American LegalNet, Inc.

FIGURE 8-5 *Civil subpena.*

part of the party having him or her served. If witnesses fail to appear, they are considered to be in **contempt of court,** and they must pay the party on whose behalf they were to testify the damages suffered by their failure to appear.

Generally, subpenas are printed forms supplied by the clerk of the court (see Figure 8-5). They indicate the terms therein on the party to be served, and if the conditions are not followed, the party so served is in contempt of court. Subpenas must

PLAINTIFF/PETITIONER: MARILYN MENDEZ	CASE NUMBER:
DEFENDANT/RESPONDENT: CHARLES HERNANDEZ	58932

PROOF OF SERVICE OF CIVIL SUBPOENA (DUCES TECUM)
FOR PERSONAL APPEARANCE AND PRODUCTION OF DOCUMENTS
AND THINGS AT TRIAL OR HEARING AND DECLARATION

1. I served this *Civil Subpoena (Duces Tecum) for Personal Appearance and Production of Documents and Things at Trial or Hearing and Declaration* by personally delivering a copy to the person served as follows:

    a. Person served *(name)*: Custodian of Records of Thriftway Foods, Inc.

    b. Address where served: 3980 Harbor Boulevard, Fullerton, CA 92635

    c. Date of Delivery: August 30, 20--

    d. Time of delivery: 9:00 a.m.

    e. Witness fees *(check one)*:
        (1) ☒ were offered or demanded
            and paid. Amount: . . . . . $ ___30.00___
        (2) ☐ were not demanded or paid.

    f. Fee for service: . . . . $ ___30.00___

2. I received this subpoena for service on *(date)*: August 29, 20--

3. Person serving:
    a. ☐ Not a registered California process server.
    b. ☐ California sheriff or marshal.
    c. ☐ Registered California process server.
    d. ☐ Employee or independent contractor of a registered California process server.
    e. ☐ Exempt from registration under Business and Professions Code section 22350(b).
    f. ☐ Registered professional photocopier
    g. ☐ Exempt from registration under Business and Professions Code section 22451.
    h. Name, address, and telephone number and, if applicable, county of registration and number:

I declare under penalty of perjury under the laws of the State of California that the foregoing is true and correct.	**(For California sheriff or marshal use only)** **I certify** that the foregoing is true and correct.
Date:	Date:
▶ _____ (SIGNATURE)	▶ _____ (SIGNATURE)

982(a)(15.1) [Rev. January 1, 2000]t	PROOF OF SERVICE OF CIVIL SUBPOENA (DUCES TECUM) FOR PERSONAL APPEARANCE AND PRODUCTION OF DOCUMENTS AND THINGS AT TRIAL OR HEARING AND DECLARATION	Page three of three

FIGURE 8-5   *Continued*

be served in person, and there is space on the back of the document to indicate when, where, and how service is made.

Persons being summoned as witnesses are entitled to a witness fee and mileage as established by state law. Some jurisdictions require that the witness fee deposit be paid before a subpena can be issued.

A subpena is served in much the same manner as a summons, and the attorney's office is responsible for having it served by a private individual or an officer of the court. There is space on the back of the subpena for the serving party to indicate the date and facts of service. After service, a conformed copy is made for the office.

Subpoena Re Deposition

Some states require that a subpena be issued if a deposition is to be taken of a non-party witness. Such a subpena is different from the original because it indicates the place, other than the courtroom, where the deposition will be taken. If the **deponent** (the person giving sworn testimony out of court) is a party to the action, he or she is served with a *notice of taking deposition*.

Subpoena Duces Tecum

If the attorney wants to introduce certain records or items as evidence to be included in the trial or in a deposition, a **subpoena duces tecum** is prepared. *Duces tecum* is a Latin phrase meaning "bring with you." A *subpoena duces tecum* requires that a certain person appear at a trial or deposition and must bring along specific designated records, books, papers, documents, or other writings and testify regarding these exhibits. Certain information may be considered privileged, such as a psychiatric examination of a patient, but hospital and financial records may be subpenaed. This process can be a very useful device in discovery proceedings. See Figure 8-6 for a *subpoena duces tecum* form.

PRETRIAL PROCEDURES

As noted earlier, all cases do not go to trial; some may be settled out of court. The reasons for this vary: Both parties may agree that the expenses of going to trial or the emotional strain are too much to endure, or the parties may come to an agreement as to the damages involved. However, if it becomes necessary to go to trial, certain procedures must be followed.

PRETRIAL CONFERENCE

When the case has been set for trial, the attorneys of record will meet with the judge in a **pretrial conference** to discuss the issues involved in the lawsuit. These conferences are required in some states and in other states they are optional. Pretrial conferences are helpful because they provide the attorneys of record an opportunity to become familiar with all the allegations and information involved in the case. In some cases, certain aspects of the case may be settled by stipulation, or the facts exchanged may result in a dismissal or settlement of the case. Some judges hold these conferences in their chambers, whereas others hold them in the courtroom.

At the conclusion of the conference, a pretrial order, or stipulation, is prepared and filed with the court, and the lawsuit is ready to go to trial (Figure 8-7).

SETTING THE TRIAL DATE

In a jury trial, it is important that the jury not overlook anything the attorneys consider significant to the case. Each of the parties prepares a set of instructions, and, after exchange, argument, and judicial decision, one combined set is used.

FIGURE 8-6 *Subpoena duces tecum.*

ATTORNEY OR PARTY WITHOUT ATTORNEY *(Name and Address)*	TELEPHONE NO.: (714) 555-2440	FOR COURT USE ONLY

ROBERT MORGAN #12345
Attorney at Law
320 Main Street
Fullerton, CA 92634
BAR NO.: 12345
ATTORNEY FOR *(Name)*: MARILYN MENDEZ

NAME OF COURT SUPERIOR COURT, STATE OF CALIFORNIA
STREET ADDRESS: FOR THE COUNTY OF ORANGE
MAILING ADDRESS: 700 Civic Center Drive West
CITY AND ZIP CODE: Santa Ana, CA 92701-4079
BRANCH NAME: CENTRAL

PLAINTIFF/PETITIONER: MARILYN MENDEZ

DEFENDANT/RESPONDENT: CHARLES HERNANDEZ

DECLARATION APPLICATION FOR SUBPENA DUCES TECUM	CASE NUMBER 58932

The undersigned hereby applies for a subpena duces tecum and declares:

1. Trial of this matter has been set for *(date)*: September 5, 20-- In Dept. No.: 5 of the above-entitled court

2. *(Name)*: The Custodian of Records of Thriftway Foods, Inc.
has in his or her possession or under his or her control the following *(specify exact documents, matters, and things to be produced)*: Any and all payroll records of CHARLES HERNANDEZ showing gross salary, itemized deductions, and net salary, together with any and all records including but not limited to the following: any vested interest in retirement plan, and/or profit sharing plan, insurance, stock option plan, stocks, bonds, vacations, sick leave, bonuses, and advances, for the period January 1, 20-- to date.

3. The above are material to the issues in the case as follows *(set forth facts fully detailing materiality)*: Said documents are the main source of information to be introduced into evidence at the time of the hearing.

4. Good cause exists for the production of the above documents, matters, and things as follows: Said documents are the main source of information to be introduced into evidence at the time of the hearing.

I declare under penalty of perjury under the laws of the State of California that the foregoing is true and correct.

Date: August 28, 20--

ROBERT MORGAN
(TYPE OR PRINT NAME)   ▶   *(SIGNATURE OF DECLARANT)*

DECLARATION
APPLICATION FOR SUBPENA DUCES TECUM
LS-030

The attorney may have a number of instructions to give to the jury, and they are usually dictated to the support staff. These instructions consist of the relevant law that the attorney wants the judge to tell the jury. They also ensure that the judge does not overlook anything the attorney considers significant regarding the case. The instructions must be prepared in a certain legal style, but the particulars of this style may vary from office to office. It is important to check with your office to see which style to use. Each instruction, no matter how short, usually is typed on a separate sheet.

Judgment

When there is no jury trial, the judge will make the ruling in the case on the basis of the arguments and merits of the parties to the action. The decision of the judge is called a **judgment**, or decree. When the case is heard before a jury, the jury will

FIGURE 8-7 *Notice of trial.*

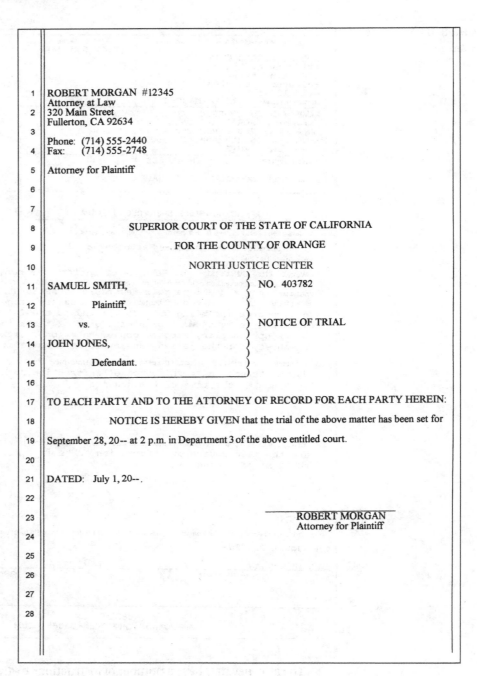

ROBERT MORGAN #12345
Attorney at Law
320 Main Street
Fullerton, CA 92634

Phone: (714) 555-2440
Fax: (714) 555-2748

Attorney for Plaintiff

SUPERIOR COURT OF THE STATE OF CALIFORNIA

FOR THE COUNTY OF ORANGE

NORTH JUSTICE CENTER

SAMUEL SMITH,   NO. 403782

        Plaintiff,

    vs.   NOTICE OF TRIAL

JOHN JONES,

        Defendant.

TO EACH PARTY AND TO THE ATTORNEY OF RECORD FOR EACH PARTY HEREIN:

        NOTICE IS HEREBY GIVEN that the trial of the above matter has been set for

September 28, 20-- at 2 p.m. in Department 3 of the above entitled court.

DATED: July 1, 20--.

_____
ROBERT MORGAN
Attorney for Plaintiff

render a decision in favor of one of the parties on the basis of either the **preponderance of evidence** in civil cases or beyond a **reasonable doubt** in criminal actions. The decision of the jury is called the **verdict**; the judge applies the law to the verdict and pronounces the judgment. In our legal system, the philosophy concerning civil cases and criminal cases differs. In a civil case, a verdict or judgment is based on the preponderance of evidence, whereas in criminal cases the accused must be proven guilty beyond a reasonable doubt.

Nonjury Trial

At the conclusion of a nonjury trial, the successful party files a paper (unless waived) entitled *Findings of Fact and Conclusions of Law*. This document provides the facts on which the judgment was reached and on which the law was applied. This document is signed by the judge and filed with the court.

Jury Selection

If a request is made for a jury trial a jury must be selected. Depending on the court and the matter, the jury usually consists of six to twelve members. Potential jurors are selected at random from a driver's license list or voter registration for the area in which they will serve. Those selected for jury duty are requested to come to court on a particular day. If a person selected for jury duty does not appear and does not have a good reason for not appearing, he or she is said to be in contempt of court.

The process of selecting a jury for a particular case is called *voir dire*. An information sheet on each prospective juror is given to the attorneys on both sides. The judge may ask questions of the jury (called a panel) and dismiss members for prejudice.

The attorneys interview the remaining prospective jurors after some of the panel members have been dismissed. Either attorney may dismiss a person *for cause* if the attorney feels that a person may be biased. If an attorney dismisses a person and does not give a reason, this is called a **peremptory challenge**. A certain number of peremptory challenges are allowed by court rules. Some trials require that more than one panel be called for jury selection.

Jury Trials

After a jury trial, the attorney for the prevailing party or the clerk prepares a legal paper entitled *notice of entry of judgment* (see Figure 8-8) or *judgment on the verdict*. This document includes the verdict of the jury and judgment pronounced by the court. Conformed copies are served on the adverse counsel, and the original is filed with the court.

Judgment After Trial

If the plaintiff is successful, at the conclusion of the trial the plaintiff is called the **judgment creditor**, and the defendant against whom the judgment has been rendered becomes known as the **judgment debtor**. The plaintiff to whom the favorable judgment has been granted is also known as the **prevailing party**.

The judgment is a court order that requires the losing party to provide some **satisfaction** for the judgment. The form of the satisfaction may be the payment of monetary damage and court costs or the performance of a specific act on the part of the judgment debtor. The judgment creditor provides the court with a list of the damages and the itemized costs, and all these costs and expenses must be approved by the court if the judgment debtor objects to them. If the judgment debtor refuses to pay the judgment voluntarily, any of her or his assets not subject to exemption from execution may be seized to satisfy the judgment.

WRIT OF EXECUTION

In order for the judgment creditor to seize or sell the property of a judgment debtor through a sheriff or marshal, a **writ of execution** must be obtained from the court. A writ of execution is a paper issued by the clerk that provides the authority for a sheriff or marshal to take into possession specific property belonging to the judgment debtor and not exempt from execution and to sell such property at a public auction upon proper notice. The proceeds from such a sale are then applied to the

FIGURE 8-8 *Notice of entry of judgment.*

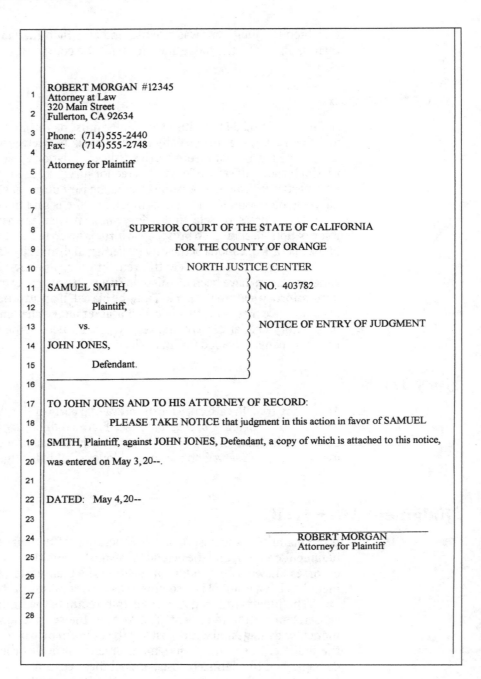

```
 1  ROBERT MORGAN  #12345
    Attorney at Law
    320 Main Street
 2  Fullerton, CA 92634

 3  Phone:  (714) 555-2440
    Fax:    (714) 555-2748
 4
 5  Attorney for Plaintiff

 6

 7

 8              SUPERIOR COURT OF THE STATE OF CALIFORNIA

 9                     FOR THE COUNTY OF ORANGE

10                       NORTH JUSTICE CENTER
                                                )
11  SAMUEL SMITH,                               )   NO.  403782
                                                )
12          Plaintiff,                          )
                                                )
13       vs.                                    )   NOTICE OF ENTRY OF JUDGMENT
                                                )
14  JOHN JONES,                                 )
                                                )
15          Defendant.                          )

16

17  TO JOHN JONES AND TO HIS ATTORNEY OF RECORD:

18          PLEASE TAKE NOTICE that judgment in this action in favor of SAMUEL

19  SMITH, Plaintiff, against JOHN JONES, Defendant, a copy of which is attached to this notice,

20  was entered on May 3, 20--.

21

22  DATED:  May 4, 20--

23

24                                          _____
                                                     ROBERT MORGAN
25                                                  Attorney for Plaintiff

26

27

28
```

court costs and the liquidation of the judgment. If there are excess proceeds, these are returned to the judgment debtor.

Examination of Judgment Debtor

If the judgment creditor does not know of any assets belonging to the judgment debtor, an *examination of the judgment debtor* can be initiated. This is a proceeding in which the judgment debtor is ordered to appear in court and submit to an examination pertaining to his or her assets. If the judgment debtor refuses to answer the questions pertaining to the assets, the judgment debtor is held to be in contempt of court. The court has the power, upon the request of the judgment creditor, to issue a bench warrant for the arrest of the judgment debtor if the judgment debtor does not appear in response to the order.

CONCLUDING PROCEDURES

Satisfaction of Judgment

When the prevailing party has been paid all the money due, the attorney files a *satisfaction of judgment*. An attorney failing to file a satisfaction of judgment on time may be fined. This document is prepared to the benefit of the debtor; it states the amount of money received by the claim and that full satisfaction has been made. The document indicates that the judgment is entered in the official records. It must be signed, filed, and served on the judgment debtor.

Rights of the Losing Party

After a judgment has been handed down by the court, the losing party has several alternatives. The losing party may satisfy the judgment or appeal, while the prevailing party takes the necessary steps to ensure payment, or appeal the case to the higher court. If the latter alternative is chosen, the losing party will not make any payment to the prevailing party. The attorney for the losing party must, however, make the appeal within the time specified by law or the right to appeal will be lost.

Appellate Procedures

There is a good deal of consistency in appellate procedures, and many of the state laws on these procedures are based on the *Federal Rules of Civil Procedure*. Although the forms may vary from state to state, the process and time limits are somewhat uniform. The procedures for conducting an appeal are similar, whether the appellate court is federal, state, intermediate, or a higher court. There are no witnesses and no jury in an appellate court hearing. The decision of the justices is based on the attorney's arguments in support of their briefs and the record of the proceedings from the original trial.

After all the arguments have been heard, the court may **affirm**, **reverse**, or **modify** the opinion of the lower court. If there is legal deficiency, the case may be dismissed.

The appealing party in the prior litigation becomes the **appellant**, and the responding party to the appeal becomes the **respondent**.

The first step in filing the appeal after the judgment is entered is the *notice of appeal*. In California, this notice must be filed within sixty (60) days after the date of mailing the notice of entry of judgment. The caption of the document in the appeal is similar to that of the original documents, and the original notice of appeal is filed with the trial court.

Briefs

A **brief** may be defined as a complete statement of the client's case, including the written argument of the attorney. After presenting the facts and legal issues, the main purpose of the brief is to present the attorney's interpretation of the law, supported by pertinent authorities. It is the option of the attorney to have the brief typed or printed.

There are two types of briefs. Trial court briefs usually are filed on the date that the matter goes to trial. Appellate briefs are filed in the appellate court, the state supreme court, or the federal court. The appellate attorney has a specified number of days to file the brief, or argument, after initially filing the notice of appeal.

The support staff should check to see what the court rules specify in the style and preparation of these briefs.

SUMMARY

Though many procedures are involved in a lawsuit after the initial complaint has been filed, most cases never go to trial. If the defendant does not make an appearance, the case may result in a default judgment. If the parties agree out of court, there may be a voluntary abatement, or the case may be dismissed. Occasionally, the plaintiff may find it advantageous to settle the case without a trial. This often can be accomplished through mediation or arbitration procedures.

When the case goes to trial, however, certain procedures need to be followed. If the defendant wants to have the plaintiff set forth all the items in the litigation, there may be a request for a bill of particulars. When depositions need to be taken from witnesses, they may need to be served with a subpena indicating the time, place, and date for the appearance. If the witness fails to appear, he or she is considered to be in contempt of court.

If the trial goes to court, there are certain procedures for uncovering evidence, and these are called discovery proceedings. Discovery proceedings may include written interrogatories; depositions or oral interrogatories; a demand for a detailed account of the plaintiff's claim, called a bill of particulars; motions; notice of hearings; and orders.

When depositions need to be taken from the adverse parties, they may be served with a subpena. These subpenas may be to summon a witness or request a deposition or a *subpoena duces tecum* that may require a certain person to appear and bring along specific designated records or documents.

If there is no jury trial, the judge will make the ruling. If there is a jury trial, the jury will arrive at a decision in favor of one of the parties on the basis of the preponderance of evidence or beyond a reasonable doubt. After the judgment has been determined, the losing party may satisfy the judgment or appeal the case to a higher court.

VOCABULARY

adverse party   One resisting or opposing a claim, judgment, or appeal.

affirm   Confirm; when a higher court declares that a lower court action is valid and right.

appearance   To come into court as a party to a lawsuit.

appellant   The appealing party in the prior litigation during appellate procedures.

bill of particulars   A detailed statement of the items of plaintiff's demand in an action or of the defendant's counterclaim.

brief   Concise summary of the main points of a law case.

certificate of readiness   Certificate filed with the court clerk indicating that the case is ready for trial.

contempt of court   An act or omission tending to obstruct or interfere with the orderly administration of justice or to impair the dignity of the court or respect for its authority.

default   Occurs when the defendant does not make an appearance or take the correct legal steps to respond to a properly served complaint and summons.

deponent   Person giving sworn testimony out of court.

deposition   The testimony of a witness taken under oath and pursuant to law that, when reduced to writing and authenticated by a notary, may be used at the trial.

discovery   The process of uncovering evidence and learning about the issues involved in a case.

evidence   Proof legally presented at the trial of a case through witnesses, exhibits, and so forth.

extension of time to plead   A stipulation to extend the time for appearance.

interrogatory   A formal list of questions required to be answered either in writing or orally. An interrogatory can be either oral, called a deposition, or written.

involuntary dismissal   The law requires that the action be discontinued when the plaintiff fails to meet certain legal requirements.

judgment   The decision of the judge. Also called a decree.

judgment creditor   The person favored by the judgment.

judgment debtor   The person against whom the judgment is rendered and who must pay the other party.

modify   To alter; to change.

motion for summary judgment   A legal procedure that will obtain a judgment on a case without the necessity of going to trial

overrule   To refuse to grant, to deny or annul.

peremptory   Not requiring any explanation or cause to be shown. For example, a peremptory challenge to a juror means that either side in a trial has the right to excuse a certain number of possible jurors before the trial without giving any reason.

peremptory challenge   The right to eliminate a juror for no stated reason.

preponderance of evidence   Evidence that carries the greater weight; the evidence that has the most validity.

pretrial conference   Informal hearing held by the attorneys before the trial judge prior to the trial of a case, in which any matters that might aid in the disposition of the action are discussed and resolved.

prevailing party   The one in whose favor the decision or verdict is rendered and judgment entered.

respondent   The party responding to an appellate case.

reasonable doubt   It is that state of the case which, after the entire comparison and consideration of evidence, the jurors cannot feel a conviction of the truth of the charge.

reverse   Set aside; for example, when a higher court reverses a decision of a lower court.

satisfaction   Discharge of an obligation by paying what is due or what is awarded by judgment of the court.

subpena   A process to compel a witness to appear and give testimony (also spelled subpoena).

subpoena duces tecum   *Duces tecum* is a Latin term meaning "bring with you"; a subpena ordering the witness to bring along specified materials or documents.

sustain (by the court)   Uphold a motion or a claim and to grant it.

sustained   Granted, established, kept, or maintained.

voluntary abatement   The process by which both parties agree to settle out of court.

witness   Someone who has information pertinent to the case, but who is neither a plaintiff nor defendant.

writ of execution   A paper issued by the court providing authority for a sheriff or marshal to take specific property from the judgment debtor and sell that property at public auction.

STUDENT ASSESSMENT 1

Instructions: Circle T if the statement is true or F if the statement is false.

T   F   1.   Laws are rules that govern society in its daily existence.

T   F   2.   The summons notifies the plaintiff in a civil suit that an action has been brought against him or her.

T   F   3.   If the complaint has been verified, it is not necessary to verify the answer.

T   F   4.   Giving false testimony under oath is considered contributory negligence.

T   F   5.   A dissatisfied party to a civil action has the right to appeal.

T   F   6.   Characteristics of the common law system include the jury system, the adversary system, and the presumption of innocence in criminal cases.

T   F   7.   When a person is served with a subpena and does not appear at the specified time, he or she may be found in contempt of court, a criminal charge.

T   F   8.   The summons is a dictated document, not a form, that must be served on the defendant.

T   F   9.   The legal terms *prayer* and *verification* have the same meaning.

T   F   10.   The successful plaintiff in a court trial is referred to as a judgment debtor.

T   F   11.   Calculating time is of little importance to the legal staff.

T   F   12.   Interrogatories are written questions about a case submitted by one side of the lawsuit to the other.

T   F   13.   Lack of jurisdiction over the subject matter of the case means that the case was filed after the deadline.

T   F   14.   If a witness fails to appear after receiving a subpena, he or she is considered to be in contempt of court and may be fined.

T   F   15.   Interrogatories are always to be answered within twenty (20) days after service of the summons and complaint.

T   F   16.   A deposition is sworn testimony of a party or witness taken by a court reporter.

T   F   17.   Discovery documents can be served by the plaintiff on the defendant or by the defendant on the plaintiff.

T   F   18.   A summons is a document commanding the witness to appear and give testimony at the stated time and place.

T   F   19.   Only the plaintiff's attorney can serve interrogatories.

T   F   20.   The judge usually asks the prevailing attorney to prepare the final judgment.

STUDENT ASSESSMENT 2

Instructions: Circle the letter that indicates the most correct answer.

1. The law office heading usually is printed on legal stationery
   A. because it is required by law
   B. to identify the document
   C. as a public relations tool to identify the firm
   D. to name the state where the document was written

2. All communication between the parties to a lawsuit should be through
   A. the legal secretary
   B. the judge and the litigant
   C. the attorneys
   D. the litigant

3. Conform means to
   A. make similar
   B. collate and assemble
   C. make identical
   D. file with the court

4. The party taking a case up on appeal is the
   A. appellant
   B. respondent
   C. appellee
   D. none of these

5. The right or authority of a court to hear and adjudge cases is referred to as
   A. service
   B. venue
   C. jurisdiction
   D. none of these

6. The pleading that states the defendant's defense against the plaintiff's claims is the
   A. prayer
   B. answer
   C. bill of particulars
   D. complaint

7. The detailed facts on which a complaint is based, which are usually supplied by the plaintiff upon the defendant's request, are contained in the
   A. summons
   B. answer
   C. bill of particulars
   D. prayer

8. The delivery of a summons to the person named therein is called
   A. service
   B. filed
   C. demurrer
   D. venue

9. Papers that are placed with the clerk of a court are said to be
   A. served
   B. filed
   C. answered
   D. prayed for relief

10. To be present in court as a party to a lawsuit is to make a(n)
    A. caption
    B. service
    C. appearance
    D. response

STUDENT ASSESSMENT 3

Instructions: Match the most correct letter to the number.

Section I	*Section I*
_____ 1. appearance	A. proceeding eliminating objectionable allegations of a complaint
_____ 2. motion to strike	B. arguments or contentions to support demurrer
_____ 3. points and authorities	C. filing a pleading on a party's behalf
_____ 4. garnishment	D. designation of a source of a statement of law or statute
_____ 5. citation	E. order requiring property to be sold

(continued)

_____ 6. interrogatories

F. questions submitted in writing by one party requiring answers by the other

_____ 7. writ of execution

G. the right to eliminate

_____ 8. peremptory challenge

H. order used against salary or wages

_____ 9. bill of particulars

I. detailed statement of matters set forth in a pleading

_____ 10. conform

J. to make identical

Section II

_____ 1. deposition

_____ 2. default

_____ 3. jurisdiction

_____ 4. subpena

_____ 5. venue

_____ 6. judgment creditor

_____ 7. _subpoena duces tecum_

_____ 8. judgment debtor

_____ 9. interrogatories

_____ 10. contempt of court

Section II

A. a process to compel a witness to appear

B. power to hear and determine

C. a process by which the court commands a witness who has in his or her possession or control written documents that are pertinent to the issues of a legal action to produce the documents at the time of the trial and to testify

D. losing party in court action

E. the place or county in which the case is to be tried

F. testimony of a witness under oath, reduced to writing

G. neglect or failure of a party to take the necessary steps in a legal action

H. successful party in court action

I. intentionally doing something that is against court rules

J. written questions that a witness must answer under oath

STUDENT ASSIGNMENTS

Note 1: This is a continuation of Practice Set I on page 144 that you started in Chapter 7. Use the information from that practice set for reference in preparing these papers. Check with your instructor as to the court captions to use in preparing these papers.

Note 2: In the following projects, with the exception of the verdict, you can use the template you created in Chapter 6 (**ch06_TMP**). This will save you from using repetitive keystrokes.

PROJECT 1: NOTICE OF INTENTION TO TAKE DEPOSITION

Instructions: Using your word processing software and the template that you created for pleadings in Chapter 6, prepare the following "Notice of Intention to Take Deposition."

   Save as **ch8_NOTC** and print one copy for your instructor.

PROJECT 2: PLAINTIFF'S INTERROGATORIES TO DEFENDANT

Instructions: Using your word processing software and the template you created for pleadings in Chapter 7, prepare the following "Plaintiff Albert Aggrieved's Interrogatories to Defendant Charlie Careless."

   Save as **ch8_INT** and print one copy for your instructor.

PROJECT 3: DEFENDANT'S ANSWERS TO PLAINTIFF'S INTERROGATORIES

Instructions: Using your word processing software and the template you created for pleadings in Chapter 7, prepare the following "Defendant Charlie Careless's Answers to Plaintiff Albert Aggrieved's Interrogatories."

   Save as **ch8_ANSW** and print one copy for your instructor.

PROJECT 4: VERDICT

Instructions: Using your word processing software prepare the following "Verdict."

   Save as **ch8_VERD** and print one copy for your instructor.

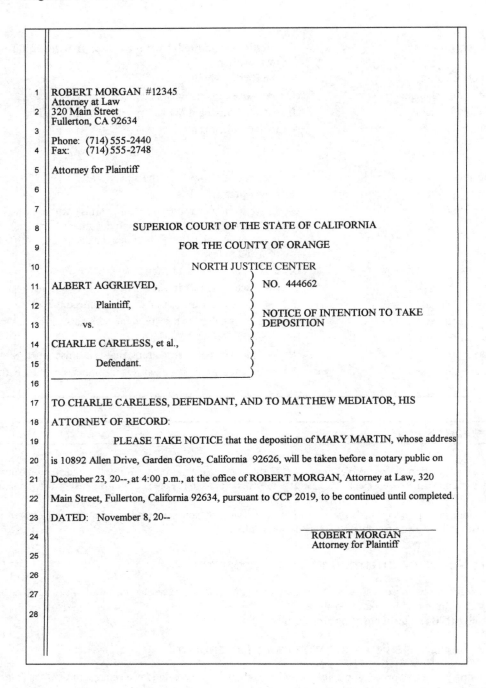

1   ROBERT MORGAN #12345
     Attorney at Law
2   320 Main Street
     Fullerton, CA 92634
3
     Phone: (714) 555-2440
4   Fax: (714) 555-2748
5   Attorney for Plaintiff
6
7
8   SUPERIOR COURT OF THE STATE OF CALIFORNIA
9   FOR THE COUNTY OF ORANGE
10   NORTH JUSTICE CENTER
11   ALBERT AGGRIEVED,   NO. 444662
12   Plaintiff,
                             NOTICE OF INTENTION TO TAKE
13   vs.   DEPOSITION
14   CHARLIE CARELESS, et al.,
15   Defendant.
16
17   TO CHARLIE CARELESS, DEFENDANT, AND TO MATTHEW MEDIATOR, HIS
18   ATTORNEY OF RECORD:
19   PLEASE TAKE NOTICE that the deposition of MARY MARTIN, whose address
20   is 10892 Allen Drive, Garden Grove, California 92626, will be taken before a notary public on
21   December 23, 20--, at 4:00 p.m., at the office of ROBERT MORGAN, Attorney at Law, 320
22   Main Street, Fullerton, California 92634, pursuant to CCP 2019, to be continued until completed.
23   DATED: November 8, 20--
24   ROBERT MORGAN
                                           Attorney for Plaintiff
25
26
27
28

1 ROBERT MORGAN #12345
   Attorney at Law
2 320 Main Street
   Fullerton, CA 92634
3
   Phone: (714) 555-2440
4 Fax: (714) 555-2748

5 Attorney for Plaintiff

6

7

8   SUPERIOR COURT OF THE STATE OF CALIFORNIA

9   FOR THE COUNTY OF ORANGE

10   NORTH JUSTICE CENTER

11 ALBERT AGGRIEVED,   )   NO. 444662
)
12   Plaintiff,   )
)   PLAINTIFF ALBERT AGGRIEVED'S
13   vs.   )   INTERROGATORIES TO DEFENDANT
)   CHARLIE CARELESS
14 CHARLIE CARELESS, et al.,   )
)
15   Defendant.   )
)

16

17 TO DEFENDANT CHARLIE CARELESS AND TO MATTHEW MEDIATOR, HIS

18 ATTORNEY:

19   Plaintiff requests Defendant CHARLIE CARELESS to answer under oath within

20 thirty (30) days, the following interrogatories:

21   IMPORTANT NOTE: All questions relate to the accident described in Plaintiff's

22 Complaint. Any questions directed to "you" includes you, your insurance company, your

23 attorneys, your investigators, and your representatives. You must take full inquiry to your

24 insurance company, attorneys, investigators, and representatives before attempting to answer

25 these questions. Your answers are under oath.

26   1.   State name and address of driver of your vehicle.

27   2.   State name and address of registered owner(s) of your vehicle.

28   3.   Was vehicle being operated with consent of owner(s)?

4.   State name, address, and age of all persons in your vehicle.

5.   Was the driver of your vehicle the agent, employee, or joint adventurer of anyone? If yes, state:

(a)   Of whom.

(b)   Whether the driver was acting within the scope of the agency, employee, or joint venture.

6.   Was your vehicle covered by a policy of liability insurance? If yes, state:

(a)   Name and address of insurance company.

(b)   Named insured.

(c)   Policy limits per person/per accident

7.   If the operator of your vehicle was not the owner, was the operator covered by another policy of automobile liability insurance? If yes, state:

(a)   Name and address of insurance company.

(b)   Named insured.

(c)   Policy limits per person/per accident

8.   State name, business address, residence address, and telephone number of all persons who saw, heard, witnessed, or claimed to have seen, heard, or witnessed the accident, or any of the events surrounding it.

9.   State name, address, and telephone number of every person who has been interviewed on your behalf concerning this accident (whether or not a statement or report was taken).

10.   Have "you" a statement or report from any witness? If yes, as to each statement or report, give name of witness, whether written, signed or unsigned, recorded or unrecorded, and who has custody now.

11.   Have "you" a statement or report from Plaintiff? If so, as to each statement or report, state whether written, signed or unsigned, recorded or unrecorded. If taken, please attach a complete photocopy (if written) or transcript (if recorded).

1   12.   Have "you" any photographs of the scene of the accident?

2   If yes, state:

3   (a)   Total number of photographs taken.

4   (b)   By whom taken.

5   (c)   Date.

6   (d)   Who has custody now.

7   13.   Have "you" any photographs of any vehicle in the accident?

8   If yes, state:

9   (a)   Total number of photographs taken and of what.

10   (b)   By whom taken.

11   (c)   Date.

12   (d)   Who has custody now.

13   14.   Was your vehicle damaged? If so, what is the estimate of

14   repairs, or amount if repaired, and where was the vehicle repaired?

15   DATED: October 29, 20--

16   ROBERT MORGAN
Attorney for Plaintiff

17

18

19

20

21

22

23

24

25

26

27

28

1 MATTHEW MEDIATOR #98765
   Attorney at Law
2 1212 Valley View Street
   Garden Grove, CA 92645
3
   Phone: (714) 555-1111
4 Fax: (714) 555-1122
5 Attorney for Defendant
6
7
8   SUPERIOR COURT OF THE STATE OF CALIFORNIA
9   FOR THE COUNTY OF ORANGE
10   NORTH JUSTICE CENTER

11 ALBERT AGGRIEVED,   )   NO. 444662
)
12   Plaintiff,   )
)   DEFENDANT CHARLIE CARELESS'S
13   vs.   )   ANSWERS TO PLAINTIFF ALBERT
)   AGGRIEVED'S INTERROGATORIES
14 CHARLIE CARELESS, et al.,   )
)
15   Defendant.   )
16
17   Defendant CHARLIE CARELESS answers Plaintiff ALBERT AGGRIEVED'S

18 interrogatories as they are numbered as follows:

19   1.   CHARLIE CARELESS, 404 Pico Place, Huntington Beach, California,

20 92646.

21   2.   Same as answer to No. 1.

22   3.   Yes.

23   4.   Only me.

24   5.   No.

25   6.   Yes.

26   (a)   STATE FARM INSURANCE COMPANY, 1234 Main Street,

27 Garden Grove, California 92640.

28   (b)   CHARLIE CARELESS.

1

(c) $100,000.00/$300,000.00

2   7.   Operator was the owner.

3   8.   Plaintiff and me.

4   9.   No one to my knowledge.

5   10.   No.

6   11.   No.

7   12.   No.

8   13.   No.

9   14. $300.00 estimate - car not repaired.

10   I declare, under penalty of perjury, that the foregoing is true and correct.

11   Executed on November 9, 20-- , at Garden Grove, California.

12

13   _____
                                          CHARLIE CARELESS
14   Defendant

15

16

17

18

19

20

21

22

23

24

25

26

27

28

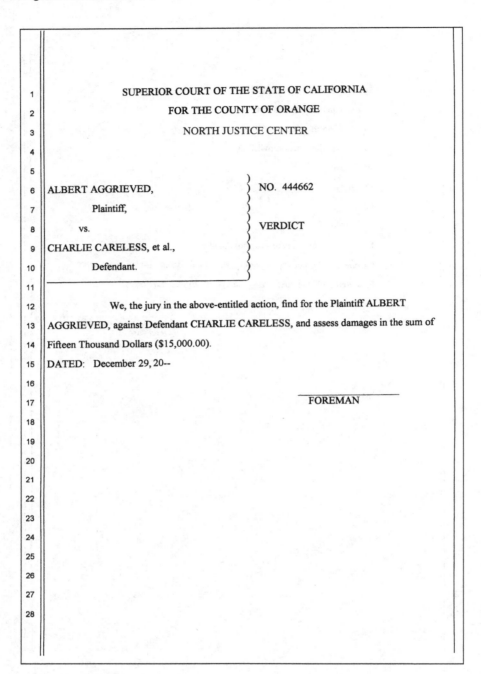

1   SUPERIOR COURT OF THE STATE OF CALIFORNIA

2   FOR THE COUNTY OF ORANGE

3   NORTH JUSTICE CENTER

4

5

6   ALBERT AGGRIEVED,   )   NO. 444662
)
7   Plaintiff,   )
)
8   vs.   )   VERDICT
)
9   CHARLIE CARELESS, et al.,   )
)
10   Defendant.   )

11

12   We, the jury in the above-entitled action, find for the Plaintiff ALBERT

13   AGGRIEVED, against Defendant CHARLIE CARELESS, and assess damages in the sum of

14   Fifteen Thousand Dollars ($15,000.00).

15   DATED: December 29, 20--

16

17   _____
                                               FOREMAN

18

19

20

21

22

23

24

25

26

27

28

Part 4

SUBSTANTIVE LAW

Last Will and Testament
of

Dated

RALPH I. CALLEN
ATTORNEY AT LAW
2141-C WEST LA PALMA AVENUE
ANAHEIM, CALIFORNIA 92801
(714) 555-5222

9

FAMILY LAW

OBJECTIVES

Upon completion of this chapter, you should be able to:

1. Discuss some of the historical aspects of marriage
2. Describe how marriage licenses are obtained
3. Define the differences between a valid, void, and voidable marriage
4. Discuss the value of a prenuptial agreement
5. Explain the differences between a divorce and dissolution of marriage
6. Describe the grounds for divorce
7. Discuss the procedures for a dissolution of marriage
8. Explain the difference between community property and separate property
9. Describe domestic partnerships
10. List the different kinds of adoptions
11. Explain the procedures for adoptions
12. Discuss the differences between a guardianship and a conservatorship

MARRIAGE

In England, marriage was historically the exclusive concern of ecclesiastical courts and canon law, while marriage in the United States always has been regulated by the civil authorities. In spite of the religious interest in the United States in the marital status and its obligation, the regulation of marriage has been considered essential for the public welfare; therefore, marriage has been regulated by the police power of the state.

Monogamy is a marriage relationship between one man and one woman at one time. **Bigamy** is the criminal offense of marrying a second time while a previous marriage is still in effect. **Polygamy** is the state of having two or more spouses at the same time.

Licenses

Most states require that the parties obtain a license before the marriage, although in a few jurisdictions exceptions have been made, for example, when the parties have been living together as husband and wife while not being legally married. Marriage licenses are issued by various officials, such as the county clerk, a minor court judge, or a justice of the peace, and there are no uniform rules governing where the licenses must be obtained. A nominal fee is charged for licenses in all states, and customarily both parties must apply for the license. Licensing statutes outline the information that must be provided on the form and require that it be given under oath. Some of the information required is used in the compilation of vital statistics, while the other information required is used to determine if the parties are legally eligible to marry each other. Bigamy and polygamy are criminal offenses in the United States.

Most states impose a waiting period between the application for the license and the actual marriage. This period varies from twenty-four hours to five days, but the typical waiting period is three days.

Almost all states require some sort of physical examination as a condition to the issuance of a marriage license. Most states limit the examination to tests for venereal diseases, but other jurisdictions may require a broader examination for various physical and mental illnesses.

State statutes recognize the solemnization of marriages, and the civil officer most frequently authorized to perform marriages is the justice of the peace. Most states require witnesses for the marriage ceremony, and the usual number is two. Each state has procedures regarding the recording of marriage licenses or certificates; the general procedure is for the party solemnizing the marriage to complete the blanks usually printed on the back of the marriage license. The marriage official, in turn, sends the completed license to the proper authorities to be recorded.

Common-Law Marriages

A **common-law marriage** is not solemnized by religious or civil ceremony, but instead it is effected by cohabitation as husband and wife for a time sufficient to create a legal marriage. Common-law marriages currently are recognized in some states and are not recognized in others, although nonrecognition may be qualified in various ways. California does not recognize common-law marriages.

Valid, Void, and Voidable Marriages

The validity of a marriage is determined by the laws of the state or the country where the marriage is contracted. A **valid marriage** is one that meets all the requirements of marriage in the state in which the marriage is contracted. Such a marriage may be dissolved only by death, divorce, or dissolution.

A **void marriage** is one that is wholly void from the beginning, never can become valid, and confers no rights or obligations. Generally, marriages between the following classes of persons are considered void.

1. Children and parents
2. Ancestors and descendants of any degree
3. Brothers and sisters of the whole blood or half-blood
4. Uncles and nieces
5. Aunts and nephews
6. Those in which one of the persons is already married under a valid marriage. (There are some exceptions if one of the persons is absent for a stated number of years and is not known to be living.)

A **voidable marriage** may be declared a **nullity** or **annulled** on the petition of one of the parties. If the voidable marriage is not annulled or declared a nullity within the time specified, it becomes a valid marriage and can be dissolved only by a divorce or **a judgment of dissolution** (cancellation of the marriage contract). While the grounds for annulment differ from state to state, the following are the most common grounds for voidable marriages:

1. Either party was under the age of legal consent and contracted marriage without consent of parent or guardian.
2. Former husband or wife was living, although believed to have been dead.

3. Either party was of unsound mind as of the time of the marriage.
4. Consent was obtained by fraud.
5. Consent to the marriage was obtained by force.
6. Physical incapacity existed at the time of the marriage, and such incapacity continues and appears to be incurable.

Prenuptial Agreement

A **prenuptial agreement or premarital** is prepared when two people about to be married desire to change some of the conditions imposed by the law when they marry. (Some marriage contracts include and are based on a prenuptial agreement.) Three reasons for entering into such an agreement may be the following:

1. One or both of the parties to be married have been married before and may have property from the previous marriage that they wish to leave to the children of the previous marriage rather than to a new spouse.
2. One of the parties to the marriage is a partner in a business organization. If that person is to die, the law might allow the surviving spouse to function as that partner. This situation may not be in the best interest of that business or those parties concerned; therefore, a prenuptial agreement could be made to change those conditions.
3. One or both of the parties to the marriage have assets or obligations acquired prior to the marriage that he or she wishes to clearly remain separate property.

A prenuptial agreement can more clearly define what will happen in the event of the death of a spouse or a termination of the marriage. The courts have held that full disclosure of all circumstances bearing on a prenuptial agreement must be made to all parties concerned.

The prenuptial agreement helps the couple predict and settle possible disputes over property. It also may provide for inheritance plans for children from a prior marriage or enable one party to retain ownership of a valuable piece of property, heirloom, or inheritance. The presiding judge in a disputed divorce action decides how property is to be divided if there is no prenuptial agreement.

The prenuptial agreement is essentially a contract (Figure 9-1) and is therefore prepared in the same manner and style as other legal documents. The title usually is centered and typed in bold at the top of the page. The paragraphs outlining the rights and obligations of the parties are numbered and double spaced. The conclusion of the document includes the signature lines of the parties and witnesses, as well as the notary's acknowledgment for each person signing the document. Some states have specific statutory language, acknowledgements, and waivers that must be incorporated into the document.

DIVORCE AND DISSOLUTION OF MARRIAGE

A marriage may be terminated in two ways:

1. By death of one of the partners
2. By divorce or dissolution

It is not unusual for the terms *divorce* and *dissolution* to be used interchangeably where both fault and no-fault divorces are granted.

In states where divorces are granted, the person initiating the divorce is the plaintiff and the opposing party is the defendant. The termination of the marriage is referred to as divorce, and the documents filed are complaint and answer. In states

FIGURE 9-1   *Prenuptial agreement.*

PRENUPTIAL AGREEMENT

THIS AGREEMENT is entered into by and between ANN PHONG, a resident of Orange County, California (hereinafter referred to as "ANN") and TOM NGUYEN, a resident of Orange County, California (hereinafter referred to as "TOM") in contemplation and consideration of their forthcoming marriage.

WITNESSETH:

WHEREAS, the parties are engaged and intend to be married to each other; and

WHEREAS, the parties to this Agreement intend and desire to define their respective rights in the property of the other, and to avoid such interest which they might acquire in the property of the other as incidents of their forthcoming marital relationship; and

WHEREAS, . . .

NOW, THEREFORE, in consideration of the above-stated premises and of their marriage, it is agreed as follows:

1.   Each party, desiring to define the interest she and he shall have in the estate of the other during the marriage and after the death of the other party, restate and adopt the preamble as set forth above in its entirety and, by this reference, incorporate it herein.

2.   TOM hereby waives and releases all right, title, and interest, statutory or otherwise, in all of the premarriage property owned by ANN at the time of the marriage and all of the property, both real and personal, tangible and intangible, acquired by her at any time thereafter from gifts or inheritance. . .

3.   ANN hereby waives and releases all right, title, and interest, statutory or otherwise, in all of the premarriage property owned by TOM at the time of the marriage and all of the property, both real and personal, tangible and intangible, acquired by him at any time thereafter from gifts or inheritance. . .

---

that allow no-fault divorces, the party initiating the action is the petitioner and the answering party is the respondent.

State laws may vary with respect to divorce and the dissolution of marriage. The word divorce in some states has come to be replaced by the more neutral dissolution of marriage terms. The concept of no-fault divorce has gained acceptance (see Dissolution of Marriage section), and many states have followed California's lead in revising their divorce laws. The philosophy in California is that blame need not be assigned if a couple cannot live together. Therefore, dissolving a marriage is generally no longer an **adversary proceeding**—a proceeding initiated by one party against another by means of a complaint—and no longer requires the accusations of fault and testimony that used to leave both parties in a divorce angry and bitter.

FIGURE 9-1   *Continued*

4.   The parties further acknowledge and agree. . . .

IN WITNESS WHEREOF, the parties hereto have set their hands and seals

to this Agreement on the _____ day of _____, _____.

Signed, sealed, and delivered
in the presence of:

_____   _____
Witness   ANN PHONG

_____
Printed Name of Witness

_____   _____
Witness   TOM NGUYEN

_____
Printed Name of Witness

STATE OF CALIFORNIA
                                          ss:
COUNTY OF ORANGE

BEFORE ME, the undersigned authority, personally appeared ANN

PHONG and TOM NGUYEN who, after first being duly sworn, deposes and say

that they have read the foregoing Agreement and acknowledge that they have

executed the same for the purposes herein expressed.

SWORN TO AND SUBSCRIBED before me this _____ day of

_____, _____.

_____
Notary Public

Many forms and documents must be completed by the legal staff in conjunction with either a divorce or a dissolution proceeding. Latin terms are sometimes used in referring to the parties to the action. *Et uxor* means "and wife" and *et vir* means "and husband."

It is important to remember that undergoing a divorce or dissolution of marriage may be a very emotional experience for the clients requesting this action, and support staff may be required to exercise unusual patience and understanding in their interactions with these clients.

Divorce

Complaint and Summons   In some states, divorce is an adversary proceeding and follows the pattern of pleadings and litigation. An answer to the complaint is required within a specified number of days or the defendant may lose the case by default. The first document served on the defendant is accompanied by a summons and may be known as a **complaint for divorce, petition for divorce** (Figures 9-2 and 9-3), or **bill of divorcement.** If the defendant cannot be located, the complaint must be served by publication.

Grounds for Divorce To end a marriage, the law requires a reason. Each state has a list of these reasons, called **grounds for divorce,** which are sufficient in the courts of that state. The court's requirement that *legally sufficient grounds* exist for divorce means that the particular state's legislature has decided a divorce may be granted only under specific circumstances. In other words, the lawmakers have decided that only for specific reasons may a person obtain a divorce. The most common grounds for divorce are adultery, willful neglect or desertion, conviction of a felony, extreme cruelty, and incompatibility. The grounds for divorce (dissolution) in California vary and are discussed later in the chapter.

Adultery Adultery usually is defined as the voluntary sexual intercourse of a married person with someone other than the married person's spouse.

Willful Neglect or Desertion A second ground for cause for divorce is referred to as **willful neglect.** This ground is defined as the neglect and failure of the husband with ability to provide life's necessities for the wife.

FIGURE 9-2 *Petition for divorce—Texas.*

GREG BAILEY #09876
Attorney at Law
460 Main Street
Austin, TX 77418

Phone: (409) 555-5912
Fax: (409) 555-5906

No. _____

SALLY SMITH, PLAINTIFF	§	IN THE DISTRICT COURT
	§	
VS	§	FIRST JUDICIAL DISTRICT
	§	
SAMUEL SMITH, DEFENDANT	§	AUSTIN, TEXAS

ORIGINAL PETITION FOR DIVORCE

TO THE HONORABLE JUDGE OF SAID COURT:

This suit is brought by SALLY SMITH, Petitioner, Social Security No. 346-36-1534, who is 35 years of age, and who resides at 123 Range Road, Austin, Texas, 77018. SAMUEL SMITH, Respondent, Social Security No. 348-15-1240, is 37 years of age and resides at 3245 Navajo Trail, Austin, Texas, 77019.

I.

Petitioner has lived in this state for the preceding six-month period and has been a resident of this county for the preceding 90-day period.

II.

No service is necessary at this time.

III.

The parties were married on or about May 15, ---- , and ceased to live together as husband and wife on or about January 13, _____.

IV.

The marriage has become insupportable because of discord or conflict of personalities between Petitioner and Respondent that destroys the legitimate ends of the marriage relationship and prevents any reasonable expectation of reconciliation.

V.

Petitioner and Respondent are parents of the following children of this marriage, who are not under the continuing jurisdiction of any other court:

FIGURE 9-2   *Continued*

NAME:	Susan Smith
SEX:	Female
BIRTHPLACE:	Houston, Texas
DOB:	August 25, ____
PRESENT ADDRESS:	123 Range Road, Austin, Texas 77018
SOCIAL SECURITY NO.:	123-10-1789

NAME:	Patrick Smith
SEX:	Male
BIRTHPLACE:	Austin, Texas
DOB:	January 2, ____
PRESENT ADDRESS:	123 Range Road, Austin, Texas 77018
SOCIAL SECURITY NO.:	238-10-6253

There are no court-ordered conservatorships, court-ordered guardianships, or other court-ordered relationships affecting the children.

VI.

Petitioner believes that Petitioner and Respondent will enter into a written agreement containing provisions for conservatorship and support of the children. If such agreement is not made, Petitioner requests the Court to make orders for conservatorship and support of the children.

VII.

Petitioner believes Petitioner and Respondent will enter into an agreement for the division of their estate. If such agreement is made, Petitioner requests the Court to approve the agreement and order a division of their estate in a manner consistent with the agreement. If such agreement is not made, Petitioner requests the Court to order a division of their estate in a manner that the court deems just and right, as provided by law.

PRAYER

Petitioner prays that citation and notice issue as required by law and that the Court grant a divorce and such other relief requested in this petition.

Petitioner prays for general relief.

Respectfully submitted,

_____

GREG BAILEY

Willful desertion by either party is also used by some states as a ground for divorce. Desertion has many possible meanings. One of these is a persistent refusal by one spouse to have sexual intercourse when his or her physical condition does not make the refusal a reasonable necessity.

There appears to be no uniform definition for the word *desertion*, and in some states the offense is called **abandonment**. Most states require that the desertion continue for a specified period of time before an action can be filed. The length of time varies from one to five years, with one year being the most common.

Conviction of a Felony   Another ground for divorce exists if one spouse has been convicted of a felony during the marriage. The legislature's reasoning is that a successful marital relationship hardly can be conducted when one party is serving a prison sentence.

Extreme Cruelty   A widely used ground for divorce in most states is extreme mental or physical cruelty. This is used as a ground for divorce in almost every state. As originally adopted, it means precisely what it says. The plaintiff must show that the spouse is extremely cruel by physical means or by constant mental harassment.

FIGURE 9-3 *Complaint for divorce—New York.*

KEN KVITKA
Attorney at Law
460 Harbor View
Long Island, NY 10580

Phone: (603) 555-5912
FAX: (603) 555-5906

SUPREME COURT OF THE STATE OF NEW YORK
COUNTY OF NEW YORK

_____

SALLY SMITH, Plaintiff,

-against-   VERIFIED COMPLAINT

SAMUEL SMITH, Defendant   Index No. _____

_____

Plaintiff, SALLY SMITH, by her attorney, KEN KVITKA, Esq., as and for her Amended Verified Complaint, respectfully alleges as follows:

FIRST: Plaintiff and Defendant were married on August 1, ____, in the City of New York, County of New York, State of New York.

SECOND: Plaintiff was a resident of the State of New York when this action was commenced and has been a resident of the State of New York for a continuous period of more than two years immediately preceding the commencement of this action.

THIRD: Defendant was a resident of the State of New York when this action was commenced and has been a resident of the State of New York for a continuous period of more than two years immediately preceding the commencement of this action.

FOURTH: The within action was commenced by the service of a Summons personally served upon the Defendant, SAMUEL SMITH, on February 1, ____, and that said Summons had inscribed on the face thereof the words, "Action for a Divorce."

FIFTH: There are two issues born of this marriage, to wit: SUSAN SMITH, born August 25, ____, and PATRICK SMITH, born January 2, ____.

SIXTH: The Plaintiff and Defendant own, as tenants by the entirety, the marital residence located at 456 North Plains, Woods, New York.

SEVENTH: At the following times, none of which is earlier than five (5) years prior to the commencement of this action, the Defendant committed the following acts which endangered Plaintiff's physical and mental well-being and rendered it unsafe and improper for Plaintiff to continue to reside with Defendant; said acts of cruel and inhuman treatment were committed without just cause or provocation and include the following:

(a) as a continuous course of conduct since October, ----, three years after the purchase of the marital residence, the Defendant advised the Plaintiff that he no longer wished to live with her in the house in New York City, since he did not want to be stuck in the woods and wanted to return to the city.

(b) as a continuous course of conduct for the past five years, Defendant constantly put down the Plaintiff's family and told the Plaintiff, "You're only a plumber's daughter."

(c) as a continuous course of conduct for the past five years, the Defendant told the Plaintiff that she was not up to his intelligence.

(d) as a continuous course of conduct for the past five years, the Defendant refused to discuss or communicate as to any family or marital problems; and

(e) as a continuous course of conduct for the past five years, Defendant has accused Plaintiff of "not being a good lover," has called her "boring," and has told her that he does not love her.

FIGURE 9-3   *Continued*

EIGHTH: Defendant's conduct, as aforesaid, has caused Plaintiff great physical and mental anguish, thereby rendering it unsafe and improper for Plaintiff to cohabit with Defendant.

NINTH: No other action is now pending between Plaintiff and Defendant for divorce, separation, or annulment in any Court in the State of New York or of any other state, territory, or dependency of the United States or any foreign country.

TENTH: No decree of divorce, separation, or annulment or any other decree dissolving the marriage between Plaintiff and Defendant has ever been obtained in any court of the State of New York or of any other state, territory, or dependency of the United States or any foreign country.

ELEVENTH: Plaintiff and Defendant have entered into an agreement of settlement, dated as of February 14, _____, in which the parties have resolved, by agreement, all of the issues arising in respect of their marital relationship, including, but not limited to, maintenance, child support, equitable distribution, and counsel fees.

TWELFTH: Plaintiff alleges that to the best of her knowledge, she has taken or will take, prior to the entry of final judgment, all steps solely within her power to remove any barrier to Defendant's remarriage following the divorce requested herein.

WHEREFORE, Plaintiff demands judgment of absolute divorce dissolving forever the bonds of matrimony heretofore existing between Plaintiff and Defendant, and for such other, further, and different relief as to the Court may seem just and proper.

Dated: New York, New York
   March 12___, _____.

Respectfully Submitted,

_____
KEN KVITKA
Attorney at Law

TO: _____
Attorney for Defendant

Practically speaking, this ground has been used as a "catchall" in most cases, since the degree of proof required by the court is something less than the legislature had originally anticipated.

Incompatibility   Another ground for divorce is **incompatibility**. Only a few states use this as a ground for divorce, and the statutes that outline the requirement for this ground usually fall into three categories: (1) divorce is authorized only when the parties have lived apart for the prescribed period of time under a decree of separation from the court; (2) divorce is authorized when the parties have *voluntarily* lived apart for a prescribed time; and (3) divorce is granted only upon proof that the parties have lived apart for the prescribed time. The period of separation varies considerably from state to state, with three to five years being the most common statutory period.

Residence Requirements   Most states, with the exception of Alabama, require that the plaintiff be a resident of the state for a specified period of time before initiating divorce proceedings. The time requirements vary from six weeks to three years. The term **residence** usually refers to a domicile, which is defined as the place where the plaintiff is physically present and plans to make his or her home. In some states, the statutes require that only the defendant need be a resident of that state to meet the requirements for residence and jurisdiction.

Contested Divorces   While many divorces are not contested by the defendant, some divorces are bitterly contested because one of the parties does not want the divorce, does not want to give up custody of the children, does not want to make child support or alimony payments, or does not agree with the property settlement agreement. If the divorce is contested, the procedures followed are the same as in any case in litigation. An answer and perhaps a cross-complaint are filed. There may be motions and discovery proceedings, and finally a hearing is held in the superior or higher court of jurisdiction. If there is mutual agreement to the divorce, the defendant usually forgoes his or her right to appear at the hearing and to answer the complaint.

Order to Show Cause   Most states require that the parties to a divorce file a financial statement when they file the complaint for divorce. A preliminary hearing is then held, and this procedure is called an **order to show cause (OSC)**. This procedure will secure temporary orders, including orders for spousal support, child custody, child support and visitation, restraining orders, attorney's fees, and court costs pending trial of the case.

The OSC requires the opposing party to appear in court for examination pertaining to the granting of the requested temporary orders. The opposing party must show cause why the court should not issue the orders requested.

Alimony and Support   Alimony or spousal support is a court-ordered allowance paid by a husband to his ex-wife (or, occasionally, by wife to ex-husband) after separation or divorce. **Child support** is an allowance paid to provide for one's children.

The amount of alimony or **support** awarded in divorces varies among jurisdictions and is based on the statutes of each state. The age of the parties, the ability to pay, the length of the marriage, the standard of living, and the number of children born during the marriage all are factors considered when the court awards alimony or spousal support. The purpose of awarding alimony is not punitive, but it is a means of providing a substitute for the support that would ordinarily have been provided through the marriage had the marriage continued. The amount of the award depends on the circumstances of each case.

The amount of the support for minor children depends on the ability of the parent to pay, the needs of the children, and the relative standard of living that the children have enjoyed, and in some states the amount of time the children spend with each parent. Support awards occupy a special place in the law. Most general debts are discharged in bankruptcy proceedings, but spousal and child support cannot be discharged if the husband goes into bankruptcy.

In some circumstances, the husband may be entitled to receive support payments from his wife if he is unable to support himself and if she has sufficient means to support him. The most important points to remember about alimony and support are the needs of the person who receives it and the financial ability of the person who pays it.

The Uniform Child Custody Jurisdiction and Enforcement Act (UCCJEA)
The Uniform Child Custody Jurisdiction and Enforcement Act concerns jurisdiction over child custody matters, including visitation. The general purposes of the act are to avoid jurisdictional conflicts with courts of other states in matters of child custody, to promote cooperation with the courts of other states, to ensure that litigation concerning the custody of a child takes place in the proper state, to avoid hearings on custody decisions of other states, and to promote and expand the exchange of information and assistance between the courts of one state with other states concerning the child. Basically, the act comes into effect only if custody proceedings are pending in another court in another state. Some states apply these principles to intercounty jurisdictional disputes as well.

Decree of Divorce   In order to obtain the final decree of divorce, there must be a hearing on the complaint. Most states require a waiting period before the final decree is granted. After the specified time has passed, the final decree of divorce is prepared, signed, filed, and served. State laws vary as to the amount of time required between the granting of the interlocutory and the final decree, but it usually runs between six months and one year.

Dissolution of Marriage (California)

The concept of **no-fault divorce** has gained acceptance concerning the dissolution of marriage. No-fault divorce is just what the name implies: Neither party is at fault, but one or both of the partners want the marriage dissolved. In a no-fault divorce, the divorce itself is no longer an adversary action where one person has to be right and the other person has to be wrong; it means merely that two people cannot get along under the terms of the marriage agreement and want it dissolved. With the adoption of the Family Law Act in California in 1970 and the integration of this act into the enactments of the Family Code in 1992, many of the terms and procedures dealing with the termination of a marriage have been changed (see Table 9-1). In addition to the Family Law Act, the new code contains provisions regarding domestic violence; minor, parent, and child relationships; freedom from parental custody and control; adoptions; and domestic partnerships. The term **divorce** has been changed to **dissolution**, *complaint* to **petition**, *answer* to *response*, *plaintiff* to **petitioner**, *defendant* to **respondent**, and *alimony* to **spousal support**.

Grounds for Dissolution   As noted earlier, to end a marriage, the law requires a reason, and each state has its own list of legally acceptable reasons. Under California dissolution of marriage law, the only two grounds are (1) **irreconcilable differences** that have caused the **irremediable breakdown** of the marriage and (2) **incurable insanity**.

Residence Requirements   The petitioner is required to be a resident of California for six months prior to the filing of the petition and to be a resident of the county in which the petition is filed for three months. The Superior Court has exclusive jurisdiction in family law matters.

Procedures for Dissolution   The party initiating a dissolution is designated the petitioner and begins the action by filing the petition (Figure 9-4). Accompanying the petition is a summons (for issuance by the clerk), and, in some instances, a declaration under the Uniform Child Custody Jurisdiction and Enforcement Act. As in any litigation case, a summons is prepared to notify the respondent of the pending action. Some individual counties may have additional forms requirements.

At the same time the initial documents are filed to commence an action for dissolution of marriage and during the action, the petitioner may file additional documents requesting the court to make temporary orders concerning child support, custody, visitation, spousal support, attorney's fees, and such other orders as may be requested. The request for such orders is made by means of an **order to show** cause proceeding.

TABLE 9-1   Terms Relevant to California Family Law

	Under the Law	*Under California's Family Law Act*
Pleadings	complaint	petition
	answer	response
Parties	plaintiff	petitioner
	defendant	respondent
Relief, defenses, causes of action, etc.	action	proceeding
	alimony	spousal support
	annulment	declaration of nullity
	fault grounds	irreconcilable differences
	pendente lite	temporary
	prayer	proposed judgment
	separate maintenance	legal separation
	stranger	nonparent

FL-100

ATTORNEY OR PARTY WITHOUT ATTORNEY (Name, State Bar number, and address):	FOR COURT USE ONLY

ROBERT MORGAN   SBN 12345
Attorney at Law
320 Main Street
Fullerton, CA 92634

TELEPHONE NO.: (714) 555-1234   FAX NO. (Optional): (714) 555-5678
E-MAIL ADDRESS (Optional):
ATTORNEY FOR (Name): SALLY SMITH

SUPERIOR COURT OF CALIFORNIA, COUNTY OF ORANGE
STREET ADDRESS: COUNTY OF ORANGE
MAILING ADDRESS: 341 THE CITY DRIVE
CITY AND ZIP CODE: ORANGE, CA 92868
BRANCH NAME: LAMOREAUX JUSTICE CENTER

MARRIAGE OF
PETITIONER: SALLY SMITH

RESPONDENT: SAMUEL SMITH

PETITION FOR

[X] **Dissolution of Marriage**
[ ] **Legal Separation**
[ ] **Nullity of Marriage**   [ ] **AMENDED**

CASE NUMBER:

1. RESIDENCE (Dissolution only) [X] Petitioner   [ ] Respondent   has been a resident of this state for at least six months and of this county for at least three months immediately preceding the filing of this *Petition for Dissolution of Marriage.*

2. STATISTICAL FACTS
   a. Date of marriage: August 1, 20--
   b. Date of separation: August 5, 20--
   c. Time from date of marriage to date of separation *(specify):*
      Years: 15   Months: 0

3. DECLARATION REGARDING MINOR CHILDREN *(include children of this relationship born prior to or during the marriage or adopted during the marriage):*
   a. [ ] There are no minor children.
   b. [X] The minor children are:

Child's name	Birthdate	Age	Sex
SUSAN SMITH	August 25, 20--	--	F
PATRICK SMITH	January 2, 20--	--	M

   [ ] Continued on Attachment 3b.
   c. If there are minor children of the Petitioner and Respondent, a completed *Declaration Under Uniform Child Custody Jurisdiction and Enforcement Act (UCCJEA)* (form FL-105) must be attached.
   d. [ ] A completed voluntary declaration of paternity regarding minor children born to the Petitioner and Respondent prior to the marriage is attached.

4. SEPARATE PROPERTY
   Petitioner requests that the assets and debts listed [ ] in *Property Declaration* (form FL-160)   [ ] in Attachment 4
   [X] below   be confirmed as separate property.

Item	Confirm to
All property acquired prior to the date of marriage, subsequent to the date of separation, or by gift, bequest, devise, or descent, and the rents, issues and profits therefrom, to be determined at the time of trial.	

NOTICE: You may redact (black out) social security numbers from any written material filed with the court in this case other than a form used to collect child or spousal support.

Page 1 of 2

Form Adopted for Mandatory Use
Judicial Council of California
FL-100 [Rev. January 1, 2005]

PETITION—MARRIAGE
(Family Law)

Family Code, §§ 2330, 3409

FIGURE 9-4   *Response (dissolution of marriage)—California.*

Petition   The petition (Figure 9-4) commences an action for dissolution, nullity, or **legal separation**. It sets forth the facts and the relief or judgment sought by the petitioner. Separate, community, and quasi-community property and the obligations of the parties must be listed on the petition.

The petitioner also may require temporary relief from some activity by the respondent, such as harassment or physical harm. In this case, the court may issue

MARRIAGE OF *(last name, first name of parties):*	CASE NUMBER:
SMITH, SALLY and SAMUEL	

5. DECLARATION REGARDING COMMUNITY AND QUASI-COMMUNITY ASSETS AND DEBTS AS CURRENTLY KNOWN
   a. ☐ There are no such assets or debts subject to disposition by the court in this proceeding.
   b. ☒ All such assets and debts are listed ☐ in *Property Declaration* (form FL-160) ☒ in Attachment 5b.
      ☐ below *(specify):*

6. **Petitioner requests**
   a. ☒ dissolution of the marriage based on
      (1) ☒ irreconcilable differences. (Fam. Code, § 2310(a).)
      (2) ☐ incurable insanity. (Fam. Code, § 2310(b).)
   b. ☐ legal separation of the parties based on
      (1) ☐ irreconcilable differences. (Fam. Code, § 2310(a).)
      (2) ☐ incurable insanity. (Fam. Code, § 2310(b).)
   c. ☐ nullity of void marriage based on
      (1) ☐ incestuous marriage. (Fam. Code, § 2200.)
      (2) ☐ bigamous marriage. (Fam. Code, § 2201.)
   d. ☐ nullity of voidable marriage based on
      (1) ☐ petitioner's age at time of marriage. (Fam. Code, § 2210(a).)
      (2) ☐ prior existing marriage. (Fam. Code, § 2210(b).)
      (3) ☐ unsound mind. (Fam. Code, § 2210(c).)
      (4) ☐ fraud. (Fam. Code, § 2210(d).)
      (5) ☐ force. (Fam. Code, § 2210(e).)
      (6) ☐ physical incapacity. (Fam. Code, § 2210(f).)

7. **Petitioner requests** that the court grant the above relief and make injunctive (including restraining) and other orders as follows:

		Petitioner	Respondent	Joint	Other
a.	Legal custody of children to	☒	☐	☐	☐
b.	Physical custody of children to	☒	☐	☐	☐
c.	Child visitation be granted to	☐	☒	☐	☐

As requested in form: ☐ FL-311 ☐ FL-312 ☐ FL-341(C) ☐ FL-341(D) ☐ FL-341(E) ☐ Attachment 7c.

   d. ☐ Determination of parentage of any children born to the Petitioner and Respondent prior to the marriage.
   e. Attorney fees and costs payable by .... ☐ ☒
   f. Spousal support payable to (earnings assignment will be issued) .... ☐ ☒
   g. ☒ Terminate the court's jurisdiction (ability) to award spousal support to Respondent.
   h. ☒ Property rights be determined.
   i. ☐ Petitioner's former name be restored to *(specify):*
   j. ☐ Other *(specify):*

      ☐ Continued on Attachment 7j.

8. **Child support**–If there are minor children born to or adopted by the Petitioner and Respondent before or during this marriage, the court will make orders for the support of the children upon request and submission of financial forms by the requesting party. An earnings assignment may be issued without further notice. Any party required to pay support must pay interest on overdue amounts at the "legal" rate, which is currently 10 percent.

9. **I HAVE READ THE RESTRAINING ORDERS ON THE BACK OF THE SUMMONS, AND I UNDERSTAND THAT THEY APPLY TO ME WHEN THIS PETITION IS FILED.**

I declare under penalty of perjury under the laws of the State of California that the foregoing is true and correct.
Date:

SALLY SMITH
(TYPE OR PRINT NAME) ▶ (SIGNATURE OF PETITIONER)

Date:

ROBERT MORGAN   SBN 12345
(TYPE OR PRINT NAME) ▶ (SIGNATURE OF ATTORNEY FOR PETITIONER)

NOTICE: Dissolution or legal separation may automatically cancel the rights of a spouse under the other spouse's will, trust, retirement plan, power of attorney, pay on death bank account, survivorship rights to any property owned in joint tenancy, and any other similar thing. It does not automatically cancel the right of a spouse as beneficiary of the other spouse's life insurance policy. You should review these matters, as well as any credit cards, other credit accounts, insurance polices, retirement plans, and credit reports to determine whether they should be changed or whether you should take any other actions. However, some changes may require the agreement of your spouse or a court order (see Family Code sections 231–235).

FL-100 [Rev. January 1, 2005] **PETITION—MARRIAGE** Page 2 of 2
(Family Law)

FIGURE 9-4 *Continued*

an *ex parte* (an order granted with the opposing party having little or no notice of it) restraining order.

Contested Proceedings The respondent may not contest the dissolution of marriage but may contest other requests made by the petitioner, such as child custody, support, and division of community property. If the respondent opposed any of the requests made in the petition, a response to the petition must be made within thirty (30) days after service the summons and petition or a default will be entered.

Uncontested Proceedings A proceeding is considered to be uncontested if:

1. The respondent does not file a response or make a general appearance within thirty (30) days after service of the summons and petition.
2. The parties have executed a **marital settlement agreement** conforming to the statutory requirements (Figure 9-5) resolving all issues, or
3. The parties enter into an agreement after the respondent files a response and the parties stipulate that the matter can be heard as an uncontested matter.

MARITAL SETTLEMENT AGREEMENT

This Marital Settlement Agreement ("Agreement") is made and entered into this _____ day of September, 19--, at Los Angeles, California, by and between IRMA L. ESCOBAR (hereinafter referred to as "Wife"), and RICHARD L. ESCOBAR (hereinafter referred to as "Husband"), both hereinafter collectively referred to as "The Parties." In consideration for the mutual promises and other considerations set forth below, the parties agree as follows:

1.   Effective Date of Agreement: The effective date of this Agreement is

September _____, 20--. Unless otherwise specifically provided, all statements, warranties and representations in this Agreement are true and correct as of that date.

2.   Recitals: This Agreement is made with reference to the following facts:

A.   Date of Marriage.   Husband and Wife were married in New York, New York, on August 1, 20--.

B.   Date of Separation.   Husband and Wife separated on August 5, 20--.

C.   Children.   The parties have two children; namely, MARIA A. ESCOBAR, born August 5, ----, age ten (10); and JOSE P. ESCOBAR, born January 2, ----, age six (6).

. . .

18.   Each party has read the foregoing Agreement and fully accepts and understands the same. There has been no promise, agreement, or undertaking of either of the parties to the other, except as herein set forth, relied upon by either as a matter of inducement to enter into this Agreement.

19.   Each party agrees, upon demand, and as necessary or convenient, to execute any and all documents required to effect the transfers herein provided for.

FIGURE 9-5 *Marital settlement agreement.*

20.   This Agreement may, subject to the approval of the Court, be made a part of any decree of dissolution between the parties.

21.   <u>Binding on Heirs</u>.   This Agreement shall be binding upon and inure to the benefit of the parties hereto and to their heirs, executors, administrators, assigns and other successors in interest of each of them.

22.   <u>Entire Agreement</u>.   This Agreement supersedes any and all other agreements, either oral or in writing between the parties relating to the rights and liabilities arising out of their marriage.   This Agreement contains the entire agreement of the parties.

This Agreement is entered into on September _____, 20--, at Los Angeles, California.

_____
IRMA L. ESCOBAR, Wife

_____
RICHARD L. ESCOBAR, Husband

State of California,   )
) ss.
County of _____   )

On this _____ day of _____, 20--, before me, the undersigned, a Notary Public, in and for said County and State, personally appeared IRMA L. ESCOBAR, and RICHARD L. ESCOBAR, known to me to be the persons whose names are subscribed to the within instrument and acknowledged to me that they executed the same.

WITNESS my hand and seal.

_____
Notary Public in and for said County and State

FIGURE 9-5   *Continued*

COMMUNITY PROPERTY

Community property is a system of property ownership that evolved from the Spanish and Mexican law and came into effect when certain states became part of the United States. Community property was the original marital property system in California and a number of other states, and this law governs the control and ownership of marital property.

In spite of common Spanish and Mexican law origins, the community property system differs from state to state because of varying interpretations of the law. The net result is that the community property law in California, for instance, is not the same as it is in Texas. In discussing community property here, then, we are strictly speaking about California law.

In general, community property is property acquired during marriage, either by the husband or wife, through the efforts or the labor of either. Community property can include money, stock, real estate, or any kind of tangible or intangible property.

Property owned before marriage or property acquired by gift or inherited from someone who has died is not community property, but is called **separate property**. Property may be changed from separate property to community property, or vice versa, through a written agreement between the husband and wife. The manner in which the property is classified is very important. When judges divide the community property upon termination of the marriage, they give half to each spouse. The separate property remains with the person who had it originally.

Generally, property acquired by a party after the date of separation is also deemed that person's separate property. The date of separation is determined by the lack of a party's intent to resume the marital relationship and by conduct evidencing the final breakup thereof.

QUASI-COMMUNITY PROPERTY

California law also recognizes what is called **quasi-community property**. This property is found only when the husband and wife are divorced in California after having lived previously in another state. In dissolution proceedings, the California court treats property acquired by the couple before they moved to California (which would have been community property if it had been acquired in California) as if it were community property and divides it between the parties according to the rules governing community property.

DOMESTIC PARTNERSHIPS

Some states recognize **domestic partnerships**. In California, a domestic partnership is established when both persons file a Declaration of Domestic Partnership with the secretary of state and meet all of the following requirements:

1. Both persons have a common residence.
2. Neither person is married to someone else and neither is a member of another domestic partnership with someone else that has not been terminated, dissolved, or adjudged a nullity.
3. The two persons are not related by blood in a way that would prevent them from being married to each other in this state.
4. Both persons are at least eighteen years old.
5. Either of the following:
   a. Both persons are members of the same sex.
   b. One or both of the persons meet the eligibility requirements for Social Security old age benefits. Persons of the opposite sex may not constitute a domestic partnership unless one or both of them are over the age of sixty-two.
6. Both persons are capable of consenting to the domestic partnership.

FL-120

ATTORNEY OR PARTY WITHOUT ATTORNEY *(Name, State Bar number, and address):*	FOR COURT USE ONLY

RICHARD MARTIN   SBN 54321
Attorney at Law
340 Main Street
Fullerton, CA 92634

TELEPHONE NO.: (714) 555-4321   FAX NO. *(Optional):* (714) 555-8765
E-MAIL ADDRESS *(Optional):*
ATTORNEY FOR *(Name):* SAMUEL SMITH

SUPERIOR COURT OF CALIFORNIA, COUNTY OF ORANGE
STREET ADDRESS: COUNTY OF ORANGE
MAILING ADDRESS: 341 THE CITY DRIVE
CITY AND ZIP CODE: ORANGE, CA 92868
BRANCH NAME: LAMOREAUX JUSTICE CENTER

MARRIAGE OF
PETITIONER: SALLY SMITH

RESPONDENT: SAMUEL SMITH

RESPONSE [X] and REQUEST FOR
[X] Dissolution of Marriage
[ ] Legal Separation
[ ] Nullity of Marriage   [ ] AMENDED

CASE NUMBER:

1. RESIDENCE (Dissolution only) [X] Petitioner [X] Respondent   has been a resident of this state for at least six months and of this county for at least three months immediately preceding the filing of the *Petition for Dissolution of Marriage.*

2. STATISTICAL FACTS
   a. Date of marriage: August 1, 20--
   b. Date of separation: August 5, 20--
   c. Time from date of marriage to date of separation *(specify):*
      Years: 15   Months: 0

3. DECLARATION REGARDING MINOR CHILDREN *(include children of this relationship born prior to or during the marriage or adopted during the marriage):*
   a. [ ] There are no minor children.
   b. [X] The minor children are:

Child's name	Birthdate	Age	Sex
SUSAN SMITH	August 25, 20--	--	F
PATRICK SMITH	January 2, 20--	--	M

   [ ] Continued on Attachment 3b.
   c. If there are minor children of the Petitioner and Respondent, a completed *Declaration Under Uniform Child Custody Jurisdiction and Enforcement Act (UCCJEA)* (form FL-105) must be attached.
   d. [ ] A completed voluntary declaration of paternity regarding minor children born to the Petitioner and Respondent prior to the marriage is attached.

4. SEPARATE PROPERTY
   Respondent requests that the assets and debts listed [ ] in *Property Declaration* (form FL-160) [ ] in Attachment 4
   [X] below   be confirmed as separate property.
Item	Confirm to

   All property acquired prior to the date of marriage, subsequent to the date of separation, or by gift, bequest, devise, or descent, and the rents, issues and profits therefrom, to be determined at the time of trial.

NOTICE: You may redact (black out) social security numbers from any written material filed with the court in this case other than a form used to collect child or spousal support.

Page 1 of 2

Form Adopted for Mandatory Use
Judicial Council of California
FL-120 [Rev. January 1, 2005]

RESPONSE—MARRIAGE
(Family Law)

Family Code, § 2020

FIGURE 9-6 *Petition (dissolution of marriage)—California.*

Effective January 1, 2005, domestic partners are subject to many responsibilities and rights concerning their finances and property, including laws governing community property, support, and so on. A domestic partnership may be dissolved by mutual agreement—filing a Notice of Termination of Domestic Partnership

MARRIAGE OF *(last name, first name of parties):* SMITH, SALLY and SAMUEL	CASE NUMBER:

5. DECLARATION REGARDING COMMUNITY AND QUASI-COMMUNITY ASSETS AND DEBTS AS CURRENTLY KNOWN
   a. ☐ There are no such assets or debts subject to disposition by the court in this proceeding.
   b. ☒ All such assets and debts are listed ☐ in *Property Declaration* (form FL-160) ☒ in Attachment 5b.
   ☐ below *(specify):*

6. ☐ **Respondent contends** that the parties were never legally married.
7. ☐ **Respondent denies** the grounds set forth in item 6 of the petition.
8. **Respondent requests**
   a. ☒ dissolution of the marriage based on
      (1) ☒ irreconcilable differences. (Fam. Code, § 2310(a).)
      (2) ☐ incurable insanity. (Fam. Code, § 2310(b).)
   b. ☐ legal separation of the parties based on
      (1) ☐ irreconcilable differences. (Fam. Code, § 2310(a).)
      (2) ☐ incurable insanity. (Fam. Code, § 2310(b).)
   c. ☐ nullity of void marriage based on
      (1) ☐ incestuous marriage. (Fam. Code, § 2200.)
      (2) ☐ bigamous marriage. (Fam. Code, § 2201.)
   d. ☐ nullity of voidable marriage based on
      (1) ☐ respondent's age at time of marriage.
          (Fam. Code, § 2210(a).)
      (2) ☐ prior existing marriage.
          (Fam. Code, § 2210(b).)
      (3) ☐ unsound mind. (Fam. Code, § 2210(c).)
      (4) ☐ fraud. (Fam. Code, § 2210(d).)
      (5) ☐ force. (Fam. Code, § 2210(e).)
      (6) ☐ physical incapacity. (Fam. Code, § 2210(f).)

9. **Respondent requests** that the court grant the above relief and make injunctive (including restraining) and other orders as follows:

	Petitioner	Respondent	Joint	Other
a. Legal custody of children to	☐	☐	☒	☐
b. Physical custody of children to	☐	☐	☒	☐
c. Child visitation be granted to	☐	☐	☐	☐

   As requested in form: ☐ FL-311 ☐ FL-312 ☐ FL-341(C) ☐ FL-341(D) ☐ FL-341(E) ☐ Attachment 9c.
   d. ☐ Determination of parentage of any children born to the Petitioner and Respondent prior to the marriage.

	Petitioner	Respondent
e. Attorney fees and costs payable by	☒	☐
f. Spousal support payable to (wage assignment will be issued)	☐	☒

   g. ☒ Terminate the court's jurisdiction (ability) to award spousal support to Petitioner.
   h. ☒ Property rights be determined.
   i. ☐ Respondent's former name be restored to *(specify):*
   j. ☐ Other *(specify):*

   ☐ Continued on Attachment 9j.

10. **Child support–** If there are minor children born to or adopted by the Petitioner and Respondent before or during this marriage, the court will make orders for the support of the children upon request and submission of financial forms by the requesting party. An earnings assignment may be issued without further notice. Any party required to pay support must pay interest on overdue amounts at the "legal" rate, which is currently 10 percent.

I declare under penalty of perjury under the laws of the State of California that the foregoing is true and correct.
Date:

SAMUEL SMITH
_____   ▶ _____
(TYPE OR PRINT NAME)   (SIGNATURE OF RESPONDENT)
Date:

RICHARD MARTIN
_____   ▶ _____
(TYPE OR PRINT NAME)   (SIGNATURE OF ATTORNEY FOR RESPONDENT)

The original response must be filed in the court with proof of service of a copy on Petitioner.

FL-120 [Rev. January 1, 2005]   **RESPONSE—MARRIAGE**   Page 2 of 2
                                                          (Family Law)

FIGURE 9-6 *Continued*

signed by both parties with the secretary of state under certain conditions, or by obtaining a formal Dissolution of Domestic Partnership through the courts.

California does recognize validly formed domestic partnerships or other similar legal unions, other than marriage, between members of the same sex from other jurisdictions.

The forms for filing and responding to a dissolution of domestic partnership are similar to those for a dissolution of marriage: summon (FL-110), petition (specific to dissolution of domestic partnership), UCCJEA Form (FL-105), and the response (specific to dissolution of domestic partnership).

ADOPTION

Adoption can be defined as the legal process by which a child acquires parents other than his or her natural parents, and parents acquire a child other than their own biological child. The decree of adoption terminates the legal rights and obligations that formerly existed between the child and the natural parents, and these rights and obligations are acknowledged as existing between the child and the new adoptive parents. It is important in discussing adoptions to emphasize the formation of the legal relationship between the child and the adoptive parents, but it is also important to note the termination of the legal relationship with the child's natural parents. In some states, this is a two-step process; first the parents' rights are terminated, and then the child is legally adopted.

Each state has statutes designating which court will grant adoptions. This jurisdiction may be granted to a general court, such as a superior court, or to a specialized court, such as probate, juvenile, or domestic relations. Some of the more common types of adoptions are independent, stepparent, agency, intercountry, and adult.

Independent Adoption

An **independent adoption** is one in which the child to be adopted is placed by the natural parent or parents, who consent to the adoption by specific individuals. The arrangements for the adoption are made between one or both of the natural parents and the new parents or sometimes through another party. In most states, however, an adoption agency usually becomes involved before the final decree of adoption is granted. Although the adoption agency may be public or private, it must operate within the state laws and be properly licensed by the state.

Stepparent Adoption

A **stepparent adoption** is one in which a stepparent is the petitioner, and one natural or adoptive parent retains his or her custody and control of the child. If the other natural parent is living, it is usually necessary to obtain consent to the adoption, whereby the natural parent relinquishes all rights to the child or has that relationship terminated by the courts. Stepparent adoptions are common where one of the natural parents has remarried and the partners to the marriage want to provide the child with all the rights and privileges of a natural child.

Agency Adoption

An **agency adoption** is one in which the father and/or mother has relinquished a child to a licensed adoption agency for placement. One or both of the parents must sign a form provided by the agency relinquishing the child for adoption. The agency then approves and verifies the qualifications of the prospective parents and arranges for the adoption. Before the adoption is completed, the agency makes home studies to determine if the circumstances are suitable for the care and adoption of the child. If the home conditions meet with the agency's approval, the final decree of adoption is approved.

Intercountry Adoption

Federal law makes a special immigration visa available for adoption of a foreign-born minor. **Intercountry adoption** includes the completion of the adoption in the child's native country.

Adult Adoptions

Often there are circumstances when it may be necessary to adopt someone who is no longer a minor. Most states require that the adoptive parents be at least ten years older than the adoptee. This type of adoption, called **adult adoption**, may be used when the person adopting and the person to be adopted each have attained the age of majority. The circumstances of this type of adoption may be that the person adopted may inherit from the adoptive parent or may be entitled to other financial benefits by virtue of the adopted relationship. Adult adoption also may take place when a family has taken care of a child for a number of years and, even though the child then attains the age of majority, they want to confer on this child to be adopted all the rights of a natural child.

Most states require the consent of the spouse of the adopting party in adult adoptions, unless such spouse is lawfully separated or incapable of giving consent.

ADOPTION PROCEEDINGS

An adoption proceeding is not an adversary proceeding, and the caption in the adoption papers is different from that of a litigation proceeding. Instead of indicating EDWARD RODRIGUEZ vs. EUNICE RODRIGUEZ, the caption reads, "In the Matter of the Adoption Petition of EDWARD RODRIGUEZ and EUNICE RODRIGUEZ, Adopting Parents."

The Petition for Adoption or Adoption Request   Though adoption proceedings vary somewhat from state to state, usually they are initiated by the filing of a **petition for adoption** or adoption request (Figure 9-7). This document is signed by the petitioners and verified. In a stepparent adoption, only the signature of the stepparent may be required on the petition. The petition includes the names and marital status of the parents and prays that the court approve the adoption.

Consent and Agreement Form   The parents must sign a *consent and agreement form* (Figure 9-8) stating that they agree to adopt the child and give the child every right of a natural child, including the right of inheritance. Nearly every state requires a consent form and in some cases a form listing the adoption expenses (Figure 9-10) is required. If the adoption is an agency adoption, the agency signs a *consent of agency to adoption form*. If the child is over a certain age, he or she may be required to sign a consent and agreement form. Nearly every state requires the consent of natural parents, guardians, and others as a prerequisite to adoption. The general rule is that a legitimate child only may be adopted with the consent of both parents, unless one of them has lost parental rights through abandonment or other conduct releasing the necessity of his or her consent. Some states require that consents be signed in the presence of an adoption social worker.

Decree of Adoption   The final document filed in the adoption proceeding is the decree of adoption or **certificate of adoption** (Figure 9-9). This decree is dated and signed by the judge and indicates the name by which the child shall be subsequently known. A copy of this decree is sent to the state so that the child's birth certificate may be sealed, and a new certificate is issued indicating the child's new name and the new parents as the legal parents.

ADOPT-200   Adoption Request

If you are adopting more than one child, fill out an adoption request for each child.

1   Your name(s) (adopting parent(s)):
a.   EDWARD RODRIGUEZ
b.   EUNICE RODRIGUEZ

Relationship to child: UNCLE/AUNT

Your address:

Street: _____

City: _____ State: _____ Zip: _____

Your phone #: (___) _____

Your lawyer (if you have one): (Name, address, phone #, and State Bar #):
ROBERT MORGAN   12345
320 MAIN STREET
FULLERTON, CA 92634

(714)555-1234

Clerk stamps below when form is filed.

Court name and street address:

Superior Court of California, County of
ORANGE
341 THE CITY DRIVE
ORANGE, CA 92868
LAMOREAUX JUSTICE CENTER

Case Number:
AD-12583

2   Type of adoption: (Check one)
☐ Agency (name): _____
☐ Relative
☒ Independent
☐ International (name of agency): _____
☐ Stepparent/Domestic Partner

3   Information about the child:

a.   The child's new name will be:
ELIZABETH RODRIGUEZ

b.   ☐ Boy ☒ Girl

c.   Date of birth: MAY 5, 20--   Age: --

d.   Child's address (if different from yours):
Street: _____ City: _____ State: ____ Zip: _____

e.   Place of birth (if known):
City: LOS ANGELES
State: CA   Country: USA

f.   If the child is 12 or over, does the child agree to the adoption? ☐ Yes ☐ No

4   Child's name before adoption (Fill out ONLY if this is an independent, relative, or stepparent/domestic partner adoption.): ELIZABETH SANCHEZ

5   Does the child have a legal guardian? ☐ Yes ☒ No
If yes, attach a copy of the Letters of Guardianship and fill out below:
a.   Date guardianship ordered: _____
b.   County: _____
c.   Case number: _____

6   Is the child a dependent of the court? ☐ Yes ☒ No
If yes, fill out below:
Juvenile case number: _____
County: _____

(To be completed by the clerk of the superior court if a hearing date is available.)

Hearing Date ➡ Hearing is set for:
Date: _____ Time: _____
Dept.: _____ Room: _____
Name and address of court if different from above:
_____
_____

To the person served with this request: If you do not come to this hearing, the judge can order the adoption without your input.

Judicial Council of California
Rev. January 1, 2004, Mandatory Form
Family Code, § 8714, 8714.5, 8802, 8912, 9000; Welfare &
Institutions Code, § 16119; Cal. Rules of Court, rule 1464

Adoption Request

ADOPT-200, Page 1 of 3
➡

FIGURE 9-7   *Petition for adoption.*

GUARDIANSHIP AND CONSERVATORSHIP

There are several types of **guardianships**, including the natural guardian, the child's parents. A **guardian of the person** is one who has custody of the child with the obligations of support and education. This type of guardian may have no authority to

Your name(s): <u>EDWARD RODRIGUEZ</u>
<u>EUNICE RODRIGUEZ</u>

Case Number:
AD-12583

7 Child may have Indian ancestry: ☐ Yes ☒ No
If yes, attach Form ADOPT-220, Adoption of Indian Child.

8 If this is an Agency Adoption:

a. I/We have received information about the Adoption Assistance Program, Regional Center, and mental health services available through Medi-Cal or other programs. ☐ Yes ☐ No

b. All persons with parental rights agree the child should be placed for adoption by the California Department of Social Services or a licensed adoption agency (Fam. Code, § 8700) and have signed a *Relinquishment* form approved by the California Department of Social Services except:

Name: _____ Relationship to child: _____

Name: _____ Relationship to child: _____

9 If this is an Independent Adoption:

a. A copy of the Adoptive Placement Agreement is attached. (Required in most independent adoptions; see Fam. Code, § 8802.)

b. I/We will file promptly with the department or delegated county adoption agency information required by the department in the investigation of the proposed adoption. ☒ Yes ☐ No

c. All persons with parental rights agree to the adoption and have signed the Adoptive Placement Agreement *Consent to Adoption* on a form approved by the California Department of Social Services except:

Name: _____ Relationship to child: _____

Name: _____ Relationship to child: _____

10 If this is a Stepparent/Domestic Partner Adoption:

a. The birth parent is ☐ in state ☐ out of state
(If out of state and unable to sign in the presence of the required official, the parent may sign his or her consent before a notary. (Fam. Code, § 9003 (b).))

b. Adopting parents married: _____ *(date)* OR Domestic partnership registered: _____ *(date)*.
(This does not affect the social worker's recommendation. Information is for court only. There is no waiting period.)

11 ☐ There is no presumed or biological father because the child was conceived by artificial insemination using semen provided to a medical doctor or a sperm bank. (Fam. Code, § 7613.)

12 Form ADOPT-310, *Contact after Adoption Agreement:*
☐ Is attached ☐ Will not be used ☐ Will be filed at least 30 days before the adoption hearing
☒ Undecided at this time

13 Name of birth parents if you know:
a. <u>MARGARET SANCHEZ</u> *(mother)*
b. <u>RICHARD SANCHEZ</u> *(father)*

14 ☐ The consent of the ☐ birth mother ☐ presumed father is not necessary because *(specify Fam. Code, § 8606 subdivision):* _____

Rev. January 1, 2004 | **Adoption Request** | ADOPT-200, Page 2 of 3 →

FIGURE 9-7 *Continued*

manage or possess the child's property. Another kind of guardian is the **guardian of the estate,** who is responsible for the care, management, protection, and investment of the **ward's** property. A **testamentary guardian** is one authorized by the appointment of the person or estate by will. Such guardians have the same duties as the guardians of the person or the estate.

Your name(s): <u>EDWARD RODRIGUEZ</u>
<u>EUNICE RODRIGUEZ</u>

Case Number:
AD-12583

15 A court ended the parental rights of:

Name: _____   Relationship to child: _____

Name: _____   Relationship to child: _____

16 ☐ I/We will ask the court to end the parental rights of:

Name: _____   Relationship to child: _____

Name: _____   Relationship to child: _____

17 Each of the following persons with parental rights has not contacted his or her child in one year (Fam. Code, § 8604(b)):

Name: _____   Relationship to child: _____

Name: _____   Relationship to child: _____

18 Each of the following persons with parental rights has died:

Name: _____   Relationship to child: _____

Name: _____   Relationship to child: _____

19 Suitability for Adoption:

Each adopting parent:

a. Is at least 10 years older than the child

b. Will treat the child as his or her own

c. Will support and care for the child

d. Has a suitable home for the child *and*

e. Agrees to adopt the child

20 I/We ask the court to approve the adoption and to declare that the adopting parent(s) and the child have the legal relationship of parent and child, with all the rights and duties of this relationship, including the right of inheritance.

21 If a lawyer is representing you in this case, he or she must sign here:

Date: _____   <u>ROBERT MORGAN</u>   ▶ _____
Type or print your name   *Signature of Attorney for Adopting Parent*

22 I declare under penalty of perjury under the laws of the State of California that the information in this form is true and correct to my knowledge. This means if I lie on this form, I am guilty of a crime.

Date: _____   <u>EDWARD RODRIGUEZ</u>   ▶ _____
Type or print your name   *Signature of Adopting Parent*

Date: _____   <u>EUNICE RODRIGUEZ</u>   ▶ _____
Type or print your name   *Signature of Adopting Parent*

Rev. January 1, 2004   **Adoption Request**   ADOPT-200, Page 3 of 3

FIGURE 9-7 *Continued*

A guardian *ad litem* is appointed to represent the ward in litigation because a minor or incompetent cannot enter into litigation on his or her own behalf; a guardian *ad litem* may be appointed to act for him or her. The person who wants to act on a minor's or incompetent's behalf petitions the court for an *Order for Appointment of Guardian Ad Litem*. This document serves as both a petition and an order. After the guardian *ad litem* has been appointed, the litigation proceeds as usual, with the guardian *ad litem* signing the verification and the other papers on behalf of the minor or incompetent.

ADOPT-210   Adoption Agreement

Clerk stamps below when form is filed.

1   Your name(s) (adopting parent(s)):
a.   EDWARD RODRIGUEZ
b.   EUNICE RODRIGUEZ

Relationship to child : UNCLE/AUNT

Your address *(skip this if you have a lawyer):*
Street: _____

City: _____   State: _____   Zip: _____

Your phone #: (_____) _____

Your lawyer *(if you have one): (Name, address, phone #, and State Bar #):*
ROBERT MORGAN   12345
320 MAIN STREET
FULLERTON, CA 92634

(714) 555-1234

2   Child's name:

Before adoption: ELIZABETH SANCHEZ

After adoption: ELIZABETH RODRIGUEZ

Date of birth: MAY 5, 20--   Age: --

Court name and street address:

Superior Court of California, County of
ORANGE
341 THE CITY DRIVE
ORANGE, CA 92868
LAMOREAUX JUSTICE CENTER

Case Number:

AD-12583

3   I am the child listed in **2** and I agree to the adoption.

Date: _____   _____
Type or print your name

▶ _____
Signature of Child (child must sign at hearing if 12 or older;
optional if child is under 12)

4   *If only one* **adopting parent,** *read and sign below:*

a.   I am the adopting parent listed in **1** , and I agree that the child will:

   (1)   Be adopted and treated as my legal child (Fam. Code § 8612(b)); *and*

   (2)   Have the same rights as a natural child of mine, including the right of inheritance.

Date: _____   _____
Type or print your name

▶ _____
Signature of Adopting Parent (sign at hearing)

b.   I am the spouse of the adopting parent listed in **1** , and I agree to his or her adoption of the child.

Date: _____   _____
Type or print your name

▶ _____
Signature of Spouse

Judicial Council of California
Rev. January 1, 2004, Mandatory Form
Family Code, §§ 8602-8606, 8612, 9003;
Cal. Rules of Court, rule 1464

Adoption Agreement

ADOPT-210, Page 1 of 2
→

FIGURE 9-8   *Consent and agreement.*

If there is a judgment in favor of the minor or incompetent, the guardian ad litem must indicate how the awarded funds will be managed and deposited and must petition the court for permission to withdraw the funds.

Guardianship Proceedings   Guardianship proceedings are initiated when the person or institution desiring to become the guardian of the minor files a form

Your name(s):   EDWARD RODRIGUEZ
                 EUNICE RODRIGUEZ

Case Number:
AD-12583

5   *If two adopting parents, read and sign below:*

We are the adopting parents listed in **❶** , and we agree that the child will:

(1)   Be adopted and treated as our legal child (Fam. Code, § 8612(b));

(2)   Have the same rights as a natural child of ours, including the right of inheritance;

and I agree to the other parent's adoption of the child.

Date: _____   EDWARD RODRIGUEZ _____   ▶ _____
                       Type or print your name   *Signature of Adopting Parent (sign at hearing)*

and I agree with the other parent's adoption of the child.

Date: _____   EUNICE RODRIGUEZ _____   ▶ _____
                       Type or print your name   *Signature of Adopting Parent (sign at hearing)*

6   For stepparent/domestic partner adoptions only:

If you are the legal parent of the child listed in **❷** *, read and sign below:*

I am the legal parent of the child and the spouse or domestic partner of the adopting parent listed in **❶** , and I agree to his or her adoption of my child.

Date: _____   _____   ▶ _____
                       Type or print your name   *Signature of Adopting Parent (sign at hearing)*

7   **Executed:**

Date: _____   ▶ _____
                       Judge (or Judicial Officer)
                       HON. JANE DOE

Rev. January 1, 2004   **Adoption Agreement**   ADOPT-210, Page 2 of 2

FIGURE 9-8   *Continued*

entitled **Petition for Appointment of Guardian.** The names and addresses of close relatives who may be concerned with the welfare of the minor must be included in the petition. Thus their names become a matter of record, and they must be given written notice of the guardianship proceedings.

The law office should prepare a *Notice of Hearing for Appointment of Guardian* when preparing the petition for guardianship. The petition and notice are filed with

ADOPT-215   Adoption Order

Clerk stamps below when form is filed.

1 Your name(s) (adopting parent(s)):

a.   EDWARD RODRIGUEZ

b.   EUNICE RODRIGUEZ

Relationship to child: UNCLE/AUNT

Your address *(skip this if you have a lawyer)*:

Street:

City: _____ State: _____ Zip: _____

Your phone #: (_____) _____

Your lawyer *(if you have one): (Name, address, phone #, and State Bar #)*:

ROBERT MORGAN   12345

320 MAIN STREET

FULLERTON, CA 92634

(714) 555-1234

Court name and street address:

Superior Court of California, County of
ORANGE
341 The City Drive
Orange, CA 92868
LAMOREAUX JUSTICE CENTER

Case Number:

AD-12583

2 Type of adoption: *(Check one)*

☐ Agency *(name):* _____

  ☐ Relative

☒ Independent

☐ International *(name of agency):* _____

☐ Stepparent/Domestic Partner

3 Child's name after adoption:

ELIZABETH RODRIGUEZ

Date of birth: MAY 5, 20--   Age: --

City: LOS ANGELES   State: CA   Country: USA

4 Name of adoption agency: _____

5 People present in court today *(date):* APRIL 30, 20--   in:

Dept.: L73   Div.: _____ Rm.: _____   Judge: DOE

☐ Adopting parent(s)   ☐ Lawyer for adopting parent(s)

☐ Child   ☐ Child's lawyer

☐ Parent keeping parental rights (stepparent/domestic partner): _____

☐ Other people present *(list name and relationship to child):*

  a. _____

  b. _____

If more, attach a sheet of paper, write "ADOPT-215, Item 5" at the top, and list additional name(s) and relationship(s) to child.

Judge will fill out section below.

6 The judge finds that the child: *(Check all that apply)*

a. ☐ Is 12 or older and agrees to the adoption.

b. ☐ Is under 12.

FIGURE 9-9   *Decree of adoption.*

the court. Enough copies of the notice should be made to be sent to all the persons listed on the petition. The conformed notice, along with a proof of service, should be sent to all the persons listed on the petition.

An *Order Appointing Guardian* and several copies of the letters of guardianship should be prepared for the attorney to take to the hearing. The judge signs the original

Your name(s):   EDWARD RODRIGUEZ
                 EUNICE RODRIGUEZ

Case Number:
AD-12583

7 The judge has reviewed the report and other documents and evidence and finds that each adopting parent:

a. Is at least 10 years older than the child

b. Will treat the child as his or her own

c. Will support and care for the child

d. Has a suitable home for the child *and*

e. Agrees to adopt the child.

8 ☐ This case is a relative adoption petitioned under Family Code section 8714.5.

☐ The adopting relative   ☐ The child, who is 12 or older   has requested that the child's name before adoption be listed on this order under section 8714.5(g).

The child's name before adoption was: ELIZABETH SANCHEZ

9 ☐ The child is an Indian child. The judge finds that this adoption meets the placement requirements of the Indian Child Welfare Act and that there is good cause to give preference to these adopting parents. The clerk will fill out **12** below.

10 ☐ The judge approves the *Contact After Adoption Agreement* (ADOPT-310)
         ☐ As submitted   ☐ As amended on ADOPT-310

11 The judge believes the adoption is in the child's best interest and orders this adoption.
The child's name after adoption will be: ELIZABETH RODRIGUEZ
The adopting parent(s) and the child are now parent and child under the law, with all the rights and duties of the parent-child relationship.

Date: April 30, 20--   ▶ _____

                           Judge (or Judicial Officer)
                           HON. JANE DOE

Clerk will fill out section below.

12 **Clerk's Certificate of Mailing**

For the adoption of an Indian Child, the Clerk certifies:
I am not a party to this adoption. I placed a filed copy of:

☐ ADOPT-200, *Adoption Request*

☐ ADOPT-215, *Adoption Order*

☐ ADOPT-220, *Adoption of Indian Child*

☐ ADOPT-310, *Contact After Adoption Agreement*

in a sealed envelope, marked "Confidential," and addressed to:

Chief, Division of Social Services
Bureau of Indian Affairs
1849 C Street, NW
Mail Stop 310-SIB
Washington, DC 20240

The envelope was mailed, with full postage, by U.S. mail from:

Place: _____   on *(date)*: _____

Date: _____   Clerk, by: _____, Deputy

| Rev. January 1, 2004 | **Adoption Order** | ADOPT-215, Page 2 of 2 |

FIGURE 9-9   *Continued*

order and the clerk issues the letters of guardianship. Certified copies of the letters will be made to be used by the guardian. These copies provide authorization for the guardian to act in this capacity and perform the responsibility required of this position.

When the minor reaches the age of majority, the guardianship relationship terminates. The age of majority varies from state to state, although in some states the minor is considered to have reached the age of majority if he or she is married. When

ADOPT-230	**Adoption Expenses**			

Clerk stamps below when form is filed.

If you are adopting your stepchild or your domestic partner's child, do not fill out this form.

1 Your name(s) (adopting parent(s)):
a. EDWARD RODRIGUEZ
b. EUNICE RODRIGUEZ

Relationship to child: UNCLE/AUNT

Your address *(skip this if you have a lawyer):*
Street: _____

City: _____ State: _____ Zip: _____

Court name and street address:

Superior Court of California, County of
ORANGE
341 THE CITY DRIVE
ORANGE, CA 92868
LAMOREUAX JUSTICE CENTER

Your phone #: (____) _____

Your lawyer *(if you have one): (Name, address, phone #, and State Bar #):*
ROBERT MORGAN   12345
320 MAIN STREET
FULLERTON, CA 92634

(714) 555-1234

Case Number:
AD-12583

2 Name of child after adoption:
ELIZABETH RODRIGUEZ

3 List services you obtained related to the adoption of the child listed
in **2**

Service	Name and Address of Service Provider	How Much Paid or Value of Service	Payment Date
a. Hospital	_____ _____	$ _____	_____
b. Prenatal care	_____ _____	$ _____	_____
c. Legal fees	ROBERT MORGAN 320 MAIN STREET FULLERTON, CA 92634	$ ___1,200___	01/02/20--
d. Adoption agency fee	_____ _____	$ _____	_____
e. Transportation	_____ _____	$ _____	_____
f. Adoption facilitator fees	_____ _____	$ _____	_____

Judicial Council of California
Rev. January 1, 2003, Mandatory Form
Family Code, § 8610

Adoption Expenses

ADOPT-230, Page 1 of 2
→

FIGURE 9-10 *Adoption expenses.*

the minor reaches the age of majority, a petition is prepared by the attorney terminating the guardianship relationship, although in some states the guardian is not entitled to a final discharge until one year after the ward reaches the age of majority. This discharge requires a hearing, and the minor must be given notice in writing of this hearing. The guardian is then required to present to the court a formal accounting of the minor's finances during the guardianship period. The guardian is

Your name(s):   EDWARD RODRIGUEZ
                EUNICE RODRIGUEZ

Case Number:
AD-12583

Service	Name and Address of Service Provider	How Much Paid or Value of Service	Payment Date
g. Counseling fees		$	
h. Adoption service provider	John Roe 9876 Santa Ana Boulevard Santa Ana, CA 92701	$ 1,200	02/01/20--
i. Pregnancy expenses		$	
j. Court filing fees and fingerprinting fees	Orange County Superior Court 341 The City Drive Orange, CA 92868	$ 350	02/01/20--
k. Other		$	

If you need more space, attach a sheet of paper and write "ADOPT-230, Item 3—Payment for Services" at the top.
Number of pages attached: _____

4 I declare under penalty of perjury under the laws of the State of California that I have listed all payments (or anything of value) that I have paid or agreed to pay, or that were paid on my behalf, related to the child I want to adopt. I declare under penalty of perjury under the laws of the State of California that the information in this form is true and correct, which means that if I lie on this form, I am guilty of a crime.

Date: _____   EDWARD RODRIGUEZ _____
                    Type or print your name

➤ _____
Signature of Adopting Parent

Date: _____   EUNICE RODRIGUEZ _____
                    Type or print your name

➤ _____
Signature of Adopting Parent

Rev. January 1, 2003   **Adoption Expenses**   ADOPT-230, Page 2 of 2

FIGURE 9-10   *Continued*

entitled to a fee, and the method of determining the fee is prescribed by law. When the judge signs the *Order Settling Final Account of the Guardian*, the guardianship is terminated. As soon as the guardianship is terminated, all the money in the minor's account is turned over to the minor.

Conservatorship

Basically, the procedures for appointing a **conservator** are the same as those for appointing a guardian. A conservator may be appointed upon the request of the conservatee if the conservatee realizes that he or she is no longer capable of handling his or her own business and affairs. All the relatives must be notified of the time of the hearing on the petition. The court will decide if the conservatee is making a wise decision in the appointment of the conservator and thereby protect the conservatee against fraud or undue influence.

SUMMARY

This chapter discusses some of the historical aspects of marriages and how marriage licenses are obtained. Valid, void, and voidable marriages are explained and the conditions for using prenuptial agreements are presented.

Explanations of how states vary in their divorce laws and the philosophical differences between divorce and dissolution of marriage are presented. The grounds for divorce may vary from state to state, whereas the concept of the no-fault divorce (dissolution) considers no one to be at fault. The only grounds for a dissolution of marriage are irreconcilable differences or incurable insanity. The disposition of property is important, and the definitions for community and separate property are given.

This chapter also provides a discussion on domestic partnerships and the requirements for establishing and dissolving domestic partnerships.

This chapter includes a discussion on adoption and the different types of adoptions that can be granted, such as independent, stepparent, agency, intercountry, and adult. The circumstances for appointing a guardian or conservator are described, and proceedings for these appointments are discussed.

Although the states have different laws that relate to divorce and dissolution of marriage, it is important to have an overview of these procedures.

VOCABULARY

abandonment   Act of relinquishing with no intention to reclaim.

adopt   Take by choice; accept formally; take a child as one's own.

adoption   Act of adopting.

adult adoption   The adoption of a person who is no longer a minor.

adultery   Sexual intercourse between a married person and one other than his or her spouse.

adversary proceeding   One having opposing parties. A contested action; having opposing interests.

agency adoption   When one or both of the natural parents have released the child for adoption by signing a form provided by the agency.

alimony   Term for money paid by one spouse for the support of the other after legal separation or dissolution.

annulment   The act of making void.

bigamy   The crime of contracting a marriage by one whose previous marriage is still in force.

certificate of adoption   The final legal document filed in an adoption.

child support   An allowance paid to provide for one's children.

common-law marriage   A legally recognized marriage that has not been sanctioned by the formality of a legal license.

community property   Property held jointly by a husband and wife.

complaint for divorce   The first legal paper or pleading filed in a divorce action that is an adversary action.

conservatee   An adult person, who by reason of age, illness, mental weakness, intemperance, or other cause is unable to care for him or herself or property.

conservator   A person who is legally responsible to conserve or protect one who, for reasons of age or infirmity, is unable to manage his or her own property or affairs.

desertion   To forsake, to abandon, to leave with no intention of returning.

dissolution   The term used for divorce under California law.

divorce   Legal dissolution of the marriage ties.

domestic partnership   Both persons are members of the same sex and are capable of consenting to a domestic partnership.

et uxor Latin term meaning "and wife." Abbreviation is *et ux*.

et vir A Latin term meaning "and husband."

ex parte A Latin term meaning "one side only; in the interest of one party only."

grounds for divorce The foundation, basis, or points relied on for requesting a divorce.

guardian *ad litem* A Latin term for a guardian who is appointed by the court to take charge of another person's interests during a lawsuit involving that person.

guardian of the estate A special guardian with limited powers with respect to a person's estate.

guardian of the person A special guardian with limited powers with respect to the person, but not the estate.

guardianship Legal responsibility established to protect the property of minors and others who are unable to administer their affairs.

incompatibility The inability of two people to live together in marriage; the quality or state of being incompatible.

incompetent One who is incapable of managing his or her own affairs because of insanity, feeble-mindedness, or a similar condition.

incurable insanity One of the two grounds in California for dissolution or legal separation.

independent adoption The act of placing a child with adopting parents where no adoption agency is involved.

irreconcilable differences Differences between husband and wife that are not reconcilable; one ground for dissolution or legal separation in California.

irremediable breakdown Marital relations that cannot be remedied, reestablished, or mended. A term used in California.

intercountry adoption The adoption of a foreign-born child for whom federal law makes a special immigration visa available.

judgment of dissolution The act of revoking or canceling of a contract and restoring each party to their original rights.

legal separation Court decree establishing the right of a married couple to live apart without divorce or dissolution.

letters of conservatorship Court papers designating the conservator.

letters of guardianship Court papers designating the guardian.

marital settlement agreement An agreement between the parties providing for the disposition and distribution of their community property, custody of children, payment of attorney fees and court costs, and allowance of one party to the other for support and maintenance.

no-fault divorce A situation in which both parties want the marriage dissolved and neither party is at fault for the dissolution.

nullity A proceeding to declare a marriage void from its inception. The nullity is final upon the granting of the judgment of nullity.

order to show cause (OSC) An order requiring husband or wife to appear for examination pertaining to the granting of spousal support, support and maintenance of children, attorney fees, restraining orders, and court fees.

petition The document filed to commence an action for dissolution, nullity, or legal separation in California.

petition for adoption The first legal paper filed in adoption proceedings.

Petition for Appointment of Guardian A legal paper requesting the court to appoint someone who is responsible for the general control and care of another.

petition for divorce The first legal paper or petition filed in a divorce action that is not adversary.

petitioner The party who initiates the proceeding for dissolution of marriage in California.

polygamous Involving polygamy.

polygamy The offense of having several spouses at the same time.

prenuptial agreement A signed agreement between two parties before marriage as to the conditions of that marriage.

quasi-community property Property acquired in another state by husband or wife as if it were community property; resembling community property.

residence Act or fact of residing; place where one lives.

respondent A defendant in an action under California's Family Law Act.

restraining order An order of the court preventing the one named from doing a certain thing.

separate property Property owned by a husband or wife that is not community property; property acquired by either spouse prior to marriage or by gift or inheritance after marriage or acquired after the date of separation.

spousal support Court-ordered payments to the spouse. A term used in California.

stepparent adoption The adoption of a child by a stepparent that provides the child with all the privileges and rights of a natural child.

support Court-ordered payments made by either party of a marriage for the support and maintenance of the children of that marriage.

surrogate A person who takes the place of or represents another.

temporary restraining order Sometimes included with an OSC to restrain someone from doing something (for example, to prevent one spouse from harassing the other or from removing money from bank accounts).

testamentary guardian One appointed by the deed or last will of the parents of a child.

valid marriage A marriage that can be dissolved only by death or judgment of dissolution.

void marriage A marriage that is void from the beginning and can never become a valid marriage.

voidable marriage A marriage that may be declared a nullity by a proceeding brought on voidable grounds. If a voidable marriage is not declared a nullity within a specified time, it becomes valid and can only be dissolved by a judgment of dissolution.

ward The minor in a guardianship relationship.

willfull desertion A ground for divorce having many meanings. One is persistent refusal by one spouse to have sexual intercourse when there is no physical condition necessitating such refusal.

willful neglect A grant for divorce defined as the neglect and failure of the husband with ability to provide life's necessities for the wife.

STUDENT ASSESSMENT 1

Instructions: Circle T if the statement is true or F if the statement is false.

T   F   1.   The person filing the petition in a dissolution of marriage proceeding is called the respondent.

T   F   2.   In some states, the divorce proceeding is commenced by the filing of the complaint.

T   F   3.   Most states require the parties to the marriage to obtain a license.

T   F   4.   Most states require a waiting period between the application for a marriage license and the ability to marry. The typical waiting period is about ten days.

T   F   5.   A void marriage can never become a valid marriage, whereas a voidable marriage may become a valid marriage if it is not nullified within a specified period of time.

T   F   6.   Adultery is considered to be grounds for divorce in some states.

T   F   7.   One of the grounds for divorce in some states is when one of the partners to the marriage has been convicted of a felony offense.

T   F   8.   Marital dissolution agreements are also known as property settlement and property and support agreements.

T   F   9.   In certain circumstances, a husband may be entitled to support payments from his wife if she has sufficient means to support him.

T   F   10.   While some states require that a plaintiff in a divorce proceeding be a resident of that state to meet the residency requirements, other states require that only the defendant need be a resident in order to file for a divorce.

T   F   11.   Action is commenced in a dissolution proceeding by the filing of a petition.

T   F   12.   A petition for adoption does not have to be verified.

T   F   13.   A legally adopted child acquires the same relationship with the adopting parent as that of a natural child, including the right of inheritance.

T   F   14.   The basic adoption policy is that the primary consideration is the general welfare of the child.

T   F   15.   In some states, a couple or an unmarried person may qualify as adopting parent(s).

T   F   16.   In independent adoptions, the natural parents have the privilege of selecting the adopting parents. This is not true of an agency adoption.

T   F   17.   The identity of the adopting parent is always confidential in an independent adoption.

T   F   18.   In an independent adoption, the child is not capable of being adopted until the natural parents' consent form is signed.

T   F   19.   The consent of the spouse of the adopting parent is not required in an adult adoption.

T   F   20.   An illegitimate child can be adopted without the consent of the mother, even though the mother is living.

T   F   21.   Adoption hearings are private, and the adopting parents and child must appear before the court at the hearing.

T   F   22.   A child or adult may take the family name of the adopting parents.

T   F   23.   In some states, a child over a certain age may be required to sign a form consenting to the adoption.

T   F   24.   The adoption proceeding usually is initiated by the filing of a form entitled Decree of Adoption.

T   F   25.   In guardianship proceedings, an institution may be appointed guardian of the estate and the person.

T   F   26.   Guardianship proceedings are initiated by a minor desiring to have a guardian appointed by the court.

T   F   27.   The guardianship relationship usually terminates when the minor reaches the age of majority.

T   F   28.   The final decree of adoption is signed by the judge.

T   F   29.   In adult adoptions, most states require that the adopting parent(s) be older than the adoptee.

T   F   30.   A person must be under eighteen years of age to be adopted.

STUDENT ASSESSMENT 2

Instructions: Fill in the word that best completes the statement.

1. While adoption proceedings vary from state to state, they are usually initiated by the filing of the _____.
2. The final legal paper filed in an adoption proceeding is called the_____.

List four of the six grounds given in the text for voidable marriages:

3. _____
4. _____
5. _____
6. _____
7. The practice of having several spouses at the same time is called _____.
8. A divorce (dissolution) in which the person filing does not have to prove the spouse at fault is called _____.
9. A(n) _____ marriage is created according to the requirements of the law.
10. _____ is the term used to describe the marriage between one man and one woman at one time.

STUDENT ASSESSMENT 3

Instructions: Match the most correct letter to the number.

Section I	*Section I*
_____ 1. community property	A. property acquired as a gift
_____ 2. incompetent	B. legal responsibility to protect the person or property of another
_____ 3. conservator	C. property acquired in another state
_____ 4. separate property	D. a person incapable of handling his or her own affairs
_____ 5. quasi-community	E. property acquired through a marriage
_____ 6. guardian	F. legal responsibility to manage the affairs of an adult

Section II	*Section II*
_____ 1. guardian *ad litem*	A. one side only
_____ 2. *ex parte*	B. and husband
_____ 3. *et vir*	C. guardian appointed by the court to handle the affairs of a minor
_____ 4. testamentary guardian	D. guardian appointed under the terms of a will

STUDENT ASSIGNMENTS

PROJECT 1: CREATE A PREMARITAL AGREEMENT

Create an abbreviated Premarital Agreement similar to Figure 9-1 on pages 179–180 and substitute the following information:

Parties:	Maria Gonzales
	Jesus Rodriguez
Location:	Santa Ana, CA
	Orange County
Date:	Use the current date

Save your document as **Ch9_Premarital Agreement** and print one copy for your instructor. Close your document.

PROJECT 2: CREATE A MARITAL SETTLEMENT AGREEMENT

Create an abbreviated Marital Settlement Agreement similar to Figure 9-5 on pages 189–190 and substitute the following information.

Wife:	Dee Wilson
Husband:	Robert Wilson
Date:	Use the current date
Effective Date of Agreement:	Use current date
Place of Marriage:	Los Angeles, CA
Date of Marriage:	December 1, 20—
Date of Separation:	June 10, 20—
Children:	John L. Wilson, August 14, 19—, age 20
	Kathy J. Wilson, September 20, 19—, age 24

Save your document as **Ch9_Marital Settlement Agreement** and print one copy for your instructor. Close your document.

WILLS, TRUSTS, AND PROBATE

OBJECTIVES

Upon completion of this chapter, you should be able to:

1. Describe the nature and purpose of estate planning
2. Identify the formalities and requirements for making a will
3. Discuss the various types of wills
4. Provide the basic guidelines for the preparation of a will
5. Prepare a will
6. Describe a codicil and when it is used
7. Identify the different parts of the will document
8. Discuss the difference between a will and a trust agreement
9. Compare the differences between a testamentary trust and a living (*inter vivos*) trust
10. Discuss the nature of a trust
11. List the procedures in processing a probate

ESTATE PLANNING

It is important that consideration be given to the preparation of wills or trusts before a person dies in order to enable the heirs to retain as much of that person's estate as possible. Estate planning describes the area of law that deals with the disposition of a person's property after death. Estate planning is the method of handling, disposition, and administration of an estate when a person dies. Through estate planning, a person can direct the disposal of his or her estate to heirs.

Estate planning provides the legal tools for those who have exercised the right to dispose of their property upon death, as well as those who have not. Estate planning involves many types of documents, and the most common of these is the will. A will permits a person to distribute the estate property in whatever manner desired and may even be helpful in limiting the amount of taxes that may be required to be paid after a person's death.

WILLS

Wills are documents in which individuals indicate how they would like to have their property and estate distributed after death. Many people die without making provisions for their property, and millions of dollars in personal and **real property** are unclaimed in our probate courts (also known in some states as **surrogate** or orphan's courts) because the deceased did not make a will. Though some attorneys specialize in the preparation of wills and probate proceedings only, most general practice

FIGURE 10-1 *Sample will cover.*

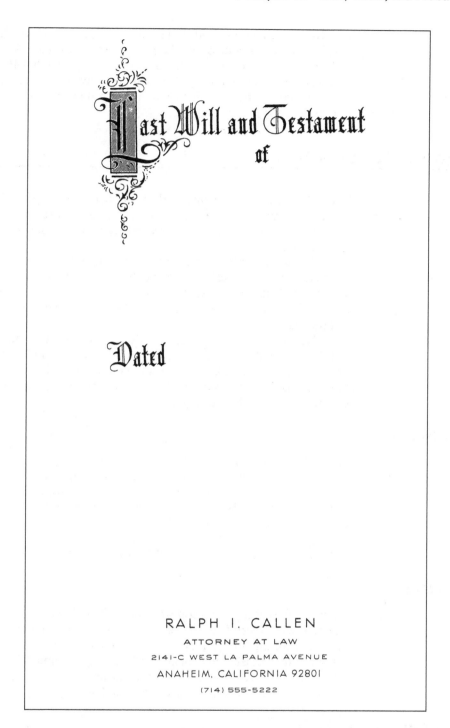

Last Will and Testament

of

Dated

RALPH I. CALLEN
ATTORNEY AT LAW
2141-C WEST LA PALMA AVENUE
ANAHEIM, CALIFORNIA 92801
(714) 555-5222

attorneys are asked to prepare wills for their clients from time to time. Properly prepared wills can prevent litigation and family arguments and provide for the manner in which the deceased would have liked to have his or her estate distributed. The *proving up* of the will—that is, probate proceedings—assures that the estate of the **decedent** is distributed as requested in the will and that the rights of the heirs are protected.

The **testator** is the individual who makes the will and sets forth the manner in which his or her property should be disposed of after death (Figure 10-1). Although the terms *will* and *testament* are synonymous, traditionally *wills* are entitled **Last Will and Testament**, but are commonly referred to as *wills*. A person who has made a will is said to have died **testate**; a person who dies without leaving a will is said to have died **intestate**. The terms *give, devise,* and **bequeath** have special significance in a will. A gift of personal property left through a will is called a **legacy,** or **bequest,** while a gift of real property is referred to as a **devise.** A **legatee,** or **beneficiary,** is the recipient of personal property, and the **devisee** is the recipient of real property.

FORMALITIES IN MAKING A WILL

The will must be in writing, either handwritten or typewritten. The original will must be submitted for probate, and it must not be torn, mutilated, or show any signs of burning, as such conditions may be accepted as evidence of the testator's intent to revoke the instrument.

The will must be signed by the testator, and if there are witnesses, it must have been signed (by the testator) in the presence of those witnesses (usually two) who sign the will in the testator's presence and in the presence of each other. If the testator is not able to write his or her name, he or she can make a mark, which can be attested to by the witnesses.

Alterations or erasures made after a will has been signed are causes for declaring the will void. It is difficult to prove whether such alterations were made before or after the signing of the will, so such methods of changing a will are discouraged. Any additions or revisions to the conditions of the will should be included in a supplementary section called a *codicil*.

Codicil

An addition made to a will for the purpose of altering or revoking it is called a **codicil.** The same formalities used in preparing the original will also must be followed in preparing a codicil. If the original will was typewritten and signed by two witnesses, the codicil must be typewritten and signed by two witnesses (although the witnesses do not necessarily have to be the same persons). If the original will is handwritten and legal in the state in which it was drafted, the codicil does not have to be witnessed if it is handwritten, dated, and signed by the testator.

Living Wills

A **living will** is really not a conventional will at all, but a document that outlines how a person with a terminal illness or a condition that requires decisions about the use of life-sustaining procedures wants to be medically treated. Provisions are now being established in most states for writing a living will and defining the treatments that qualify as artificial life support, such as the use of mechanical respirators, intravenous feeding tubes, and other forms of artificial life-support systems.

Preparing the Will

Since a will is a very important document, it is necessary that it be attractively and accurately typed. The use of word processors in legal offices can produce an error-free copy of the will. To ensure that there will be no question as to the validity of the will, each page must be numbered and the will must be worded so that each sentence ties into the next, thus preventing the insertion of a different page. Some attorneys request that the typist end each page with a hyphenated word and that the testator initial each page of the will to guard against the fraudulent insertion of pages. As extra protection against possible fraud, the signatures must not be placed on a separate page, but must immediately follow the final paragraph of the will.

Use of Aliases

To protect the testator, the attorney generally will list in the will all the names by which the testator has been known and under which he or she may currently own property. These additional names are known as **aliases** and are often introduced by the abbreviation **a.k.a.**, which means "also known as." For example, Daniel Davis might be listed as Daniel D. Davis, Daniel David Davis, Jr., or Dan Davis.

WHO CAN MAKE A WILL

Any adult can make a will, but not all persons have what is known as *testamentary capacity*. This term relates to a person's age, mental ability to comprehend the meaning of that which is written in the instrument, and intent as a testator. If the testator is without testamentary capacity, the will is void.

Persons of legal age and sound mind may generally make a valid will. Legal age varies depending on state statutes. Legal age for making a will in California and New York is eighteen, whereas legal age for making a will in Indiana is twenty-one. Some state statutes permit younger persons to make bequests of personal property while restricting them from devising any interest in real property.

Creditors

A will does not necessarily take precedence over the rights of the person to whom the testator may have had an obligation and in whose favor the law guarantees a right to the estate. Creditors and those to whom the decedent owes money may present their claims for payment against the estate before the distribution of assets.

Undue Influence

A will may be attacked or held invalid if a probate court finds that the testator made his or her will under **undue influence**. Undue influence is unfair persuasion. For example, an elderly person might be cheated by a younger relative. The court must distinguish between undue influence and the kindness, attention, advice, and friendliness shown toward the testator by the one named in the will.

Escheat

If there is no will and if there are no heirs capable of inheriting the estate, the property and estate of the decedent revert back to the state, or **escheat**.

TYPES OF WILLS

Generally, three types of wills are recognized by law: formal wills, holographic wills, and nuncupative wills. A **formal will** (Figure 10-2) is a typewritten document prepared according to statute and common law. It must be signed by the testator and witnessed. Formal wills are valid in all states. The number of witnesses necessary to sign a will varies from state to state, but most states require at least two or three witnesses.

Many states also allow the addition of a *self-proving affidavit* to a will. This affidavit states that the will was properly signed. Providing there is no objection, this affidavit avoids the necessity of bringing one or more of the witnesses before the court following the death of the testator to testify as to the signing. If a will contains a self-proving affidavit, a notary's acknowledgment will follow the will, because the affidavit is a sworn statement that must be notarized.

A **holographic will** is a handwritten will prepared by the testator and, if dated and signed, may be as binding as a formal typewritten will. Wills such as this may be

FIGURE 10-2 *Last Will and Testament.*

LAST WILL AND TESTAMENT

of

IRMA VASQUEZ

I, IRMA VASQUEZ, a resident of the City of Los Angeles, State of California, being of lawful age and sound and disposing mind and memory, and not acting under duress, menace, fraud, or the undue influence of any person whomsoever, do hereby make, publish, and declare this to be my Last Will and Testament, hereby expressly revoking any and all other Wills and Codicils heretofore made by me.

FIRST: Declaration of Family Relationship.

I hereby declare that I am married; that my husband's name is ERWIN VASQUEZ, that my husband and I have two now living children; that their names are IVAN VASQUEZ and ESTHER MENDEL, that I have no other living children; that I have one deceased child and that his name is IKE VASQUEZ, who died leaving no issue.   I further declare that I have neither adopted any children nor stood in the mutually acknowledged relationship of parent and child with any persons other than my above-named children.   Any provision herein which may inure to the benefit of my children shall not include any children hereafter adopted by me.

SECOND: Payment of Debts and Expenses.

I direct that my Executor, hereinafter named, as soon as there shall

legally binding, but they are often incomplete and need legal interpretation. Generally it is recommended that an attorney be consulted to make certain that the will is complete in every detail.

A **nuncupative will** is a will that is declared orally and not in writing. Such wills should be reduced to writing as soon as possible, for they are difficult to prove in a court of law. For example, a possible valid nuncupative will might be made by the victim of an automobile accident. Another example of a nuncupative will is when a member of the armed services injured in action wants to make arrangements for the disposition of his or her belongings. Before those present, the individual might state the names of those who are to receive his or her property upon death. This oral statement, when reduced to writing, could be presented to the court and witnessed by those hearing it.

Mention should also be made of a **reciprocal will**, or one in which a husband or wife leaves his or her entire estate to the other. These wills usually consist of a series of standardized clauses that can be adapted to the particular circumstances of the parties. With the use of a word processor, the secretary can easily customize standard paragraphs and clauses to a particular client's needs.

Wills generally proceed in a standard sequence of paragraphs, or **clauses**. The order and usage of these clauses may vary depending on the needs of the testator and

FIGURE 10-2 *Continued*

as witnesses thereto; and we further declare that at the time of the signing of this

Will the said IRMA VASQUEZ appeared to be of sound and disposing mind and

memory and not acting under duress, menace, fraud, or the undue influence of

any person whomsoever.

_____

Residing at   6445 Mountain View Avenue

Anaheim, CA 92807

_____

Residing at   2780 Braeburn Street

Placentia, CA 92670

_____

Residing at   6720 Edgemont Drive

Brea, CA 92621

the attorney's preferences. The following standard clauses may be used in the preparation of a will.

1. *Introductory clause.* The introductory clause of the will states the name of the testator and indicates that he or she is of sound mind and not acting under duress; affirms the document to be the testator's last will and testament; and revokes all wills or codicils (additions to the will) previously made.

     I, _____ , residing in the City of _____ , County of _____ , and State of _____ , being of lawful age, and of sound and disposing mind and memory, and not acting under duress, do hereby make, publish, and declare this instrument to be my Last Will and Testament; and I do hereby revoke all other wills and codicils to wills heretofore made by me.

2. *Payments of debts and funeral expenses.* Because all debts of the estate must be paid before the remaining assets can be distributed to the heirs, most wills usually include a paragraph directing that the representative pay all debts and funeral expenses of the decedent.

     FIRST: I direct that all my just debts and expenses of my last illness and funeral expenses be paid from my estate as soon after my demise as can lawfully and conveniently be done.

3. *Statement of relationships.* The next paragraph usually indicates the marital status of the testator; the name of the spouse, if married; and the names and ages of children, if any. Children are referred to as the **issue** of the marriage. If there are no children, it should be so stated in the will.

SECOND: I declare that at the time of the execution of this Will, I am married to _____ and have [children; give names and dates of birth].

4. *Nomination of representative.* One of the clauses of the will should indicate who will serve as the executor of the estate. Formerly, if such a person was male, he was known as the **executor**, and if female as the **executrix**. Presently, the term *executor* is used for either a male or female representative.

Most wills usually indicate an alternative executor in case the first person so appointed cannot serve. If the executor is a close relative and the testator has complete trust in the integrity of the executor, the testator may request that the executor serve in this capacity *without bond,* saving the estate the expense of bonding the executor. If there is a question of trust, the testator may require that the executor serve in this capacity *with bond.* If an executor is not indicated in the will, a representative for the estate will be appointed by the court. Such a representative is called the **administrator with will annexed** or administrator *cum testamento annexo* (**c.t.a.**). These terms are discussed more fully in the next section.

THIRD: I hereby nominate and appoint as Executor of my Last Will and Testament, _____ of _____, California, to serve [with or without bond]. In the event _____ cannot or will not serve, for any reason whatsoever, I then nominate and appoint as Executor of my Last Will and Testament, _____ of _____, California, to serve [with or without bond].

5. *Distribution of estate.* The purpose of a will is to dispose of the estate according to the wishes of the testator. The amounts and kinds of property the testator leaves are called bequests, or devises. This clause indicates the distribution and can be one simple statement, or in a large estate may consist of many pages.

FOURTH: I give and bequeath to _____ all the money I have on deposit at the time of my death in the _____ Bank at _____.

6. *Trust clauses.* The testator may leave money or property, or both, in trust for minor children or beneficiaries of any age. The beneficiaries do not receive the property or money held in trust at the time of the testator's death, but they may receive a portion from the investment at certain intervals.

A very popular type of trust used today is the ***inter vivos trust*** or living trust. This is a separate document from the will, is not probated, and may be referenced by the will for purposes of making a pour-over provision. This trust is established while the person granting the trust is still alive, and the grantor usually retains control of the trust during his or her lifetime. When the grantor dies, the assets of the trust become the property of the person or persons designated by the trust.

A sample trust clause might be drafted as follows:

FIFTH: I appoint _____ as Trustee of the trusts established under this, my Will, and direct that (s)he shall not be required to file a bond for the faithful performance of [his, her] duties.

7. *Guardianship clauses.* The guardianship clause is necessary for testators who are responsible for minor children or incompetent adults. It is important that a **guardian**, the person or institution responsible for the care of the children or incompetent adults or their property, be mentioned, or bitter custody battles could

ensue. It is also a good idea to indicate alternative guardians in case the guardian so indicated is unable to serve.

SIXTH: If my [husband, wife] should predecease me, I nominate and appoint _____ to be Guardian of the property on any of my minor children who shall survive me. In the event the said _____ shall predecease me, or be unable to act as such, I appoint _____ Guardian of such minor children and I direct that no bond or other undertaking shall be required of either Guardian for the performance of the duties of such office.

8. *One-dollar clause.* (Also referred to as "no contest clause.") To protect the beneficiaries from anyone who may contest the will, many wills include a *one-dollar clause.* This clause offers one dollar or states that no provision is made for a particular person who has a legal claim to any portion of the estate, but whom the testator wishes to ignore in the distribution of his or her estate.

   If the testator wishes to disinherit one of his or her own children, the testator must make mention of the child in the will. This is usually done by leaving such a child a token amount, such as one dollar. Even the one dollar is not necessary if a statement is made in the will showing that the child is being disinherited.

   SEVENTH: I have intentionally, and with full knowledge, failed to provide for any other person living at the time of my demise except as otherwise provided herein. If any person, whether a beneficiary under this Will or not, shall contest this Will or object to any of the provisions hereof, I give to such person so contesting or objecting, the sum of One Dollar ($1.00) and no more, in lieu of the provisions which I have made herein or which I might have made herein, to such person or persons so contesting or objecting.

9. *Testimonium clause.* The last clause in the will preceding the signature is called the *testimonium clause.* This clause refers to the execution of the will by the testator and the time and place when the will is signed.

   IN WITNESS WHEREOF, I have hereunto subscribed my name this _____ day of _____, at _____, California.

   _____
   (Name of Testator)

10. *Attestation clause.* Holographic wills need not be witnessed in states where they are considered legal. However, formal wills must be signed by the testator in the presence of two or three witnesses (depending on state requirements), and the witnesses must sign in the presence of the testator and each other. Although the body of the will is double spaced, **attestation clauses** may be single spaced. The signatures of the testator and the witnesses must all appear on the same page, and if there is not enough room, the body of the document may have to be ruled to ensure that all the signatures appear on the same page.

   The foregoing instrument, consisting of _____ pages, including this page, was at the date hereof, by _____ signed as and declared to be his Will, in the presence of us who, at his request and in his presence, and in the presence of each other, have subscribed our names as witnesses thereto. Each of us observed the signing of this Will by _____ and by each other subscribing witness and knows that each signature is the true signature of the person whose name was signed.

   Each of us is now more than _____ ( ) years of age and a competent witness and resides at the address set forth after his name.

We are acquainted with _____ At this time, (s)he is over the age of _____ ( ) years, and to the best of our knowledge (s)he is of sound mind and is not acting under duress, menace, fraud, misrepresentation, or undue influence.

_____
Residing at

_____

_____

_____
Residing at

_____

_____

_____
Residing at

_____

_____

11. *Self-proving affidavit (optional).* If the will includes a self-proving affidavit, it follows the witness attestation clause.

WE, _____, _____ and _____, the Testator and the witnesses, respectively, whose names are signed to the attached or foregoing instrument, having been sworn, declared to the undersigned officer that the Testator, in the presence of witnesses, signed the instrument as his Last Will and Testament, that he signed, and that each of the witnesses, in the presence of the Testator and in the presence of each other, signed the Will as a witness.

_____
(Name of Testator)

_____
Witness

_____
Witness

Subscribed and acknowledged before me by _____, the Testator, and subscribed and sworn to before me by _____ and _____ , the witnesses, on the _____ day of _____, _____, all of whom personally appeared before me and are personally known.
My Commission Expires:

_____
Notary Public

After the will is completed and formally executed, the original and one copy should be given to the client and a copy should be retained for the office files.

TRUSTS

The fundamental nature of a trust consists of the creation of a separate legal entity to hold property for the benefit of another, resulting in a legal entity called a **trust**. A trust is a legal arrangement in the form of a written contract in which a person called a **trustor**, grantor, or settlor transfers property to another person or organization, called the **trustee**, who then holds the property for the benefit of the trustor or the beneficiaries. The trustee has fiduciary responsibility to act in the beneficiary's best interest. It is also incumbent on the trustee to avoid conflicts of interest between the trustee and the beneficiary. The beneficiary of a trust is the person who receives the benefits or property of the trust. Trusts provide more flexibility than wills and are usually longer and more detailed. A person can be the trustee of a trust until death or until incapacitated.

A trust can hold any kind of real or **personal property** belonging to the trustor, such as cash, stocks, bonds, real estate, and other tangible assets. The trust can be a part of a will, or it can be created while the trustor is still alive. Trusts do not fall under the state's probate laws and therefore avoid the probate procedure. This can lower the cost of administering an estate after the death of the trustor and expedite the transfer of assets of trustor to beneficiaries.

A will disposes of a person's property after death, whereas a trust is more flexible and enables the trustor to bequeath gifts of property or money to loved ones while still living. Also, assets of an estate can be protected in a trust from lawsuits, divorces, or unforeseen circumstances. The trust arrangement places legal title to property in the hands of one person who owes a fiduciary duty to administer that property for the benefit of another. The following types of trusts are the most common.

Testamentary Trust

A **testamentary trust** does not take effect until the death of the testator. Upon the testator's death, the trust becomes effective and is handled as a typical trust situation. At this time, the assets are distributed to the trustee to be held for the beneficiaries named in the will. A trust instrument is essentially a contract and is prepared similarly to a contract document. The title is typed at the top of the page, centered, and typed in boldface. The text is typed double spaced, and the paragraphs are separated into articles.

Living Trust

A living trust, or an *inter vivos* trust (meaning "between two persons"), is established while the person establishing the trust is still alive, with the purpose of placing all the funds and property under the trustee's control during that person's lifetime. In a revocable living trust, the trustor reserves the right to change the terms of the trust at any time or may even take back the trust assets. In an irrevocable trust, the elements of the trust cannot be revoked by the trustor at any time.

Though the trustor may dictate the complexity of the agreement, the trust must be in compliance with the law. A successor trustee can be appointed to serve in the event the initial trustee becomes incapacitated, dies, or opts not to act. When the trustor dies, the property is distributed in accordance with the terms of the trust. This type of trust is useful in estate planning due to its flexibility and has been sometimes called a *will substitute*. It has more advantages than a will because it avoids the expense and delay of probate administration and allows estate tax planning.

Revocable and Irrevocable Trusts

In a **revocable living trust** (Figure 10-3), the trustor reserves the right to change the trust at any time or even take back the assets of the trust. Upon the death of the trustor, the right of revocation is terminated, and the terms of the trust become irrevocable.

In an **irrevocable trust**, the trustor cannot change the terms and conditions of the trust once the trust is signed. Irrevocable trusts are used to protect assets from waste and to save income and estate taxes. This type of trust allows life insurance proceeds and other accumulated income to be taxed at a lower rate.

FIGURE 10-3 *Revocable trust.*

**The Revocable Trust
of
ROBERT EDWARD WILSON**

THIS TRUST AGREEMENT is made between ROBERT EDWARD WILSON of Orange County, California, ("hereinafter called Trustor"), and DEE VIRGINIA WILSON, of Orange County, California, (hereinafter called "Trustee").

WITNESSETH:

That for and in consideration of the promises and the covenants set forth in this agreement, Trustor has deposited with the Trustee the property set forth on Schedule A, IN TRUST, which, together with any other property which may be received by the Trustee, shall constitute the subject matter of the Trust and be referred to as the "Trust Estate." The Trustee acknowledges the receipt of said property and agrees to hold the same, together with any other property that may be received by the Trustee, and to perform the duties of the Trustee as provided in this document.

**ARTICLE I
STATEMENT OF PURPOSE**

1.1   Purpose. Trustor has established this Trust in order to provide a means for the management of Trustor's properties deposited with the Trustee, and of such property interests as may be deposited with the Trustee in the future; to provide during the life of Trustor for his health, maintenance, and support; and to provide for Trustor's family after Trustor's death.

**ARTICLE II
NAME AND SITUS OF TRUST**

2.1   Name. This Trust shall, for the convenience of reference, be known as "THE REVOCABLE TRUST OF ROBERT EDWARD WILSON." It shall be sufficient to refer to it as such in any instrument of transfer, deed, assignment, bequest or devise.

. . .

13.2   Children Inclusive. Unless otherwise clearly indicated, the word "child" or "children" shall mean Trustor's lawful child or children. The words "issue," "lineal descendants," or "descendants" shall mean lawful blood descendants of all degrees of the individual designated, and adopted children of

---

PROBATE

Probate is the court proceeding of proving the validity of the testator's will upon death and distributing the estate with this will. If the estate is small, it may not be necessary to go through probate. Probate is not an adversary proceeding as is civil litigation, but it requires court approval and that certain legal procedures be followed for the protection of the heirs and the proper distribution of the estate.

Although probate proceedings may differ somewhat from state to state, the basic process is essentially the same throughout the United States. The qualified legal staff has a very important responsibility in probate proceedings with respect to the preparation of the court papers, conferring with the clients, and watching court deadlines. This is one area of the law in which many paralegals or legal assistants work because of the number of procedures that must be followed and the expertise required in the preparation of the court documents.

FIGURE 10-3 *Continued*

Trustor and of Trustor's issue shall be considered and treated in all respects as children or issue.

13.3 <u>Code</u>. Unless otherwise stated, all statutory references in this Trust are to Sections of the Internal Revenue Code of 1986 ("Code"), as amended, and include any corresponding provisions of the federal tax law which may, from time to time, be in effect.

13.4 <u>Headings for Reference</u>. The headings or titles preceding the text of the Articles and Sections of this instrument are inserted solely for convenience of reference and shall not affect the meaning or construction of this instrument.

IN WITNESS WHEREOF, I have set my hand and seal to this, THE REVOCABLE TRUST OF ROBERT EDWARD WILSON, consisting of pages numbered 1 through __, including this page, plus __ succeeding pages, this __ day of _____, __.

_____
TRUSTOR

ACCEPTANCE BY TRUSTEE

The undersigned accepts the Trust imposed by the foregoing THE REVOCABLE TRUST OF ROBERT EDWARD WILSON and agrees to serve as Trustee upon the terms and conditions set forth in the Trust Agreement.

IN WITNESS WHEREOF, I have set my hand and seal on this __ day of - _____, __.

_____
DEE VIRGINIA WILSON
TRUSTEE

Basically, the purposes of probate administration are as follows:

1. To ensure that the terms of the decedent's will are followed
2. To ensure that the decedent's estate is distributed only to those designated in the will
3. To collect and inventory all the assets of the estate
4. To ensure that all the legitimate debts of the decedent are paid
5. To ensure that all proper taxes are paid

The first stage of probate consists of an examination of the will by the probate court for approval. If approval of the will is granted, the court orders that the terms of the will be carried out. This provides for the second stage in the probate proceeding, which is to carry out the terms of the will and the appointment of the executor or administrator.

Executor

A person named in a will to carry out the wishes of the testator is known as an executor. (This term refers to either a male or female executor. The term *executrix* formerly referred to a female.) An executor may be the spouse, a beneficiary, an attorney, a representative of the bank, or any person serving as a **fiduciary**, or in a relationship of trust. If the estate is a large one requiring complicated tax and distribution problems, the executor may be a professionally trained person or may require the expertise of an attorney. If the will so states, an executor may serve without bond. Unless these words appear in the will, the executor must purchase a bond, the expense of which may be paid from the funds of the estate. Bonding guarantees that the executor will act honestly and in good faith in the administration of the estate.

Administrator

An **administrator** is a person appointed by the probate court to administer the estate if there is no will, or if an executor is not named in the will, or if an executor is either incapable or unwilling to serve. If there is a will, but the party named in the will cannot or will not assume this responsibility, the court will appoint an administrator to serve in this capacity. (The term *administrator* refers to either a male or a female. The term **administratrix** formerly referred to a female who administered the terms of the will.) This person then becomes known as an administrator *c.t.a.*, meaning "administrator with will annexed." The letters *c.t.a.* come from the Latin phrase *cum testamento annexo,* meaning "with will annexed."

Because the terms *executor* and *administrator* have different meanings in the execution of the probate proceedings, the term *representative* will be used here to indicate the person responsible for the management of the probate proceedings.

The attorney is responsible for providing the legal advice and fulfilling the legal requirements, and the representative deals with the practical problems that arise in the administration of the estate. The representative may be responsible for the care and maintenance of the family home or automobiles, while the attorney provides the legal advice for the sales or exchanges of the real and personal property. The legal staff is essential in the preparation of the court papers and in calendaring important deadlines.

Probate Checklist

Most legal offices follow a probate checklist in the preparation of the papers (Figure 10-4). After each step is completed, it is indicated by date. These checklists serve an important function in the law office to assure that none of the steps are overlooked and that all the deadlines are met.

Attorney's Conference

After the death of the testator, the family and the representative of the estate will meet with the attorney to discuss probate procedures and the terms of the will. Often this is a sad occasion for the family and for those close to the family, and it is important that the attorney and legal staff be sympathetic and understanding, as well as helpful, in following legal procedures and preparing the necessary documents. Certified copies of the death certificate must be obtained by the representative so that the necessary legal papers and insurance policies in the administration of the estate can be obtained. Certified copies of the death certificate can be obtained from the proper county official for a small fee. The certificate indicates the time, place, and date of death, along with the signature of the responsible physician or coroner.

After the attorney's conference, and when the attorney has been able to gather as much information as possible regarding the ownership of the assets of the estate, property involved in the estate, records, legal papers, and personal property included in the estate, the attorney's office will set up a case file for the decedent and file the petition for the probate of the estate.

PROCEDURAL STEPS FOR THE ADMINISTRATION OF PROBATE

Petition and Order Appointing Representative

The first formal step is the filing of a petition with the clerk of the respective court (Figure 10-5), usually in the county in which the **decedent** resided. This petition usually asks the court to do the following: admit the will to probate, determine if there is a will, and appoint the executor or administrator, depending on the circumstances

No.	PROBATE PROCEEDINGS			
1	Deceased		Date	
2	Petition for Probate of Will or Administration	Date of Hearing?		
3	Publication of Notice of Hearing	Date?	Date Filed	Aff. of Publication
4	Order Appointing Executor/Administrator	Date?		
	Bond?	Company?	Amount?	
5	Letters Testamentary or of Administration	Date?		
6	Notice to Creditors	Dates of Publication	to	
	Late day for Filing Claims?			
7	Creditor's Claims:		Date Filed	
	Creditor	Amount		Approved or Rejected
8	Petition for Family Allowance	Date of Hearing		
	Period?	Amount?	Date of Order?	
9	Petition for Probate Homestead	Date of Hearing?		
	Period Allowed?	Order date?		
10				
11				
12	Inventory and Appraisement	Appraiser's Name		
	Fee $	Date Filed?	Value of Estate $	
13	Inheritance Tax Releases			
14	Inheritance Tax Affidavit	Date		
	Community Property Affidavit			
15	Report of Inheritance Tax Appraiser	Tax	Amount $	
16	Federal Estate Tax $	Due	Prelim. Return Due	
17	Petition for sale of Parcel	Date of Hearing	Order Dated	
	Special Notice	Publication	Date Filed	
18	Petition for sale of Parcel	Date of Hearing		
	Special Notice	Publication	Order Dated	
19	Petition for sale of Parcel	Date of Hearing	Order Dated	
	Special Notice	Publication	Date Filed	
20				
21				
22				
23				
24	Final Account and Petition for Distribution	Date of Hearing		
25	Order Settling Final Account			
26	Receipts on Distribution			
27	Final Discharge	Date		
28				

FIGURE 10-4 *Probate proceeding form.*

DE-111

ATTORNEY OR PARTY WITHOUT ATTORNEY *(Name, state bar number, and address)*:	FOR COURT USE ONLY
ROBERT MORGAN ATTORNEY AT LAW 320 MAIN STREET FULLERTON, CA 92634 TELEPHONE NO.: (714) 555-2440 FAX NO. *(Optional)*: (714) 555-2748 E-MAIL ADDRESS *(Optional)*: ATTORNEY FOR *(Name)*: IVAN IMMORTAL	

SUPERIOR COURT OF CALIFORNIA, COUNTY OF ORANGE
STREET ADDRESS: 341 THE CITY DRIVE
MAILING ADDRESS: P. O. BOX 14169
CITY AND ZIP CODE: ORANGE, CA 92868-3209
BRANCH NAME: LAMOREAUX JUSTICE CENTER

ESTATE OF *(Name)*: IRMA IMMORTAL

                                                    DECEDENT

PETITION FOR	[X] Probate of Will and for Letters Testamentary
	[ ] Probate of Will and for Letters of Administration
	    with Will Annexed
	[ ] Letters of Administration
	[ ] Letters of Special Administration [ ] with general powers
	[X] Authorization to Administer Under the Independent
	    Administration of Estates Act [ ] with limited authority
		CASE NUMBER:
		A52731
		HEARING DATE:
		JUNE 30, 20__

		DEPT.: L72 TIME: 10:00 A.M

1. Publication will be in *(specify name of newspaper)*: ORANGE COUNTY REPORTER
   a. [X] Publication requested.   b. [ ] Publication to be arranged.

2. Petitioner *(name of each)*: IVAN IMMORTAL   **requests**
   a. [X] decedent's will and codicils, if any, be admitted to probate.
   b. [x] *(name)*: IVAN IMMORTAL
       be appointed (1) [X] executor   (3) [ ] administrator
                    (2) [ ] administrator with will annexed   (4) [ ] special administrator [ ] with general powers
       and Letters issue upon qualification.
   c. [X] that [X] full [ ] limited   authority be granted to administer under the Independent Administration of Estates Act.
   d. (1) [X] bond not be required for the reasons stated in item 4d.
      (2) [ ] $_____ bond be fixed. It will be furnished by an admitted surety insurer or as otherwise provided by law.
          (Specify reasons in Attachment 2 if the amount is different from the maximum required by Prob. Code § 8482.)
      (3) [ ] $_____ in deposits in a blocked account be allowed. Receipts will be filed. *(Specify institution and location)*:

3. a. **Estimated value of the estate for filing fee purposes** *(Complete in all cases. The estimated value of the estate is the fair market value of the real and personal property of the estate at the date of the decedent's death, without reduction for encumbrances. See Gov. Code, § 26827.)*:
    (1) [X] Less than $250,000   (6) [ ] At least $1.5 million and less than $2 million
    (2) [ ] At least $250,000 and less than $500,000   (7) [ ] At least $2 million and less than $2.5 million
    (3) [ ] At least $500,000 and less than $750,000   (8) [ ] At least $2.5 million and less than $3.5 million
    (4) [ ] At least $750,000 and less than $1 million   (9) [ ] $_____ *
    (5) [ ] At least $1 million and less than $1.5 million   * *(Specify total estimated value of estate.)*

   b. [ ] This petition is not the first petition for appointment of a personal representative with general powers filed in this proceeding. The first petition was filed on *(date)*:

4. a. Decedent died on *(date)*: 5/18/__   at *(place)*: SANTA ANA, CA (ORANGE COUNTY)
    (1) [X] a resident of the county named above.
    (2) [ ] a nonresident of California and left an estate in the county named above located at *(specify location permitting publication in the newspaper named in item 1)*:
   b. Street address, city, and county of decedent's residence at time of death *(specify)*: 165 MAIN STREET, SANTA ANA, CA 92165 (ORANGE COUNTY)

(Continued on reverse)   Page 1 of 3

Form Adopted for Mandatory Use
Judicial Council of California
DE-111 [Rev. August 17, 2003]

PETITION FOR PROBATE

Legal Solutions Plus

Probate Code, §§ 8002, 10450
Government Code, § 26827

FIGURE 10-5 *Petition for probate.*

of the case. The petition is set for hearing, and the notice of time and place of the hearing is given by mailing a copy of the notice to all the heirs, as well as the beneficiaries named in the will. Assuming that there is a will, notice also will be made either by publication in a newspaper or by posting notice at the courthouse. In most probate cases, the petition is not opposed and the judge routinely approves the petition; admits the will, if there is one; and appoints the personal representative.

ESTATE OF *(Name)*: IRMA IMMORTAL

CASE NUMBER: A52731

DECEDENT

4. c. **Character and estimated value of the property of the estate for bond purposes:**

    (1) Personal property: $ 20,000

    (2) Annual gross income from

        (a) real property: $

        (b) personal property: $

        Total: $ 20,000

    (3) Real property: $ *(If full authority under the Independent Administration of Estates Act is requested, state the fair market value of the real property less encumbrances.)*

  d. (1) [X] Will waives bond. [ ] Special administrator is the named executor and the will waives bond.

    (2) [ ] All beneficiaries are adults and have waived bond, and the will does not require a bond. *(Affix waiver as Attachment 4d(2).)*

    (3) [ ] All heirs at law are adults and have waived bond. *(Affix waiver as Attachment 4d(3).)*

    (4) [ ] Sole personal representative is a corporate fiduciary or an exempt government agency.

  e. (1) [ ] Decedent died intestate.

    (2) [X] Copy of decedent's will dated: 6/1/__ [ ] codicils dated: are affixed as Attachment 4e(2).
(Include in Attachment 4e(2) a typed copy of a handwritten will and a translation of a foreign language will.)

      [X] The will and all codicils are self-proving (Prob. Code, § 8220).

  f. **Appointment of personal representative** *(check all applicable boxes):*

    (1) Appointment of executor or administrator with will annexed:

      (a) [X] Proposed executor is named as executor in the will and consents to act.

      (b) [ ] No executor is named in the will.

      (c) [ ] Proposed personal representative is a nominee of a person entitled to Letters. *(Affix nomination as Attachment 4f(1)(c).)*

      (d) [ ] Other named executors will not act because of [ ] death [ ] declination [ ] other reasons *(specify in Attachment 4f(1)(d).)*

    (2) Appointment of administrator:

      (a) [ ] Petitioner is a person entitled to Letters. *(If necessary, explain priority in Attachment 4f(2)(a).)*

      (b) [ ] Petitioner is a nominee of a person entitled to Letters. *(Affix nomination as Attachment 4f(2)(b).)*

      (c) [ ] Petitioner is related to the decedent as *(specify):*

    (3) [ ] Appointment of special administrator requested. *(Specify grounds and requested powers in Attachment 4f(3).)*

  g. Proposed personal representative is a [X] resident of California [ ] nonresident of California *(affix statement of permanent address as Attachment 4g).* [ ] resident of the United States [ ] nonresident of the United States.

5. [X] Decedent's will does not preclude administration of this estate under the Independent Administration of Estates Act.

6. a. The decedent is survived by *(check at least one box in each of items (1)-(4)).*

    (1) [X] spouse [ ] no spouse as follows: [ ] divorced or never married [ ] spouse deceased

    (2) [ ] domestic partner [X] no domestic partner *(See Prob. Code, §§ 37(b), 6401(c), and 6402.)*

    (3) [X] child as follows: [X] natural or adopted [ ] natural adopted by a third party [ ] no child

    (4) [ ] issue of a predeceased child [X] no issue of a predeceased child

  b. Decedent [ ] is [X] is not survived by a stepchild or foster child or children who would have been adopted by decedent but for a legal barrier. *(See Prob. Code, § 6454.)*

7. *(Complete if decedent was survived by (1) a spouse or domestic partner but no issue (only a or b apply), or (2) no spouse, domestic partner, or issue. Check the **first** box that applies):*

  a. [ ] Decedent is survived by a parent or parents who are listed in item 9.

  b. [ ] Decedent is survived by issue of deceased parents, all of whom are listed in item 9.

  c. [ ] Decedent is survived by a grandparent or grandparents who are listed in item 9.

  d. [ ] Decedent is survived by issue of grandparents, all of whom are listed in item 9.

  e. [ ] Decedent is survived by issue of a predeceased spouse, all of whom are listed in item 9.

  f. [ ] Decedent is survived by next of kin, all of whom are listed in item 9.

  g. [ ] Decedent is survived by parents of a predeceased spouse or issue of those parents, if both are predeceased, all of whom are listed in item 9.

  h. [ ] Decedent is survived by no known next of kin.

DE-111 [Rev. August 17, 2003] **PETITION FOR PROBATE** Page 2 of 3

FIGURE 10-5   *Continued*

Request for Special Notice

Any person may file a Request for Special Notice and serve a copy on the executor. This means that the executor must notify such person of the time, date, and place of all the hearings of motions or petitions during the administration of the estate. The original notice must be filed before the date of hearing, together with proof of service by mail.

ESTATE OF *(Name)*: IRMA IMMORTAL	CASE NUMBER:
DECEDENT	A52731

8. *(Complete only if no spouse or issue survived decedent.)* Decedent ☐ had no predeceased spouse ☐ had a predeceased spouse who (1) ☐ died not more than 15 years before decedent owning an interest in **real property** that passed to decedent, (2) ☐ died not more than five years before decedent owning **personal property** valued at $10,000 or more that passed to decedent, (3) ☐ neither (1) nor (2) apply. *(If you checked (1) or (2), check only the **first** box that applies)*:

  a. ☐ Decedent is survived by issue of a predeceased spouse, all of whom are listed in item 9.
  b. ☐ Decedent is survived by a parent or parents of the predeceased spouse who are listed in item 9.
  c. ☐ Decedent is survived by issue of a parent of the predeceased spouse, all of whom are listed in item 9.
  d. ☐ Decedent is survived by next of kin of the decedent, all of whom are listed in item 9.
  e. ☐ Decedent is survived by next of kin of the predeceased spouse, all of whom are listed in item 9.

9. Listed below are the names, relationships, ages, and addresses, so far as known to or reasonably ascertainable by petitioner, of (1) all persons named in decedent's will and codicils, whether living or deceased; (2) all persons named or checked in items 2, 6, 7, and 8; and (3) all beneficiaries of a devisee trust in which the trustee and personal representative are the same person.

Name and Relationship	**Age**	**Address**

SEE ATTACHMENT 9

☒ Continued on Attachment 9.

10. Number of pages attached: 1

Date: JUNE 5, 20___

* (Signature of all petitioners also required. (Prob. Code, § 1020, California Rules of Court, rule 7.103).)

▶ _____
(SIGNATURE OF ATTORNEY*)
ROBERT MORGAN

I declare under penalty of perjury under the laws of the State of California that the foregoing is true and correct.

Date:

IVAN IMMORTAL
(TYPE OR PRINT NAME)

▶ _____
(SIGNATURE OF PETITIONER)

_____
(TYPE OR PRINT NAME)

▶ _____
(SIGNATURE OF PETITIONER)

DE-111 [Rev. August 17, 2003]   **PETITION FOR PROBATE**   Page 3 of 3

FIGURE 10-5 *Continued*

Proving the Will

In some states, it is necessary to have the witnesses to the will appear at the hearing to attest to the fact that they did witness the will and that it was known to them to be the last will and testament of the testator. In California, the witness may appear in person, or the attorney may present to the court a form entitled Proof of Subscribing Witness (Figure 10-6) signed by the **witness** and attesting to the fact that he or she did witness the will. If the witnesses are not available, an affidavit attesting to the authenticity of the testator's signature must be presented.

Hearing

Appointment of Federal Inheritance Tax Referee   The appointment of the inheritance tax referee usually is done as a part of the order appointing the representative. It is the referee's job to appraise certain categories of assets in the estate and also to prepare a report calculating any **inheritance tax**.

Filing the Bond and Issuance of Letters   Representatives are formally appointed once they file their bond (if required) and sign their oath of office, and the court signs the Order for Probate (Figure 10-7) and issues either the Letters Testamentary (Figure 10-8) or Letters of Administration.

ADMINISTRATION OF THE ESTATE

Publication of Notice to Creditors

Immediately following the appointment of the representative, a formal notice to creditors is published in a newspaper giving public notice that anyone claiming to be a creditor of the estate should submit a claim within the required time limit. The same legal newspaper that published the notice of the hearing of the petition for probate of will may publish the notice to creditors, and the publisher will file proof of publication.

Safe Deposit Box Inventory and Release

If the safe deposit box was not previously opened to check for a will, the attorney or relative makes arrangements with the proper public official to inventory its contents. This inventory and release usually can be accomplished within a week or two after the initial request.

Joint Tenancy

If the decedent was a joint tenant of real property, the attorney will carry out proceedings to terminate the joint tenancy of record. Transfers of joint tenancy personal property will be made to the survivor or survivors.

Community Property (California)

If part of the estate is community property, a petition to determine its community property character and to have it handled without formal probate administration may be filed and processed (depending on the terms of the will). If all the decedent's property is community property or if all of it was held in joint tenancy, no administration may be necessary at all. Property that is proved to be community property is exempt from inheritance taxes. This includes all property acquired through the efforts of either spouse during the marriage and during their residence in the state.

DE-131

ATTORNEY OR PARTY WITHOUT ATTORNEY *(Name, state bar number, and address)*:	TELEPHONE AND FAX NOS	FOR COURT USE ONLY
(714) 555-2440	(714) 555-2748	

ROBERT MORGAN
ATTORNEY AT LAW
320 MAIN STREET

FULLERTON, CA 92634

ATTORNEY FOR *(Name)*: IVAN IMMORTAL

SUPERIOR COURT OF CALIFORNIA, COUNTY OF ORANGE
STREET ADDRESS: 341 THE CITY DRIVE
MAILING ADDRESS: P. O. BOX 14169
CITY AND ZIP CODE: ORANGE, CA 92868-3209
BRANCH NAME: LAMOREAUX JUSTICE CENTER

ESTATE OF *(Name)*: IRMA IMMORTAL

DECEDENT

PROOF OF SUBSCRIBING WITNESS	CASE NUMBER: A52731

1. I am one of the attesting witnesses to the instrument of which Attachment 1 is a photographic copy. I have examined Attachment 1 and my signature is on it.
   a. [X] The name of the decedent was signed in the presence of the attesting witnesses present at the same time by
      (1) [X] the decedent personally.
      (2) [ ] another person in the decedent's presence and by the decedent's direction.
   b. [X] The decedent acknowledged in the presence of the attesting witnesses present at the same time that the decedent's name was signed by
      (1) [X] the decedent personally.
      (2) [ ] another person in the decedent's presence and by the decedent's direction.
   c. [X] The decedent acknowledged in the presence of the attesting witnesses present at the same time that the instrument signed was decedent's
      (1) [X] will.
      (2) [ ] codicil.

2. When I signed the instrument, I understood that it was decedent's   [X] will   [ ] codicil.

3. I have no knowledge of any facts indicating that the instrument, or any part of it, was procured by duress, menace, fraud, or undue influence.

I declare under penalty of perjury under the laws of the State of California that the foregoing is true and correct.

Date: JUNE 30, 20___

SALLY SLOAN
_____ (TYPE OR PRINT NAME)   ▶   _____ (SIGNATURE OF WITNESS)

6445 MOUNTAIN AVENUE
ANAHEIM, CA 92907
_____ (ADDRESS)

ATTORNEY'S CERTIFICATION
(Check local court rules for requirements for certifying copies of wills and codicils)

I am an active member of The State Bar of California. I declare under penalty of perjury under the laws of the State of California that Attachment 1 is a photographic copy of every page of the   [ ] will   [ ] codicil   presented for probate.

Date: JANUARY 15, 20___

ROBERT MORGAN
_____ (TYPE OR PRINT NAME)   ▶   _____ (SIGNATURE OF ATTORNEY)

Form Approved by the Judicial Council of California DE-131 [Rev. January 1, 1998] Mandatory Use [1/1/2000]	**PROOF OF SUBSCRIBING WITNESS** (Probate)	Legal Solutions Plus	Probate Code, § 8220

FIGURE 10-6 *Proof of Subscribing Witness.*

DE-140

ATTORNEY OR PARTY WITHOUT ATTORNEY *(Name, state bar number, and address):*   TELEPHONE AND FAX NOS.   FOR COURT USE ONLY
(714) 555-2440   (714) 555-2748

ROBERT MORGAN
ATTORNEY AT LAW
320 MAIN STREET

FULLERTON, CA 92634
ATTORNEY FOR *(Name):* IVAN IMMORTAL

SUPERIOR COURT OF CALIFORNIA, COUNTY OF ORANGE
STREET ADDRESS: 341 THE CITY DRIVE
MAILING ADDRESS: P. O. BOX 14169
CITY AND ZIP CODE: ORANGE, CA 92868-3209
BRANCH NAME: LAMOREAUX JUSTICE CENTER

ESTATE OF *(Name):* IRMA IMMORTAL

DECEDENT

ORDER FOR PROBATE
ORDER [X] **Executor**   CASE NUMBER
APPOINTING [ ] Administrator with Will Annexed
[ ] Administrator   [ ] Special Administrator   A52731
[X] Order Authorizing Independent Administration of Estate
[X] with full authority [ ] with limited authority

WARNING: THIS APPOINTMENT IS NOT EFFECTIVE UNTIL LETTERS HAVE ISSUED.

1. Date of hearing: JUNE 30, 20__   Time: 9:30 A.M   Dept./Room: L72   Judge: RICHARD O. FRAZEE, SR
THE COURT FINDS
2. a. All notices required by law have been given.
   b. Decedent died on *(date):* 5/18/__
      (1) [X] a resident of the California county named above.
      (2) [ ] a nonresident of California and left an estate in the county named above.
   c. Decedent died
      (1) [ ] intestate
      (2) [X] testate
      and decedent's will dated: 6/1/__   and each codicil dated:
      was admitted to probate by Minute Order on *(date):*
THE COURT ORDERS
3. *(Name):* IVAN IMMORTAL
   is appointed **personal representative**:
   a. [X] executor of the decedent's will   d. [ ] special administrator
   b. [ ] administrator with will annexed   (1) [ ] with general powers
   c. [ ] administrator   (2) [ ] with special powers as specified in Attachment 3d(2)
   (3) [ ] without notice of hearing
   (4) [ ] letters will expire on *(date):*
   and letters shall issue on qualification.
4. a. [X] **Full Authority** is granted to administer the estate under the Independent Administration of Estates Act.
   b. [ ] **Limited authority** is granted to administer the estate under the Independent Administration of Estates Act (there is no authority, without court supervision, to (1) sell or exchange real property or (2) grant an option to purchase real property or (3) borrow money with the loan secured by an encumbrance upon real property).
5. a. [X] Bond is not required.
   b. [ ] Bond is fixed at: $ to be furnished by an authorized surety company or as otherwise provided by law.
   c. [ ] Deposits of: $ are ordered to be placed in a blocked account at *(specify institution and location):*
      and receipts shall be filed. No withdrawals shall be made without a court order. [ ] Additional orders in Attachment 5c.
   d. [ ] The personal representative is not authorized to take possession of money or any other property without a specific court order.
6. [X] *(Name):* BRUCE HANSON   is appointed probate referee.

Date: 6/21/__

JUDGE OF THE SUPERIOR COURT

7. Number of are attached: _____   [ ] SIGNATURE FOLLOWS LAST ATTACHMENT

Form Approved by the
Judicial Council of California
DE-140 [Rev. January 1, 1998]
Mandatory Use [1/1/2000]   **ORDER FOR PROBATE**   Legal Solutions Plus   Probate Code, §§ 8006, 8400

FIGURE 10-7 *Order for Probate.*

DE-150

ATTORNEY OR PARTY WITHOUT ATTORNEY *(Name, state bar number, and address):*	TELEPHONE AND FAX NOS.: (714) 555-2440 (714) 555-2748	FOR COURT USE ONLY

ROBERT MORGAN
ATTORNEY AT LAW
320 MAIN STREET

FULLERTON, CA 92634
ATTORNEY FOR *(Name):* IVAN IMMORTAL

SUPERIOR COURT OF CALIFORNIA, COUNTY OF ORANGE
STREET ADDRESS: 341 THE CITY DRIVE
MAILING ADDRESS: P. O. BOX 14169
CITY AND ZIP CODE: ORANGE, CA 92868-3209
BRANCH NAME: LAMOREAUX JUSTICE CENTER

ESTATE OF *(Name):* IRMA IMMORTAL

DECEDENT

LETTERS

X	TESTAMENTARY		OF ADMINISTRATION
	OF ADMINISTRATION WITH WILL ANNEXED		SPECIAL ADMINISTRATION

CASE NUMBER: A52731

LETTERS	**AFFIRMATION**

1. [X] The last will of the decedent named above having been proved, the court appoints *(name):* IVAN IMMORTAL
  a. [X] executor.
  b. [ ] administrator with will annexed.
	1. [ ] PUBLIC ADMINISTRATOR: No affirmation required (Prob. Code, § 7621(c)).
	
	2. [X] INDIVIDUAL: **I solemnly affirm that I will perform the** duties of personal representative according to law.

2. [ ] The court appoints *(name):*
 	
  a. [ ] administrator of the decedent's estate.
  b. [ ] special administrator of decedent's estate
    (1) [ ] with the special powers specified in the *Order for Probate.*
    (2) [ ] with the powers of a general administrator.
    (3) [ ] letters will expire on *(date):*
	3. [ ] INSTITUTIONAL FIDUCIARY *(name):*
	
	  I solemnly affirm that the institution will perform the duties of personal representative according to law. I make this affirmation for myself as an individual and on behalf of the institution as an officer. *(Name and title):*

3. [X] The personal representative is authorized to administer the estate under the Independent Administration of Estates Act [X] **with full authority** [ ] **with limited authority** (no authority, without court supervision, to (1) sell or exchange real property or (2) grant an option to purchase real property or (3) borrow money with the loan secured by an encumbrance upon real property).	4. Executed on *(date):* JUNE 30, 20___ at *(place):* SANTA ANA , California. ▶ _____ (SIGNATURE)
4. [ ] The personal representative is not authorized to take possession of money or any other property without a specific court order.	**CERTIFICATION** I certify that this document is a correct copy of the original on file in my office and the letters issued the personal representative appointed above have not been revoked, annulled, or set aside, and are still in full force and effect.
WITNESS, clerk of the court, with seal of the court affixed.	
(SEAL) Date: JUNE 30, 20___ Clerk, by _____ (DEPUTY)	(SEAL) Date: JUNE 30, 20___ Clerk, by _____ (DEPUTY)

Form Approved by the Judicial Council of California DE-150 [Rev. January 1, 1998] Mandatory Use [1/1/2000]	**LETTERS** (Probate) Legal Solutions Plus	Probate Code, §§ 1001, 8403, 8405, 8544, 8545; Code of Civil Procedure, § 2015.6

FIGURE 10-8 *Letters Testamentary.*

Inventory and Appraisement

It is essential that an **appraisal** be made listing all the property and assets of the **estate.** The attorney should take steps to gather this information together as soon as possible. If stocks and bonds are included in the estate, the legal staff may need to refer to a copy of a newspaper from the date of death to determine the value of the decedent's securities (stocks and bonds) on that date. This value is not difficult to calculate if all the stocks and bonds are listed on stock exchanges, as their value is published daily in the newspapers. To obtain an appraisal, figure the high and low prices of the stocks on that date by averaging the *bid* and *ask* price as quoted in the newspaper. Then multiply this average price by the number of shares that the decedent held in each company. Though there are other ways of determining this value, this procedure is approved by the Internal Revenue Service and may be used on the inventory. These figures are important because they indicate the value of the gross estate and the amount of taxes that must be paid.

The inventory of all the assets must be very detailed and specific and list all the items separately. The style for typing the inventory and appraisement varies from office to office, although this information generally is typed on unruled, letter-sized bond paper.

In California, this typed, detailed inventory accompanies an official document sometimes called an **Inventory and Appraisement.** After this printed form has been prepared and values have been placed on it for those types of assets that do not require appraisement by the probate referee, the inventory is submitted to the referee. Assets that have a fixed value, such as cash, bank accounts, and certain bonds, do not have to be appraised by the referee. Only those items that have an unknown value, such as property, coin collections, antiques, and jewelry, would be appraised by the referee or a designate. After the referee appraises the items requiring appraisement, a value is placed on the total inventory and it is returned to the representative's attorney. The attorney then files it with the clerk.

Creditors' Claims

In some states, a Notice to Creditors must be published in a local newspaper of general circulation a certain number of times and for a specified time period. In other states, no official notification to creditors may be required. In New York, for example, seven months is considered to be sufficient time to present claims from creditors against the estate. The time is reduced to three months, however, if a notice to creditors is published. After proper notice of the testator's death is given to all creditors, it becomes the responsibility of the creditors to submit all claims. State laws specify the time allowed for creditors to present their claims. In California, the limit is four months. Creditors' claims must be verified and approved by the executor before they are paid.

Generally, in an uncomplicated estate, few claims are submitted, and usually those are for funeral expenses, medical expenses incurred during the decedent's last illness, utility bills, and other types of indebtedness that are not disputed. However, some claims for debts or liabilities may be disputed. These will be rejected, litigated, or compromised in due course.

Preservation and Disposition of Estate Assets

After his or her appointment, the representative should preserve and care for those assets requiring care and attention. Decisions will be made about disposition of assets that will depreciate in value or physically deteriorate or that, for some other reason, should not be held in the estate. In addition, if the cash needs of the estate for creditors—claims, funeral expenses, costs of administration, taxes, and so forth—exceed the cash available, the executor, in consultation with the attorney, will have to decide how to raise the money. This may be done by borrowing from one or more of the beneficiaries of the estate or from a third party or simply by liquidating additional estate assets (e.g., sell stock or real estate.) Petitions must be presented to the court for the authorization to make the sale, lease, or loan to confirm the action. Details for carrying out such transactions are arranged by the representative and the attorney.

Setting Aside Estate

Family Allowance and Homestead   The surviving spouse, minor children, and adult children who are incapable of earning a living and who are actually dependent in whole or in part upon the decedent for their support are entitled to a reasonable allowance from the estate. This allowance may be filed before the inventory and appraisement has been filed and must be paid in preference to certain other charges.

In addition to the family allowance, it may be necessary to set apart from the estate a homestead for the spouse and/or children.

Distribution

Inheritance Tax   When the necessary information has been obtained, certain forms must be completed for the state controller's office (in California), or other representative state agency, by the representatives. This will enable the probate referee to submit a report to the controller's office for audit and approval. The referee then submits the report to the attorney for review and approval and files it with the court.

The inheritance tax documents can be submitted to the referee at the same time that the inventory is submitted to him or her for appraisement purposes. After the inheritance tax has been fixed, payment should be made within the statutory deadline. Unless the will contains a provision that all taxes will be paid from estate funds, each individual usually pays the inheritance taxes due before receiving the bequest.

Federal Estate Tax   If the value of property subject to federal estate tax is high enough, a federal estate tax return will have to be prepared and filed. The federal estate tax is paid out of estate funds. The due date is nine months from the date of death.

The value of the estate on which federal taxes must be paid is much higher than the amount for which state inheritance taxes must be paid. The legal staff should be familiar with both state and federal tax forms and procedures. The name of the full federal return is United States Estate (and generation-skipping transfer) Tax Return. It is a booklet that includes a set of detailed schedules listing administration expenses, the net value of the estate, and the taxes payable. The Internal Revenue Service (IRS) may audit this form, and it may ask for records or documents to substantiate the items on the return. If the Internal Revenue Service accepts the form after having audited it, the IRS will send the attorney a *closing letter,* which is necessary to close the estate. The forms for filing the estate taxes may be obtained from the Internal Revenue Service or any U.S. post office or online at IRS.Gov.

Federal and State Income Taxes and Gift Taxes   Federal and state income taxes must be paid on the decedent's estate up to the time of death. Standard income tax forms must be filed for this purpose, and if the proceeding extends over a year, taxes must be paid annually.

Accounting and Distribution of the Estate   The estate is ready to be closed when the following conditions have been met:

1. The time for filing the creditors' claims has expired.
2. The inheritance tax has been fixed and paid.
3. The federal and state taxes have been fixed and paid.
4. The funeral expenses and creditors' claims have been paid.
5. All litigation or any other problem preventing the closing of the estate is completed.

If all these conditions have been met, the estate should be in good condition to close.

If all the persons to whom the estate will be distributed are adults and if they all waive any requirement for a formal accounting of the financial transactions during administration of the estate, a petition for final distribution may be filed without an accounting. Without such a waiver, an accounting is required showing the representative's cash receipts and cash disbursements, date by date and item by item.

When the court is satisfied that everything has been properly handled in the best interest of the heirs and all taxes paid, an order is signed allowing for the final distribution of the assets. The commissions of both the attorney and probate representative may be reduced by the court in some cases if a final distribution is not made within the limitations of certain statutes.

Distribution and Final Discharge   After final discharge is ordered and the order has been signed and filed with the court (see Figure 10-9), the actual distribution must be carried out. This involves the transferring of the stocks and bonds into the names of the beneficiaries and the fees and compensations being paid to the attorney and the representative. The law specifies that a certain percentage of the value of the estate must be paid to the attorney and the executor as fees for their services.

The executor may waive his or her right to a fee, which often occurs if the executor is a spouse, child, or other relative of the deceased. If there have been unusual problems in connection with the administration of the estate, the attorney or executor may petition the court for additional or **extraordinary fees.**

Application for a final discharge, which relieves the representative from any further liability and responsibility, is made after payment to the representative and the attorney and transfer of the assets to the beneficiaries and receipts for the assets have been signed by the beneficiaries and filed with the court. See Figure 10-9 for an example of a final discharge.

SUMMARY

Estate planning is an area of the law that deals with the disposition of a person's property after death. Through estate planning, an individual can direct the disposal of his or her estate to heirs, as well as maintain financial security while living.

Wills are documents in which individuals indicate how they would like to have their property and estate distributed after death. The Last Will and Testament is a very important document, and it is one of the most important documents the law office prepares. The validity of the will depends on the testamentary capacity of the testator, the expression of intent, and the execution of the document.

Generally there are three types of wills recognized by law, and they include formal, holograph, and nuncupative wills. Wills generally contain a series of standardized clauses that are customized to the individual and the circumstances.

A trust is an estate-planning tool that allows the trustor to distribute the property to the heirs without the delay and expense of probate administration. Trusts are more sophisticated than wills and are only drafted for people whose net assets require estate tax planning. The trust instrument is an expression in written form of the trustor's intentions that sets forth the specific powers of the trustee and the nature of the beneficiary's equitable interest.

Probate is the court proceeding for proving the validity of the testator's will and the distribution of the estate. The probate code for each state provides the requirements for the probate of the estate, but basically ensures that the terms of the decedent's will are followed and all the taxes are paid. A final discharge is filed with the court after all the assets have been distributed, compensations have been paid, and all the receipts have been signed and filed with the court.

1 | NAME, ADDRESS AND TELEPHONE NUMBER OF ATTORNEY(S)

2 | ROBERT MORGAN
ATTORNEY AT LAW
320 MAIN STREET

3 |

4 | FULLERTON, CA 92634
(714) 555-2440   (714) 555-2748
Attorney(s) for IVAN IMMORTAL

5 |

6 | **SUPERIOR COURT OF CALIFORNIA, COUNTY OF**   ORANGE

7 | IN THE MATTER OF THE   ESTATE OF IRMA   CASE NUMBER

8 | IMMORTAL   A52731

9 |

_____
(Deceased/Minor/Incompetent, Etc.)

10 | **DECLARATION FOR FINAL DISCHARGE**

11 | I, IVAN IMMORTAL   , say:

12 | I am the EXECUTOR   of the above entitled estate; that I have, under approval, authoriza-
(Executor/Administrator/Guardian, Etc.)

13 | tion and order of the Court, paid all sums of money due from me as such EXECUTOR
(Executor/Administrator/Guardian, Etc.)

14 | and all required receipts and vouchers for same are on file in said estate; that distribution and delivery has been made of all
the property and assets of said estate in accordance with the decree therefor made and that receipts from all the respective

15 | distributees are on file in said estate and that I have performed all acts lawfully required of me as such
EXECUTOR

16 | (Executor/Administrator/Guardian, Etc.)

17 | I declare under penalty of perjury under the laws of the State of California that the foregoing is true and correct.

18 |

19 | Executed on _____ at _____ , California.
(Date)   (Place)

20 |

21 | **ORDER OF FINAL DISCHARGE**

22 | It appearing from the aforesaid declaration that the above entitled estate has been fully administered and that a final decree
of discharge is in order.

23 |

24 | It is therefore ORDERED, ADJUDGED AND DECREED that _____
(Name)

25 | as _____ of the above entitled estate is hereby released and discharged
(Executor/Administrator/Guardian, Etc.)

26 | and that _____ and _____ sureties are discharged and released from all liability to be incurred hereafter.
(He/She)   (His/Her)

27 |

28 | Dated: FEBRUARY 10, 20_____   _____
                                                                                JUDGE OF THE SUPERIOR COURT

DECLARATION AND ORDER OF FINAL DISCHARGE   Legal Solutions Plus   LS-1328

FIGURE 10-9   *Final discharge.*

VOCABULARY

administrator   An individual or corporate entity appointed by the court to manage the estate when the deceased dies without leaving a will.

administrator with will annexed   A party appointed by the court to handle an estate when there is a will but the named executors cannot or will not serve, or when none are named in the will.

administratrix   A term formerly used to denote a female person appointed by the court to manage the estate when the deceased died without leaving a will.

a.k.a.   An abbreviation for "also known as."

alias   A name by which a person may have been known at some time, although he or she has been known by other names.

ancillary proceedings   Auxiliary proceedings, usually in another state, for the purpose of carrying out the provisions of the will or to provide authority for the disposition of real property located in such other state.

appraisal   Placing a valuation on property by persons qualified to do so.

attestation clause   The clause following the testator's signature signed by the witnesses attesting to the testator's true will and signature.

beneficiary   Recipient of a legacy or devise; a person to receive property from an estate.

bequeath   To dispose of personal property by a will.

bequest   A gift of personal property by a will.

bond   An obligation made binding by a money forfeit.

clause   Part of a written instrument or document.

codicil   An addition to a will that makes changes in it, added after the will is executed.

cum testamento annexo (c.t.a.)   A Latin phrase meaning "with will annexed or attached."

decedent   One who died.

descendant   One who is descended from another; children near or remote.

devise   To dispose of by a will; sometimes used only for real property.

devisee   One who receives real property through a will.

escheat   The reverting of property to the state when there are no legal heirs and no will.

estate   The property of a decedent; the interest that anyone has in real or personal property.

executor   Man or woman or corporate executor appointed by deceased in his or her will to carry out the terms of the will; the personal representative of the testator.

executrix   A term formerly used to denote a female person appointed by the deceased to carry out the terms of the will.

extraordinary fee   Fee charged beyond what is usual or regular.

fiduciary   A legal relationship based on trust in the integrity of an individual.

formal will   A typewritten document prepared according to statute and common law, directing the disposition of one's property after death.

guardian   One appointed to take care of the person or property of another.

hereditament   Any property that may be inherited.

holographic will   A will entirely written, dated, and signed by the testator in his or her own handwriting.

inherit   Acquire or succeed to as an heir.

inheritance   That which is inherited.

inter vivos trust   The living trust. Method by which certain assets are placed in trust during the lifetime of the decedent.

intestate   A person is said to have died intestate when he or she dies without leaving a will.

Inventory and Appraisement   A statement of all the assets of an estate with their officially determined values.

irrevocable trust   A trust that is established to protect assets and to save income and estate taxes.

issue   Lineal descendants; children.

Last Will and Testament   A document specifying the manner in which property is to be disposed of upon the owner's death.

legacy   A gift or bequest of personal property by a will.

legatee   One to whom money or personal property is bequeathed in a will.

Letters of Administration   Orders of the court, signed by the judge, authorizing the administrator to proceed with the settling of the estate.

Letters Testamentary   Similar to letters of administration, except that they name an executor instead of an administrator.

lineal heirs   Heirs who are related to the deceased in a direct ascending or descending line as children and grandchildren, parents and grandparents.

living will   A will containing direction to a physician regarding medical treatment for an individual relative to imminent death.

nuncupative will   A will declared orally and not in writing.

personal property   Everything that is subject to ownership, except real property.

per stirpes   A Latin term meaning that the children of one heir of the testator may take only the portion of the estate that the parent would have taken if living.

probate   Proving a will; all matters over which probate courts have jurisdiction.

public administrator   A public official who has prior right to administer an estate when no other qualified person seeks appointment as administrator.

real property   Land and, generally, anything attached to the land, such as buildings.

reciprocal will   A will in which a husband and wife leave their entire estate to the other.

revocable living trust   A trust that is established when the trustor is still alive, with the purpose of having all funds and property remaining under the trustor's control until death.

succession   The order in which persons have a right to acquire title to the property of one who dies intestate.

surrogate   In certain states, a judge or court having charge of the probate of wills and the administration of the estate.

testamentary trust   A trust created by a will, which usually takes effect after the death of the testator.

testate   Having made a valid will.

testator   Male or female person who makes a will.

testratrix   Formerly used to denote a female who makes a will.

trust   Property held by one person for the benefit of another.

trustee   The person who holds legal title to property for the benefit of another person.

trustor   The person who establishes the trust.

undue influence   Unfair persuasion.

will   An instrument directing the disposition of one's property after death.

witness   A person who subscribed to a will following the testator's signature.

STUDENT ASSESSMENT 1

Instructions: Circle T if the statement is true or F if the statement is false.

T   F   1. If the decedent has maintained a safe deposit box, it must be opened in the presence of a proper official.

T   F   2. Personal property would include such items as furniture, rugs (unlaid), land, and automobiles.

T   F   3. Statutes regarding the legal age of the testator vary from state to state.

T   F   4. The legal representative of a decedent who dies testate is called an executor.

T   F   5. Probate codes outline the substantive and procedural requirements of estate settlement.

T   F   6. A nuncupative will is effective only under certain circumstances.

T   F   7. A holographic will is one entirely written, dated, and signed in the handwriting of the testator.

T   F   8. A codicil is a rewriting of an original will.

T   F   9. The Latin term *cum testamento annexo* means "with will annexed."

T   F   10. Because the testator will proofread the will, careful proofreading by the legal staff is not essential.

T   F   11. Some law offices require the testator's signature or initials on all pages of the will.

T   F   12. The following is correctly punctuated: I, SALLY SMITH, do hereby. . . .

T   F   13. Only one executor may be named in a will.

T   F   14. A bond is required of all executors.

T   F   15. The "LETTERS" referred to in probate matters are printed court forms.

T   F   16. If a minor's parents are unable to care for him or his property, a conservatorship would be established.

T   F   17. An incompetent is one who is incapable of handling his or her property and managing his or her own affairs.

T   F   18. The following are spelled correctly: decedant, administrator, codicil.

T   F   19. The same formalities used in preparing the original will must be followed in preparing the codicil.

T   F   20. The names of the recently deceased person and the executor appear in the caption on legal papers in testate matters.

T   F   21. Most legal papers and court forms in probate matters are prepared by the law office.

T   F   22. A written accounting is required of the executor before the estate may be distributed, unless it is waived by the beneficiaries.

T   F   23. Some states allow minors to make devises of real property while restricting them from making bequests of personal property.

T   F   24. The executor must petition the court before transferring or selling real property.

T   F   25. Federal estate taxes are paid from estate funds and are computed on the assets of the estate.

T   F   26. The beneficiary is individually taxed by state inheritance taxes.

T   F   27. A trust is an estate planning tool allowing the trustor to distribute property for the benefit of the trustor's heirs.

T   F   28. A notice to creditors is given by writing each of the decedent's creditors and notifying them of the appointment of the executor.

(continued)

T	F	29.	Before the executor may assume his or her responsibility of carrying out the provisions of the will, he or she must obtain certified copies of Letters Testamentary.
T	F	30.	The probate proceeding is an adversary proceeding.
T	F	31.	The court clerk's office assigns a docket number to probate cases.
T	F	32.	Before the executor may be discharged of his or her duties, all the debts of the estate and the decedent must be discharged.
T	F	33.	Only certain individuals may file a Request for Special Notice in a probate proceeding.
T	F	34.	If undue influence is used on the testator, a will may be declared to be invalid.
T	F	35.	Unless the client is to be furnished copies, the minimum number of copies required of probate documents is two.
T	F	36.	The original will of the decedent is kept by the executor and a copy of the original will is filed with the court clerk's office.
T	F	37.	Real property is distributed in accordance with the provisions of the will in an intestate matter.
T	F	38.	A listing of all the assets of the decedent is called an inventory.
T	F	39.	The federal estate tax is imposed on the transfer of the entire estate and not on the share received by a particular beneficiary.
T	F	40.	It is important that a holographic will be witnessed.
T	F	41.	The terms *incompetent* and *minor* have the same meaning.
T	F	42.	A petition and an order of the court serve the same purpose.
T	F	43.	In order to close a probate proceeding, all taxes must be paid.
T	F	44.	In a probate proceeding, the inheritance tax is determined by the probate referee.
T	F	45.	All states require that an official notification to creditors be given.
T	F	46.	Forms for filing the estate tax may be obtained from the U.S. Postal Service or the Internal Revenue Service.
T	F	47.	The abbreviation a.k.a. means "also known as."
T	F	48.	A legacy is a gift of real property.
T	F	49.	In order to save attorney fees, it is a good idea to draw up a joint will.
T	F	50.	The signatures of witnesses cannot appear separately, but must immediately follow the final paragraph of the will.
T	F	51.	Formal wills are valid in all states.
T	F	52.	The last clause of the will preceding the testator's signature is called the attestation clause.
T	F	53.	Administrator c.t.a. means an administrator has been appointed by the court even though there is a will.
T	F	54.	The petition for probate is usually filed in the county in which the decedent resided.
T	F	55.	Proper names usually are typed in all caps on legal documents.

STUDENT ASSESSMENT 2

Instructions: Circle the letter that indicates the most correct answer.

1. The term that means the children of one heir may only inherit that heir's portion of the estate is called
   A. escheat
   B. *per stirpes*
   C. codici
   D. *inter vivos*
   E. none of these

2. Letters are issued to the administrator
   A. at the hearing on the first petition for probate of will
   B. at the time the petition is filed at the clerk's office
   C. at the final accounting
   D. after all taxes have been paid

(continued)

3. A will in which a husband or wife leaves an entire estate to the other is called a
   A. nuncupative will
   B. formal will
   C. testamentary will
   D. holographic will
   E. none of these
4. The term "issue of the marriage" refers to
   A. children
   B. assets
   C. taxes
   D. debts
   E. none of these
5. A person appointed by the court to serve as a representative even though the decedent left a will is called a(n)
   A. testator
   B. administrator
   C. executor
   D. administrator c.t.a.
   E. none of these

STUDENT ASSESSMENT 3

Instructions: Fill in the word that best completes the statement.

1. A(n) _____ trust does not take effect until the death of the testator.
2. A(n) _____ trust enables the trustor to change the trust at any time.
3. Preferably, there should be at least _____ witnesses to a will.
4. The right of the state to take property when there are no heirs is known as the right of _____.
5. The statement signed by the witnesses to the will is called the _____ clause.
6. An oral will is called a(n) _____ will.
7. A totally handwritten will is called a(n) _____ will.
8. _____ is a Latin term meaning "between two persons."
9. Those named in a will to receive property are called _____.
10. The term for the person who makes and signs a will is _____.

STUDENT ASSESSMENT 4

Instructions: Match the most correct letter to the number.

_____ 1. intestate
_____ 2. nuncupative
_____ 3. attestation
_____ 4. codicil
_____ 5. holographic
_____ 6. administrator
_____ 7. executor
_____ 8. devise
_____ 9. decedent
_____ 10. will

A. a person who died without leaving a will
B. legal document that disposes of property of the decedent
C. gift of real property
D. person who dies
E. person appointed by court for decedent who died intestate
F. an oral will
G. written addition that modifies existing will
H. handwritten will
I. summary at end of will stating its validity
J. person appointed by court for decedent who died testate

STUDENT ASSIGNMENTS

Note: Refer to Chapter 6 or check with your instructor for directions on how to set up these papers.

PRACTICE SET 2: PROBATE (TESTATE)

Case Particulars

Attorney:	Robert Morgan, #12345, Attorney at Law
	320 Main Street
	Fullerton, CA 92634
Telephone/Fax:	(714) 555-2440 Phone
	(714) 555-2748 Fax
Deceased:	Sally Smith
Date of Death:	April 18, _____
Petitioner/Executor:	Samuel Smith (Son)
	2876 Paseo Road
	Laguna Hills, CA 92653
Alternate:	Bill Burris
Family:	
Husband:	Steven Smith
Son:	Doug Smith (Deceased)
Daughter:	Jean Jones
	1600 Indian Road
	Piedmont, CA 94600
Son:	Samuel Smith
	2876 Paseo Road
	Laguna Hills, CA 92653
Grandchildren:	Jim, John, Jay, and Stephanie Smith
	1517 Westcliff Drive
	San Marino, CA 91108
Estate:	Consists of community and separate property

Project 1: Prepare a Will

Instructions: Find and replace. Using your word processor, open file **ch010_WL.doc** (Last Will and Testament) on your data disk. Using the find and replace feature on your word processor, replace the variables with the items listed below:

Attorney:	BILL BURRIS
Testator:	SALLY SMITH
Executor:	SAMUEL SMITH
Alternate Executor:	BILL BURRIS
Second Alternate Executor:	SECURITY NATIONAL BANK
Husband:	STEVEN SMITH
First Son:	DOUG SMITH
Second Son:	SAMUEL SMITH
Daughter:	JEAN JONES

Run a spell check and save your document as **ch10_WL**. Print one copy of Last Will and Testament for your instructor.

Project 2: Create a Template for Probate Documents and Prepare a Waiver of Notice of Hearing

Instructions: Create a template. Using your word processor, set up a template for the following Sample 10-1, p. 241. This template or wizard will be used in this project and Projects 3, 4, and 5 to save you from using repetitive keystrokes. Key in the information for the template as indicated and save your template as **ch010_TMP**. Print a copy. Retrieve your template file and create a document for Sample 10-2, p. 242. Save your document as **ch10_WAV** and print one copy for your instructor.

(continued)

Project 3: Fill in Property Description for a Judgment Settling First and Final Account in a Probate

Instructions: Append text to existing document. Retrieve file **ch010_JU** from your student data disk and fill in the personal property description on page 3 starting with ITEM NO. 2 as follows:

2. CALIFORNIA SAVINGS & LOAN ASSOCIATION,
Certificate of Deposit No. 7080, 2-year
term ending June 16, _____,
MIRACLE MILE OFFICE
5870 Wilshire Blvd.   16,208.61
Los Angeles, CA 90054

3. GREAT WESTERN LOAN ASSOCIATION
Guaranteed Rate Certificate Account
No. 6380, 2-year term ending June 13, _____,
Laguna Hills, California   16,141.22
TOTAL CASH   33,568.40
$5,000.00 of above cash is separate property
of the deceased; therefore, one-half (1/2) of
the balance of $28,568.40 is deducted as
community property interest of surviving
husband, STEVEN SMITH.   − 14,284.20
NET CASH $19,284.20

STOCKS AND BONDS:

4. 130 shares STANDARD OIL COMPANY
OF CALIFORNIA $3,786.25
Less one-half (1/2) community property
interest of STEVEN SMITH, surviving
husband   − 1,893.13
NET STOCKS AND BONDS   1,893.12

MISCELLANEOUS:

(Following is separate property of decedent)
Distributive interest in the Estate of DICK
DOUGLAS, (predeceased brother of
decedent herein),
81 South Street
New York, New York
Case No. 2843/71   30,000.00
TOTAL PROPERTY ON HAND $51,177.32

Save your document as ch10_JU, and print one copy for your instructor.

Project 4: Create Receipt for Executor's Commission

Instructions: Reuse an existing template. Retrieve the template you created as **ch010_TMP** and key in the information for Sample 10-3, Receipt for Executor's Commission.
Save your document as **ch10_EXE**, and print one copy for your instructor.

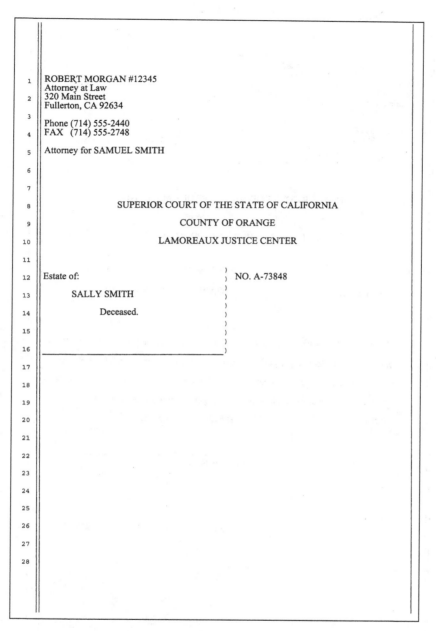

1 ROBERT MORGAN #12345
   Attorney at Law
2 320 Main Street
   Fullerton, CA 92634

3
   Phone (714) 555-2440
4 FAX   (714) 555-2748

5 Attorney for SAMUEL SMITH

6

7

8   SUPERIOR COURT OF THE STATE OF CALIFORNIA

9   COUNTY OF ORANGE

10   LAMOREAUX JUSTICE CENTER

11

12 Estate of:)   NO. A-73848
)
13   SALLY SMITH   )
)
14   Deceased.   )
)
15   )
)
16 _____   )

17

18

19

20

21

22

23

24

25

26

27

28

SAMPLE 10-1

```
 1   ROBERT MORGAN #12345
     Attorney at Law
 2   320 Main Street
     Fullerton, CA 92634
 3
     Phone (714) 555-2440
 4   FAX   (714) 555-2748

 5   Attorney for SAMUEL SMITH

 6

 7            SUPERIOR COURT OF THE STATE OF CALIFORNIA

 8                       COUNTY OF ORANGE

 9                     LAMOREAUX JUSTICE CENTER

10

11   Estate of:                    )  NO. A-73848
                                    )
12      SALLY SMITH                 )  WAIVER OF NOTICE OF HEARING
                                    )
13          Deceased.               )
                                    )
14   _____)

15        The undersigned, named as one of the alternate Executors of the Will of SALLY SMITH,

16   deceased, hereby acknowledges receipt of a copy of decedent's Will, the original of which is on

17   file with the Court, and  hereby waives Notices of the Hearing of the Petition for Probate of Will.

18        I declare, under penalty of perjury, that the foregoing is true and correct.

19   Executed on this 26ᵗʰ day of May, 20---, at Fullerton, California.

20

21                                    _____

22                                    BILL BURRIS

23

24

25

26

27

28
```

SAMPLE 10-2

```
 1 │ ROBERT MORGAN #12345
   │ Attorney at Law
 2 │ 320 Main Street
   │ Fullerton, CA 92634
 3 │
   │ Phone (714) 555-2440
 4 │ FAX  (714) 555-2748
   │
 5 │ Attorney for SAMUEL SMITH
   │
 6 │
   │
 7 │
   │
 8 │         SUPERIOR COURT OF THE STATE OF CALIFORNIA
   │
 9 │                 COUNTY OF ORANGE
   │
10 │             LAMOREAUX JUSTICE CENTER
   │
11 │
   │                                     )
12 │ Estate of:                          )   NO. A-73848
   │                                     )
13 │        SALLY SMITH                  )   RECEIPT FOR EXECUTOR'S
   │                                     )   COMMISSION
14 │           Deceased.                 )
   │                                     )
15 │                                     )
   │                                     )
16 │ _____   )
   │
17 │        SAMUEL SMITH hereby acknowledges receipt of the sum of $1,661.64 as Executor's
   │
18 │ Commission as set forth in Judgment Settling First and Final Account and Report of Executor,
   │
19 │ and Allowing Statutory Commissions and Attorney's Fees and of Final Distribution, from said
   │
20 │ SAMUEL SMITH as Executor.
   │
21 │ DATED:  January 5, 20---
   │
22 │
   │                                    _____
23 │                                    SAMUEL SMITH
   │
24 │
25 │
26 │
27 │
28 │
```

SAMPLE 10-3

11

BUSINESS ORGANIZATIONS

OBJECTIVES

Upon completion of this chapter, you should be able to:

1. Describe the elements of a sole proprietorship
2. Describe the elements of a partnership
3. Discuss the characteristics of a limited liability company and a limited liability partnership
4. Explain the differences between proprietorships, partnerships, corporations, and limited liability companies
5. Discuss the advantages and disadvantages of sole proprietorships, partnerships, and corporations
6. Discuss the characteristics of a corporation
7. List the steps involved in starting a corporation
8. Prepare basic corporate legal documents
9. Prepare a simple general partnership agreement

FORMS OF BUSINESS OWNERSHIP

The best form of ownership for an individual or group of persons depends on a number of factors, such as the type of business or service rendered, management preference, the number of owners, the method of financing, the cost of undertaking the business, the continuity of existence of the venture, and the applicable federal and state tax laws. The four basic forms for a business enterprise are:

- Sole proprietorship
- Partnership
- Corporation
- Limited liability company

Sole Proprietorships

The **sole proprietorship** is a business owned and operated by one person, or a husband and wife. It is the oldest, simplest, and least-complicated type of business organization. In this form, the owner is the business; thus, anyone who does business without creating a separate business organization has a sole proprietorship. Over two-thirds of all American businesses are sole proprietorships, which are typically small enterprises. Sole proprietors can own and manage any type of business, from an informal home office undertaking to a large restaurant or construction firm.

Some of the advantages of a sole proprietorship include the following:

- The sole proprietor receives all the profits from the business.
- The sole proprietor has full management authority and does not need to obtain permission from a partner or a board of directors.
- Fewer legal forms are required, and it is often easier and less costly to start a business.
- The sole proprietorship allows more flexibility than a partnership or corporation.
- The sole proprietor makes all the business decisions as to whom to hire, how to schedule hours, and where to locate the business.
- The sole proprietor pays personal income taxes on profits that are reported on the person's individual tax returns.
- The sole proprietor can establish tax-exempt retirement accounts.

When compared to the other business enterprises, the sole proprietorship also shares many disadvantages, which may include the following:

- Unlimited liability—the owner is solely responsible for all debts and liabilities incurred in the operation of the business and the owners personal assets may be at risk in the satisfaction of those debts. Sole proprietors are also personally liable for the torts and civil wrongs they or their employees commit in the course of doing business.
- Less expertise in business organization than a partnership or corporation.
- The proprietor's opportunity to raise capital is limited to personal funds, and the funds of those willing to make loans.
- Difficulty in selling the business because the sole proprietor is the business and the goodwill between the sole proprietor and his/her customers may not easily transfer to a new owner, particularly in business while personal services are provided and personal relationships are important and valued.

Another disadvantage of the sole proprietorship is that when the owner dies, so does the business—it is automatically dissolved. A new proprietorship is created if the business is transferred to family members or other heirs. The sole proprietorship is really an extension of the individual, who is solely responsible for all aspects of the enterprise.

Sole proprietorships are governed by state and local law. If a sole proprietor chooses to operate his or her business under a name other than his or her surname (last name), the business will be operating under what is known as an assumed, or fictitious, business name. The public has a right to know with whom they are doing business, and for that reason sole proprietors operating under a business name are generally required to file a fictitious business name statement. In most cases, this filing is done in the office of the county clerk or recorder in the county in which the sole proprietor is conducting its business. In some states fictitious names are required to be filed with the secretary of state or equivalent state agency.

When selecting a fictitious business name, the sole proprietor may not choose another name that is already in use or is confusingly similar to another business already in existence. For that reason, a name availability search of the records of the governing agency where the fictitious business name statement will be filed should be undertaken. Many counties have the fictitious business names already filed on record listed on their websites. If not, a search may be conducted at the agency's office either in person or through an attorney service. For a more thorough search in various jurisdictions, a sole proprietor may contact one of the many service companies that specialize in such name searches. These companies will check phone book listings, public records, trade associations, and the Internet. A search of the U.S. Patent and Trademark Office's website (www.uspto.gov) can also be done to locate trademarks applied for or registered for interstate business—business across state lines.

Once a business name has been chosen and determined to be available, a fictitious business name statement (Figure 11-1) is filed with the appropriate agency and then published in a newspaper of general circulation for a period of time in local rules. Most agencies have the appropriate form and filing and publishing requirements on their websites. Fictitious business name statements typically expire some time in the future. In California, they are effective for five (5) years. Other states have shorter or longer periods of effectiveness. Prior to expiration, a renewal filing must be made with the appropriate agency and possibly publication as well.

When the sole proprietor either closes the business or sells it to someone else, a Statement of Abandonment of Fictitious Business must be filed and published in the same manner as the initial statement. The new owner would then file and publish a new fictitious business name statement.

Partnerships

A **partnership** has been defined as a voluntary association of two or more persons formed to carry on as co-owners of a business for profit. The foundation of partnerships has been traditionally classified as either general or limited partnerships. These two forms of partnerships differ considerably in regard to the legal requirements.

A partnership arises out of an agreement, either oral or written, between two or more individuals to carry on a business for profit and is not an entity separate and apart from its partners. The partners are the co-owners of the business and share the control of the business and the profits derived from that business. While a partnership agreement may be oral, it is highly suggested that it be in writing (Figure 11-2) as it provides certainty in the event the partners have a dispute in the future. The partners may establish the terms of the agreement as long as the terms are not illegal or contrary to public policy. The partnership is a legal entity, and partners are liable for the payment of all the debts and obligations incurred by the partnership, as well as the payment of all taxes. This means that a partner, as an individual, becomes liable for the entire amount owed by the partnership, and not just his or her proportionate share of the debts, obligations, and taxes. In addition, each individual partner is personally responsible for the business action of all partners acting on behalf of the partnership.

General Partnership   A **general partnership** consists of a contract between two or more individuals to carry on a business for profit. The partners are the co-owners of the business and have joint control to share the operation of the business and the profits or losses. The essence of a partnership is an intention to earn a profit and share in the proceeds of the business, as well as a willingness to share the risks or losses. The partnership agreement determines the proportionate distribution of the profits or losses. Depending on the business and financial status of the individual partners, an advantage of doing business as a partnership is in the tax advantage, as opposed to that of other types of business entities. The benefits and burdens of the partnership need not be equal between the partners.

Some advantages of a partnership include the following:

- Ease of creation
- Shared responsibility

THIS FORM IS TO BE FILED
* VIA MAIL ONLY *

TOM DALY
ORANGE COUNTY CLERK-RECORDER
12 CIVIC CENTER PLAZA, ROOM 106
POST OFFICE BOX 238
SANTA ANA, CA 92702-0238

FICTITIOUS BUSINESS NAME STATEMENT <u>FILING INSTRUCTIONS</u>
To ensure a prompt and accurate record of your filing, type or print in black ink only.
DO NOT ABBREVIATE.

THE FOLLOWING PERSON(S) IS (ARE) DOING BUSINESS AS:

1.	Fictitious Business Name(s)	(optional) Business Phone No. (_____) _____
1A.	☐ New Statement ☐ Refile—List Previous No._____ ☐ Change	
2.	Street Address, City & State of Principal place of Business City State Zip Code (Do **NOT** use a P.O. Box or P.M.B.)	
3.	Full name of Registrant (If Corporation, enter corporation name)	If Corporation/L.L.C. State of Incorporation or organization
	Res./Corp. Address (Do **NOT** use a P.O. Box or P.M.B.) City State Zip Code	
	Full name of Registrant (If Corporation, enter corporation name)	If Corporation/L.L.C. State of Incorporation or organization
	Res./Corp. Address (Do **NOT** use a P.O. Box or P.M.B.) City State Zip Code	
	Full name of Registrant (If Corporation, enter corporation name)	If Corporation/L.L.C. State of Incorporation or organization
	Res./Corp. Address (Do **NOT** use a P.O. Box or P.M.B.) City State Zip Code	
4.	(CHECK ONE ONLY) This business is conducted by (○) an individual (○) a general partnership (○) a limited partnership (○) an unincorporated association other than a partnership (○) a corporation (○) a business trust (○) co-partners (○) husband and wife (○) joint venture (○) Limited Liability Co. (○) Other—Specify _____	
5.	Have you started doing business yet? Yes___ Insert the date you started: _____ No ___	**NOTICE: THIS FICTITIOUS NAME STATEMENT EXPIRES FIVE YEARS FROM THE DATE IT WAS FILED IN THE OFFICE OF THE COUNTY CLERK-RECORDER. A NEW FICTITIOUS BUSINESS NAME STATEMENT MUST BE FILED BEFORE THAT DATE. THE FILING OF THIS STATEMENT DOES NOT OF ITSELF AUTHORIZE THE USE IN THIS STATE OF A FICTITIOUS BUSINESS NAME IN VIOLATION OF THE RIGHTS OF ANOTHER UNDER FEDERAL, STATE, OR COMMON LAW (SEE SECTION 14411 ET SEQ., BUSINESS AND PROFESSIONS CODE).**
6.	If Registrant is NOT a corporation, sign below: (See instructions on the reverse side of this form.) Signature_____ _____ (Type or Print Name) I declare that all information in this statement is true and correct. (A registrant who declares as true information which he or she knows to be false is guilty of a crime.)	If Registrant is a corporation, an officer of the corporation signs below: If Registrant is a limited liability company, a manager or an officer signs below. _____ Limited Liability Company Name/Corporation Name _____ Signature and Title of Officer or Manager I declare that all information in this statement is true and correct. (A registrant who declares as true information which he or she knows to be false is guilty of a crime.) _____ Print or Type Officer's/Manager's Name and Title

(THIS FEE APPLIES AT THE TIME OF FILING)
FILING FEE $23.00 FOR ONE BUSINESS NAME.
$7.00 FOR EACH ADDITIONAL BUSINESS NAME.
$7.00 FOR EACH ADDITIONAL PARTNER AFTER FIRST TWO.
PROVIDE A SELF-ADDRESSED, STAMPED, RETURN ENVELOPE.
➡◆ F059-FictitiousBus.Stmt. (R12/02)

FIGURE 11-1 *Fictitious Business Name Statement.*

- Good tax advantages
- Fewer government regulations
- Less costly to create
- Larger capital base than sole proprietorship

FIGURE 11-2
Partnership agreement.

GENERAL PARTNERSHIP AGREEMENT

THIS PARTNERSHIP AGREEMENT ("Agreement") made and effective this _____, by and between the following individuals, referred to in this Agreement as the "Partners": _____.

The Partners wish to set forth, in a written agreement, the terms and conditions by which they will associate themselves in the Partnership.

NOW, THEREFORE, in consideration of the promises contained in this Agreement, the Partners affirm in writing their association as a partnership in accordance with the following provisions:

1. **Name and Place of Business**.
The name of the partnership shall be called _____ (the "Partnership"). Its principal place of business shall be _____, until changed by agreement of the Partners, but the Partnership may own property and transact business in any and all other places as may from time to time be agreed upon by the Partners.

2. **Purpose**.
The purpose of the Partnership shall be to _____. The Partnership may also engage in any and every other kind or type of business, whether or not pertaining to the foregoing, upon which the Partners may at any time or from time to time agree.

3. **Term**.
The Partnership shall commence as of the date of this Agreement and shall continue until terminated as provided herein.

4. **Capital Accounts**.
A. The Partners shall make an initial investment of capital, contemporaneously with the execution of this Agreement, as follows:

    Partners and Capital
    _____

In addition to each Partner's share of the profits and losses of the Partnership, as set forth in Section 5, each Partner is entitled to an interest in the assets of the Partnership.

B. The amount credited to the capital account of the Partners at any time shall be such amount as set forth in this Section 4 above, plus the Partner's share of the net profits of the Partnership and any additional capital contributions made by the Partner and minus the Partner's share of the losses of the Partnership and any distributions to or withdrawals made by the Partner. For all purposes of this Agreement, the Partnership net profits and each Partner's capital account shall be computed in accordance with generally accepted accounting principles, consistently applied, and each Partner's capital account, as reflected on the Partnership federal income tax return as of the end of any year, shall be deemed conclusively correct for all purposes, unless an objection in writing is made by any Partner and delivered to the accountant or accounting firm preparing the income tax return within one (1) year after the same has been filed with the Internal Revenue Service. If an
. . .

Some individuals find the partnership a very attractive form of business enterprise, while others may find it undesirable. Some disadvantages of a partnership include the following:

- Unlimited personal liability
- Possible lack of business continuity
- Possible dissolution upon the death of a partner
- Lack of agreement between partners

General partnerships are governed by state and local law. As discussed earlier, there are few formalities associated with the formation of a general partnership and generally no state filings are required, although in some cases state filing is required. A review of the applicable state statutes should be undertaken to ensure the appropriate formalities are followed.

There are, however, a few formalities to attend to in forming a general partnership. If all of the partners' surnames are included in the name of the partnership, it is not considered a fictitious name. For example, if Susan Brown, James Hillman,

FIGURE 11-2 *Continued*

11. **Procedure on Dissolution of Partnership**.
Except as provided in Section 10.B.(3) above, this Partnership may be dissolved only by a unanimous agreement of the Partners. Upon dissolution, the Partners shall proceed with reasonable promptness to liquidate the Partnership business and assets and wind-up its business by selling all of the Partnership assets, paying all Partnership liabilities, and by distributing the balance, if any, to the Partners in accordance with their capital accounts, as computed after reflecting all losses or gains from such liquidation in accordance with each Partner's share of the net profits and losses as determined under Section 5.

12. **Title to Partnership Property**.
If for purposes of confidentiality, title to Partnership property is taken in the name of a nominee or of any individual Partner, the assets shall be considered to be owned by the Partnership and all beneficial interests shall accrue to the Partners in the percentages set forth in this Agreement.

13. **Leases**.
All leases of Partnership assets shall be in writing and on forms approved by all the Partners.

14. **Controlling Law**.
This Agreement and the rights of the Partners under this Agreement shall be governed by the laws of the State of _____.

15. **Notices**.
Any written notice required by this Agreement shall be sufficient if sent to the Partner or other party to be served by registered or certified mail, return receipt requested, addressed to the Partner or other party at the last known home or office address, in which event the date of the notice shall be the date of deposit in the United States mails, postage prepaid.

16. **General**.
This Agreement contains the entire agreement of the Partners with respect to the Partnership and may be amended only by the written agreement executed and delivered by all of the Partners.

17. **Binding Upon Heirs**.
This Agreement shall bind each of the Partners and shall inure to the benefit of (subject to the Sections 9 and 10) and be binding upon their respective heirs, executors, administrators, devisees, legatees, successors and assigns.

IN WITNESS WHEREOF, the Partners have executed this Agreement the date first above written.

_____

_____

and Joseph Smith operate a partnership under the name Brown, Hillman, and Smith, they would not be considered to be doing business under a fictitious name. However, if only two of the partners' names were included in the partnership name (e.g., Brown and Hillman) or if a word such as "Associates" or "Company" is used in the name (e.g., Brown, Hillman, Smith, and Associates), this would signify to the public the possibility that other partners exist, and the partnership would be considered to be operating under a fictitious name, requiring the filing of a fictitious business name statement.

The filing of a fictitious business name statement for a general partnership is very much like that of a sole proprietorship, including searching the appropriate records to determine name availability. The fictitious business name statement shown in Figure 11-1 is the same statement used for partnerships. Once again, you would file the statement with the appropriate agency and then publish it in a newspaper of general circulation.

If partners withdraw from the partnership or new partners are admitted, a new fictitious business name statement will need to be filed to provide the public with current information. Once again, you would file the statement with the appropriate agency and then publish it in a newspaper of general circulation.

When the partnership either closes the business or sells it to a new group of people, a Statement of Abandonment of Fictitious Business must be filed and published in the same manner as the initial statement. The new owners would then file and publish a new fictitious business name statement.

Limited Partnership   A limited partnership is a form of partnership that requires at least one general partner and one limited partner. The *general partner* manages the business and assumes all liability for all partnership debts. A *limited partner* has no management role and no right to participate in the operation of the business, but has contributed capital and shares in the profits of the business. Limited partners face no liability beyond their monetary contributions to the business.

A major advantage of becoming a limited partner is the limitation on liability with respect to lawsuits brought against the partnership and the amount of money placed at risk.

Unlike sole proprietorships and general partnerships, limited partnerships are formed in compliance with state law. Most of the laws governing limited partnerships come from the Uniform Limited Partnership Act approved in 1916 and the Revised Uniform Limited Partnership Act, approved in the mid-1970s and further amended in 1985.

To form a limited partnership, the general partner would cause a Certificate of Limited Partnership to be prepared and filed with the Secretary of State of the state in which the partnership will operate its business. Some states utilize preprinted forms and provide them on their websites; others do not and it is necessary to draft the certificate from scratch. Prior to this filing, however, the desired name of the limited partnership would need to be checked for availability with the appropriate Secretary of State.

As with general partnerships, a limited partnership agreement may be either oral or written; however, it is suggested that an attorney be used to draft a limited partnership agreement that conforms to state statutes. In addition, the limited partners investing their money in the partnership will want a detailed agreement, particularly because they will not be engaging in the day-to-day running of the business and will want to know that their financial interests are being properly managed.

If the name of the limited partnership changes or one or more of its general partners change, an amendment to the certificate of limited partnership must be filed with the Secretary of State. When the partnership closes its business, the partnership must file appropriate dissolution documentation with the Secretary of State. Again, many states will have the requisite forms on their websites. If not, the attorney for the partnership will draft them as necessary.

THE CORPORATE ORGANIZATION

A **corporation** is a legal entity, existing in accordance with the laws of the state where formed. A corporation may be likened to a person, but it is separate from its incorporators, **officers, directors, stockholders,** or employees. It may sue and be sued in its own name, may make contracts, may acquire and dispose of personal and real property, and may do all the other things that a natural person may do if engaged in the same type of business. It is different from business organizations such as sole proprietorships or partnerships, but also shares some of their advantages and disadvantages.

There are three essential aspects to a corporation:

1. *Creation by the state.* A corporation is created by the state in which it is organized, in contrast to a general partnership, which comes into existence as the result of a contract.
2. *Legal entity.* A corporation is an entity separate and distinct from its incorporators, stockholders, officers, directors, or employees. The corporate assets belong to the corporation and not to the stockholders, just as the debts and

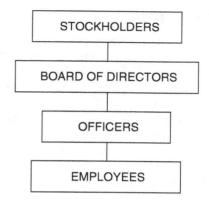

liabilities are not the obligation of the stockholders but the responsibility of the corporation.

3. *Perpetual life.* One distinct advantage of a corporation is its perpetual life or continuous existence. The corporation continues regardless of the death of the officers, directors, stockholders, or employees. The only way a corporation ceases to exist is through its dissolution, either voluntarily or involuntarily.

The group of persons interested in forming a corporation is known as its incorporators. They outline the type of business in which the corporation will engage and other information that the attorney will need in preparing the legal papers. The state in which the corporation is organized is called the *state of incorporation.* The corporation operates in that state as a **domestic corporation.** In all other states, it is referred to as a **foreign corporation,** even though it may qualify to do business in those states. Corporations organized outside the United States are referred to as **alien corporations.** Even though the executive offices of a corporation may be located in a particular state, the corporation has not necessarily been incorporated under the laws of that state. If the corporation is very small and all the stock in that corporation is held by a small group of closely knit people or by the members of one family, it is called a **close corporation.** The close corporation may have a single shareholder, or a closely knit group of shareholders, who hold the positions of directors and officers. As a corporation, however, the firm must still meet specific requirements.

In general, a corporation may do the same things that an individual may do, such as

1. Appoint necessary officers and agents
2. Enter into contracts
3. Acquire and dispose of property
4. Borrow and pledge corporate assets as security
5. Sue and be sued

Stockholders

Because a corporation is a "legal being" created by law, it can act only through its directors and officers, who are appointed or designated by the stockholders, and **board of directors,** respectively. Through their voting rights, stockholders participate in the management of the corporation. Stockholders who are not able to attend stockholders' meetings may give someone else the authority for voting. Such written authority is called a **proxy.**

Board of Directors

Even though an individual may own stock in the corporation, he or she may not bind the corporation in contracts. The corporation is governed by the board of directors. The directors are elected by the shareholders and operate as a board and not as individuals. They are the supreme authority of the corporation, and they set and determine policy as well as fix and direct the operations. The directors also have the responsibility for selecting, electing, and supervising officers: determining the salaries of the officers; and declaring dividend payments. Directors are called on to make many decisions that cannot be delegated to anyone else.

Corporate Officers

The officers of the corporation are chosen by the board of directors and provide the management of the corporation. The officers typically include a president, vice-president, secretary, and treasurer. A corporation may have other officers, and generally two or more of the officers may be the same person unless provided otherwise by the articles or bylaws or by state statute. In general, the powers of the officers are conferred on them by the bylaws.

President   The president may or may not be the chairperson of the board of directors. If so, the president is the chief executive officer of the corporation. If not, the president is second in command, with the chairperson of the board being the controlling person. The president's powers depend on the structure of the corporation, but the president usually has charge of the corporation's business and presides over the meetings of the corporation.

Vice-President   The vice-president serves as a substitute for the president when circumstances require. In some corporations, the vice-president may serve as a department head.

Secretary   The secretary is responsible for the minutes of the meetings and maintains the records of the corporation.

Treasurer   The treasurer is responsible for keeping the finances and the books of the corporation. In California, this position is often referred to as *chief financial officer.*

ADVANTAGES OF A CORPORATION

The principal advantages of a corporation as contrasted with other business organizations are as follows:

- *Limitation of liability.* As a general rule, the stockholders of a corporation are not personally liable for the debts of the corporation. The financial liability of stockholders in a corporation is limited to their investment in the corporation. In most cases, creditors may not go beyond the corporation's own assets in enforcing payment of valid debts of the corporation.
- *Perpetual life.* The corporation form of business has perpetual life. A corporation can outlive those who form it. The death or disability of one or more of the owners does not jeopardize its existence. Thus the employees, owners, and creditors are assured a certain degree of security.
- *Financial flexibility.* The pooling of the financial strength invested in the business by the stockholders permits financial ventures that would otherwise be impossible.

Corporations may grow and expand through the sale of additional shares of stock to new and present shareholders in the company.

- *Transfer of ownership.* As a general rule, the ability of stockholders to sell all or part of their interest in the company through the sale of their stock is a definite advantage. This procedure may be transacted without disturbing the operation of the company or affecting its corporate organization.

- *Tax advantages.* The owners of a small, closely held corporation may find current federal income tax laws less burdensome than the taxes that are applicable to a partnership.

- *Immunity from liability of corporate acts.* Stockholders are not agents of the corporation or of each other; therefore, a stockholder ordinarily is not criminally or civilly liable for the acts of the corporation or its directors, officers, employees, or agents.

DISADVANTAGES OF A CORPORATION

The disadvantages of a corporation, as contrasted with other business organizations, are as follows:

- *Expense of organization.* Compared with other forms of business organizations, a corporation is probably the most expensive type to organize. In addition to the initial attorney's fees, the corporation usually must pay incorporation taxes, filing fees, permits, and organizational expenses.

- *Government regulation.* Because of the federal and state laws governing corporations, they are subject to close scrutiny in all their financial planning. This is not as true in a partnership or sole proprietorship.

- *Division of profits.* The profits of a corporation are divided among the stockholders, who may number into the hundreds of thousands. Partners or individual proprietors personally receive all the profits from their enterprise and efforts.

- *Taxation.* Though a corporation may be treated more favorably than other forms of business organizations, the minimum federal corporate income tax rate is higher than the minimum personal income tax rate applicable to owners of other types of business organizations. In addition, corporations must pay state income or franchise taxes as well as special business taxes that other businesses may not be required to pay.

LAWS GOVERNING CORPORATIONS

State laws govern corporations conducting business within that state. Such laws govern names used by corporations, content of articles of incorporation, issuance of stock, and other matters pertaining to functions of a corporate entity.

In addition to state laws, federal laws also govern the operation of corporations, especially if the stock of the corporation is listed on a stock exchange or if its shares of stock are publicly held or widely sold. The **Securities and Exchange Commission (SEC)** is one government agency that is very important to all corporations. This governing body is responsible for the operation of all publicly held corporations.

TYPES OF CORPORATIONS

Corporations may be classified as public, private, and quasi-public; stock and non-stock; and domestic, foreign, and alien. A corporation may fall into one or more of these classifications:

- *Federal or state corporations* are formed for the purpose of governing cities, towns, or villages and are referred to as municipal corporations or sometimes public corporations, although this term can be confused with a corporation whose stock is sold to the public on stock markets such as NYSE or NASDAQ.
- *Private corporations* are formed by persons for their own purposes and may be either nonstock or stock corporations. Examples of private stock corporations formed for business purposes and operated for profit include the Newport Construction Company, Balboa Savings and Loan, Barr Jewelers, and similar businesses.
- *Quasi-public corporations* are formed by private persons for the purpose of carrying on some form of public service. An electric company, gas company, or public transportation company are examples.
- *Nonstock corporations* do not operate for profit and have no capital stock. A charitable corporation is sometimes called an **eleemosynary** corporation. Examples of this type of corporation would be an incorporated hospital, an orphans' home, or a college formed for charitable, educational, religious, or social purposes. The following are private nonstock corporations: Salvation Army, Fullerton Community Hospital, and Children's Home Society.
- *Stock corporations* are formed for business purposes; they operate for profit and issue capital stock. A construction company, a bank, and a manufacturing firm operating under these conditions are all examples of stock corporations.

A *de jure* corporation is a corporation that has received its state charter after having satisfied every requirement for the formation of a corporation under the laws of the state. It is organized and operates in complete compliance with these laws.

A *de facto* corporation is an organization that operates as a corporation but has failed to comply with one or more minor requirements of the state law governing the organization of a corporation in that state. Such a corporation may operate in the same manner as a *de jure* corporation with regard to making contracts, suing and being sued, and buying and selling. The state alone may question its status as a corporation.

FORMATION OF A CORPORATION

Incorporation procedures are governed by the laws of each state. Though minor variations may exist from state to state, the general outlines for incorporation procedures are similar throughout the United States.

Incorporators

When one or more persons decide that they would like to engage in some form of business and that a corporation would be the best business organization to serve their needs, they will probably consult an attorney and initiate the necessary proceedings for forming a corporation. These persons are the incorporators, or organizers. Once the corporation is formed, they may remain with the corporation as officers, directors, or stockholders, or they may have nothing more to do with the corporation. The formation of each corporation is different and depends on the needs of the corporation and those who serve as the initial incorporators.

Reserving a Corporate Name

Most states prohibit a newly organized corporation from selecting and using a corporate name that is identical to or confusingly similar to or that of an existing corporation, so as to avoid confusion on the part of the general public. Therefore, the incorporators should select several names in advance, listing them in order of preference, and contact the secretary of state or other public official requesting that a check be made as to the availability of these names.

This contact can be done by one of many ways, depending on the state. Some states offer prepaid telephone accounts where information is available immediately. Other states have similar services via their websites. In the alternative, you can use a local attorney service or one of the many corporation service companies that provide filing services.

Finally, you can send your request via mail with the requisete filling fee; however, depending on the volume of mail received by the secretary of state, this could be a time-consuming process. Certain words such as *bank*, *trust*, and *trustee* may not be used as part of the corporate name unless a certificate of approval by the superintendent of banks is obtained and attached to the articles of incorporation.

After the secretary of state has advised the incorporators as to which of their chosen names are available for corporate use, they may reserve a name from those available if they will not be immediately forming the corporation. This will ensure that no one else uses the name in the meantime. The laws of most states allow a specified period of time for the reservation of corporate names. This allows the organizers time to draw up their articles of incorporation or charter and include the name that has been reserved in their formal application for incorporation.

Articles of Incorporation

After the name has been reserved, the incorporators will want to prepare the **articles of incorporation**, **charter**, or *certificate of incorporation* (see Figure 11-3). These names are all used to refer to the basic legal document under which the corporation will operate. The statutes of the state of incorporation dictate what the name of the document will be. When this document is approved by the secretary of state or other public official, it enables the corporation to operate as a legal entity within the state.

The powers, rights, and privileges of a corporation are contained in the articles of incorporation. Any acts of a corporation that go beyond the authority given it by the state are called ***ultra vires*** acts. If a corporation performs an *ultra vires* act, it may be possible to "pierce the corporate veil" and go beyond the power of the corporation and sue the stockholders personally. Similarly, if corporate formalities are not followed (such as annual meetings) or the finances of the corporation are comingled with those of the owners (the stock holders), it may also be possible to "pierce the corporate veil," and the corporation is not protected as a legal entity.

The contents of the articles of incorporation usually include the name of the corporation as well as the articles of incorporation. This document may be prepared through the use of fill-in forms, or it may be completely dictated by the attorney.

The procedure for preparing the articles of incorporation is as follows:

1. The legal support staff types the original and makes the necessary number of copies of the articles of incorporation.
2. The incorporators sign the articles of incorporation. Some states require that these be signed before a notary.
3. The articles are submitted to the secretary of state for filing, with a request that the copies be certified and returned. Depending on the state, filing the articles of incorporation can be done by the following methods: fax, in person, through an

FIGURE 11-3 *Articles of Incorporation.*

ARTICLES OF INCORPORATION

OF

SOUTH COAST CONSTRUCTION COMPANY, INC.

I

The name of this corporation is SOUTH COAST CONSTRUCTION COMPANY, INC.

II

The purpose of this corporation is to engage in any lawful act or activity for which a corporation may be organized under the General Corporation Law of California other than the banking business, trust company business, or the practice of a profession permitted to be incorporated by the California Corporations Code.

III

The name and address in the State of California of this corporation's initial agent for the service of process is:

JIM POWERS
278 North Euclid
Fullerton, CA 92634

IV

The corporation is authorized to issue only one class of shares of stock; and the total number of shares for which this corporation is authorized to issue is 6,000.

DATED: August 1, ----

_____
JIM POWERS

---

attorney or corporation service company at mail, which will, of course, take extra time to process (sometimes months depending on the state).

4. Filing normally includes the submission of the original and required number of copies for certification. *Certification* means that someone with the proper authority compares the original with the copies and confirms them to be the same. Some states require that a copy of the articles be recorded and filed in the county in which the corporation has its principal office. A few states also require that the corporation must file and record certified copies of the articles in all counties in which the corporation does business or owns real estate.

5. A remittance covering the filing and certification fee, franchise tax, and organization tax is usually required by the office of the secretary of state when the articles of incorporation are filed.

6. When the corporation has been approved and the certified copies have been returned to the attorney's office, all copies must be conformed. In some states, such as New York, the certified copies of the charter are not adequate notice of the official state approval of the corporation.

Corporation Kit

When the official notification has been received from the state, the corporate records must be set up and a corporation kit ordered from a legal stationery supplier. The kit usually includes an embosser with the corporate seal on it, a three-ring loose-leaf binder typically called a "minute book" to contain the charter, bylaws, minutes of stockholder and director meetings and other corporate records, a stock certificate book, and a stock transfer ledger.

The supplier needs to know the exact name of the corporation, the state and year of incorporation and the number and par value (if any) of the shares authorized in the charter, as this information will appear on the corporate seal and/or stock certificates.

Bylaws

The **bylaws** of the corporation are the basic rules and regulations governing operation of the company (see Figure 11-4 for an example). The bylaws are usually rather specific, while the articles (Figure 11-3) are broad and general. To amend the bylaws is a much more simple procedure than to amend the articles of incorporation, which requires a filing with the secretary of state.

Generally the bylaws are prepared by the attorney, although printed forms are available in which the blanks can be filled in. After the bylaws are adopted at the first meeting, a copy is inserted in the corporation minute book.

The bylaws generally include the following information:

1. The location of the principal office of the corporation
2. The functions, duties, and responsibilities of the directors of the corporation; the rules governing the number of directors, election of directors, **quorum** for meetings, regulations for special and regular meetings; and the rules governing the transactions of the board of directors

FIGURE 11-4   *Bylaws.*

BYLAWS

OF

SOUTH COAST CONSTRUCTION COMPANY, INC.

(A California Corporation)

ARTICLE I

SHAREHOLDERS' MEETINGS

Section 1.   TIME.   An annual meeting for the election of directors and for the transaction of any other proper business and any special meeting shall be held on the date and at the time as the Board of Directors shall from time to time fix.

Time of Meeting: 2:00 P.M.   Date of Meeting: The 1st day of June of each year.

Section 2.   PLACE.   Annual meetings and special meetings shall be held at such place, within or without the State of California, as the Directors may, from time to time, fix.   Whenever the Directors shall fail to fix such place, the meetings shall be held at the principal executive office of the corporation.

Section 3.   NOTICE.   Written notice stating the place, day, and hour of each meeting, and, in the case of a special meeting, the general nature of the business to be transacted or, in the case of an Annual Meeting, those matters which the Board of Directors, at the time of mailing of the notice, intends to present for action by the shareholders, shall be given not less than ten (10) days (or not less than any such other minimum period of days as may be prescribed by the General Corporation Law) or more than sixty (60) days (or more than any such maximum period of days as may be prescribed

[* * *]

FIGURE 11-4 *Continued*

ARTICLE VIII

BOOKS AND RECORDS - STATUTORY AGENT

<u>Section 1.</u> RECORDS: STORAGE AND INSPECTION. The corporation shall keep at its principal executive office in the State of California, or, if its principal executive office is not in the State of California, the original or a copy of the Bylaws as amended to date, which shall be open to inspection by the shareholders at all reasonable times during office hours. If the principal executive office of the corporation is outside the State of California, and, if the corporation has no principal business office in the State of California, it shall, upon request of any shareholder, furnish a copy of the bylaws as amended to date.

The corporation shall keep adequate and correct books and records of account and shall keep minutes of the proceedings of its shareholders, Board of Directors, and committees if any, of the Board of Directors. The corporation shall keep at its principal executive office, or at the office of its transfer agent or registrar, a record of its shareholders, giving the names and addresses of all shareholders and the number and class of shares held by each. Such minutes shall be in written form. Such other books and records shall be kept either in written form or in any other form capable of being converted into written form.

<u>Section 2.</u> RECORD OF PAYMENTS. All checks, drafts, or other orders for payment of money, notes, or other evidences of indebtedness, issued in the name of or payable to the corporation, shall be signed or endorsed by such person or persons in such manner as shall be determined from time to time by resolution of the Board of Directors.

[* * *]

<u>Section 4.</u> AGENT FOR SERVICE. The name of the agent for service of process within the State of California is JIM POWERS.

---

3. The titles and duties of the officers of the corporation
4. The functions, duties, and responsibilities of the shareholders and the regulations governing their meetings, transactions, and voting procedures
5. The procedures for amending the bylaws

The First Organizational Meeting

At the beginning stages of the corporation's existence, it is necessary that certain meetings be held, and the law requires that written notice of these meetings be given to all those concerned. The meeting requirement can be satisfied by a unanimous written consent of the directors. If the parties concerned are in constant communication with each other, it may not be necessary to send a formal written notice of the time, place, and purpose of the meeting. If, however, a written notice is not sent out, a **waiver of notice** signed by all the interested parties must be attached to the minutes of the meeting. The law requires that each corporation hold an official organizational meeting at which minutes must be taken (Figure 11-5). In most states, this first meeting may be held any time after the articles of incorporation have been filed. A few states do require, however, that this meeting be held before the application for incorporation is approved by the secretary of state. The form for taking these minutes is standardized and may be dictated by the attorney or prepared on the printed forms provided in the corporate kit. The **minutes** of the first organizational meeting usually include the following business:

FIGURE 11-5 *Minutes—first organizational meeting.*

MINUTES OF FIRST ORGANIZATIONAL MEETING

OF DIRECTORS OF

SOUTH COAST CONSTRUCTION COMPANY, INC.

(A California Corporation)

The undersigned, being the Incorporator named in the Articles of Incorporation of the above-named California corporation, duly formed by the filing of said Articles of Incorporation in the office of the California Secretary of State on the 1st day of August, ----, and desiring to hold the first organizational meeting for the purpose of completing the organization of its affairs, in accordance with the powers conferred upon Incorporators by Section 210 of the General Corporation Law, held such meeting at 278 North Euclid, in the City of Fullerton, California, on the 11th day of August, ----, at 2:00 P.M. of said day.

Present at this session of the meeting:

JIM POWERS

being the incorporator of said corporation named in its Articles of Incorporation.

On motion and by unanimous vote, LINDA SMITH was elected temporary Chairman, and TRACY HERBERT was elected temporary Secretary of the meeting.

ARTICLES OF INCORPORATION FILED

The Chairman stated that the original of Articles of Incorporation of the corporation had been filed in the office of the California Secretary of State, and had been assigned the following filing date and State Corporation number:

Official filing date: August 1, ----

Official Filing Number: 21700

She presented to the meeting a certified copy of said Articles of Incorporation, showing filings as stated, and the Secretary was directed to insert said copy in the Book of Minutes of the corporation.

[* * *]

1. Adoption of the bylaws
2. Election of officers of the corporation
3. Adoption of the form of stock certificates
4. Adoption of the form of corporate seal
5. Selection of the principal place of business for the corporation
6. Authorization for payment of corporation expenses and attorney's fees
7. Authorization to establish bank accounts
8. Authorization to issue securities
9. Adoption of tax year

After the corporation has been officially formed and the first organizational meeting held, the law requires that the board of directors and stockholders of a corporation hold an annual meeting on a regular basis. An example of the minutes of an annual meeting of the board of directors and the kind of business that might be transacted at this meeting are shown in Figure 11-6.

FIGURE 11-5   *Continued*

<u>LOSSES ON SMALL BUSINESS STOCK</u>

The meeting next considered the advisability of adopting a plan to qualify the shares of the corporation so as to enable the shareholders to obtain ordinary loss treatment for tax purposes in the event said shares suffered full loss. After full discussion, and upon motion duly made, seconded, and carried, the following resolution was adopted:

RESOLVED: That the corporation shall, and hereby does, adopt the following plan to qualify under Section 1244 of the Internal Revenue Code and Section 18208 of the Revenue and Taxation Code, effective this date:

1. The maximum number of shares to be issued under this plan shall not exceed 6,000 shares and the aggregate consideration, which shall consist only of cash, cancellation of indebtedness, and property, to be received therefore, shall not exceed Sixty Thousand Dollars ($60,000.00).

[* * *]

4. No shares other than those sold and issued under this plan shall be offered or sold during the period that this plan is effective.

<u>MISCELLANEOUS BUSINESS</u>

The Chairman then asked if there was any other business to come before the meeting.

<u>ADJOURNMENT</u>

There being no further business to come before the meeting, upon motion duly made, seconded, and unanimously carried, the meeting was adjourned.

_____
LINDA SMITH
President and Chairman

Attest:

_____
TRACY HERBERT
Secretary

CORPORATION STOCK

The articles of incorporation set forth the number of shares authorized to be sold by the corporation. Those people who buy these shares of **stock** thereby become the owners of the company, and the evidence of their ownership is the stock certificate issued to them.

Regulation of the Sale of Securities

Because of the ease with which corporations may be formed and the possibility of fraud in the sale of securities, strict regulations governing the sale of securities at both the state and federal level have been introduced.

Blue Sky Laws

Blue sky laws are state statutes that regulate the issue and sale of stock of *intrastate* corporations. These laws protect the public from fraud in the offering of securities in the individual states through laws that are state statutes pertaining to the registration and sale of stock. Under these laws, the seller of the securities is required to

FIGURE 11-6 *Minutes—annual meeting.*

MINUTES OF ANNUAL MEETING OF

DIRECTORS OF

SOUTH COAST CONSTRUCTION COMPANY, INC.

(A California Corporation)

The annual meeting of Directors of South Coast Construction Company, Inc., a California corporation, was held at the principal office of the corporation on June 1, ----, for the purpose of electing officers, considering reports of the affairs of the corporation, and transacting such other business as may be required.

There were present at the meeting the following Directors:

LINDA SMITH, SUE ANDERSON, and TRACY HERBERT

There were no Directors absent.

The Chairman announced that the meeting was held pursuant to a written waiver of notice and consent; such waiver and consent was presented to the meeting and upon motion duly made, seconded, and unanimously carried, was made a part of the records of the meeting and now precedes the minutes of this meeting in the Book of Minutes of the corporation.

The Chairman stated that it was necessary to elect officers of the corporation for the ensuing year. Upon motion duly made, seconded, and unanimously carried, the following individuals were elected to the office set forth opposite their names:

LINDA SMITH	President
SUE ANDERSON	Vice President
TRACY HERBERT	Secretary

There being no further business to come before the meeting, the meeting was adjourned.

_____
TRACY HERBERT
Secretary

make a public statement of responsibility and disclose the general financial conditions of the corporation, as well as make a full accounting of how the proceeds of the new stock issue are to be used by the corporation. The facts governing the issuance of stock and its sale are submitted to the appropriate public official, and both civil and criminal penalties may be applied if there is a violation of the law.

Federal Securities Act

Sales of securities are also governed by the Securities and Exchange Commission (SEC) and must be registered before such sales are made.

A corporation desiring to issue new securities must file a detailed and complicated registration statement. Under the Securities Act, the Securities and Exchange Commission was established in 1934 to regulate the sale of securities in interstate commerce. This act applies only to the sale of securities to the public, and it does not apply to sales between individuals. Under this act, a prospectus of any new issue must be filed with the SEC for examination before the actual sale of any securities. The commission requires information on the types of securities already outstanding, the terms of sale, profit-sharing arrangements, and options created in connection with the issue, as well as any other information the commission considers necessary.

The SEC also requires a registration statement about the new stock being offered. The first part of this statement is actually the prospectus, while the second part includes every aspect of the corporate operations not covered in the prospectus. If a sale is found to be improper because of false information or fraud, the investor may have the right to sue the persons who have signed the registration statement for all resulting damage. Responsible officials who fail to comply with the law are subject to criminal prosecution.

Following registration of the securities the corporation is also governed by the Securities and Exchange Act of 1934, which governs the resale of securities following initial registration.

Par Value Stock

The value that the incorporators place on the stock issued by a corporation must be specified in the articles of incorporation. This value is the same for each issue and is called **par value**. In general, par value is the minimum consideration for which a share can be sold.

Transfer of Stock

Stock is like any other form of personal property or **negotiable instrument** and may be transferred or assigned at any time. Such transfer must be recorded in the corporate minute book in order to be binding on the corporation. Owning stock is the same as owning an interest in the corporation, and the transfer of interest must be recorded as a transfer of the stock certificate. The sale and transfer of shares, in some instances, are subject to the approval of the Corporations Commission or other regulatory body of the state in which the corporation is formed. See Figure 11-7 for an example of a stock certificate with a warning about the sale of securities.

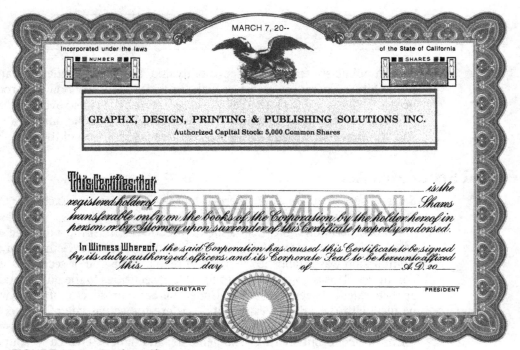

FIGURE 11-7 *Stock certificate.*

FIGURE 11-7 *Continued*

For value relieved _____ hereby sell, assign and transfer unto

PLEASE INSERT SOCIAL SECURITY OR OTHER
IDENTIFYING NUMBER OF ASSIGNEE

(NAME AND ADDRESS OF TRANSFEREE SHOULD BE PRINTED OR TYPEWRITTEN)

_____ Shares

represented by the within certificate and, if required, do hereby irrevocably

constitute and appoint _____ Attorney

to transfer the said Shares on the books of the within named Corporation, with full power of

substitution in the premises.

Dated _____

In presence of _____

NOTICE: THE SIGNATURE ON THIS ASSIGNMENT MUST CORRESPOND WITH THE NAME AS WRITTEN UPON THE FACE OF THE CERTIFICATE, IN EVERY PARTICULAR, WITHOUT ALTERATION OR ENLARGEMENT, OR ANY CHANGE WHATEVER.

THE SECURITIES EVIDENCED BY THIS CERTIFICATE HAVE NOT BEEN REGISTERED UNDER THE SECURITIES ACT OF 1933, AS AMENDED (THE "SECURITIES ACT"), AND MAY NOT BE SOLD, TRANSFERRED, ASSIGNED OR HYPOTHECATED EXCEPT PURSUANT TO AN EFFECTIVE REGISTRATION STATEMENT UNDER THE SECURITIES ACT COVERING SUCH SECURITIES OR IF SUCH SALE, TRANSFER, ASSIGNMENT OR HYPOTHECATION IS EXEMPT FROM THE REGISTRATION AND PROSPECTUS DELIVERY REQUIREMENTS UNDER THE SECURITIES ACT.

CORPORATE DISSOLUTIONS

As the result of a **merger** or **consolidation**, corporate dissolutions may occur. Dissolutions also may occur because the corporation may not be solvent or successful. While the formation of the corporation may be relatively simple, the dissolution of a corporation may be very difficult and complex. Dissolutions may be voluntary or involuntary.

Voluntary Dissolutions

In some states a corporation may be dissolved voluntarily by the consent of the shareholders. A statement of the intent to dissolve is filed with the secretary of state, and after all the debts and obligations of the corporation have been paid or discharged and the remaining assets of the corporation have been distributed to the shareholders, a *certificate of dissolution* is filed and the corporation is considered officially dissolved by the secretary of state.

Involuntary Dissolutions

Involuntary dissolutions may be initiated by the creditors of the corporation or by a petition from a percentage of the stockholders. In involuntary dissolutions, the court enters a decree after the corporate debts have been paid or discharged, and the remaining assets are distributed to the shareholders. After this has occurred, the court issues a *decree of dissolution,* and the corporation is dissolved.

LIMITED LIABILITY COMPANY

Limited liability companies (abbreviated as **LLC** or **LC** depending on the state) are a relatively new type of entity. They were first created in 1977, and by 1996 all states and the District of Columbia had enacted legislation recognizing LLCs. This form of organization combines the best benefits from corporate and partnership laws. First, its owners, called members, are provided with limited liability just as shareholders are and are protected from liability for the LLCs acts and acts of other members in the course of business. Second, all money earned by the LLC is passed directly to the members, who pay tax on the money at individual tax rates, just as partnerships are taxed. In most states, and depending on the revenues of the LLC, the LLC does not pay a separate tax on corporations.

An LLC can be managed by its members, or the members can appoint someone or another entity (such as a corporation) to manage its business. If managed by its members, it is considered a member-managed LLC.

LLCs are formed in compliance with estate law. LLC formation is similar to that of a corporation, in that articles of organization are filed with the secretary of state. In addition, the LLC is also governed by an agreement called an operating agreement (or limited liability company agreement), which is much like a partnership agreement and corporate bylaws combined. An operating agreement is very complex and should be drafted by legal counsel competent in tax law.

To form an LLC, the articles of organization (called certificate of formation in some states) is filed with the secretary of state in which the partnership will operate its business. Some states utilize preprinted forms and provide them on their websites; others do not and it is necessary to draft the articles from scratch. Prior to this filing, however, the desired name of the LLC would need to be checked for availability with the appropriate secretary of state.

If the name of the LLC is to change, an amendment to the articles of organization must be filed with the secretary of state. When the LLC closes its business, it must also file appropriate dissolution documentation with the secretary of state. Again, many states will have the requisite forms on their websites. If not, the attorney for the partnership will draft them as necessary.

LIMITED LIABILITY PARTNERSHIP

As with LLCs, **limited liability partnerships (LLPs)** are a relatively new form of business entity. LLPs function as normal partnerships but are registered with the state and provide partners with a certain liability shield. Partners do not have liability for any partnership obligations incurred while the partnership is an LLP; however, partners do remain liable for their own conduct.

In many states, LLPs are required to meet certain minimum financial responsibility standards with respect to insurance coverage and/or capital reserves. This is to protect any one who would normally have all partners available to be sued in the case of tort or civil claims. In many states, including California, LLPs are only available to certain professions, such as lawyers and accountants.

As with LLCs, LLPs are governed by state statutes and are formed by the filing of prescribed forms with the Secretary of State, as well as the drafting of a complex partnership agreement.

SUMMARY

The best form of business ownership for an individual or group depends on the needs of the individual or group and the purpose of the organization. The three basic forms for a business enterprise are sole proprietorship, partnership, and corporation. The sole proprietorship form of business is the oldest, simplest, and least complicated. Most small businesses today are sole proprietorships.

The partnership form of business is based on an agreement between two or more persons to engage in some form of business enterprise. The partners agree to share the control of the business and the profits derived from that business. It is a legal entity, and the partners are personally liable for the debts and obligations of the partnership. Generally, partnerships are classified as general or limited.

A corporation is a legal entity that exists within the laws of the state where it is formed. It may be likened to a person, but it is separate from its incorporators, officers, directors, stockholders, or employees. As it is a creation of the state, it may sue and be sued, enter into contracts, and do anything a person might do. The formation of a corporation begins with a decision as to the type of corporation to be established, which is sometimes dictated by the purpose and size of the enterprise. The articles of incorporation are filed with the state and serve as a charter, providing it with a legal identity. Following the adoption of the bylaws, the organizational meetings serve to govern the corporate organization.

A limited liability company (LLC) is a relatively new entity that exists within the laws of the state in which it was formed. LLCs combine the best aspects of corporations (limited liability for its members) and partnerships (pass-through taxation for its members). The articles of organization are filed with the state to form the LLC and an operating agreement is prepared by legal counsel competent in tax law, which is much like a partnership agreement and corporate bylaws combined.

A limited liability partnership (LLP) is a relatively new business entity that functions as a normal partnership but is registered with the state, providing partners with a certain liability shield. Partners do not have liability for any partnership obligations; however, the partners remain liable for their own tortuous conduct. LLPs are governed by state statutes and are formed by the filing of prescribed forms with the secretary of state as well as the drafting of a complex partnership agreement.

The legal professional should have a fundamental knowledge of these business enterprises and become familiar with the preparation and requirements for their creation and operation.

VOCABULARY

alien corporation   A corporation chartered outside the country in which it is doing business.

articles of incorporation   The instrument by which a private corporation is formed and organized under general corporation laws.

blue sky laws   State statutes regulating investment in companies and the sale of securities to protect against fraud within the individual states.

board of directors   Elected officials who establish policies of a corporation.

bylaws   Rules and regulations of a corporation that govern its operation.

charter   Authorization to establish a corporation; known in some states as articles of incorporation or certificates of incorporation.

close corporation   A small corporation owned by a few people, often members of the same family.

consolidation   The unification of two or more corporations into a single corporation.

corporation   A business entity of limited liability empowered to do business under state law, or possibly under the power of the federal government.

de facto corporation   A business organization that operates as a corporation but has failed to comply with one or more of the provisions of state laws regarding the organization of a corporation.

de jure corporation   A corporation organized in complete compliance with the corporate laws in the state in which it operates.

director   One who has been elected or appointed to the board of directors.

dissolution   The process of dissolving a corporation.

domestic corporation   A corporation chartered in the same state in which it is doing business.

eleemosynary   (pronounced el-e-MOS-e-nary) Related to or supported by charity.

foreign corporation   A corporation chartered outside the state in which it is doing business.

general partnership   In a limited partnership, the partner who assumes responsibility for the management of the partnership and liability for all partnership debts.

incorporation   The act or process of forming a corporation.

limited liability company (LLC or LC)   An entity combining the best aspects of corporations and partnerships.

limited liability partnership (LLP)   A partnership that is registered with the state providing partners with a certain liability shield.

limited partnership   A partnership of one or more general partners (who manage the partnership and are responsible for the debts) and one or more limited partners (who only contribute assets and are liable only to the extent of their contribution).

merger   The absorption by a corporation of one or more other corporations.

minutes   The record of the business transacted at a meeting of stockholders and directors.

negotiable instruments   Securities or paper that may be transferred, or negotiated, from one person to another.

officer   An elected official of a corporation, such as a president, vice-president, secretary, or treasurer.

partnership   An agreement by two or more persons to carry on, as co-owners, a business for profit.

par value   The value of a share of stock printed on its face value at incorporation.

proxy   An authorization in writing signed by a stockholder designating another person to vote in his or her place.

quorum   The number of members of the board of directors, committee, or other organized body required to make that body, when duly assembled, legally competent to transact business.

Securities and Exchange Commission (SEC)   A federal agency that regulates and supervises the operation of public corporations.

sole proprietorship   The simplest form of business whereby the owner is the business and is legally responsible for all the debts and obligations incurred by the business.

stock   The certificate of evidence of ownership of an interest in a corporation.

stockholder   The owner of stock in a corporation.

ultra vires   A Latin term meaning "beyond the legal powers conferred upon a corporation by its charter or articles."

waiver   The voluntary relinquishment of a right.

waiver of notice   To surrender a claim or the right of being notified.

STUDENT ASSESSMENT 1

Instructions: Circle T if the statement is true or F if the statement is false.

T   F   1.   Most businesses in America are sole proprietorships.

T   F   2.   Corporate assets belong to the stockholders and not to the corporation.

T   F   3.   Corporate existence continues regardless of the death of the stockholders.

T   F   4.   General and limited partners have the same authority, but a different liability.

T   F   5.   In a small, *close* corporation, it is not necessary to obtain permission from the Corporation Commissioner in order to transfer stock.

T   F   6.   A partnership is a separate entity apart from its partners or members.

T   F   7.   It has been possible for the court to "pierce the corporate veil" and hold stockholders personally liable for obligations of the corporation.

T   F   8.   A sole proprietorship may not continue to function after the death of the owner.

T   F   9.   The secretary of state generally approves the articles of incorporation.

T   F   10.   There are so many corporations today with different names that a corporate name cannot be reserved in advance.

T   F   11.   The words *bank, trust, trustee,* or related words, may not be a part of the corporate name unless the certificate of approval of the superintendent of banks is attached to the articles of incorporation.

T   F   12.   The board of directors establishes the policy for the corporation.

T   F   13.   Some states require that the articles of incorporation be signed before a notary.

T   F   14.   It is much easier to amend the articles of incorporation than to amend the bylaws.

T   F   15.   A corporation is the oldest form of business organization.

T   F   16.   The articles of incorporation are specific in meaning, whereas the bylaws are general in meaning.

T   F   17.   Par value for stock refers to the current market value.

T   F   18.   A corporation and partnership are both created by the state.

T   F   19.   A corporation is a legal entity and a partnership is an association.

T   F   20.   A partnership may be terminated by the death of one of the partners.

T   F   21.   A partnership can expand through the sale of additional stock.

T   F   22.   Corporations are established under federal law.

T   F   23.   Each state designates the official state agency through which a corporation must be formed.

T   F   24.   The officers of the corporation may be elected or appointed by the stockholders.

T   F   25.   The Securities and Exchange Commission is responsible for the operation of all publicly held corporations.

STUDENT ASSESSMENT 2

Instructions: Circle the letter that indicates the most correct answer.

1. The individuals who set the broad policies for the corporation are the
   a. officers
   b. employees
   c. incorporators
   d. board of directors
   e. none of these

2. A corporation that acts in complete compliance with the corporate laws is
   a. *ultra vires*
   b. *de facto*
   c. *de jure*
   d. domestic
   e. none of these

3. Corporate debts are the responsibility of the
   a. shareholders
   b. incorporators
   c. corporation
   d. board of directors
   e. none of these

4. A corporation formed for the purpose of governing a municipality is called a
   a. public corporation
   b. quasi-public corporation
   c. close corporation
   d. private corporation
   e. none of these

5. A corporation formed for the purpose of providing electric service to a community is called a
   a. close corporation
   b. private corporation
   c. quasi-public corporation
   d. public corporation
   e. none of these

STUDENT ASSESSMENT 3

Instructions: Insert the word that best completes the statement.

1. One who conducts the business of a partnership and has unlimited liability is a(n) _____.
2. Authority used by stockholders to have their votes cast by others at corporation meetings is known as _____.
3. The Securities and Exchange Commission was established in _____.
4. The original copy of the articles of incorporation is filed with _____.
5. The oldest form of a business organization is a(n) _____.

STUDENT ASSESSMENT 4

Instructions: Match the most correct letter to the number.

	Section I		*Section I*
_____	1. *de jure*	A.	number of members required to transact business
_____	2. *de facto*	B.	beyond the powers of the corporation
_____	3. sole proprietor	C.	oldest form of business
_____	4. board of directors	D.	organized in complete compliance with corporate laws of state
_____	5. eleemosynary	E.	basic rules governing internal operation of corporation
_____	6. bylaws	F.	charitable corporation
_____	7. articles of incorporation	G.	establishes general policies of corporation
_____	8. quorum	H.	broad and general rules of corporation
_____	9. *ultra vires*	I.	operates as a corporation but has failed to comply with the state law regarding the organization of a corporation

	Section II		*Section II*
_____	1. domestic	A.	municipal corporation
_____	2. foreign	B.	chartered outside the state in which it does business
_____	3. federal and state	C.	chartered outside the country in which it does business
_____	4. quasi-public	D.	public transportation company
_____	5. alien	E.	chartered in the same state in which it does business
_____	6. nonstock	F.	private college

STUDENT ASSIGNMENTS

PRACTICE SET 3: CORPORATION

Case Particulars

Attorney:	Robert Morgan #12345
	Attorney at Law
	320 Main Street
	Fullerton, CA 92634
	Telephone: (714) 555-2440
	Fax: (714) 555-2748
Name of Firm:	Newport Construction Company
	1000 Newport Boulevard
	Orange, CA 92640
Incorporator:	Ila Incorporator
	104 North Harbor Boulevard
	Fullerton, CA 92634
Directors:	Sue Duple
	1114 North Anaheim
	Anaheim, CA
	Lori Faden
	1200 Miramar Drive
	Fullerton, CA

(continued)

	Theresa Hitlock	
	10072 Gilbert	
	Anaheim, CA	
Officers:	President:	Theresa Hitlock
	Vice-president:	Sue Duple
	Secretary:	Lori Faden
	Chief Financial Officer:	Ila Incorporator
Stock Structures:	Total capitalization:	7,500 shares
Date:	April 21, 20____	

Case History

Ila Incorporator has contacted Robert Morgan, Attorney at Law, and requested that he set up the necessary forms and legal papers to form a construction corporation in Orange County, California.

You will want to do the following:

1. Send a letter to the secretary of state reserving the corporate name.
2. File the articles of incorporation with the secretary of state.
3. Have the principals of the corporation adopt the bylaws.
4. Prepare a waiver of notice to hold the first meeting.
5. Type the minutes of the first meeting.
6. Send a letter and the necessary forms to the commissioner of corporations requesting issuance of stock.
7. After the corporation has been in existence for over one year, prepare the minutes of the annual meeting of the board of directors.

STUDENT ASSIGNMENTS

PROJECT 1: PREPARE A LETTER REQUESTING USE OF CORPORATE NAME

Instructions: Using your word processor and the letterhead template you created for Robert Morgan, prepare a letter similar to Sample 11-1, p. 271, to request availability of corporate name.

Save as **ch11_lt1** and print.

PROJECT 2: PREPARE THE ARTICLES OF INCORPORATION

Instructions: Retrieve **ch011_Ar** (Articles of Incorporation) from your data disk and fill in the required information as indicated in the practice set case particulars.

Save your document as **ch11_Ar** and print.

PROJECT 3: PREPARE LETTER FOR FILING ARTICLES OF INCORPORATION

Instructions: Retrieve your letterhead template and prepare a letter similar to Sample 11-2, p. 272, for filing articles of incorporation.

Save as **ch11_Lt2** and print one copy for your instructor.

(continued)

PROJECT 4: PREPARE THE BYLAWS

Instructions: Retrieve Ch011_BY from your disk. Integrate the following variables from your disk into the main document file. Your instructor may make this a merge assignment or a find and replace.

Variables

Section 1: TIME
Section 2: PLACE
Section 3: CALL
Section 4: NOTICE
Section 5: CONSENT
Section 6: CONDUCT
Section 7: PROXY
Section 8: INSPECTOR
Section 9: SUBSIDIARY
Section 10: QUORUM
Section 11: BALLOT
Section 12: AGREEMENT

Save as **ch11_BY** and print one copy for your instructor.

STUDENT ASSIGNMENTS

PROJECT 5: PREPARE CORPORATE MINUTES FROM TEMPLATE

Instructions: Retrieve the template file **ch011_MN** from your data disk and fill in the appropriate variables with the following information:

Company Name:	Newport Construction Company
Date of Meeting:	January 15, _____
Attendees:	SUE DUPLE, LORI FADEN, and THERESA HITLOCK
Elected Officers:	THERESA HITLOCK, President
	SUE DUPLE, Vice-president
	LORI FADEN, Secretary

Save as **ch11_MN**, and print one copy for your instructor. Congratulations! You have completed most of the documents for setting up a corporation.

PARTNERSHIP AGREEMENT

PROJECT 1

Instructions: Retrieve the Partnership Agreement, **ch011_PT**, from your data disk and fill in the following information:

Date:	March 25, _____
Partnership business name:	Blooms
Place of business:	578 North Street, Anaheim, California 92980
Type of business:	Flower Shop
Partners' names:	Blossom Trent and Iris Jones
Shared profits and losses:	Shared equally by each partner (50%)
Time commitment:	Hours to be equally shared by each partner (50%)
Capital:	$60,000 total, shared equally
State of governing law:	Your state

Save as **ch11_PT**, and print one copy for your instructor.

ROBERT MORGAN
Attorney at Law

320 Main Street
Fullerton, CA 92634
(714) 555-2440   FAX (714) 555-2748

April 21, 20---

Corporate Filing Division
Secretary of State
111 Capitol Mall
Sacramento, CA 95814

Gentlemen:

Enclosed for filing is the original of the Articles of Incorporation for the Newport Construction Company, Inc., together with two (2) additional copies for certification and a check in the sum of $100 to cover the filing fee for the enclosed. The Incorporator has already obtained a certificate of name registration by letter dated March 30, 20---, which is enclosed herewith.

We would appreciate your promptness in filing the Articles of Incorporation and returning the certified copies in the self-addressed, stamped envelope.

Very truly yours,

ROBERT MORGAN

urs
Enclosures

SAMPLE 11-1

ROBERT MORGAN 12345
Attorney at Law

320 Main Street
Fullerton, CA 92634
(714) 881-2440   FAX (714) 881-2748

April 21, 20--

Corporate Filing Division
Secretary of State
111 Capitol Mall
Sacramento, CA 95814

Gentlemen:

Enclosed for filing is the original of the Articles of Incorporation for the Newport
Construction Company, Inc., together with two (2) additional copies for
certification and a check in the sum of $100 to cover the filing fee for the enclosed.
The Incorporator has already obtained a certificate of name registration by
letter dated March 30, 20--, which is enclosed herewith.

We would appreciate your promptness in filing the Articles of Incorporation and
returning the certified copies in the self-addressed, stamped envelope.

Very truly yours,

ROBERT MORGAN

SAMPLE 11-2

12 REAL ESTATE

OBJECTIVES

Upon completion of this chapter, you should be able to:

1. Discuss the history of the ownership of property in the United States
2. Describe the difference between real and personal property
3. Prepare a promissory note
4. Recognize the importance of recording documents
5. Explain the methods for determining a legal description for property
6. Discuss the different classifications of property
7. Describe the different kinds of deeds
8. Discuss how ownership in real property is transferred
9. Explain the advantages of a title search
10. List the different types of deeds
11. Describe the differences between mortgages and deeds of trust
12. List the different kinds of leases
13. Explain the procedures for evicting a tenant

Most Americans take the ownership of property for granted and do not realize that this is a right not held by all the citizens in different countries throughout the world. The right to own property in the United States is expressly granted by the Fifth and Fourteenth Amendments to the U.S. Constitution and by the constitutions of most states. The purchase of a home is the largest investment most families make. This investment involves financial and residential burdens that continue throughout the course of the buyer's lifetime.

Law offices are often called on to prepare documents that transfer the title (legal ownership) of real estate or the leasing of real property. The laws governing the transfer of title are extremely precise and vary from state to state. In California, for example, most real estate transactions are handled through real estate brokers working with private companies that specialize in the paperwork involved in transferring title. These companies are called *escrow companies* and *title companies*. In New York, attorneys handle the transfer of real property, and they frequently represent clients in the buying and selling of real estate.

CLASSIFICATION OF PROPERTY

Property may be classified as either personal or real property.

Personal property may be defined as property other than real property. Personal property is often thought of as movable property and includes such items as automobiles, boats, furniture, household items, jewelry, unlaid carpeting (rugs), and other items that may be transported easily from one place to another. The seller usually does the paperwork involved in the buying and selling of personal property. Installment loans, chattel mortgages (mortgages on personal property), and negotiable instruments, such as promissory notes (see Figure 12-1), are examples of this kind of paperwork. The states have adopted the **Uniform Commercial Code** to regulate transactions involving personal property. When businesses involved in selling personal property are unable to collect money due to them from their customers, they turn these accounts over to collection agencies. If the collection agency is not able to collect the debt, they turn the account over to an attorney, who may initiate a lawsuit.

Real property includes not only the land but also what is below and above the land. You may have purchased land without the **mineral rights** (rights to what is below the ground) or with an **easement** (such as permission to run utilities across your property). These transactions may have taken place prior to your purchase of the land but are a part of the sale of the real property. You may also have purchased the land

FIGURE 12-1 *Promissory note.*

PROMISSORY NOTE

____$20,000.00____   White Plains, New York

FOR VALUE RECEIVED, the undersigned, _____DEE WILSON_____, of _149 Hill Street, White Plains, New York_, promises to pay to the order of **BETH JOHNSON**, at _876 Pinto Lane, White Plains, New York_, or such other place as the holder may designate in writing to the undersigned, the principal sum of ___$20,000.00___, together with interest thereon from date hereof until paid, at the rate of __seven (7) percent__ per annum as follows: ___Monthly___ consecutive installments of _principal and interest_ in the amount of _$153.00_ on the _first day of April_ commencing _April 1, ----_, and continuing on the first day of each month thereafter until fully paid.

Payments shall be applied first to accrued interest and the balance to principal.

All or any part of the aforesaid principal sum may be prepaid at any time and from time to time without penalty.

In the event of any default by the undersigned in the payment of principal or interest when due, or in the event of the suspension of actual business, insolvency, assignment for the benefit of creditors, adjudication of bankruptcy, or appointment of a receiver, of or against the undersigned, the unpaid balance of the principal sum of this Promissory Note shall, at the option of the holder, become immediately due and payable.

The maker and all other persons who may become liable for the payment hereof, severally waive demand, presentment, protest, notice of dishonor or nonpayment, notice of protest, and any and all lack of diligence or delays in collection which may occur, and expressly consent and agree to each and any extension or postponement of time and payment hereof from time to time at or after maturity or other indulgence, and waive all notice thereof.

In case suit or action is instituted to collect this note, or any portion hereof, the maker promises to pay such additional sum as the court may adjudge reasonable for attorney's fees in said proceedings.

This note is made and executed under, and is, in all respects, governed by, the laws of the State of _New York_.

_____March 15, ----_____

_____DEE WILSON_____

with **improvements** on it. These improvements may include laid carpeting, buildings, sidewalks, fences, trees, landscaping, swimming pools, or anything that is affixed to the land with the intention of being permanent.

PROPERTY DESCRIPTION

It is relatively easy to describe personal property; the terms *serial number*, *model number*, *size,* and *color* can easily identify an item. However, it is much more difficult to describe real property. All transactions involving real property require an accurate description of that property. Documents referring to a specific piece of property, such as a deed, mortgage, easement, or lease, require a description of that parcel of property to identify it as the subject of the transaction.

The description by which a piece of property is identified is called a **legal description.** Therefore, the legal description of a piece of property becomes important in determining the enforceability of any document dealing with property transactions. While the manner of a legal description of a parcel of property may vary from state to state, the legal description identifies that piece of property in a consistent and uniform manner.

Public records are kept by a county clerk or other public official of property transactions, and the general public has access to the information contained in these public records. The parties to a transaction are, in effect, protected by recording these documents with a public official. Recording property transactions protects the parties against the claims of a subsequent buyer or seller.

The methods used to describe real property are metes and bounds, rectangular (government) survey, and plats and subdivisions. The exact method may vary from location to location, and while each method may be used independently, some properties may have a property description using all three.

Metes and Bounds

The original thirteen colonies, plus Tennessee, Kentucky, Maine, Vermont, West Virginia, and Texas, used the terms *metes* and *bounds* for property descriptions.

A metes and bounds description measures property by measuring distances and angles from designated landmarks and in relation to adjoining properties. The description starts at a designated place on the property called the point of beginning (POB) and proceeds around the boundaries, referencing linear measurements or compass point (metes) and the natural and artificial fixed object (bounds). Distances are measured in terms of **metes** (chains, links, rod, or feet); inches are never used. Directions are measured by **bounds** in terms of degrees, minutes, and seconds. A circle has a total of 360 degrees and each degree contains 60 minutes. A direction of 30 degrees, 14 minutes, and 20 seconds might be written as

30°14'20"
30 degrees, 14 minutes, 20 seconds
thirty degrees, fourteen minutes, twenty seconds

A metes and bounds description might look like this:

Beginning at a point on the Northerly side of that tract described in Book 175, page 534 Deed Records; thence North 67°98'10" South 637.80 feet, more or less, to the East line of Land Claim No. 56 . . .

Rectangular (Government) Survey

Historically, when the United States used to sell public lands, reference to property locations was made on the basis of landmarks such as trees, rocks, and monuments. In 1787, the United States government established a conventional method of identifying the lots sold, and Congress developed a rectangular system of measurement for land called the government survey, which is more commonly known as the **rectangular (government) survey**, and based on using latitude and longitude lines. Some of the longitude (north and south) lines were used to serve as prime **meridians**. Some of the latitude (east and west) lines were used to serve as **base lines**. This system of measurement is based on a rectangular tract located with reference to base lines running east and west and meridian lines running north and south. An evaluation of real property to determine its boundaries and physical limits is called a **survey**.

The rectangular tract created by these lines is known as a **township**. A row of townships running north and south is called a *range*, and the ranges are numbered east to west. Property is measured north and south of the base line and east and west of the prime meridian. A legal description of a government survey may read like this:

> The South Half of the Northeast Quarter of Southwest Quarter of Section Four, Township 35 North, Range 68 West . . .

The townships are divided into thirty-six **sections**; a section is one square mile and contains approximately 640 acres.

Plats and Subdivisions

A **plat** map has to be approved by the county when land is subdivided. This map is then filed and may be referred to as follows: Plat Book 81 of Los Angeles County, California, Page 450. The metes and bounds descriptions of the total parcel of land and of each subdivided piece of land are shown on the plat map. The subdivided pieces are called **lots**, and a group of lots is referred to as a **block**. The following is a property description of a platted piece of land.

> Lot Fifty Seven (57), Block Three (3) of the Sand Canyon Addition to the City of Laguna Niguel, County of Orange, State of California, as recorded in Plat Book 37, Page 564.

Care should be taken in the preparation of legal descriptions. It is very important for the legal office staff to keyboard accurate legal descriptions and to proofread each other's work. One typographical error can result in a lawsuit that may take years to resolve. Many legal office employees make it a point to carefully check property descriptions and read them aloud to another person in the office to check the keyed text for any description or typographical error.

OWNERSHIP OF PROPERTY

The form of ownership of property is not determined by the use of that property or who occupies it, but by how title to the property is indicated in the form of ownership specified in the deed recorded in connection with the acquisition or purchase.

Fee Simple

Fee simple ownership is absolute, unconditional, and perpetual. It is the highest type of ownership that a person can have. Upon the death of the immediate owner, the property passes on to the heirs. Most real estate transactions involve **fee simple** ownership, which means that the owner owns the property without reservation. Corporations, partnerships, individuals, estates, or trusts may acquire fee simple real estate either alone or with others.

Concurrent Ownership

If two or more persons own real estate jointly, it is said to be held "**concurrently**." There are two major classifications of concurrent ownership: *joint tenancy* and *tenancy in common*. Ownership of *community property* and *tenancy by entirety* also exist in some states.

Joint Tenancy   A joint tenancy is created when real property is transferred to two or more people simultaneously and equally. Each owns an individual, equal, undivided share in the property. In the event of the death of one of the owners, the decedent's share reverts to the other owner(s) without the necessity of going through probate.

Although husbands and wives may take title to property as joint tenants, it is not limited to married couples. The right of survivorship is one of the principal advantages of joint tenancy. One joint tenant may not change the right of survivorship by will, and neither the heirs nor creditors have any claim against property held in joint tenancy with others. The joint tenancy continues until there is only one owner who then takes ownership and who has all the rights of sole ownership, including the right to have property to pass to the heirs.

Tenancy in Common   Tenancy in common is an undivided ownership of interest in property by two or more people in any proportion. The interests are a fraction of the whole, and there is no specific division of the property. Therefore, none of the tenants in common can claim any specific portion in the event that one of the tenants in common dies. The undivided interest of the tenant is willable and passes on to the heirs by law, thereby making the heirs tenants in common with the other owners.

Community Property   Refer to the section on community property in Chapter 10 for a detailed definition of this term. **Community property** law governs the control and ownership of marital property in some states. California, because of Spanish influence from Mexico, and Louisiana, because of French influence, have community property laws that govern the ownership and sale of property. In these states, the general rule is that any property acquired during marriage by either the husband or wife, except property acquired by gift or devise, belongs one-half to the husband and one-half to the wife. The community property concept is based on the civil law system of continental Europe.

Quasi-community property (as discussed in Chapter 10) is property that may be acquired outside a community property state, but which in a dissolution of marriage (divorce) proceeding passes in the same manner as community property.

Tenancy by the Entirety   A tenancy by the entirety is created when real property is acquired by a husband and wife jointly after marriage. Each is the owner of the entire property, subject to the right of the other. Neither has the right to sell without the full knowledge and consent of the other, and such tenancy is therefore more restrictive than joint tenancy. Each has the right of survivorship so that, upon the death of one, the surviving spouse becomes the sole owner. In the event of divorce, the property is then owned by them as tenants in common. Not all states recognize tenancy by the entirety, and in some states this form of ownership has been abolished.

REAL ESTATE TRANSACTIONS

A typical real estate transaction begins with an offer to buy from a proposed purchaser to the seller. In some states, the real estate purchase contract usually is obtained from a real estate broker or an agent. In other states, this contract may be prepared by an attorney. Under the provisions of the statute of frauds, all contracts for the sale of an interest in real property must be in writing to be enforceable. The broker completes the contract of sale, usually prepared on a printed form. Individual contracts are drafted by the attorney. After the buyer and seller sign the contract, the buyer is said to have an *equitable interest* in the property of the seller.

The real estate purchase contract should contain the names of the buyer and seller, the location and legal description of the property to be transferred, the purchase price and method of financing to be used, and the date of settlement on which the deed is to be delivered and possession given. The contract usually stipulates the payment of a token sum known as deposit, the size of which depends on the amount of the purchase price. If the buyer should fail to meet the terms of the contract, this token payment may be awarded to the seller.

Title Search

To own land, you must have **title** to it, and when you sell that land, you must prove that you have title to it. A title search usually requires a search of the public records to make certain that the land has no claims or **liens** against it and rightfully belongs to the seller. The conditions to look for in a title search include unpaid taxes and other liens against the property; assessments (an apportionment of certain taxes or charges levied against the property); easements (any rights of others to use the land for a special purpose such as a driveway or utility easement); restrictions placed on the property by previous owners; covenants, conditions, and restrictions (aka CC&R's) in connection with homeowners' associations, and cases pending in the courts or unpaid judgments against the seller.

Other purposes of the title search are to determine the rights of the present owner as defined by former deeds or wills and numerous other matters disclosed only through a careful inspection of the records in the county courthouse or federal or state offices.

When attorneys make a title search, they provide the buyer with a statement of the result of the search known as an **abstract of title**. The abstract contains a complete history of the property, including all previous encumbrances and the evidence of their settlement, and all present liens and encumbrances, unpaid taxes, and any other matters of importance to the security of the buyer. The attorney advises the client whether to accept the deed to the property based on the information in the abstract of title.

Abstract companies and title companies make title searches for a fee. If the title company determines that the title to the property is clear, the title company may offer the buyer a title insurance policy that guarantees that the buyer is granted clear title to the property. Should the purchaser of a title policy ever be called on to answer for any liabilities created through the other owner's title, the title insurance company will indemnify the insured against all damages in connection with a clear title. Abstract companies do not offer title insurance policies.

Escrow

While the buyer and seller may be brought together for the sale through the arrangement of a broker or agent, an escrow company or law firm handles the actual transfer of title. In California, the property is said to be in **escrow** during the period between the signing of the real estate purchase contract and the final transfer of title. This means that the escrow company or law firm holds in trust the deed supplied by the seller and the deposit supplied by the buyer until the final papers are completed. In New York, however, the buyer's deposit is placed in a limited escrow until the loan commitment is obtained.

DEEDS

Types of Deeds

An individual, partnership, corporation, or limited liability company may own property or acquire an interest in real estate. One common way this process occurs is through a transfer by a sale or deed. A **deed** is a **conveyance** of an interest in real property by which one party, the **grantor** (seller), conveys property to another party, the **grantee** (buyer), for a price (consideration). A deed provides proof of ownership of real property and transfers the *title*, a form showing evidence of legal ownership of property. Most deeds are prepared on printed forms that indicate the parties to the sale (buyer and seller), the operative words of conveyance, the legal description of the property (lot and tract number), and the amount of payment (consideration). The parties to the deed are referred to as the *grantor* (seller) and the *grantee* (buyer).

The most common types of deeds are:

1. Simple warranty deed
2. Full covenant and warranty deed
3. Grant deed
4. Quitclaim or release deed
5. Bargain and sale deed

A *simple warranty deed* warrants that the seller has valid title to the property and, expressly or impliedly, warrants that the seller grants to indemnify if the buyer suffers any damage because of the grantor's defective title.

A full covenant and **warranty deed** is a deed in which the seller conveys property to the buyer giving special warranties known as **covenants** and usually includes the words "conveys and warrants." In most real property sales, a full covenant and warranty deed is required. The buyer who accepts anything less is not taking advantage of the valuable protection offered in this type of deed for the ownership and use of the purchased property.

The seller of real property makes the following covenants of warranties in a full covenant and warranty deed:

1. That he or she is the owner of the property and has the right to convey title to another
2. That the buyer shall have quiet enjoyment of the property
3. That there are no encumbrances on the property, unless otherwise stated
4. That the seller guarantees the title and will provide any legal documents to the buyer necessary to perfect the title

---

QUITCLAIM DEED

FOR A VALUABLE CONSIDERATION, receipt of which is hereby acknowledged,

QUINCY QUIETTITLE

does hereby REMISE, RELEASE AND FOREVER QUITCLAIM to

ANDREW ACCLAIMED

the real property in the City of Fullerton
County of Orange

State of California, described as

1109 Seacastle Lane, Fullerton, California

Beginning at a point on the northwestern line of Seacastle Lane, distant thereon northwesterly 158 feet from the intersection thereof with the northeastern line of Harbor View Road, as said Lane and Street as shown in the Map hereinafter referred to; running then northwesterly along said line of Seacastle Lane 50 feet; thence northwesterly parallel with said line of Harbor View Road 100 feet; thence southwesterly parallel with said line of Seacastle Lane 50 feet.

Being the northeastern 50 feet of Lot 12 upon the certain Map entitled, "Map of Harbor View Tract, Fullerton, California," filed March 3, 1918, in Book 12 of Maps, at page 36, in the Office of the County Recorder of the County of Orange, State of California.

Dated June 1, 20--

STATE OF CALIFORNIA
COUNTY OF Orange] ss.

On June 1, 20--
before me, the undersigned, a Notary Public in and for said State, personally appeared QUINCY QUIETTITLE

known to me to be the person ___ whose name is subscribed to the within instrument and acknowledged that he executed the same.

WITNESS my hand and official seal.

Signature *Nancy Notary*
NANCY NOTARY

Quincy Quiettitle
QUINCY QUIETTITLE

(This area for official notarial seal)

1085 (10/69)

FIGURE 12-2 *Quitclaim deed.*

The seller may be held liable in damages for the full value of the real estate at the time of the sale for any breach of the warranties.

A **grant deed** transfers title in return for a consideration. The term *grant* warrants that the grantor has not previously conveyed title to any other person and that the estate conveyed is free from any undisclosed liens or encumbrances.

A **quitclaim** or **release deed** transfers to the buyer only the interest that the seller may have in a property. Some land is deeded without oil or mineral rights.

This type of deed merely conveys whatever rights, title, or interest, if any, the grantor has in the property. This deed typically is used when someone gives up some right in a property, such as an easement (see Figure 12-2).

A **gift deed** transfers title on the basis of a special relationship to the grantee, generally on the bonds of affection. Generally a gift deed is executed and delivered without consideration.

A *bargain and sale deed* transfers title of the property but makes no warranties with respect to the title or use of the property. A bargain and sale deed merely gives, grants, bargains, sells, and conveys the land to the grantee to have and to hold forever, without any stated warranties.

Requirements of a Deed

The statutes of most states require the following in the execution of a deed:

1. A deed must be in writing and must be signed by the seller.
2. The deed must contain words indicating the intention to transfer title to the property.
3. The deed must contain a sufficient description of the real property to identify it unmistakably.
4. In some states the deed must be witnessed.
5. The deed must be acknowledged (signed in the presence of a notary public or other authorized official who marks it with a seal) before it is recorded in a designated public office. This public office is usually the recorder's office or the county clerk's office.

MORTGAGES AND DEEDS OF TRUST

Purchasers of real property usually are unable to pay the full purchase price at the time that they buy the property and may use the property as security for a loan. They usually pay a portion of the purchase price (the down payment) and the remainder is given to the seller by a lending agency, usually a bank or savings and loan company. When this is done, the property owner gives the lender a document, known as a *real estate mortgage* (Figure 12-3), as evidence of such security. The person who signs and gives the mortgage is the **mortgagor**, or debtor. The one to whom the mortgage is given is the **mortgagee**, or creditor.

Accompanying a mortgage is a bond, or promissory note, executed by the mortgagor in favor of the lender, making the mortgagor personally liable for the debt. The mortgage represents the lien against the property in the event that the loan is not repaid as agreed. In California and some other states, a **deed of trust** is used instead of a mortgage. The difference between a deed of trust and a mortgage is that with a deed of trust there is a present conveyance of the legal title for the benefit of the lender, whereas with a mortgage the borrower has title to the property and the lending agency has a lien against the property. As a result of this difference, the lending company with a deed of trust has a more effective means of recovering the amount of the loan if the borrower defaults. Both forms are very similar. They are usually prepared on preprinted legal forms, and the names of the lending institution, the person or persons borrowing the money, the terms of the sale, and the legal description of the property are typed on these forms by the secretary. For example, see Figure 12-4.

A *promissory note* is usually prepared as the legal agreement for the repayment of the money borrowed. In some states this note is known as a mortgage, while in other states it is called a note secured by a deed of trust (Figure 12-5). The mortgage, like a deed, must be in writing, and it must be executed, acknowledged, and recorded.

A 283—Mortgage Statutory Form M2 with Special Clauses.
Long Form, Individual or Corporation.

JULIUS BLUMBERG, INC., LAW BLANK PUBLISHERS
80 EXCHANGE PLACE AT BROADWAY, NEW YORK

THIS MORTGAGE, made the 20th day of January , nineteen hundred and

BETWEEN HARVEY CLARK, who resides at 127 Heliothrope, New Rochelle,

New York,

herein referred to as the mortgagor,

and PAUL HENNEBERRY, 672 Begonia, New Rochelle, New York,

herein referred to as the mortgagee,

WITNESSETH, that to secure the payment of an indebtedness in the sum of

Sixty Thousand ($60,000.00)--------------------- dollars,

lawful money of the United States, to be paid

with interest thereon to be computed from 1st day of February , 19--, at
the rate of eight per centum per annum, and to be paid in constant monthly installments of $600.00 each, beginning at the close of escrow hereof,
and continuing for a period of twenty (20) years.

according to a certain bond, note or obligation bearing even·date herewith, the mortgagor hereby mortgages to
the mortgagee, ALL that certain plot, piece, or parcel of land with
buildings and improvements thereon, situate, lying, and being
in the County of Queens, State of New York, and designated on
certain map entitled "Tract No. 30, Broadmoor Estates, New
Rochelle, New York" and filed in the Office of the Clerk of Queens
County on June 23, 19-- as Map No. 468 and described as follows:

Beginning at the point on the westerly side of
Heliothrope Road, Distant 65.80 feet Northerly
from the corner, formed by the intersection of
the Westerly side of Heliothrope Road with the
Northerly side of Main Street, running thence
Westerly parallel with Main Street, 116.89 feet;
thence Northerly on a line nearly parallel with
Heliothrope Road and along the Westerly lines
of lots No. 52 and 53 as shown in said Map, 40 feet;
thence easterly along a line parallel with Main
Street---------------------------------------

FIGURE 12-3 *Mortgage.*

STATE OF NEW YORK,

COUNTY OF }ss.:

On the   day of   20   ,

before me came

to me known, who, being by me duly sworn, did depose and say

that   he resides at

; that   he is the

of

the corporation described in and which executed, the foregoing instru-

ment; that   he knows the seal of said corporation; that the seal

affixed to said instrument is such corporate seal; that it was so affixed

by order of the Board of

of said corporation; and that   he signed h   name thereto by

like order.

STATE OF NEW YORK,

COUNTY OF }ss.:

On the   day of   20   .

before me came

the subscribing witness to the foregoing instrument, with whom I

am personally acquainted, who, being by me duly sworn, did depose

and say that   he resides at

in   , that   he knows

to be the individual   described in, and who executed, the foregoing

instrument; that   he, said subscribing witness, was present and saw

execute the same; and that   he, said witness, at the

same time subscribed   name as witness thereto.

HARVEY CLARK

TO

PAUL HENNEBERRY

Mortgage

Dated, January 20, 20

Amount, $ 60,000.00

Due, February 1, 20

Int. Payable, 8 percent

The land affected by the within instrument

lies in QUEENS COUNTY

STATE OF NEW YORK

Record and return to

Reserve this space for use of Recording Office.

FIGURE 12-3   *Continued*

SHORT FORM DEED OF TRUST AND ASSIGNMENT OF RENTS (With Future Borrowing Clause)

incorporating by reference certain provisions of a fictitious deed of trust of record.

This Deed of Trust, Made this   20th   day of   January   , between

HARVEY CLARK   . herein called TRUSTOR,

whose address is 127 Heliothrope, New Rochelle,   New York
(Number and Street)   (City)   (Zone)   (State)

ACME TITLE INSURANCE AND TRUST CO.   , herein called TRUSTEE, and

. herein called BENEFICIARY,

PAUL HENNEBERRY

Witnesseth: That Trustor IRREVOCABLY GRANTS, TRANSFERS AND ASSIGNS TO TRUSTEE IN TRUST, WITH POWER OF SALE, that property in
ORANGE   County, California, described as:

Lot 42 in Block 12, as described on the Map entitled:

"Tract No. 30, Broadmoor Estates, Fullerton,
California," which was filed in the Office of
the Recorder of the County of Orange, State
of California, on February 6, 20--, in Book
38 of Maps at p. 67.

TOGETHER WITH the rents, issues and profits thereof, SUBJECT, HOWEVER, to the right, power and authority given to and conferred upon Beneficiary by paragraph (10) of the provisions incorporated herein by reference to collect and apply such rents, issues and profits.
For the Purpose of Securing: 1. Performance of each agreement of Trustor incorporated by reference or contained herein. 2. Payment of the indebt-edness evidenced by one promissory note of even date herewith, and any extension or renewal thereof, in the principal sum of $_____ executed by Trustor in favor of Beneficiary or order. 3. Payment of such further sums as the then record owner of said property hereafter may borrow from Beneficiary, when evidenced by another note (or notes) reciting it is so secured.
To Protect the Security of This Deed of Trust, Trustor Agrees: By the execution and delivery of this Deed of Trust and the note secured hereby, that provisions (1) to (14), inclusive, of the fictitious deed of trust recorded June 1, 1953, in the book and at the page of Official Records in the office of the county recorder of the county where said property is located, noted below opposite the name of such county:

COUNTY	BOOK	PAGE	COUNTY	BOOK	PAGE	COUNTY	BOOK	PAGE	COUNTY	BOOK	PAGE
Alameda	7043	118	Kings	558	124	Placer	629	311	Sierra	6	1
Alpine	6	65	Lake	235	108	Plumas	64	277	Siskiyou	315	114
Amador	52	393	Lassen	90	305	Riverside	1477	255	Solano	670	214
Butte	875	4	Los Angeles	41866	80	Sacramento	2420	317	Sonoma	1210	816
Calaveras	81	389	Madera	582	315	San Benito	196	295	Stanislaus	1154	443
Colusa	198	142	Marin	808	420	San Bernardino	3179	87	Sutter	307	248
Contra Costa	2133	208	Mariposa	43	242	San Diego	4874	512	Tehama	244	379
Del Norte	37	241	Mendocino	345	92	San Francisco	6165	282	Trinity	52	167
El Dorado	325	506	Merced	1110	55	San Joaquin	1528	314	Tulare	1879	106
Fresno	3313	673	Modoc	109	221	San Luis Obispo	712	43	Tuolumne	62	47
Glenn	295	536	Mono	30	343	San Mateo	2425	243	Ventura	1137	136
Humboldt	252	449	Monterey	1456	561	Santa Barbara	1156	1	Yolo	395	382
Imperial	862	839	Napa	415	331	Santa Clara	2627	445	Yuba	179	299
Inyo	103	83	Nevada	186	337	Santa Cruz	816	153			
Kern	2070	417	Orange	2512	500	Shasta	402	1			

(which provisions, identical in all counties, are printed on the reverse hereof) hereby are adopted and incorporated herein and made a part hereof as fully as though set forth herein at length; that he will observe and perform said provisions; and that the references to property, obligations, and parties in said provisions shall be construed to refer to the property, obligations, and parties set forth in this Deed of Trust.
The undersigned Trustor requests that a copy of any Notice of Default and of any Notice of Sale hereunder be mailed to him at his address herein-before set forth.

Signature of Trustor

Harvey Clark

STATE OF CALIFORNIA,
County of_____Orange_____ } ss.

On____January 20, 20--_____, before me, the undersigned, a Notary Public in and for said
State, personally appeared_____HARVEY CLARK_____

known to me to be the person__ whose name__ is __ subscribed to the within instrument and acknowledged that__he__
_____executed the same.

WITNESS my hand and official seal.   (Seal)

Edith Wharton

Notary Public in and for said State

Title Order No._____   Escrow or Loan No._____

If executed by a Corporation the Corporation Form of Acknowledgment must be used

SHORT FORM DEED OF TRUST
WOLCOTTS FORM 822—REV. 10-56

FIGURE 12-4   *Deed of trust (short form).*

Form 17   Do Not Destroy This Original Note: When paid, said Original Note, together with the Deed of Trust securing same, must be surrendered to Trustee for Cancellation and retention before reconveyance will be made.

NOTE SECURED BY DEED OF TRUST
(INSTALLMENT – INTEREST INCLUDED DELINQUENT INTEREST COMPOUNDED)

$ __60,000__   _____ Fullerton _____, California, __January 20, 20--__

In installments as herein stated, for value received, I promise to pay to __HARVEY CLARK__

at _____ 127 Heliothrope _____, or order,

the sum of _____ Sixty Thousand ($60,000.00) --------------------------------DOLLARS,

with interest from __February 1, 20--__ _____ on unpaid principal at the

rate of _____ Eight (8) _____ percent per annum; principal and interest payable in installments of

_____ Six Hundred ($600.00) --------------------------------------- Dollars

or more on the _____ First _____ day of each _____ calendar _____ month, beginning

on the _____ First _____ day of _____ February, 20-- _____

_____ and continuing until said principal and interest have been paid.

Each payment shall be credited first on interest then due and the remainder on principal; and interest shall thereupon cease upon the principal so credited. Should interest not be so paid it shall thereafter bear like interest as the principal, but such unpaid interest so compounded shall not exceed an amount equal to simple interest on the unpaid principal at the maximum rate permitted by law. Should default be made in payment of any installment of principal or interest when due the whole sum of principal and interest shall become immediately due at the option of the holder of this note. Principal and interest payable in lawful money of the United States. If action be instituted on this note I promise to pay such sum as the Court may fix as attorney's fees. This note is secured by a DEED OF TRUST to ACME TITLE INSURANCE AND TRUST COMPANY, a California corporation, as Trustee.

Paul Henneberry

THIS FORM FURNISHED BY ACME TITLE INSURANCE AND TRUST COMPANY
DO NOT DESTROY THIS NOTE

FIGURE 12-5   *Note secured by deed of trust.*

RECORDING OF DOCUMENTS

Recording gives constructive notice of the rights of persons regarding the property. It indicates who owns the property or has a mortgage on it and anything else that needs to be known about the property. When it is recorded, the mortgage serves as notice to any third parties who may be interested in purchasing the property or lending money on the property to the owner that the realty is covered by a mortgage and the mortgagee has an interest in it. If the mortgage is not recorded and a subsequent mortgage is placed on the property and recorded, the new mortgage may have precedence over the former.

The recorder's office, or in some cases the clerk of the court's office, is responsible for the recording of all the documents. In order to have a document recorded, it must be sent to the appropriate office with a request for recording. A fee is charged for this service, and the charge varies by location. The fee is usually advanced by the law office or escrow company, and the client is billed later. When a document is received at a recorder's office, identifying information is placed on it that includes the time and date of arrival, the book and page number where the document is officially recorded, and the number assigned to the document. This information permits immediate identification of the document if copies are later required. Most recorder's offices microfilm all recorded documents. Once the information is recorded, it becomes public information and is available to anyone who wishes to see it. After a document has been recorded, it is returned to the sender.

LEASES

A **lease** is a transfer of possession of real estate from a **landlord (lessor)** to a **tenant (lessee)** for a consideration called **rent**. A lease may be oral or written. It may be expressed or simply implied from the facts and circumstances.

A lease may be

1. A tenancy for a stated period
2. A tenancy from period to period
3. A tenancy at will
4. A tenancy at sufferance

The *tenancy for a stated period* of time is just as the name implies. A lease in writing is required by the statute of frauds if the period of the lease exceeds one year. Payments may be established on a monthly or per annum (yearly) basis. The lease for a stated period terminates without notice at the end of that period.

A *tenancy from period to period* may be created by the terms of the lease. For example, a lease may run from January 1, 2005, to December 31, 2006, and from year to year thereafter, unless terminated by the parties. Leases from year to year or from month to month can only be terminated upon the giving of proper notice. The length of the notice is prescribed by the statutes of the state. Most states require a thirty-day notice for terminating a month-to-month lease. They also usually require that this notice be given on the day that the rent is due.

A *tenancy at will* has no period by definition and can be terminated by either party at any time with the prescribed statutory notice.

A *tenancy at sufferance* occurs when a tenant holds over without the consent of the landlord. Until the landlord decides to evict the tenants or allows them to stay, they are tenants at sufferance.

Rights of Lessees

The rights and duties of the parties to the lease are determined by the lease itself and by the statutes of the state in which the property is located. Sometimes these rights are misunderstood. For example, the lessee is entitled to exclusive possession and control of the premises unless the lease provides to the contrary. The landlord has no right to go upon the premises unless it is written in the lease. This means that the owners of an apartment building cannot go into the leased apartments and inspect them unless the lease specifically reserves the right to do so. At the end of the rental period, however, the landlord may retake possession of the premises and at this time may inspect for damages. The landlord also has the right to retake possession of the property if the tenant abandons it.

Rights of Lessors

Upon the termination of the tenancy, the landlord is entitled to possession of the premises. If the tenancy is lawfully terminated, the right of the landlord's possession is absolute, and the motive for the termination of the tenancy does not matter.

Upon expiration of the lease, the tenant is required to return the premises in the same condition as received except for ordinary wear and tear. Unless a state statute provides to the contrary, lessees have the duty to make ordinary repairs, but they are not required to make any improvements.

EVICTION OF A TENANT

If a tenant breaches (fails to perform any of the duties concerning any covenant or the terms of the lease or is in default in the payment of the rent) the landlord may want to repossess the property and **evict** the tenant. The process for evicting a tenant varies from state to state. In some states, it is a very simple process, while in others a formal complaint has to be filed and served on the tenant. In New York, the eviction procedure is a fairly simple process known as a *summary proceeding*. In California, however, this proceeding is a formal procedure and requires a **notice to quit** followed by an unlawful detainer action.

Summary Proceeding

In a **summary proceeding**, used in New York, the landlord or the landlord's attorney completes the printed forms giving the facts of the case and then takes them to the courthouse to be issued. After the fee has been paid, the issued documents are served on the tenant, and he or she is given a specific number of days to answer or appear. If the tenant does not respond within a specified period of time, an officer of the court evicts the tenant.

Unlawful Detainer

If a tenant is to be evicted from rental property in California, the landlord serves the tenant with a preliminary notice entitled Notice to Pay Rent or Quit (Figure 12-6). After the expiration of the appropriate period of time, the tenant is personally served with a verified Complaint for Unlawful Detainer (Figure 12-7) and Summons for Unlawful Detainer (Figure 12-8). The complaint will already have been filed in court and may ask for (1) immediate possession of the rented premises, (2) rent up to and including the time of the trial, (3) damages amounting to three times the amount of money claimed, and (4) attorney's fees.

The tenants are given five days to answer the complaint. If they do not file an answer to the complaint within the five days, the landlord can enter a default judgment (Figure 12-9).

If the tenants file an answer, they will receive notification from the court that a date and time have been set for a hearing. On the day specified, they must appear in court and present their defense. After hearing the evidence, the court will decide who is right and what should be done.

If the court rules in favor of the landlord, it issues (1) a **Writ of Possession** and (2) a judgment for the amount of rent due, plus damages, which is left to the discretion of the judge. Upon receipt of payment of fees by the landlord, the sheriff will serve the *Writ of Execution (Possession of Real Property)* (Figure 12-10) upon the tenants, commanding them to move within five days. If they fail to vacate after five days, the sheriff removes them from the premises.

NOTICE TO PAY RENT OR QUIT

(C. C. P., Sec. 1161)

TO___ TOM TENANT and THERESA TENANT _____

_____

_____

Tenant — In Possession

Within THREE DAYS, after the service on you of this notice, you are hereby required to PAY THE RENT of the premises hereinafter described, of which you now hold possession, amounting to the sum of_____

_____ Four Hundred and 00/100 _____ Dollars, ($ 400.00 ___)

at the rental rate of___ Two Hundred and 00/100 _____ Dollars, ($ 200.00 ___)

per month (or week), being the_ two months' ___rent due from the____ 1st _____day of

____ March ____, 20 -- , to the 31st day of____ July _____ , 20 -- ,

or you are hereby required to DELIVER UP POSSESSION of the hereinafter described premises, within THREE DAYS after service on you of this notice, to the undersigned, or____ BOB SMITH, _____agent, who is

authorized to receive the same or the undersigned will institute legal proceedings against you to recover possession of said premises with ALL RENTS DUE and DAMAGES. The undersigned as a landlord, hereby declares a forfeiture of the lease and agreement under which you occupy the hereinbelow described property:

The premises herein referred to are situated in the_____ City _____of

_____ Villa Park _____County of___ Orange _____

STATE OF CALIFORNIA, designated by the number and street as___ 967 Goldenrod Street _____

_____and more particularly

Dated this___ 4th _____day of____ July _____, 20 --

_____

Jim Kelly
JIM KELLY

FIGURE 12-6   *Notice to Pay Rent or Quit (Courtesy of Wolcotts Legal Forms and Stationary).*

```
 1   ROBERT MORGAN #12345
     Attorney at Law
 2   320 Main Street
     Fullerton, CA 92634
 3   Telephone: (714) 555-2440
     Facsimile: (714) 555-2748
 4
     Attorneys for Plaintiff
 5

 6

 7              SUPERIOR COURT OF THE STATE OF CALIFORNIA

 8                   FOR THE COUNTY OF ORANGE

 9                     NORTH JUSTICE CENTER

10

11   JIM KELLY,                      CASE NO. 46270

12              Plaintiff,
                                     COMPLAINT FOR UNLAWFUL DETAINER
13       v.

14   TOM TENANT, THERESA TENANT, and
     DOES 1 through 5, Inclusive,
15
                Defendants.
16

17

18       Plaintiff complains of defendants and for cause of action

19   alleges:

20       1.   Plaintiff is the owner of the real property located at

21   967 Goldenrod Street, Villa Park, North Orange County Judicial

22   District, Orange County, California.

23       2.   Defendants reside in the City of Villa Park, North Orange

24   County Judicial District, Orange County, California.

25       3.   The real property, possession of which is sought in this

26   action, is situated at 967 Goldenrod Street, Villa Park, North

27   Orange County Judicial District, Orange County, California.

28
```

COMPLAINT FOR UNLAWFUL DETAINER

FIGURE 12-7   *Complaint for Unlawful Detainer.*

1	13. The reasonable value of attorney's fees in this matter is
2	the sum of Three Hundred Fifty Dollars ($350.00) if the matter is
3	uncontested and the sum of Five Hundred Dollars ($500.00) if trial
4	of the matter is necessary.
5	WHEREFORE, plaintiff prays for judgment as follows:
6	1. For restitution of said premises;
7	2. For damages at the rate of Six and 60/100 Dollars ($6.60)
8	per day from March 1, 20--, for each day defendants continue in
9	possession of said premises, and that such amount be trebled;
10	3. For the rent of said premises now due and unpaid for the
11	periods set forth in Paragraph 6 hereof in the sum of Two Hundred
12	Dollars ($200.00);
13	4. For interest on said rent at the legal rate from the date
14	each installment became due and payable;
15	5. For attorney's fees in the sum of Three Hundred Fifty
16	Dollars ($350.00) if the matter is uncontested and the sum of Five
17	Hundred Dollars ($500.00) if trial of the matter is necessary;
18	6. For costs of the suit herein; and
19	7. For such other and further relief as the Court deems just
20	and proper.
21	DATED: July 4, 20--
22	
23	By: _____
24	ROBERT MORGAN Attorney for Plaintiff
25	
26	
27	
28	

Gibson, Dunn & Crutcher LLP

2

COMPLAINT FOR UNLAWFUL DETAINER

FIGURE 12-7 *Continued*

SUMMONS
(CITACION JUDICIAL)

UNLAWFUL DETAINER--EVICTION
(PROCESO DE DESAHUCIO -- EVICCION)

NOTICE TO DEFENDANT: *(Aviso a acusado)*
TOM TENANT, THERESA TENANT, and DOES 1 through 5, Inclusive

YOU ARE BEING SUED BY PLAINTIFF:
(A Ud. le esta demandando)
JIM KELLY

FOR COURT USE ONLY
(SOLO PARA USO DE LA CORTE)

You have *5 DAYS* after this summons is served on you to file a typewritten response at this court. (To calculate the five days, count Saturday and Sunday, but do not count other court holidays.)	*Despues de que le entreguen esta citacion judicial usted tiene un plazo de 5 DIAS pare presenter una respuesta escrita a maquina en esta carte. (Para calcular las cinco alas, cuente el sabado y el domingo, pero no cuente ningun otro dla feriado observado por la corte.)*
A letter or phone call will not protect you. Your typewritten response must be in proper legal form if you want the court to hear your case. If you do not file your response on time, you may lose the case, you may be evicted, and your wages, money and property may be taken without further warning from the court.	*Una carte o una llamada telefonica no le of recera proteccion; su respuesta escrita a maquina tiene que cumplir con las formalidades regales apropiadas si usted quiere que la corte escache su cave. Si usted nopresenta su respuesta a tiempo, puede perder el cave, le pueden obliger a desaloJar su case, y le pueden quitar so salary, so dinero y outrace codas de so propiedad sin Avis adicional par parte de la carte.*
There are other legal requirements. You may want to call an attorney right away. If you do not know an attorney, you may call an attorney referral service or a legal aid office *(listed in the phone book).*	*Existed outrace requisitos regales. Puede que usted quiera llamar a un abogado inmediatamente. Si no conoce a un abogado, puede llamar a un servicio de referencia de abogados o a una oficina de ayuda legal (vea el directorio telefonico).*

The name and address of the court is: *(El nombre y direccion de la corte es)*
SUPERIOR COURT OF THE STATE OF CALIFORNIA, COUNTY OF ORANGE
1275 North Berkeley Avenue
Fullerton, CA 92635-0097
NORTH JUSTICE CENTER

CASE NUMBER: *(Numero del cave)*
46270

The name, address, and telephone number of plaintiff's attorney, or plaintiff without an attorney, is:
(El nombre, la direccion y el numero de telefono del abogado del demandante, o del demandante que no tiene abogado, es)
ROBERT MORGAN   12345   (714) 555-2440
320 Main Street
Fullerton, CA 92634

(Must be answered in all cases) An **unlawful detainer assistant (B&P 6400-6515)** ☐ did **not** ☒ did for compensation give advice or assistance with this form. *(If plaintiff has received **any** help or advice for pay from an unlawful detainer assistant, state):*
a. Assistant's name: b. Telephone No:
c. Street address, city, and ZIP:

d. County of registration: e. Registration No.:   f. Expires on *(date):*

DATE: July 28, 20--   Clerk by _____ Deputy
(Fecha)   *(Actuario)*   *(Delegado)*

[SEAL]

NOTICE TO THE PERSON SERVED: You are served
1. ☒ as an individual defendant.
2. ☐ as the person sued under the fictitious name of *(specify):*

3. ☐ on behalf of *(specify):*

    under: ☐ CCP 416.10 (corporation)   ☐ CCP 416.60 (minor)
        ☐ CCP 416.20 (defunct corporation)   ☐ CCP 416.70 (conservatee)
        ☐ CCP 416.40 (association or partnership)   ☒ CCP 416.90 (individual)
        ☐ other:
4. ☒ by personal delivery on *(date):* July 30, 20--
        (see reverse for Proof of Service)

Form Adopted by Rule 982
Judicial Council of California
982(a)(11) [Rev January 1, 1997]

SUMMONS--UNLAWFUL DETAINER

Code of Civil Procedure, §§ 412.20, 1167

2001 © American LegalNet, Inc.

FIGURE 12-8 *Summons for Unlawful Detainer.*

| PLAINTIFF: JIM KELLY | CASE NUMBER: |
| DEFENDANT: TOM TENANT, THERESA TENANT, et al. | 46270 |

PROOF OF SERVICE

1. At the time of service I was at least 18 years of age and not a party to this action, and **I served copies** of the *(specify documents)*:
SUMMONS, COMPLAINT - UNLAWFUL DETAINER

2. a. Party served *(specify name of party as shown on the documents served)*:
TOM TENANT

   b. Person served: ☒ party in item 2a   ☐ other *(specify name and title or relationship to the party named in item 2a)*:

   c. Address:
   125 Main Street, La Habra, CA 90631

3. I served the party named in item 2
   a. ☒ **by personally delivering** the copies (1) on *(date)*: July 30, 20--   (2) at *(time)*: 8:30 a.m.
   b. ☐ **by leaving** the copies with or in the presence of *(name and title or relationship to person indicated in item 2b)*:

   (1) ☐ **(business)** a person at least 18 years of age apparently in charge at the office or usual place of business of the person served. I informed him or her of the general nature of the papers.
   (2) ☐ **(home)** a competent member of the household (at least 18 years of age) at the dwelling house or usual place of abode of the person served. I informed him or her of the general nature of the papers.
   (3) on *(date)*:   (4) at *(time)*:
   (5) ☐ A **declaration of diligence** is attached. *(Substituted service on natural person, minor, conservatee, or candidate.)*

   c. ☐ **by mailing** the copies to the person served, addressed as shown in item 2c, by first-class mail, postage prepaid,
   (1) on *(date)*:   (2) from *(city)*:
   (3) ☐ with two copies of the *Notice and Acknowledgment of Receipt* and a postage-paid return envelope addressed to me.
   (4) ☐ to an address outside California with return receipt requested.   ◄ *(Attach completed form.)*   ►

   d. ☐ **by causing** copies to be mailed. A declaration of mailing is attached.
   e. ☐ **other** *(specify other manner of service and authorizing code section)*:

4. The "Notice to the Person Served" (on the summons) was completed as follows:
   a. ☒ as an individual defendant.
   b. ☐ as the person sued under the fictitious name of *(specify)*:
   c. ☐ on behalf of *(specify)*:
      under: ☐ CCP 416.10 (corporation)   ☐ CCP 416.60 (minor)   ☐ other:
             ☐ CCP 416.20 (defunct corporation) ☐ CCP 416.70 (conservatee)
             ☐ CCP 416.40 (association or partnership) ☒ CCP 416.90 (individual)

5. **Person serving** *(name, address, and telephone number)*:
   DON SMITH
   929 Goldenrod
   Villa Park, CA 92780
   (924) 555-3366

   a. Fee for service: $ 15.00
   b. ☐ Not a registered California process server
   c. ☐ Exempt from registration under B&P § 22350(b)
   d. ☒ Registered California process server
      (1) ☒ Employee or independent contractor
      (2) Registration No.: 555222
      (3) County: Orange
      (4) Expiration *(date)*: December 31, 20--

6. ☒ I **declare** under penalty of perjury under the laws of the State of California that the foregoing is true and correct.

7. ☐ I am a California sheriff, marshal, or constable and I certify that the foregoing is true and correct.

Date: July 30, 20--

►

(SIGNATURE)

| 982(a)(11) [Rev. January 1, 1997] | **PROOF OF SERVICE**
(Summons--Unlawful Detainer) | Page two
Code of Civil Procedure, 417.10(f)
2001 © American LegalNet, Inc. |

FIGURE 12-8   *Continued*

ATTORNEY OR PARTY WITHOUT ATTORNEY *(Name, Address, Telephone No.)*:	FOR COURT USE ONLY
ROBERT MORGAN (714) 555-2440 Attorney at Law (714) 555-2748 320 Main Street Fullerton, CA 92634 ATTORNEY FOR *(Name):* Plaintiff Bar No: 12345	

SUPERIOR COURT OF CALIFORNIA, COUNTY OF ORANGE
JUSTICE CENTER:

- ☐ Central - 700 Civic Center Dr. West, Santa Ana, CA 92701
- ☐ Harbor-Newport Beach Facility - 4601 Jamboree Rd., Newport Beach, CA 92660-2595
- ☐ Harbor-Laguna Hills Facility - 23141 Moulton Pkwy., Laguna Hills, CA 92653
- ☒ North - 1275 N. Berkeley Ave., Fullerton, CA 92835
- ☐ West - 8141 13ᵗʰ Street, Westminster, CA 92683

PLAINTIFF: JIM KELLY

DEFENDANT: TOM TENANT, et al.

JUDGMENT BY DEFAULT BY COURT ☒ Limited Civil ☐ Unlimited Civil	CASE NUMBER: 46270

Upon application to the Honorable CHARLES KNOWLAND _____ on (date): July 28, 20-- _____.

☒   After having heard the testimony and considered the evidence,

☐   A declaration under Section 585(d) of the Code of Civil Procedure, in lieu of testimony, having been considered,

Judgment entered for plaintiff(s) JIM KELLY _____

to recover from defendant(s) TOM TENANT, et al. _____

☒   The sum of:

	$ 200.00	Principal or Rent and damages
	$ 350.00	Attorney fees
	$ 30.00	Costs
	$	Interest
	$	Other (specify): _____
	$ 580.00	TOTAL, plus interest after judgment at the legal rate.

☐   Restitution and possession of those premises situated in the County of Orange, State of California, and described as: 125 Main Street, La Habra, CA 90631

    ☒   Judgment includes tenants, subtenants, named claimants, and any other occupants of the premises.

☐   Judgment Includes possession of the following personal property: _____

    or its value, which is fixed at $ _____ in case possession cannot be had.

☐   Other: _____

Date: July 28, 20-- _____

_____
Judge/Commissioner/Court Clerk

This judgment was entered on (date): July 28, 20-- _____

ALAN SLATER, Clerk of the Court

By: _____
Deputy Clerk

611 (Rev 1/01)	**JUDGMENT BY DEFAULT BY COURT**	CCP 585(d), 1169

2001 © American LegalNet, Inc.

FIGURE 12-9 *Judgment by Default.*

ATTORNEY OR PARTY WITHOUT ATTORNEY *(Name and Address)*:	TELEPHONE NO.:	FOR RECORDER'S USE ONLY
☒ Recording requested by and return to: ROBERT MORGAN #12345 Attorney at Law 320 Main Street Fullerton, CA 92634	(714) 555-2440 (714) 555-2748	

☒ ATTORNEY FOR ☒ JUDGMENT CREDITOR ☐ ASSIGNEE OF RECORD BAR#

NAME OF COURT: ORANGE COUNTY SUPERIOR COURT
STREET ADDRESS: 1275 N. Berkeley Avenue
MAILING ADDRESS: 1275 N. Berkeley Avenue
CITY AND ZIP CODE: Fullerton, CA 92635
BRANCH NAME: NORTH JUSTICE CENTER

PLAINTIFF: JIM KELLY

DEFENDANT: TOM TENANT, THERESA TENANT, and DOES 1 through 5, Inclusive

	☒ EXECUTION (Money Judgment)	CASE NUMBER:
WRIT	☒ POSSESSION OF ☐ Personal Property	46270
OF	☐ Real Property	FOR COURT USE ONLY
	☐ SALE	

1. **To the Sheriff or any Marshal or Constable of the County of:** Orange

   You are directed to enforce the judgment described below with daily interest and your costs as provided by law.
2. **To any registered process server:** You are authorized to serve this writ only in accord with CCP 699.080 or CCP 715.040.

3. *(Name):* JIM KELLY
   is the ☒ judgment creditor ☐ assignee of record whose address is shown on this form above the court's name.
4. **Judgment debtor** *(name and last known*

   TOM TENANT & THERESA TENANT
   125 Main Street
   La Habra, CA 90631

   ☐ additional judgment debtors on reverse
5. **Judgment entered on** *(date):* July 28, 20--
6. ☐ **Judgment renewed on** *(dates):*

7. **Notice of sale** under this writ
   a. ☒ has not been requested.
   b. ☐ has been requested *(see reverse).*
8. ☐ Joint debtor information on reverse.
   [SEAL]

☐ See reverse for information on real or personal property to be delivered under a writ of possession or sold under a writ of sale.
10. ☐ This writ is issued on a sister-state judgment.

11. Total judgment .... $	580.00
12. Costs after judgment (per filed order or memo CCP 685.090) .... $	0.00
13. Subtotal *(add 11 and 12)*.............. $	580.00
14. Credits .... $	0.00
15. Subtotal *(subtract 14 from 13)* ...... $	580.00
16. Interest after judgment (per filed affidavit CCP 685.050) .... $	0.00
17. Fee for issuance of writ.................. $	1.50
18. **Total** *(add 15,16, and 17)*.............. $	581.50

19. Levying officer:
   (a) Add daily interest from date of writ (at the legal rate on 15) of .... $ — 0.00
   (b) Pay directly to court costs included in 11 and 17 (GC 6103.5, 68511.3, CCP 699.520(i)) .... $ — 0.00
20. ☐ The amounts called for in items 11-19 are different for each debtor. These amounts are stated for each debtor on Attachment 20.

Issued on *(date):* _____ Clerk, by _____, Deputy.

- NOTICE TO PERSON SERVED: SEE REVERSE FOR IMPORTANT INFORMATION -

(Continued on reverse)

Form Approved by the Judicial Council of California EJ-130 [Rev. January 1,1997*]

WRIT OF EXECUTION

Code of Civil Procedure, §§ 699.520, 712.010, 715.010
*See note on reverse

2001 © American LegalNet, Inc.

FIGURE 12-10 *Writ of Execution (Possession of Real Property).*

SUMMARY

Most Americans take the ownership of property for granted and do not realize that this is a right not always enjoyed by citizens in other countries. Law offices are often called on to prepare legal documents that deal with the transfer and leasing of real property.

SHORT TITLE:	CASE NUMBER:
JIM KELLY v. TOM TENANT, et al.	46270

- Items continued from the first page-

4. ☐ **Additional judgment debtor** *(name and last known address):*

7. ☐ **Notice of sale** has been requested by *(name and address):*

8. ☒ **Joint debtor** was declared bound by the judgment (CCP 989-994)

a. on *(date):* July 28, 20--   a. on *(date):* July 28, 20--

b. name and address of joint debtor: b. name and address of joint debtor:

TOM TENANT   THERESA TENANT
125 Main Street   125 Main Street
La Habra, CA 90631   La Habra, CA 90631

    c. ☐ additional costs against certain joint debtors *(itemize):*

9. ☒ *(Writ of Possession or Writ of Sale)* **Judgment** was entered for the following:

    a. ☒ Possession of real property: The complaint was filed on *(date):* July 4, 20--   *(Check (1) or (2)):*

        (1) ☐ The Prejudgment Claim of Right to Possession was served in compliance with CCP 415.46. The judgment includes all tenants, subtenants, named claimants, and other occupants of the premises.

        (2) ☐ The Prejudgment Claim of Right to Possession was NOT served in compliance with CCP 415.46.

           (a) $_____ was the daily rental value on the date the complaint was filed.

           (b) The court will hear objections to enforcement of the judgment under CCP 11 74.3 on the following dates *(specify):*

    b. ☐ Possession of personal property

        ☐ If delivery cannot be had, then for the value *(itemize in 9e)* specified in the judgment or supplemental order.

    c. ☐ Sale of personal property

    d. ☐ Sale of real property

    e. Description of property:

- NOTICE TO PERSON SERVED -

WRIT OF EXECUTION OR SALE. Your rights and duties are indicated on the accompanying Notice of Levy.

WRIT OF POSSESSION OF PERSONAL PROPERTY. If the levying officer is not able to take custody of the property, the levying officer will make a demand upon you for the property. If custody is not obtained following demand, the judgment may be enforced as a money judgment for the value of the property specified in the judgment or in a supplemental order.

WRIT OF POSSESSION OF REAL PROPERTY. If the premises are not vacated within five days after the date of service on the occupant or, if service is by posting, within five days after service on you, the levying officer will remove the occupants from the real property and place the judgment creditor in possession of the property. Except for a mobile home, personal property remaining on the premises will be sold or otherwise disposed of in accordance with CCP 1174 unless you or the owner of the property pays the judgment creditor the reasonable cost of storage and takes possession of the personal property not later than 15 days after the time the judgment creditor takes possession of the premises.

➤A Claim of Right to Possession form accompanies this writ *(unless the Summons was served in compliance with CCP 415.46).*

EJ-130 [Rev. January 1, 1997*]   *NOTE: Continued use of form EJ-130 (Rev. July 1, 1996) is authorized through December 31, 1997.   **Page two**

WRIT OF EXECUTION

2001 © American LegalNet, Inc.

FIGURE 12-10 *Continued*

Most property can be classified into two categories, personal or real. Personal property is movable property and includes boats, jewelry, furniture, unlaid carpeting, and items that can be transported from one place to another. Real property includes land and anything attached thereto.

While it is relatively easy to describe personal property, it is much more difficult to describe real property. The enforceable description of real property is very important in dealing with property transactions. There are various methods of describing real property, and the exact method may vary from location to location.

The way that title to property is taken is in the form that ownership is specified in the deed in the purchase or acquisition. The possession of real property is transferred through a lease.

Ownership and leasing of real property can take many different forms, and it is important for the legal office assistant to have a basic understanding of real property transactions and procedures.

VOCABULARY

abstract of title   A condensed history of a land title, including all recorded conveyances, mortgages, liens, and other changes affecting a parcel of land.

assessment   The process of appointing an amount to be paid as an assessment of taxes or damages.

base lines   A line running east and west as set by the U.S. Survey System in 1785.

block   A group of lots in a plotted piece of ground.

bounds   A compass direction used for plotting land.

breach   Breaking a law or failing to perform a duty.

community property   Property belonging equally to the husband and wife acquired during the existence of a marriage.

conveyance   A transfer of legal title to land; also a written instrument, under seal, transferring the title to land, or some interest therein, from one person to another.

covenant   A written agreement or promise between two or more parties, especially for the performance of some action.

deed   A document by which one person transfers the legal ownership of land and what is on the land to another person.

deed of trust (trust deed)   A document by which a person transfers the legal ownership of land to independent trustees to be held until a debt on the land (a mortgage) is paid off.

easement   The right to make use of the land of another in some way, such as a driveway or gateway.

escrow   Deposit of something, such as a deed or negotiable instrument, with a third person to be held until some condition is met.

evict   To expel from property by due process of law; to dispossess.

fee simple   Absolute ownership of real property.

gift deed   A deed for which the consideration is love and affection and where there is no material consideration.

grant deed   A two-party deed involving grantor and grantee.

grantee   One to whom title to land is transferred.

grantor   One by whom a grant is made.

guaranty   To be responsible for; to give security to.

improvements   An addition to land or its existing structure, such as fences, curbs, sewers, and landscaping.

joint tenancy   Joint ownership by two or more persons with right of survivorship; all joint tenants own an equal and undivided interest and have equal rights in the property.

landlord   An owner who leases property or certain rights to property to another.

lease   A contract between owner and tenant setting forth conditions upon which the tenant may occupy and use the property and the term of the occupancy.

legal description   Identifies property according to legal requirements.

lessee   One who contracts to rent. See also *landlord*.

lessor   An owner who enters into a lease with a tenant.

lien   A charge imposed on property by which the property is made security for the discharge of an obligation.

lots   A lot is the smallest subdivision of property in a platted piece of land.

meridian   A line running north and south as set by the U.S. Survey System in 1785.

metes   The distance along a boundary line. Metes and bounds is a mapping method for land using boundary lines and angular measurements.

mineral rights   The rights that someone has to minerals on real property (may or may not include the right to mine the minerals).

mortgage   A document representing a claim on property in favor of a lender in case money is not repaid when due. Chattel mortgages are against personal property; real estate mortgages are against real property.

mortgagee   The person to whom a mortgage is given (the lender).

mortgagor   The person who receives a mortgage (the homeowner).

notice to quit   Written notice from a landlord to a tenant that the tenant will have to move.

per annum   A Latin term meaning "annually; by the year."

per diem   A Latin term meaning "per day"; an allowance of so much per day. Used in connection with rents, wages, or salary.

personal property   Movable property; something that is detachable without injury to real property.

plats   Divisions of real property into blocks and tracts.

public records   Records kept by a county clerk or other official.

quitclaim (release) deed   A deed to relinquish any interest in property that the grantor may have.

real property   Land and everything attached to it, such as buildings or landscaping.

rectangular (government) survey   Survey system based on using latitude and longitude lines.

rent   Payment for temporary possession of real or personal property.

sections   A unit of land measuring one square mile and containing 640 acres. There are 36 sections in a township.

summary proceeding   An abbreviated type of court hearing available in some situations, for example, in an eviction where the tenant's failure to pay rent automatically ends the lease.

survey   An evaluation of real property to determine its boundaries and physical limits.

tenancy by the entirety   Property acquired by a husband and wife after marriage in which neither has the right to sell without the full consent of the other.

tenancy in common   Ownership by two or more persons who hold undivided interest, without right of survivorship to the parties. The owner's interest passes on to his or her heirs at death.

tenant   One who has the temporary use and occupation of real property owned by another person (called the "landlord").

title   Evidence of legal ownership of property, especially real property.

township   A six-mile-square piece of land that is measured north and south of a base line.

trust deed   See *deed of trust*.

trustee   One appointed to execute a trust or who holds property for the benefit of another.

trustor   One who places property in trust.

Uniform Commercial Code   The code that has been adopted by all states to govern commercial transactions.

unlawful detainer   Unjustifiable retention of land by one whose right to possession has terminated.

warranty deed   A deed in which clear title to the property is absolutely guaranteed by the seller; a deed containing a covenant of warranty.

Writ of Possession   An order of the court requiring that possession of certain property be granted to a designated party.

STUDENT ASSESSMENT 1

Instructions: Circle T if the statement is true or F if the statement is false.

T   F   1.   A township is larger than a section.

T   F   2.   A title search is an unnecessary expense if the prospective purchaser is buying the property from friends or relatives.

T   F   3.   Base lines run north and south.

T   F   4.   Abstract companies make title searches and offer title insurance policies.

T   F   5.   In some states the promissory note prepared for the repayment of a loan is called a Note Secured by Deed of Trust.

T   F   6.   In real property transactions, it is important that the deed contain a complete description of the real property.

T   F   7.   A plat is a map showing property divided into lots and blocks.

T   F   8.   New York is a community property state.

T   F   9.   Once a real property document has been recorded, it becomes public information for anyone who wishes to see it.

T   F   10.   Landlords are entitled to go into the apartments that they own whenever necessary to inspect them.

T   F   11.   While it is better to have a written lease, leases may be either oral or written.

T   F   12.   A title search and a title insurance policy mean the same thing.

T   F   13.   In the event of the death of one of the owners in a joint tenancy, the decedent's share of the real property reverts to the heirs.

T   F   14.   Title policies protect the buyer's interest in the property purchased.

T   F   15.   In New York, the eviction process is called a summary proceeding.

STUDENT ASSESSMENT 2

Instructions: Circle the letter that indicates the most correct answer.

1. The symbols ' and " are used in real property descriptions to indicate
   - a. minutes and seconds
   - b. chains and links
   - c. feet and inches
   - d. none of these

2. Property acquired by a husband and wife in which that person's share reverts to the other party upon death is called
   - a. tenancy in common
   - b. personal
   - c. separate
   - d. joint tenancy
   - e. none of these

3. A meridian
   - a. runs north and south
   - b. was established in 1785
   - c. is sometimes called a prime meridian
   - d. all of these

4. Metes refers to
   - a. degrees
   - b. area
   - c. distance
   - d. none of these

5. Which of the following is considered to be real property?
   - a. automobile
   - b. carpeting (unlaid)
   - c. television
   - d. furniture
   - e. none of these

STUDENT ASSESSMENT 3

Instructions: Insert the word that best completes the statement.

1. Real property may include other things, but always consists of _____.
2. An affidavit is made by the person known as the _____.
3. In some states, landlords may collect _____ damages from the tenant if malicious abuse to the property can be proved.
4. If a complaint for an Unlawful Detainer is filed in California, the defendant has _____ days to respond.
5. In New York, the transfer of real property is usually handled by a/an _____.

STUDENT ASSESSMENT 4

Instructions: Match the most correct letter to the number.

Section I	Section I
_____ 1. joint tenancy	A. ownership by two or more people without right of survivorship
_____ 2. assessment	B. a charge imposed on property in which the property is made security for the discharge
_____ 3. tenancy in common	C. the valuation of property for the purpose of levying a tax
_____ 4. community property	D. ownership by two or more people with right of survivorship
_____ 5. lien	E. property accumulated through joint efforts of the husband and wife living together

Section II	Section II
_____ 1. easement	A. more restrictive than joint tenancy
_____ 2. escrow	B. the purchaser of a deed
_____ 3. grantor	C. the deposit of instruments and funds to a neutral third party to carry out the provisions of a contract
_____ 4. grantee	D. a right or privilege that one party has in the land of another
_____ 5. tenancy by entirety	E. seller of a deed

STUDENT ASSIGNMENTS

PRACTICE SET 4: UNLAWFUL DETAINER (EVICTION OF A TENANT)

Case Particulars

Attorney:	Robert Morgan Attorney at Law 320 Main Street Fullerton, CA 92634 Telephone: (714) 555-2440 Fax: (714) 555-2748 Penalty for late payment:	Manager (Agent): Monthly rent: Date of rental agreement: Total number of adults: Total number of children: Term of agreement begins: $10.00	Arnold Brown $600.00 October 23, _____ 2 0 November 1, _____
Plaintiff (Lessor):	Leon Landlord	Penalty for returned check (insufficient funds):	$10.00
Defendants (Tenants): Location:	Richard and Rose Renter 1164 Harmony Court Fullerton, CA 92635	Date of eviction notice: Unpaid rent: Rent due from:	February 2, _____ $1,200.00 (two months) January 1, _____ to February 28, _____

Case History

Richard and Rose Renter entered into an agreement with Leon Landlord to rent the premises at 1164 Harmony Court, Fullerton, CA 92635, at a rental rate of $600.00 per month.

Richard and Rose Renter have fallen behind in their monthly rental payments, and Leon Landlord has served them with a Three-Day Notice to Quit or Pay Rent. They still refuse to pay the rent, and Mr. Landlord has a very responsible prospective tenant who wants to rent the property. Mr. Landlord needs to have the premises vacated and has employed Robert Morgan, Attorney at Law, to file an unlawful detainer proceeding to remove them from the property.

(continued)

Richard and Rose Renter have not filed an answer to the Complaint and therefore have allowed the case to become a default.

PROJECT 1: RENTAL AGREEMENT

Instructions: Using your word processor, open file **ch012_AG**, Rental Agreement, from your data disk and fill in the information listed under case particulars. This is the original rental agreement between LEON LANDLORD and RICHARD and ROSE RENTER that is needed to process this case and evict the tenant. Save your document as **ch12_AG**, and print one copy for your instructor.

PROJECT 2: NOTICE TO PAY RENT OR QUIT

Instructions: Retrieve the file **ch012_NT**, Notice to Pay Rent or Quit, and follow the same instructions as indicated in Project 1. Save your document as **ch12_NT**, and print one copy for your instructor.

PROJECT 3: DECLARATION OF LANDLORD

Instructions: Using the stored caption template from Chapter 7, prepare the following Declaration of Leon Landlord in Support of Default Judgment for Unlawful Detainer (Sample 12-1, page 302-303). Save your document as **ch12_DEC**, and print one copy for your instructor. (See Sample 12-1.)

PROJECT 4: LETTER TO MARSHAL'S OFFICE

Instructions: Retrieve your letterhead template and prepare the letter on page 301 to the marshal's office. Save your document as **ch12_LT** and print one copy for your instructor.

Congratulations! You have just completed the necessary legal papers for a tenant eviction. (In addition, you would, however, need to prepare and file the court forms Complaint for Unlawful Detainer, Summons—Unlawful Detainer, Request to Enter Default, Judgment by Default, and Writ of Execution that are included in Chapter 12 to make this practice set case complete.)

PROJECT 5: PROMISSORY NOTE

Instructions: Retrieve **ch012_PN**, Promissory Note, and fill in the blanks with the information that is included in the promissory note example, Figure 12-1. Save your document as **ch12_PN** and print one copy for your instructor.

PROJECT 6: QUITCLAIM DEED

Instructions: Retrieve **ch012_QD**, Quitclaim Deed, and fill in the blanks with the information that is included in the quitclaim deed example, Figure 12-2. Save your document as **ch12_QD**, and print one copy for your instructor.

February 27, 20--

Marshal's Office
North Orange County Judicial District
1275 North Berkeley Avenue
Fullerton, CA 92635

RE: LANDLORD vs. RENTER
    North Orange County Municipal Court No. 38887

Gentlemen:

Enclosed please find original and two copies of Writ of Execution (Possession of Real Property) and our check for service.

Please consider this letter your instructions to execute on the judgment by obtaining possession of the premises known as 1164 Harmony Court, Fullerton, California.

If you have any questions, or if I can be of any assistance, please telephone me.

Yours very truly,

ROBERT MORGAN

urs
Enclosures

1 ROBERT MORGAN #12345
   Attorney at Law
2 320 Main Street
   Fullerton, CA 92634

3

   Phone: (714) 555-2440
4 Fax: (714) 555-2748

5 Attorney for Plaintiff

6

7

8   SUPERIOR COURT OF THE STATE OF CALIFORNIA

9   FOR THE COUNTY OF ORANGE

10   NORTH JUSTICE CENTER

11 LEON LANDLORD,   )   NO. 38887
)
12   Plaintiff,   )
)   DECLARATION OF LEON LANDLORD IN
13   vs.   )   SUPPORT OF DEFAULT JUDGMENT FOR
)   UNLAWFUL DETAINER
14   )
    RICHARD RENTER, ROSE RENTER,   )
15 and DOES 1 through 5, Inclusive,   )
)
16   Defendants.   )

17

18   I, LEON LANDLORD, declare:

19   I am the Plaintiff herein and the owner of the premises located at 1164 Harmony

20 Court, Fullerton, California.

21   Plaintiff leased to Defendants, RICHARD RENTER, ROSE RENTER, and DOES

22 1 through 5, Inclusive, and each of them, the premises known as 1164 Harmony Court, Fullerton,

23 California, under a month-to-month Rental Agreement at a monthly rental rate of Six Hundred

24 Dollars ($600.00) per month, payable in advance on the first day of each month.

25   Defendants, RICHARD RENTER, ROSE RENTER, and DOES 1 through 5,

26 Inclusive, and each of them, went into possession of the premises on November 1, 20--, and have

27 continued to occupy the same ever since.

28

SAMPLE 12-1

1   Since February 1, 20 --, Defendants, RICHARD RENTER, ROSE RENTER, and

2   DOES 1 through 5, Inclusive, and each of them, have failed to pay the rental then due. No part of

3   said rent has been paid, and there is now due and payable by Defendants, RICHARD RENTER,

4   ROSE RENTER, and DOES 1 through 5, Inclusive, and each of them, the sum of Six Hundred

5   Dollars ($600.00) for the month of February, 20 --.

6   On February 2, 20--, Plaintiff caused to be served on Defendants, and each of them,

7   a written notice stating the amount of rent then due, and requiring Defendants to pay the full

8   amount thereof or deliver up possession of said premises within three (3) days.

9   More than three (3) days have elapsed since service of such notice, and Defendants

10   have failed to pay the rent owed or deliver up possession of the premises.

11   On February 21, 20 --, I filed a Complaint against the Defendants for Unlawful

12   Detainer.

13   Defendant RICHARD RENTER was personally served on February 21, 20 --, at

14   7:30 p.m., and ROSE RENTER was personally served on February 21, 20 --, at 7:30 p.m.

15   More than five (5) days have elapsed since RICHARD RENTER and ROSE

16   RENTER were served with the Complaint for Unlawful Detainer, and Defendants have failed to

17   file a written pleading in response to the Complaint.

18   Accordingly, on February 27, 20--, I caused to be submitted a Request to Enter

19   Default on RICHARD RENTER and ROSE RENTER for Unlawful Detainer.

20   I declare that I personally entered into the Rental Agreement with Defendants, I

21   personally witnessed their signatures on the Rental Agreement, and if called upon to so testify in

22   open court, I could do so.

23   I declare, under penalty of perjury, that the foregoing is true and correct, and that

24   this Declaration was executed on February 27, 20 --.

25

26   LEON LANDLORD

27

28

SAMPLE 12-1 *Continued*

13

CRIMINAL LAW

OBJECTIVES

Upon completion of this chapter, you should be able to:

1. List four theories for punishing criminal behavior
2. Identify three functions of criminal law
3. Discuss four reasons for punishment
4. Explain the safeguards that protect individuals from abuse of power
5. List the steps in a criminal procedure
6. Describe the major groups of crime
7. Explain the classifications of crime
8. Discuss the defenses available to a criminal defendant
9. Prepare documents used in a criminal proceeding

A **crime** may be defined as an offense against society. Criminal law forbids conduct that harms society. The purpose of criminal law is to protect the public by keeping peace and order in the community.

People who are found to have broken the criminal law are punished. The degree of severity of this punishment may vary from a small fine to the death penalty. The type of punishment imposed will be affected by the type of crime that is committed and whether that person has committed other crimes in the past.

There are many theories for punishing criminal behavior. One theory is that punishment is imposed to get revenge or "get even" with the person who broke the law. A second theory is that punishing the wrongdoer will deter or discourage other people from breaking the law. A third theory for punishment is to rehabilitate, or reform, the criminals. A fourth theory is to incapacitate criminals by keeping them away from the community; society protects itself from their further criminal behavior by isolating them.

WHAT IS CRIMINAL LAW?

Criminal law is the branch of law that

1. Labels certain kinds of harmful (antisocial) conduct as crimes
2. Forbids such conduct
3. Provides for the punishment of people who commit crimes

A crime harms society. The kinds of conduct that are forbidden by criminal law are so harmful that they not only hurt the individual victim, but society as a whole.

Criminal laws are made and enforced by the government to protect society from these harms.

Reasons for Punishment

We do not, and we should not, punish people without a reason. The four major reasons for punishing people who break the criminal law are as follows:

1. Retribution
2. Deterrence
3. Rehabilitation
4. Incapacitation

Retribution The oldest reason for punishing someone who violates the law is **retribution**, that is, paying back criminals for the harm that they may have caused. The knowledge that the government will punish criminals makes it easier for the crime victims and their families to leave the business of punishment to the government. If no punishment were incurred, the victims and their families might try to seek revenge on their own. It is also important that criminals receive only the punishment that they deserve, and not more. A person who commits a minor crime should receive a lighter punishment than a person who commits a serious crime.

Punishment for the sake of punishment has been criticized by those who consider it a primitive or savage way to act. They feel that a better reason for punishment is rehabilitation or deterrence. There are those, however, who defend the use of punishment as retribution, arguing that in order for laws to be effective they must be enforced by arresting, convicting, and punishing those who break the law. Punishing those who break the law demonstrates that society has important values and that criminal law supports and protects these values.

Deterrence The second reason for punishment is **deterrence**, that is, discouraging people from violating the law. Those who think deterrence is a good reason for punishment point out that most people try to avoid negative experiences. Therefore, to avoid being punished, people will obey, and not violate, the law. Those who commit the crimes are punished to serve as an example for the rest of society.

Rehabilitation A third reason for punishment is **rehabilitation**. Rehabilitation provides criminals with the counseling and training that they need to live in society as law-abiding citizens. They may have committed the crime because they do not have the skills or education to get a job. Others commit crimes because they do not know the difference between right and wrong, or they may have emotional problems. Rehabilitation may require that the convicted person learn a trade or get an education so that they will not revert to antisocial behavior. Rehabilitation also may be in the form of treatment or counseling.

Incapacitation The last reason for punishment is **incapacitation**—isolating the criminals from the rest of society so that they cannot commit any more crimes. Those who support this idea feel that the best way to deter crime is to lock up criminals in prison, and the goal of criminal law is the protection of society.

The Constitution and the Justice System

The federal and state agencies that make up the administration of the justice system have a great deal of power. They have the power to take away an individual's freedom and, sometimes, even an individual's life. However, any system with so much power also must have the safeguards that protect the individual from the abuse of power. Many of these safeguards are contained in the Constitution of the United States.

FIGURE 13-1
Constitutional amendments that apply to criminal cases.

Fourth Amendment	*Fifth Amendment*
Prohibits unreasonable searches and seizures	Prohibits double jeopardy
Requires probable cause	Provides right to remain silent
Sixth Amendment	*Eighth Amendment*
Requires speedy, public jury trial	Prohibits excessive bail and cruel and unusual punishment
Provides right to be informed of charges	
Provides right to call and confront witnesses	*Fourteenth Amendment*
Provides right to counsel	Applies Bill of Rights to the states

The Bill of Rights   The United States Constitution is a unique document that not only establishes three branches of government and their powers but that also establishes the limitation of those powers. The Bill of Rights is the name given to the first ten amendments to the Constitution and provides for many citizens' rights that must be recognized.

The first eight amendments concern procedures used in criminal law. The state procedures for criminal law must follow the constitutional rules, and federal and state rules of criminal procedures must meet all constitutional requirements. The Sixth Amendment to the Constitution states that a person charged with a crime must be provided with a right to counsel. The portions of the Constitution and the amendments that deal with criminal procedure are binding on the federal government and on all states.

In reading the actual amendments, it is impossible to understand their full meaning without reading the decisions of the Supreme Court that has interpreted them. The Supreme Court is the final authority on the interpretation and meaning of the Constitution.

Figure 13-1 gives some of the amendments and a synopsis of their interpretation.

CRIMINAL PROCEDURES

Criminal law concerns itself with offenses against society or the state. The plaintiff in criminal law actions is the state or THE PEOPLE OF THE UNITED STATES or THE PEOPLE OF THE STATE OF . . . The case title might read:

```
THE PEOPLE OF THE STATE           )
OF CALIFORNIA,                     )
                                   )     No.109326
                    Plaintiff,     )
                                   )     ORDER OF ARREST
         vs.                       )
                                   )
SAMUEL SMITH,                      )
                                   )
                    Defendant.     )
_____    )
```

Many attorneys specialize in the field of criminal law, and most attorneys will at some time defend a client in a criminal law matter. The U.S. Constitution, state constitutions, and state statutes guarantee a person accused of a crime certain rights under the law. The charges against the accused must be filed in the proper courts, and the case must be brought to trial on a timely basis before the statute of limitations has expired. While a few procedures are different, most of the steps used in criminal cases are similar to those used in civil suits.

Points and authorities, depositions, and interrogatories are used extensively in criminal lawsuits, as are motions, notices of motions, stipulations, and other supporting documents.

The usual steps in a criminal procedure are as follows:

1. Warrant of arrest
2. Arrest: individual taken into custody
3. Arraignment: prisoner taken before the court to answer to the criminal charge
4. Preliminary trial or examination
5. Trial
6. Judgment or verdict: defendant found guilty or not guilty by a court or by the jury
7. Appeal (if filed)

Warrant of Arrest

A criminal action begins with the filing of an informal complaint by an individual. This complaint, charging that a crime (a violation of the law) has been committed, is filed with a law enforcement officer. A **warrant** (written permission giving authority to make an arrest) is signed by the judge, and an arrest is made.

Arrest

The legal beginning of most criminal cases is the **arrest**. If it is a minor offense, the officer of the law might not take the person into custody, and a summons may be used. The summons orders a person to appear in a certain court at a fixed date and time.

Booking   If a felony or serious misdemeanor is involved, the officer may not use a summons, and the suspect will be arrested and taken to a police station. There the arrestee will be booked. **Booking** is the process whereby the arrested person's name is entered into the police department's arrest book. This serves to show that the person was arrested, and the arrestee will have an arrest record. During the booking stage, the arrestee is also photographed, fingerprinted, and asked to answer questions relating to identification.

Interrogation   When a person is in custody, it is not unusual for the police to try to get information from the arrestee about the crime. This questioning is called **interrogation** and helps clear up any doubts about the case. It is also helpful to the prosecution if the police can get the suspect to sign a written **confession**. Our legal system allows the police to question a suspect, but they cannot force the suspect to confess. Forcing a confession violates the right of the Fifth Amendment, which states that persons shall not be forced to be witnesses against themselves.

Voluntary confessions, however, may be used against a defendant at a trial. The confession *must* be a voluntary act and must be given of the arrestee's free will.

The Miranda Rule   Interrogations do not always take place at a police station. There is a special rule that applies only to those people who are in custody. Since a person in custody might assume that he or she must answer all questions asked by the police, the United States Supreme Court has said that the suspect must be read the *Statement of Rights* before the police can begin to question the suspect. If a prosecutor wants to have the defendant's confession accepted as evidence, the prosecutor

FIGURE 13-2 *Miranda warning.*

STATEMENT OF RIGHTS
Miranda vs. Arizona
384 U.S. 436 (1966)

Before we ask you any questions, it is my duty to advise you of your rights.

- You have the right to remain silent.
- Anything you say can be used against you in court or any other proceeding.
- You have the right to consult an attorney before making any statement or answering any questions. You may have an attorney present with you during questioning.
- If you cannot afford a lawyer, one will be appointed for you before any questioning, if you wish.
- If you decide to answer questions now, without a lawyer present, you still have the right to stop the questioning at any time for the purpose of consulting a lawyer.
- *However*, you may waive the right to advice of counsel and your right to remain silent, and you may answer questions or make a statement without consulting a lawyer if you so desire.

---

must prove that the police gave the arrested person the *Miranda* warning (Figure 13-2). If the prosecutor cannot prove that the Miranda warning was given, the judge will not allow the jury to hear the confession as evidence in the trial.

When an individual accused of a crime has been taken into custody, bail is set by the court. The accused has the right to make certain telephone calls and will probably arrange for payment of bail. **Bail** may be posted in the form of cash or a guarantee referred to as a bail bond. Bail guarantees that the accused will appear in court at the time and date specified. If the accused does not appear at the specified time and date, bail is forfeited. Depending on the seriousness of the alleged crime, if the accused is prominent in the community or has a reliable record of employment, the accused may be released on his or her **own recognizance** or given what is termed an **OR**.

Writ of Habeas Corpus A *writ of habeas corpus* is an order directed to the custodian of a prisoner to produce the prisoner in court to determine if there is sufficient reason to keep the individual in custody. *Habeas corpus* is a Latin term that means "you have the body" and is a guarantee of personal freedom under English and American law. This procedure prevents the unjust detention of a person by legal authorities and is a personal liberty guaranteed by every state constitution and by the U.S. Constitution.

This procedure has historical implications and dates back to the fifteenth century when a jailer was not required to make an immediate response to a writ and could evade it by moving the prisoner from prison to prison or to another country or even another continent.

Any person restrained without full constitutional rights may begin a *habeas corpus* proceeding. The proceeding is initiated by filing a petition with the clerk of the court in which the relief is sought, and, after the service of the petition, the petitioner is brought before the court for a hearing.

Arraignment

The **arraignment** is the first step in the trial of a felony proceeding. The three purposes of the arraignment are

1. To establish the identity of the accused
2. To inform the accused of the charges
3. To allow the court to hear the plea of the accused

The plea made by an accused party may be any one of the following: not guilty, former or double jeopardy; former judgment, **conviction**, or acquittal; not guilty by reason of insanity; guilty; or *nolo contendere*. The latter plea means "no contest" and constitutes neither an admission nor denial of guilt. If the defendant does not plead guilty at this time, a date is set for trial.

Preliminary Hearing

The preliminary hearing is held to determine whether there is probable cause for holding the accused for trial. In some cases, a grand jury indictment may be used in lieu of a preliminary hearing. A preliminary hearing may also be held for the purpose of fixing bail.

Plea Bargaining   When a defendant pleads guilty, it is usually because of **plea bargaining**. This occurs when an agreement has been made with the prosecutor for the defendant to plead guilty in exchange for certain favorable treatment that the prosecutor can give the defendant. For example, a prosecutor may lower the crime charged to a less serious one, recommend to the judge a lighter sentence, or, if the defendant has been charged with more than one crime, strike out some of the charges.

Trial

The trial is the next step in the criminal proceedings. The jury is selected, and the members of the jury are generally cautioned against reading the newspapers or availing themselves of other media regarding the case. A person accused of a crime has a right to a trial by jury and is presumed innocent until proved guilty. The defendant in a criminal trial has the right to be present during all the proceedings, whether they are open or closed sessions. Any information or evidence that tends to negate the guilt or culpability of the accused must be turned over to the defense by the prosecution.

Judgment

If the defendant is found guilty, the court has the authority to impose the sentence. The sentence is based on definite written or oral findings of fact and conclusions of law. These are signed by the judge and recorded so that a transcript may be obtained.

Probation is an act of the court involving suspending the sentence of the convicted criminal while placing the individual under the supervision of a probation officer. The conditions of the court also may include restitution, counseling, or treatment as a condition of probation.

Parole is a conditional release of the offender before the expiration of the prison term while remaining under the supervision of public authority. If the conditions of the parole are violated, the offender is returned to imprisonment.

Appeal

If the accused believes that a legal error has occurred, the accused may appeal the case to a higher court. This is known as an **appeal** or a review of the decision of a lower court. Certain convictions bring an automatic appeal.

CRIMINAL ACTS

Any offense for which the law prescribes punishment by fine, imprisonment, or capital punishment is a crime. Thus a crime is an offense against society or the state. The state or federal government institutes a criminal action against the one who commits an act forbidden or refrains from performing an act commanded by the law.

Types of Crimes

There are three categories of crimes: felonies, misdemeanors, and infractions.

Felony   A felony is a serious crime against society and usually is punishable by death or imprisonment in a state prison. The federal crimes are those listed in the U.S. Criminal Code and others so declared by act of Congress. Any citizen who starts a rebellion, who aids and abets alien enemies, or who commits other acts specifically stated to be treason in the U.S. Constitution is guilty of the charge of treason. The Constitution states that the punishment for treason is death.

Since the federal government never adopted the common law, all federal crimes must be set forth in the written law. Murder, embezzlement, larceny, bribery, and arson are among the crimes classified as felonies. Any crime for which the penalty is a fine, imprisonment in a state or federal prison, or an offense punishable by death is considered to be a felony.

Misdemeanor   A misdemeanor is a lesser crime, usually punishable by a fine or imprisonment in the county jail, or both. Disorderly conduct, drunkenness, excessive driving speed, simple assault, and some types of trespassing fall into this category. Successive charges resulting from continued offenses of the same misdemeanor may result in a mandatory prison sentence. This is also true of traffic offenses due to the driver's intoxicated condition.

Infractions   An infraction is a minor offense usually punishable by a fine. Most traffic violations, littering, and loitering are just a few examples of this less serious offense.

Mental Element in Crime

There are two elements of a crime—act and **intent**. The latter refers to the guilty mind, wrongful purpose, or criminal intent. Motive is not an essential element of a crime. A bad motive does not make an act a crime. However, evidence of a motive is admissible to establish other elements that are essential.

The *act* is the other element of a crime and is generally defined as a performance, a deed, or a movement, as distinguished from remaining at rest. A crime also may be committed by a mere omission to act. Common examples include failure to file an income tax return, the failure to pay income taxes, and the failure of a public official to perform a duty imposed by law.

Classes of Crimes

Another way of classifying crimes is on the basis of the subject of the crime. This classification includes crimes against person, crimes against habitation, crimes against property, and crimes against public authority.

Crimes Against Person   The major crimes against person include homicide, manslaughter, mayhem, rape, assault, battery, kidnapping, and abduction.

Homicide is the killing of a human being by another human being and may be justifiable, excusable, or felonious. **Murder** is divided into two degrees in most states. Usually, a first-degree murder is defined as the premeditated and deliberate killing of a human being. While definitions vary from state to state, first-degree murder includes any killing that occurs in committing or attempting to commit another felony, such as lying in wait, poisoning, or the use of torture or cruelty. Second-degree murder only can be defined by exclusion. All murders that do not qualify as first-degree murders are murders in the second degree. Therefore, if the murder is *not* willful, deliberate, and premeditated, if it is not committed by poison, torture, or lying in wait, and it does *not* arise out of one of the specified felonies, it necessarily must be murder in the second degree.

Manslaughter is the unlawful killing of a human being without malice or afore-thought. Manslaughter can be voluntary or involuntary. Voluntary manslaughter is the intentional killing of one human being by another without justification or excuse and without malice. It usually occurs when the homicide is committed in sudden mutual combat or when committed in passion or hot blood. Involuntary manslaughter is usually defined as homicide unintentionally caused, but the death of the victim arises out of the defendant's criminal negligence or some other type of nonfelonious wrongful conduct.

Mayhem is the violent infliction of injury upon a person, including but not limited to disfigurement and the loss of a member of the body, such as an eye, a hand, a foot, or a finger. To be considered mayhem, the injury must be of a permanent nature.

Rape is the unlawful act of sexual intercourse with another person without the person's consent, chiefly by force and against that individual's will. The force may be actual or constructive. Examples of constructive force include acquiescence through fear, intimidation, or fraud. Absence of consent may also be actual or constructive when the victim is legally incapable of consent because of mental incompetence, intoxication, or minority. **Statutory rape** is sexual intercourse with another person under the legal age of consent, even though that person agrees to the act.

Assault is the attempt to inflict bodily injury on another person, either with force or violence. Though some courts hold that at least an apparent present ability to commit the battery attempted is required, other courts require an actual ability. There are various forms of assaults, such as aggravated assault, assault with intent to kill, assault with intent to commit rape, assault with a deadly weapon, and assault with intent to rob.

Battery is an assault in which force is actually applied to the person of another, either directly or indirectly. The degree of force used is immaterial and slight force is sufficient to constitute battery. Any touching, no matter how slight, will constitute a battery if the touching is in fact an *unlawful* one—unlawful in the sense that it is not consented to and not privileged by law.

Kidnapping consists of the false imprisonment of another, together with the removal of the victim to another country. Kidnapping is a common-law misdemeanor. Statutes in the various states have made kidnapping a felony, but differ in their provisions as to the elements of the crime. The element of removal to another country (or even removal to another state) generally is not required.

It is not an essential element of the crime of kidnapping that the victim be held for ransom. However, many states make kidnapping for ransom a special offense, generally carrying a more serious penalty.

Abduction is defined as the offense of taking a person by fraud and persuasion or by open violence, or the taking of a female without her consent, or without the consent of her parents or guardian, for the purpose of marriage or prostitution. Another definition of abduction is the criminal offense of taking away a person who is in the care of another. Statutes defining abduction differ significantly in various states.

Crimes Against Habitation The two major offenses against habitation involve wrongful conduct directed against the home of the victim: arson and burglary.

Arson is the willful and malicious burning of the property of another. At common law, arson was considered to be an offense against habitation because it was defined as the willful and malicious burning of the dwelling of another person. Under present statutes, however, the property burned is not limited to a dwelling and includes all kinds of property, such as shops, warehouses, vessels, railroad cars, lumber, hay, grain, and other kinds of buildings and property. The statutes in some states provide that the burning of one's own property constitutes arson. Furthermore, under current legislation, arson is considered a crime against property as well as a crime against habitation.

Burglary generally is defined as the breaking and entering of a dwelling of another with intent to commit a felony. The term *breaking*, as used in the law of burglary, means to open or put aside some part of the building for the purpose of effecting an entry. The breaking must involve a trespass in the sense that it is done without the consent of the victim. In some states, the entry must be at night, while in others, the entry may be made at any hour of the day.

Crimes Against Property   Principal crimes against property include larceny, embezzlement, fraud, robbery, receiving stolen goods, malicious mischief, and forgery.

Larceny is the fraudulent taking and carrying away of the personal property of another without consent and with the intent to steal. To constitute larceny, the property taken must be personal as distinguished from real property and recognized by law as capable of ownership. The property must be taken by trespass from the possession of another and removed, however slightly, from the place it occupies.

Embezzlement is the wrongful appropriation of personal property by one who has been entrusted with and has lawfully received possession. Embezzlement may be a felony or a misdemeanor, depending on the particular statute. Some statutes make this classification on the basis of the value of the embezzled property.

Fraud is a false representation made by a person, relied on by the innocent party, with the intent of wrongfully depriving a person of his or her property. This is a very general definition; specific kinds of frauds are defined by the statutes of the various states.

Robbery is the taking of, with the intent to steal, the personal property of another from his or her person or in his or her presence by means of violence or intimidation. Robbery is both a crime against property and a crime against the person. If the situation is one where the victim is not completely intimidated but voluntarily makes a choice between certain alternatives, the crime is *not* robbery, but an **extortion**.

Receiving stolen goods includes a number of elements. A defendant is chargeable with receiving stolen property when, with knowledge that the goods have been stolen, he or she takes them into possession with a wrongful intent. To constitute this, (1) the property must have been stolen and must retain such character when received; (2) the property must have been taken into possession of the receiver with the consent of the person from whom it was received; (3) the receiver must know that the property was stolen; and (4) the receiver must have felonious intent.

Malicious mischief is the destruction or injury with malice of property belonging to someone other than the accused.

Forgery is the fraudulent making or material alteration of writing that, as made or altered, defrauds another. A person who writes any statement or figures over the genuine signature of another with the intent of changing the meaning or intent of the document also commits forgery. The subject of forgery must be some writing or document that appears to have legal significance in that it purports to establish rights or obligations. Typical examples of such documents are deeds, mortgages, negotiable instruments, wills, and contracts. Court decrees and certificates of public officers also can be the subject of forgery.

Crimes Against Public Authority   The major crimes in this category are obstructing justice, compounding a crime, perjury, and bribery.

Obstructing justice is the willful obstruction of justice by resisting an officer who is attempting to perform his or her official duty. Resisting or obstructing an attempt to make an arrest, search, or maintain the peace; preventing the execution of civil process; and tampering with a witness or preventing the attendance of a witness at a trial are all acts that fall into this category.

Compounding a crime is abstaining from the prosecution of an offender for personal gain or reward. The necessary elements of this offense require that a crime has been committed and that the defendant is aware of this fact. The reward includes any advantage accruing from the accused to the person who abstains; it need not be money. The crime applies to anyone who, knowing that a crime has been committed, receives a reward for his or her agreement not to prosecute the accused and is not confined to the person particularly injured by it.

Perjury consists of knowingly giving false testimony under oath in a judicial proceeding in regard to a material matter. Defendants cannot be charged with knowingly giving false testimony if they honestly believe their statements to be true, even though they are in fact untrue.

Subornation of perjury is the procuring by one person of another person to commit the crime of perjury.

Bribery is the voluntary giving or receiving of anything of value in corrupt payment for an official act done or to be done. Both the person giving the bribe and the person receiving the bribe are guilty of the crime of bribery.

PROOF OF CRIMES

When the accused is found to have been grossly negligent of another person's safety, he or she may be found guilty of a crime. The determination of a person's guilt or innocence depends on proving a number of specific facts considered evidence of his or her guilt. As in the case of larceny, it must be proved that (1) the property does in fact belong to another, (2) the property was carried away, (3) it was personal property, and (4) the one being charged intended to keep the property. Unless all these points can be proved to the satisfaction of the jury, the accused probably would be found not guilty. All crimes must be proved beyond a reasonable doubt.

ARRESTS

Citizen's Arrest

A citizen who witnesses a crime being committed may arrest the criminal and have the individual charged, by proper police authorities, with the crime committed. To make a citizen's arrest based on suspicion places the one making the arrest in a vulnerable position: He or she later may be sued for damages on the grounds of *false arrest*.

A citizen who has reason to believe that a crime has been committed but did not witness the illegal act may sign a complaint and have a warrant issued for the arrest of the alleged criminal. A judge or magistrate will not issue such a warrant unless reasonable grounds are presented to assure that an arrest should be made. The issued warrant then is given to a police officer for execution.

Arrest by an Officer

A police officer or other duly-authorized person may make an arrest when there is *reasonable suspicion* that the person being arrested is responsible for the crime. The officer must use discretion in making the arrest if it is to be valid. The officer is not permitted to use any more force than is reasonably necessary to overcome the resistance of the person being arrested.

The term *police brutality* has resulted from the increasingly common charge, made by persons arrested, that the police used unwarranted force in executing the arrest. Most such charges are usually investigated, although such complaints have at times led to delay in the prosecution of an otherwise uncomplicated criminal complaint.

The term *hot pursuit* often is used in making an arrest. An officer in hot pursuit of an alleged criminal is permitted to follow the individual into a dwelling without the need of a warrant. If the officer loses sight of the criminal, however, a warrant must be obtained for the right to enter and search a dwelling in which the suspect may be hidden.

DEFENSES TO CRIMES

In a criminal case, the private legal practitioner represents only the defendant, while the state assumes the task of prosecuting the accused person. In representing the people, the state, through the district attorney or other representative, must prove the charge against the accused *beyond all reasonable doubt*.

The defense is of crucial importance to the defendant, and many ethical and professional duties and responsibilities on the part of the attorney and support staff are involved. The defense attorney is limited to those defenses that are recognized by the courts of the state in which the case is being tried. The following defenses are valid in the majority of states:

- *Lack of capacity* includes the defenses of infancy, insanity, involuntary intoxication, and unconsciousness.
- *Justification or excuse* includes the defenses of self-defense, defense of a third person, defense of property, prevention of crime, or apprehension of a criminal.
- *Coercion and necessity* can be used as a defense if the defendant can establish that he or she has not committed a criminal act willingly, but has been forced to act by a third person.
- **Entrapment** may be used as a defense to a criminal prosecution if the defendant can assert that he or she has been lured into the commission of the crime by a law enforcement officer, or someone acting on behalf of law enforcement, for the purpose of catching the defendant in the act of committing the crime.
- **Double jeopardy** constitutes being tried for the same crime twice. The Fifth Amendment protects a person from double jeopardy or from being tried more than once for the same offense. To constitute double jeopardy, the accused must have received a full trial resulting in a final verdict. If a mistrial is declared or a trial is halted for some acceptable legal reason, a second trial would not come within this definition. Only when a trial has been carried through to completion and the jury or court has rendered a verdict of not guilty is the prosecution restrained from further court action against the accused.
- *Corpus delicti* refers to the "body of the crime," that is, the essential elements of a criminal offense. To sustain the burden of proof in a criminal case, the prosecution's failure to establish the *corpus delicti* by competent evidence is a basic defense to a criminal charge.
- *Consent*, as a general rule, is the fact that the victim consented to the act constituting a crime and is *no defense* to the defendant. The theory is that a crime is a wrong against the state, rather than a wrong against the individual victim. The willingness of the victim to permit the wrongful act to occur is therefore immaterial.

SUMMARY

A crime is an offense against society, and the purpose of criminal law is to protect society from criminal acts. Though there are many theories for punishing criminal behavior, one of the main ideas is that society protects itself by isolating the criminal from society. Criminal laws have been made and are enforced by the government to protect society from criminal acts. The power to make laws and take away an individual's freedom and, sometimes, even an individual's life is granted to our federal and state agencies. However, there are many safeguards that protect our administration of justice system from the abuse of this power.

The U.S. Constitution and the Bill of Rights deal with the criminal procedures that are binding on the federal government and on all states. The Supreme Court is the final authority on the interpretation and meaning of the Constitution.

In criminal law, the charges against the accused must be filed in the proper courts and the case brought to trial on a timely basis. Most of the procedures in criminal law are similar to those in civil suits. The plaintiff in criminal law is "The People of the United States" or "The People of the State," and the defendant is the accused.

The different classifications of crime include crimes against the person, habitation, property, and public authority. The defenses to crimes include lack of capacity, justification, coercion, entrapment, double jeopardy, *corpus delicti*, and consent.

The legal office assistant needs to be familiar with the general procedures that govern criminal law and their specific requirements. An understanding of the nature of the crime and related constitutional guarantees will be very helpful in criminal law.

VOCABULARY

abduction In criminal law, the offense of taking a person by fraud and persuasion or by open violence; kidnapping.

act Performance, deed, or movement, as distinguished from remaining at rest.

appeal Review of decision of lower court.

arraignment The act of calling the defendant to court to answer an indictment or complaint.

arrest The act of seizing a person and detaining that person in custody.

assault Intentional causing of an apprehension of harmful or offensive contact.

bail Guarantees accused will appear in court; security given to obtain temporary release of a person under arrest.

battery Intentional infliction of a harmful or offensive contact upon a person.

booking Entering the name of the person arrested in the police department's arrest book.

bribery The receiving of an offering of any gift or favor in order to influence a person in the line of duty or trust.

coercion Compulsion or force; making a person act against free will.

confession A voluntary admission of guilt.

conviction The result of a criminal trial in which a person is found guilty.

corpus delicti A Latin term meaning the "body of the offense"; the elements necessary to prove that a crime has been committed.

crime A violation of the law that is punished as an offense against the state or government.

criminal law Law related to crime and punishment.

deterrence Discouraging people from violating the law by making an example of people convicted of crimes.

district attorney A public official, elected or appointed, whose chief duty is to prosecute suits on behalf of the state.

double jeopardy A defense that provides that no person can be tried twice for the same offense, once acquitted.

embezzlement A statutory offense consisting of one's fraudulent conversion of another's personal property by one to whom it has been entrusted.

entrapment Persuasive measures used by law enforcement officers to encourage persons suspected of engaging in criminal practices to commit a crime.

evidence Proof legally presented at the trial of a case through witnesses, exhibits, and so forth.

extortion Any illegal taking of money by using threats, force, or misuse of public office.

felony Any major crime punishable by death or imprisonment in a state prison.

forgery The fraudulent making or altering of an instrument that would, were the instrument to be accepted as genuine, impose a legal liability on another.

fraud Deception practiced to induce another to part with property or surrender some legal right that accomplishes this end.

habeas corpus A Latin term defined as a writ of personal freedom requiring that a person unlawfully held in custody or restrained of liberty be brought into court for inquiry into the matter of granting his or her release.

homicide The killing of one human being by another, whether or not the killing is lawful or justified.

incapacitation Keeping dangerous people isolated from the rest of society so that they cannot commit more crimes.

infraction A breach, violation or infringement.

intent The state of mind with which an act is done.

interrogation The questioning of people in custody.

kidnapping Forcible abduction of a person.

larceny Stealing personal property belonging to another.

manslaughter The unlawful killing of another without malice.

mayhem The intentional maiming or disfiguring of a person.

misdemeanor Any crime or offense not as serious as a felony. Generally those offenses punishable by fine, imprisonment in the county jail, or both.

murder The premeditated taking of a human life.

nolo contendere A Latin term meaning "no contest." A plea in criminal cases whereby the defendant offers no legal or factual defense to his acts, nor does he plead guilty. By doing this, he places himself at the mercy of the court.

own recognizance (OR)   Obligation of the accused to return to court for trial when he or she has been released without bail.

parole   A conditional release of a prisoner serving an unexpired sentence.

perjury   The legal offense of swearing that something is true when one knows it to be false.

plea   An accused person's answer to a charge or indictment in criminal practice.

plea bargaining   The acceptance of a guilty plea in exchange for the dismissal of more serious charges.

probation   The act of suspending the sentence of a convicted offender and placing that offender under the supervision of a probation officer.

rape   Sexual intercourse with a person without consent and chiefly by force or deception.

rehabilitation   Trying to reform criminals through training, education, and counseling.

retribution   Paying criminals back for the harm they have caused; a synonym for revenge.

robbery   The illegal taking of property from the person of another by using force or threat of force.

statutory rape   Sexual intercourse with a person under a specific age in accordance with various state laws.

warrant   A writ authorizing an arrest, search, or seizure; written permission given by a judge to arrest a person, search a house, etc.

STUDENT ASSESSMENT 1

Instructions: Circle T if the statement is true or F if the statement is false.

T   F   1.   Felonies are more serious crimes than misdemeanors.

T   F   2.   The defendant in a criminal trial may be present at the open jury sessions. The defendant may not attend the closed jury sessions.

T   F   3.   When the defendant is found guilty, the jury imposes the sentence.

T   F   4.   A criminal action is initiated similar to a civil action, by the filing of the complaint.

T   F   5.   A crime may not be committed by a mere omission to act.

T   F   6.   In a criminal action, the government is a party to the action.

T   F   7.   Infractions are usually punishable by jail or imprisonment.

T   F   8.   The Twelfth Amendment protects a person from double jeopardy, that is, being tried for the same crime twice.

T   F   9.   *Habeas corpus* is a Latin term that refers to the "body of the offense."

T   F   10.   Legal actions may be of a criminal or civil nature.

STUDENT ASSESSMENT 2

Instructions: Circle the letter that indicates the most correct answer.

1.   Which pleas may not be used by the defendant in a criminal matter?
   A.   *nolo contendere*   D.   former jeopardy
   B.   not guilty   E.   none of these
   C.   irreconcilable differences

2.   Which of the following crimes is not classified as a felony?
   A.   larceny   D.   arson
   B.   embezzlement   E.   none of these
   C.   bribery

3.   Which of the following crimes is not classified as a misdemeanor?
   A.   disorderly conduct   D.   some types of trespassing
   B.   simple assault   E.   none of these
   C.   excessive speed

(continued)

4. Which of the following crimes is not a crime against the person?
   A. battery
   B. assault
   C. mayhem
   D. arson
   E. none of these
5. Which of the following crimes is not a crime against property?
   A. fraud
   B. robbery
   C. embezzlement
   D. forgery
   E. none of these
6. Which of the following crimes is not a crime against public authority?
   A. obstructing justice
   B. compounding a crime
   C. receiving stolen goods
   D. perjury
   E. none of these
7. Which of the following terms is a valid criminal defense in most states?
   A. lack of capacity
   B. double jeopardy
   C. coercion
   D. entrapment
   E. all of these

STUDENT ASSESSMENT 3

Instructions: Fill in the word that best completes the sentence.

1. The two elements of the crime are the _____ and _____.
2. _____ _____ constitutes being tried for the same crime twice.
3. A(n) _____ is usually punishable by a fine or imprisonment in the county jail, or both.
4. _____ _____ is the term used for sexual intercourse with another person under age.
5. The _____ has the final authority to interpret the meaning of the Constitution.
6. _____ is the illegal altering of a document.
7. _____ allows a person to be released from jail while waiting for trial.

STUDENT ASSESSMENT 4

Instructions: Match the most correct letter to the number.

Section I

_____ 1. arraignment
_____ 2. warrant
_____ 3. bail
_____ 4. *nolo contendere*
_____ 5. appeal

Section I

A. guarantee accused will appear in court
B. no contest
C. review of decision of a lower court
D. first step in trial of felony proceeding
E. writ authorizing an arrest

Section II

_____ 1. treason
_____ 2. felony
_____ 3. misdemeanor
_____ 4. first-degree murder
_____ 5. second-degree murder

Section II

A. classification of larceny
B. defined by exclusion
C. premeditated and deliberate
D. imprisonment in county jail
E. starting a rebellion

(continued)

	Section III		Section III
_____	1. manslaughter	A.	guarantee of personal freedom
_____	2. probation	B.	review of decision
_____	3. parole	C.	conditional release of prisoner
_____	4. appeal	D.	without malice or aforethought
_____	5. *habeas corpus*	E.	suspending a sentence

STUDENT ASSIGNMENTS

PRACTICE SET 5: CRIMINAL LAW

Case Particulars

Attorney: Robert Morgan
              Attorney at Law
              320 Main Street
              Fullerton, CA 92634
              Telephone: (714) 555-2440
              Fax: (714) 555-2748
Client: Ivan Innocent

Case History

A complaint has been filed by the city attorney of Los Angeles against Ivan Innocent. Mr. Innocent has engaged Robert Morgan to represent him, and there is some question as to whether the evidence obtained against Mr. Innocent was legally obtained. Mr. Morgan feels it is necessary to file a Motion for the Suppression of Evidence to protect Mr. Innocent's constitutional rights.

In filing this type of motion, it is necessary that points and authorities (arguments in support of the motion) be filed. Points and authorities are the citations of the source books in which the arguments supporting the motion may be found, and they accompany and support the motion. These papers are typical of the legal papers the legal office assistant may be required to prepare in a criminal matter.

PROJECT 1: MOTION FOR SUPPRESSION OF EVIDENCE

Instructions: Retrieve the court caption template and key in the information for Sample 13-1, pp. 319–320, for a Notice of Motion and Motion for Suppression of Evidence. This constitutional right was discussed in Chapter 13. Save your document as **ch13_NOT** and print one copy for your instructor.

PROJECT 2: DECLARATION OF ROBERT MORGAN

Instructions: Retrieve the court caption template and key in the information for Sample 321, p. xxx, for a Declaration of Robert Morgan. Save your document as **ch13_DEC** and print one copy for your instructor.

PROJECT 3: POINTS AND AUTHORITIES

Instructions: Retrieve the court caption template and key in the information for Sample 13-3, pp. 322–324, for a Points and Authorities in Support of Motion to Suppress Evidence. Save your document as **ch13_PNT** and print one copy for your instructor.

1	ROBERT MORGAN #12345 Attorney at Law
2	320 Main Street Fullerton, CA 92634
3	
4	Phone: (714) 555-2440 Fax: (714) 555-2748
5	Attorney for Defendant
6	
7	
8	SUPERIOR COURT OF THE STATE OF CALIFORNIA
9	FOR THE COUNTY OF LOS ANGELES
10	

11	PEOPLE OF THE STATE OF CALIFORNIA,	) NO. 127309
12	Plaintiff,	) NOTICE OF MOTION AND MOTION FOR) SUPPRESSION OF EVIDENCE UNDER) PENAL CODE §1538.5; MOTION TO
13	vs.	) SUPPRESS EVIDENCE ON GENERAL) CONSTITUTIONAL GROUNDS
14	IVAN INNOCENT,	) INCLUDING <u>MIRANDA</u>; MOTION TO) DISMISS THE COMPLAINT;
15	Defendant.	) DECLARATION AND POINTS AND) AUTHORITIES IN SUPPORT THEREOF

16

17 To: THE PEOPLE OF THE STATE OF CALIFORNIA, and their attorney:

18   BURT PINES, City Attorney of the City of Los Angeles; WILLIE WILLIAMS,

19 Chief of Police of the City of Los Angeles:

20   PLEASE TAKE NOTICE that the Defendant in the above-entitled case will move

21 the Court in Division 101 thereof, or any other division to which it is transferred, on August 1,

22 20--, at 10:00 a.m., to suppress evidence under the authority of Penal Code §1538.5 as well as

23 under general constitutional authority, including <u>Miranda</u>, the Fifth and Fourteenth Amendments

24 to the Federal Constitution, and to dismiss the Complaint. Said evidence to be suppressed and/or

25 excluded includes, but is not limited to, the administration and the results of any Field Sobriety

26 Tests, including questions contained therein, the administration and the results of the Gas

27 Chromatograph Test and any and all other conversations between the arresting officers and the

28

SAMPLE 13-1

1   Defendant, and all observations made of the Defendant from the time of his being stopped to the

2   time of his release from custody.

3   These Motions will be based on the records on file in this matter, Declarations, and

4   Points and Authorities attached hereto, and the evidence, both oral and documentary, to be

5   introduced at the time of the hearing.

6   DATED: July 10, ----

7   ROBERT MORGAN
                           Attorney for Defendant

8

9

10

11

12

13

14

15

16

17

18

19

20

21

22

23

24

25

26

27

28

SAMPLE 13-1   *Continued*

1   ROBERT MORGAN   #12345
    Attorney at Law
2   320 Main Street
    Fullerton, CA 92634
3
    Phone: (714) 555-2440
4   Fax: (714) 555-2748

5   Attorney for Defendant

6

7

8   SUPERIOR COURT OF THE STATE OF CALIFORNIA

9   FOR THE COUNTY OF LOS ANGELES

10

11 PEOPLE OF THE STATE OF CALIFORNIA,)   NO. 127309
)
12   Plaintiff,   )
)
13   vs.   )   DECLARATION OF ROBERT MORGAN
)
14 IVAN INNOCENT,   )
)
15   Defendant.   )
    _____)

16

17   I, ROBERT MORGAN, declare as follows:

18   1. I am the attorney of record for the Defendant, IVAN INNOCENT.

19   2. On or about August 1, 20--, in the above-entitled Court, I will move the Court

20 to suppress the evidence against the Defendant, IVAN INNOCENT, on the grounds that said

21 evidence was illegally obtained. The evidence includes, but is not limited to, any Field Sobriety

22 Tests, Gas Chromatograph Tests, and any and all other conversations between arresting officers

23 and the Defendant, and any and all observations made of Defendant.

24   I declare, under penalty of perjury, that the foregoing is true and correct.

25 DATED: July 10, 20 --

26   _____
                                            ROBERT MORGAN
27   Attorney for Defendant

28

SAMPLE 13-2

ROBERT MORGAN #12345
Attorney at Law
320 Main Street
Fullerton, CA 92634

Phone: (714) 555-2440
Fax: (714) 555-2748

Attorney for Defendant

SUPERIOR COURT OF THE STATE OF CALIFORNIA

FOR THE COUNTY OF LOS ANGELES

PEOPLE OF THE STATE OF CALIFORNIA,)   NO. 127309
)
   Plaintiff,   )   POINTS AND AUTHORITIES IN
)   SUPPORT OF MOTION TO SUPPRESS
   vs.   )   EVIDENCE
)
IVAN INNOCENT,   )
)
   Defendant.   )

I

A MOTION TO SUPPRESS AND/OR EXCLUDE EVIDENCE IS PROPER

PRIOR TO TRIAL AS IS A MOTION TO DISMISS

   Under the provisions of the Penal Code of the State of California, the Court has the authority to suppress evidence which has been illegally obtained by law enforcement officers, and the Motion must be made prior to trial.

1538.5 Penal Code

   Additionally, it has been held that the courts have inherent power and jurisdiction to hear motions to suppress evidence which has been obtained illegally, such as the obtaining of an illegal confession.

Saidi-Tabatabai vs. Superior Court
253 CAL. App.2d 257.

SAMPLE 13-3

1   The case of <u>People vs. Travell</u>, in the appellate department of the Superior Court,

2   Superior Court No. CRA 8415, held:

3   "That a motion for suppression of a breath sample

4   or a blood alcohol sample is a proper motion under 1538.5."

5   The Court further held that, in interpreting <u>Thomas vs. Superior Court</u>, 262 CAL. App.2d 98,

6   a written Motion under the provisions of 1538.5 is not even required.

7   When a Defendant shows that there was neither an arrest warrant nor a search

8   warrant in the case, then the burden shifts to the People to justify the search as reasonable.

9   <u>People vs. Travell, CRA 8415;</u>

10   <u>Badillo vs. Superior Court,</u>
46 Cal.2d 269, 272.

11

12   All evidence, tangible and intangible, may be suppressed by the Court. The

evidence to be suppressed can include Field Sobriety Tests.

13

14   <u>People vs. Shepherd, Los Angeles</u>
Appellate Dept. No. CRA 9719

15   The above <u>Shepherd</u> case also, by implication, establishes the rule that it is

16   appropriate for a Defendant to move to suppress or exclude evidence of statements obtained in

17   violation of <u>Miranda</u>. Furthermore, the provisions of Evidence Code Section 400 through

18   Section 405 establish that the Court has authority to have pre-trial hearings to determine the

19   admissibility of profferred evidence. Such procedure eliminates the hazards of prejudicial error

20   occurring when certain evidence, which ultimately is excluded, may be referred to by the

21   prosecution. It also eliminates the necessity of jurors having to wait around for hearings and

22   decisions to be made relative to questions of admissibility of evidence, which can properly be

23   determined prior to empanelment. Additionally, and equally as important, is the fact that by

24   reason of the Court's ruling on admissibility of certain evidence, it may well assist in a termination

25   of the case by some type of <u>plea bargaining</u>.

26   The dismissal of the Complaint will be discussed in greater detail subsequently.

27   Suffice it to say that the Legislature has provided for dismissals, and our courts have dismissed

28

SAMPLE 13-3 *Continued*

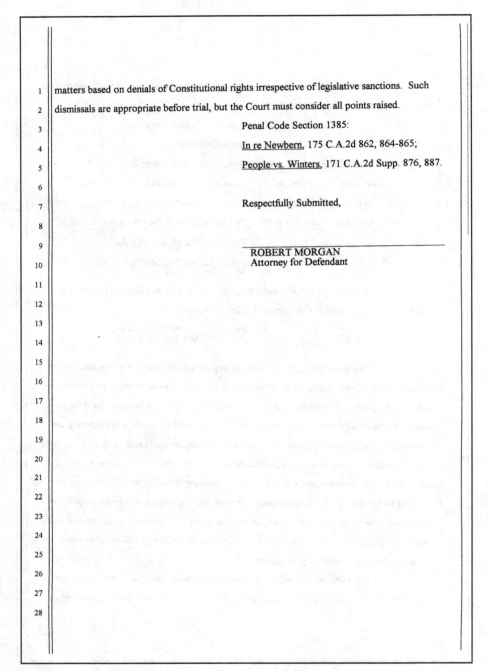

1 matters based on denials of Constitutional rights irrespective of legislative sanctions. Such

2 dismissals are appropriate before trial, but the Court must consider all points raised.

Penal Code Section 1385:

In re Newbern, 175 C.A.2d 862, 864-865;

People vs. Winters, 171 C.A.2d Supp. 876, 887.

Respectfully Submitted,

ROBERT MORGAN
Attorney for Defendant

SAMPLE 13-3 *Continued*

Part 5

LEGAL RESEARCH

Chapter 14
Legal Research

14

LEGAL RESEARCH

OBJECTIVES

Upon completion of this chapter, you should be able to:

1. Discuss the importance of legal research
2. Analyze the difference between procedural and substantive law
3. Classify the areas of legal research
4. Compare case, statutory, and administrative law
5. Describe the use of *reports* and *reporters* in legal research
6. Discuss the differences between statutes and codes
7. Interpret a citation
8. Explain how legal citations are used and why
9. Discuss the features of a citator service
10. Explain the use of computer-assisted research
11. List some of the benefits of using the Internet for legal research

A very important part of an attorney's work is the *legal research* done in preparing the client's case. The aim of legal research is to inform the attorney of the laws that apply to and govern a client's case. This is a complex procedure and requires training in using law books, computer research, and other reference materials. Legal research includes searching for **points and authorities**, such as cases and statutes, that will be cited to the court in support of the contentions being made (Figure 14-1).

Because the basis of our legal system is the law of precedents, an attorney must be able to cite prior cases and use them to support the client's case. It is impossible for attorneys to remember all the relevant laws and court decisions, and because the law is always changing, attorneys must rely on the research books that contain this information.

Legal research involves substantive law as opposed to procedural law. Substantive law deals with the rights, duties, and obligations of the law, as compared to procedural law, which determines the procedures that are followed in processing legal cases. The attorney's law library is an essential element in legal research, and it is important for the legal office assistant to understand the concepts used in legal research and the publications and materials available. Although it is unusual for a legal office assistant to perform legal research, an understanding of how to use the legal research tools is important.

U.S. LEGAL SYSTEM

The U.S. Constitution is the supreme law of the land, and neither Congress nor any of the states may enact a law that is in conflict with it. Through the power of review

FIGURE 14-1 *Attorneys spend many hours doing legal research. (Courtesy of Steelcase)*

granted to it, the U.S. Supreme Court has the authority to interpret the effect of federal and state laws to determine if they are in conflict with the U.S. Constitution. Each state has the authority to adopt its own constitution, but state constitutions cannot be in conflict with the U.S. Constitution. Likewise, statutes and codes enacted by the states cannot be in conflict with the U.S. Constitution or state constitutions.

The federal government is organized into three branches: legislative, executive, and judicial. The legislative branch of the government enacts or produces our laws. A bill is introduced into the federal or state legislature, and if it is passed and approved by the president or state governor, it becomes a law. These laws are important and regulate the rules of our society. Because these laws are published in chronological order, they are difficult to find.

In order to put these laws in logical order by subject matter, they are codified, or organized according to subject. Codification of the laws can be done by the legislature, a private publisher, or both. Federal laws are codified under the U.S. Code, and each state publishes codes such as the civil code, criminal code, or education code. Local ordinances are also organized into codes. The most common are the building, traffic, zoning, and tax codes.

THE LAW LIBRARY

Many books, periodicals, and newspapers deal with the law field, and it is necessary that each attorney maintain an adequate law library in print or via access to a legal portal on the **Internet**. The size and extent of the law library in an office varies with the size and type of practice. A single practitioner may have a very small library, while a large firm specializing in probate or civil litigation may have a very specialized and extensive library. Figure 14-2 outlines the research materials available to the law practitioner.

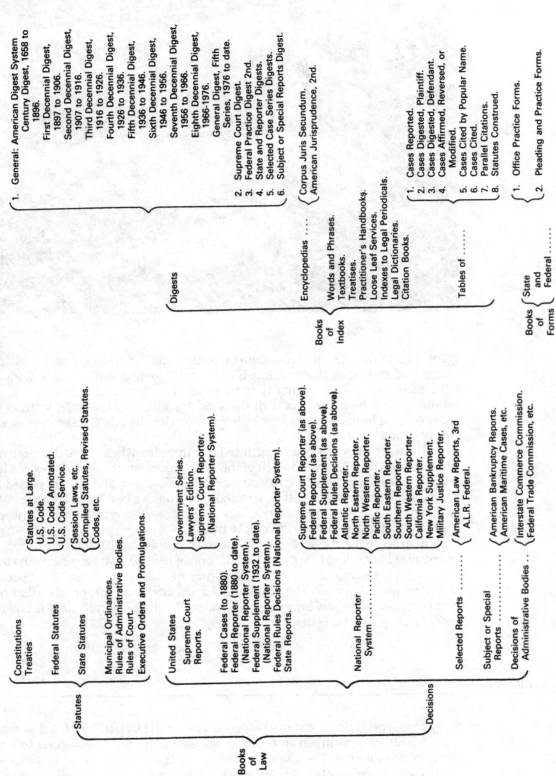

FIGURE 14-2 Outline of legal reference materials.
(Courtesy of West Publishing Company)

Pocket Supplements

It is very important that the law library be kept current (Figure 14-3). Many law books are updated with **pocket parts or supplements** that are placed in the back pocket of the hardbound books. Some law publications are maintained in binders and updated with replacement pages. It is critical that the correct page be removed and replaced in the specified order so that the publication is accurate. These updates provide the researcher with the latest information on the law, and it is important for the researcher to look up the subject in the pocket supplement as well as in the book itself. In many law offices, it is the responsibility of the legal office support person to keep the law library current by placing the updated pocket supplements in the pocket of the hardbound books.

CLASSIFICATION OF LEGAL RESEARCH

Legal research can be classified into three major categories:

1. Primary sources
2. Secondary sources
3. Finding tools

Primary Sources

The primary sources of legal research are those that are binding on the court. If the law comes from one of the primary sources, the court is required to apply that law.

FIGURE 14-3 *Attorneys make extensive use of law books in their research.*

Case law, *statutory law*, and *administrative rules* and **regulations** are primary sources of the law. Each of these sources comes from a particular branch of the government:

- *Case law* comes from the judicial branch (United States Supreme Court).
- *Statutory law* comes from the legislative branch (Congress).
- *Administrative law* comes from the executive branch (the president).

All three branches make decisions that are binding on the people.

Constitution   The highest law of the land is the U.S Constitution. Laws passed by Congress, states, counties, or cities cannot conflict with the Constitution. Amendments have been made to the Constitution, and the first ten amendments are known as the Bill of Rights. The Constitution is organized into *articles* and each article is divided into *sections*.

Case Law or Law of Precedents   The interpretation of the laws and regulations is done by the judicial branch of the government, and this is referred to as case law. Court decisions make up the basis of the case law, which is interpretation and principles that are called legal **precedents**. The judicial branch of the government decides how laws and regulations should be applied. If there is no specific law, a federal court decision will establish the prevailing principle.

Reports and Reporters   Federal and state courts may elect to publish their decisions in books called **reports** or **reporters**. A case is deemed worthy of publication if the court feels that it will help to interpret ambiguities in the law or settle a commonly disputed issue of law. Only a small fraction of the cases the courts decide are actually certified for publication by the court. Moreover, the highest court of the land, the U.S. Supreme Court, retains discretion to decertify (unpublish) a case if it determines that the holding is inaccurate or would establish bad precedent for the future.

Reporters are manufactured by publishing companies under contract with the government, such as Thomas/West. As opinions are released by the court, the legal publishing companies compile them in bound books. Some examples of reporters are the *United States Supreme Court Reporter*, *The Federal Reporter*, and the *California Official Reports*.

Organization of Reports

Cases are organized in chronological order as the decisions are released by the court. Cases on file date back to the mid-1800s. Because case reports are not organized by topic, the attorneys must use finding aids to locate cases that deal with similar propositions of law in order perform a complete analysis of an issue. The cases that appear in the Thomson/West reports are organized in the following manner:

1. Case summaries or synopsis
2. **Headnotes** or key numbers
3. Judicial opinion

A case summary is a brief, concise summary of the court's ruling that can be read quickly to glean an overview of the facts of the case, the legal issues, and the outcome (Figure 14-4).

There is one headnote number or key number assigned by the publisher to each distinct issue in every published case. A researcher can use these numbers to find the same issue in other cases in every court in the United States. This is helpful because the fact pattern of each case is slightly different. It is important for an attorney to be able to find all the cases on a particular issue to help persuade the court of the correct interpretation of the law as applied to the unique facts of a new case.

PARTIES
TO
THE
ACTION

**EGAN MARINE CONTRACTING CO.,
INC., Plaintiff,**

v.

**SOUTH SEA SHIPPING CORP., et
al., Defendants.**

Civ. No. R-82-1811.

United States District Court,
D. Maryland.

Aug. 26, 1983.

CASE
SUMMARY

Company which had performed lashing
services for vessels chartered by foreign corporation brought action against corporation
to recover payment for services rendered. On
corporation's motion to dismiss, the District
Court, Ramsey, J., held that: (1) foreign corporation which had six chartered ships visit
Maryland within a five and one-half-month
period, apparently intended to operate ships
and transport cargo to and from Maryland on
a regular basis, had incurred over $200,000
in stevedoring costs, and had two other suits
pending against it in federal District Court in
Maryland had been "doing business" within
Maryland to extent necessary to require it to
appoint a resident agent and, in absence of
such appointment, to subject it to service of
process through Maryland Department of
Assessments and Taxation, and (2) personal
jurisdiction over corporation was proper
under Maryland long-arm statute.

Motion denied.

HEADNOTE

1. Federal Civil Procedure   495

Question of whether a corporation is
doing business in Maryland for purpose of
determining whether it could be served is
one that turns on facts of each individual
case. Md.Rule 106, subd. e.

2. Federal Civil Procedure   495

Party seeking to demonstrate that corporation is doing business in Maryland for purpose of determining whether corporation
may be served as burden of proof. Md. Rule
106, subd. e.

3. Federal Civil Procedure   495, 503

Foreign corporation which had six chartered ships visit Maryland within a five and
one-half-month period, apparently intended
to operate ships and transport cargo to and
from Maryland on a regular basis, had incurred over $200,000 in stevedoring costs, and
had two other suits pending against it in
federal district court in Maryland had been
"doing business" within Maryland to extent
necessary to require it to appoint a resident
agent and, in absence of such appointment,
to subject it to service of process through
Maryland Department of Assessments and
Taxation. Md.Rule 106, subd. e; Md.Code,
Corporations and Associations, §§ 7–101 et
seq., 7–202, 7–203, 7–205.

HEADNOTE

4. Constitutional Law   305(6)

Foreign corporation which had six chartered ships visit Maryland within a five and
one-half-month period, apparently intended
to operate ships and transport cargo to and
from Maryland on a regular basis, had incurred over $200,000 in stevedoring costs, and
had two other suits pending against it in
federal district court in Maryland had transacted business in Maryland sufficient to
comport with requirements of due process,
so that personal jurisdiction over corporation
was proper under Maryland long-arm statute. Md.Code, Courts and Judicial Proceedings, § 6–103(b)(1).

David W. Skeen, Steve White, Constable, Alexander, Daneker & Skeen, Baltimore, Md., for plaintiff.

Donald E. Sharpe, Jonathan D. Smith,
Piper & Marbury, Baltimore, Md., for defendant South Sea Shipping Corp.

William F. Ryan, Jr., Whiteford, Tay-
lor, Preston, Trimbe & Johnston, Baltimore,
Md., for defendant Hansen & Tidemann,
Inc.

ATTORNEYS

OPINION

RAMSEY, District Judge. ◀——— JUDGE

Currently before the Court is defendant
South Sea Shipping's motion to dismiss the

OPINION
OR DECISION

FIGURE 14-4   *Sample page from Federal Supplement 612, Federal Supplement 1, District Court
of Maryland. (Courtesy of West Publishing Company)*

A judicial opinion is the decision of the court written by a judge in the case.
Although the appellate and supreme courts use a panel of several judges who listen
to the case and make a majority decision, only one of the judges is usually assigned
the task of writing the opinion. If one or more of the judges disagree with that
majority opinion, they may write a dissenting opinion at the end of the case, but the
dissenting opinion does not establish precedent.

Statutes and Codes   Congress introduces bills into the House and Senate.
If these bills are passed, they are submitted to the president, who may either sign or
veto the bills. If the president signs the bills, they become laws called statutes. These
statutes then are compiled chronologically, which makes them difficult to use. The
U.S. Government Printing Office prints a codified version of the laws of Congress
called the U.S. Code (Figure 14-5).

State legislators also introduce bills. When these bills are voted on, passed by
the state legislature, and signed by the governor, they become statutes. When these
state statutes are organized by subject, they become **codes**. Good examples of a code
are a building code or a health and safety code.

Regulations   The executive branch of the government creates *administrative agencies* to carry out the public laws. Some of the agencies include the Federal Transportation Agency and the Federal Drug Agency. The regulations developed by these agencies have the force of the law.

Secondary Sources

Secondary sources are the sources that discuss and analyze the law. These sources comment on, interpret, or may criticize primary authorities. These sources include legal reference books or encyclopedias and treatises. Primary authorities are the law itself, while secondary authorities do not have the force and effect of law. However, if there is not binding legal authority, secondary sources may be used to persuade the court to rule in a certain manner.

Legal Encyclopedias   Legal reference books, or encyclopedias, contain principles of law, and the legal topics are arranged alphabetically. They are usually in text form and summarize under specific subjects all the laws pertaining to a subject title with citations as to the authority or the source of the law. Some of the more widely known of these books are *Corpus Juris Secondum (CJS)*, *American Jurisprudence (Am Jur)*, and *California Jurisprudence (Cal Jur)*.

Treatises   Treatises cover specific areas of the law and are written by legal experts. They cover a single subject, such as contracts, bankruptcy, or torts.

Finding Tools

Legal research aids that locate primary and secondary sources of the law are called *finding tools*. Because of the amount of primary and secondary laws that is constantly produced, it is a tremendous job to find the authorities to support the issues. Through the use of finding tools such as codes, digests, legal directories, and computerized research tools, it is possible to access this information.

Codes/Statutes   State and federal statutes (other than the U.S. Constitution) are generally drafted by lobbyists, politicians, and special interest groups and then put into law by the government or a referendum of the voters.

Attorneys do not generally write the statutes, and this can lead to disagreement as to their meaning or interpretation. Legal publishing companies produce **annotated codes** to aid with interpretation. Annotated codes contain cross-references to treatises and cases that have interpreted the statute to help explain the meaning to the attorneys.

Digests   A digest is an index to reports arranged systematically according to subject matter. A digest provides access to all the sources of case law in a manner similar to the information provided in the table of contents or the index of a textbook. A detailed index of all the information published by West Publishing Company is the *American Digest System*. This publication contains abstracts (summaries), by subject matter, of all the cases reported in the *National Reporter System*.

Legal Dictionaries and Directories   Legal dictionaries give complete definitions of legal terms and are arranged in the manner of a standard dictionary. The legal support staff should also become familiar with the *Martindale—Hubbell Law Directory*. This multiple-volume reference, published annually, lists lawyers with their addresses and specialties, as well as a digest of the fifty states' patent, copyright, and trademark laws (Figure 14-6).

Other Sources

Form Books   Form books are a helpful addition to a law office library. They contain pleading forms (legal papers making formal, written statements on each side

TITLES OF THE UNITED STATES CODE

1. General Provisions
2. The Congress
3. The President
4. Flag and Seal, Seat of Government and the States
5. Government Organization and Employees
6. Surety Bonds
7. Agriculture
8. Aliens and Nationality
9. Arbitration
10. Armed Forces
11. Bankruptcy
12. Banks and Banking
13. Census
14. Coast Guard
15. Commerce and Trade
16. Conservation
17. Copyrights
18. Crimes and Criminal Procedure
19. Custom Duties
20. Education
21. Food and Drugs
22. Foreign Relations and Intercourse
23. Highways
24. Hospitals and Asylums
25. Indians
26. Internal Revenue Code
27. Intoxicating Liquors

28. Judiciary and Judicial Procedure
29. Labor
30. Minerals, Land, and Mining
31. Money and Finance
32. National Guard
33. Navigation and Navigable Waters
34. (Navy) (Superseded by Title 10)
35. Patents
36. Patriotic Societies and Observances
37. Pay and Allowances of the Uniformed Services
38. Veteran's Benefits
39. Postal Service
40. Public Buildings, Properties, and Works
41. Public Contracts
42. The Public Health and Welfare
43. Public Lands
44. Public Printing and Documents
45. Railroads
46. Shipping
47. Telegraphs, Telephones, and Radiotelegraphs
48. Territories and Insular Possessions
49. Transportation
50. War and National Defense

FIGURE 14-5 *Titles of U.S. codes.*

FIGURE 14-6 *Legal research is a complex procedure and requires training in using law books.*

of the case) covering all subjects and phases of the law. Some of the better known form books are *American Jurisprudence Legal Forms* and *American Jurisprudence Pleading and Practice Forms*. The states also issue form books that apply to their procedures, for example, *California Forms of Pleading and Practices* and *California Civil Procedure Forms Manual*. Attorneys often dictate information from form books in the preparation of legal proceedings.

Newspapers   *Legal newspapers* contain current legal news and articles, as well as a daily schedule of cases set for trial. Most legal newspapers contain a classified section for attorneys, paralegals, and legal secretaries. These periodicals can serve as an excellent source of job opportunities in the legal area.

LEGAL CITATIONS

A **citation** is a reference to a statement of law or legal authority. In preparing legal papers, attorneys must indicate their source by citing a code section, reference, or legal precedent. The reference to this authority is called a citation, from the verb *to cite*. References are usually cited in abbreviated form. As an example, *Smith v. Jones* reported in Volume 316 of the *Pacific Reporter 2d* series at page 115 is cited as *Smith v. Jones*, 316 P.2d 115. This procedure shortens and simplifies the use of references and makes legal research easier. Citations should be abbreviated whenever they are used as an authority for a statement of the law. Citations are used in the preparation of briefs and points and authorities and to support courtroom arguments and theories.

Typing Citations

In doing legal research and citing prior cases from law books, it is important that citations be typed carefully and accurately according to precise guidelines. Citations are essential to the **brief** (a complete statement of the client's case), and the legal professional must proof the citations to be sure that they are absolutely accurate (Figure 14-7). The following are examples of citations:

FIGURE 14-7 *Preparing accurate and complete citations is an important function of the law office staff.*

Citations from the U.S. Constitution:

U.S.Const., Art. IV, cl. 3
U.S.Const., Amend. XX

Unabbreviated, these citations would read, United States Constitution, Article IV, clause 3; and United States Constitution, Amendment 20.

Citation from U.S. Code:
31 U.S.C.A. Sec. 462

This citation deals with Title 31 (relating to legal tender and payment of debts) of the *United States Code Annotated*, Section 462.

Federal Citation:
Lee v. United States, 343 U.S. 747 (1952)

This citation shows Lee as the plaintiff against the United States in Volume 343 of the *U.S. Reports* on page 747.

State Citation:
Glock v. Howard & Wilson Colony Co., 123 Cal. 1 (1898)

The parties to this action are Glock, the plaintiff, and Howard & Wilson Colony Co., the defendant. The case is listed in Volume 123 of the *California Reports* on page 1.

The Blue Book

It is important for the legal support staff to be familiar with books and materials in the library (Figure 14-8). A useful book for any support staff person is *A Uniform System of Citations*, generally known as the *Harvard Blue Book* or *The Blue Book*. This book is edited by the *Harvard Law Review* and the *University of Pennsylvania Law Review*. It explains, in careful detail, the general rules for making citations from statutory material, judicial reports, books, pamphlets, letters, speeches, interviews, periodicals, and newspapers. It covers many areas of style and shows the general rules for punctuation, cross referencing, subdivisions, capitalizing, and other matters of style relevant to the law office.

Citator Services

Citator services, such as Shepard's and KeyCite, are used to determine if a case or a statute is still good law. The laws are constantly changing, so it is important for an attorney to determine if the legal authority relied upon is still good law. Attorneys increasingly rely on computerized research to perform this task, as discussed more fully in the next section.

COMPUTERIZED RESEARCH AND THE INTERNET

Most attorneys prefer to use computer-aided technology to perform legal research, such as **WESTLAW** or **LEXIS**. Computerized legal research is usually accessed

FIGURE 14-8 *Reference books are essential to the attorney and legal staff.*

through a secure portal on the Internet with a password that the attorney licenses from a legal publisher for a fee. The Internet address for WESTLAW is www.west-law.com and the address for LEXIS is www.lexis.com.

There are many advantages to computer-assisted legal research. One advantage is that the law can be updated more quickly. A new case may take weeks to print and ship to a law library, but it will usually appear on WESTLAW within three minutes of the court issuing a verdict in a new case.

Case law, in particular, can be difficult to find in reporters due to their chronological organization. With the aid of computer technology, the attorney can link to every case on a particular issue from one headnote in a single case. An attorney can also use word searching to search for legal authority on a particular topic through cases, treatises, codes, and even jury verdicts and settlements that were not published by the court. WESTLAW has more than 14,000 separate databases available for its users.

Internet research providers offer free assistance from 800 helplines that are staffed twenty-four hours a day to assist the researchers in finding the information they need.

Computer-assisted legal research (CALR) uses computers for legal research (Figures 14-9 and 14-10). CALR has many advantages over manual legal research. Manual legal research is performed by using a law library and research books, periodicals, statutes, indexes, and digests. When the relevant information is located, the researcher must pull the bound volume to read the entire case. Manual research also requires the use of a law library, which is expensive to acquire and keep up to date.

When CALR is used correctly, it is faster than manual methods, and it can find or retrieve cases that might not otherwise have been found due to poor indexing or other errors.

While CALR has many advantages over manual legal research, it is not free. Most legal information services charge on the basis of time connected to their systems or by using yearly subscription fees. Some services charge for each search, while others charge a minimum monthly charge even though the service may not be used.

FIGURE 14-9   *It is important for the legal staff to be familiar with the books in the law library.*

While there are many information services available, WESTLAW and Lexis Nexis are the best known and have the largest databases.

WESTLAW is the computerized research service from West Publishing Company. WESTLAW has one of the largest law libraries in the world, with more than 14,000 separate databases available for its users. Researchers using WESTLAW are able to use the key number system. A key number or a word is entered, and WESTLAW documents containing that number or word are retrieved. West Publishing Company also has CD-ROM libraries available. Compact discs with information on bankruptcy, federal civil practice, government contract, and federal taxation are available for legal research on the computer.

WESTLAW provides a transparent **interface** designed by WESTLAW and Dialog that will allow Westlaw subscribers to locate news, business, technical, and other information, in addition to legal research, through the Dialog service. Dialog is the supplier of information for business and financial publications, news sources, and scientific, technical, government, and patent literature. This information will provide attorneys with facts and background information in addition to the legal research. These services make use of modern technology and enable the legal researcher to use the speed and capacity of the computer to retrieve significant research information.

LEXIS was the first online full-text information service and is one of the largest. LEXIS contains all the federal case laws. LEXIS specializes in providing the National Insurance Law Service volumes of insurance codes, regulation, and related laws. LEXIS uses a slightly different syntax for entering search questions than WESTLAW, and both LEXIS and WESTLAW have a free hotline to help with legal research problems.

The Internet and Computer-Assisted Research in the Law Office

The law firms that have more relevant information presented in an organized manner have an advantage over those law firms that struggle to find information. Legal information services through the use of the Internet represent a huge body of

FIGURE 14-10 *Legal research can be done using computerized research software and the Internet.*

FIGURE 14-11 *WESTLAW is a computer-assisted legal research system that offers vast legal research capabilities with its extensive database. (Courtesy of West Publishing Company)*

information that is just being tapped—on the local, regional, national, and international level (see Table 14-1). These services allow the attorney to retrieve cases, statutes, and other documents from a vast global library of legal and business materials in a matter of seconds (Figure 14-11). Searches in WESTLAW and LEXIS allow the legal professional to retrieve relevant, current, accurate, and reliable results that assist in the preparation of the client's case and the practice of law (Figure 14-12).

TABLE 14-1   Law-Related Websites

Name of Web Page	Description	Web Address
Google	A search engine that returns keyword search results based on relevance of contents	http://www.google.com
Yahoo	Search engine for searching for websites	http://www.yahoo.com
Prentice Hall	Catalog of books containing a searchable database	http://prenhall.com
ABA	American Bar Association	http://www.abanet.org
Thomas	Information on the U.S. Congress	http://thomas.loc.gov/
FedWorld	A gateway to dozens of online government resources, from court opinions to government regulations	http://www.fedworld.gov/
The White House	Information on the White House and the administration, including a database of all government information on the Net	http://www.whitehouse.gov/
National Federation of Paralegal Associations	Career development and paralegal-related information	http://paralegals.org/
Indiana Law School	Indiana Law School Listing	http://www.law.indiana.edu/
Chicago–Kent	Contains the Legal Domain Network, which provides access to law-related discussion groups and mailing lists	http://www.kentlaw.edu/
Cornell University Legal Information Institute	Directory of law-related topics on the Internet	http://www.law.cornell.edu/
Nolo Press Self-Help Law Center	Online legal services for consumers	http://www.nolo.com/about.html
West Publishing	West's Legal Directory	http://west.thomson.com
Federal Express	Track your Federal Express package	http://www.fedex.com/us/

FIGURE 14-12 *Anyone who wants to research the law can use the power of the computer for research.*

SUMMARY

A very important part of an attorney's work is involved in legal research. Because our legal system is essentially based on the law of precedents, the attorney needs to cite prior cases to support the client's case. This involves doing research and using the law library. Legal office assistants familiar with legal terminology and the location of the most-used references in the law library can be an asset to the attorney and the law firm.

It is very important that the law library be kept current with the latest rulings relating to the law. The legal office assistant is often responsible for updating the law library and making sure that pocket supplements are ordered and inserted in the appropriate hardbound books. It is also very important to ensure that incorrect pages are removed and the new pages inserted correctly.

Dramatic changes are taking place in legal research as a result of the use of technology, and legal information services are available that allow users to access large databases of information. Many law firms are finding computers a valuable tool for research, both in the speed with which the information is retrieved and in the accuracy of that information. Many attorneys find the use of the Internet a valuable source of information that provides a wide variety of information and services.

VOCABULARY

annotated codes Explained and commented on by means of remarks or notes.

annotation Mark or notation by way of explanation. In annotated codes, decided cases involving the statute are cited following each section of the statute.

brief A complete statement of the client's case, including the attorney's argument and supporting authorities.

case law Laws and regulations as interpreted by the judicial branch of government.

citation Reference to laws or other cases to support a position that a person desires to establish.

code A compilation of the laws pertaining to a given topic or subject title; statue books (may or may not be annotated).

Corpus Juris Secondum (CJS) The Latin name adopted for an exhaustive encyclopedia of the law of the country; also, the body of the law.

digests Series of books that serve as indexes to the reported cases comprising the law; collections or summaries.

encyclopedias Legal reference books, in text form under specific subjects, summarizing all the law pertaining to the subject title, with citations as the source authority for the statement of law.

form books A reference book containing samples of typed forms used in legal proceedings.

headnote A note or comment prefixed to a court's decision.

hypertext Enables the user to open related Web pages by clicking them with the mouse.

information service A large host computer that stores large databases and allows access to computer users who subscribe to the service.

interface To connect between or among different machines.

Internet One of the world's largest computer networks, known as a "network of networks."

Lexis A computerized legal research database.

links Enables the user to open Web pages by clicking them with the mouse. Also referred to as *hypertext* or *hypertext* link.

National Reporter System A system of reports that divides the United States into seven regions; each *Reporter* covers a particular section of the United States.

pocket supplements Inserts used to update books. The new information is inserted in a pocket in the back cover of the book.

points and authorities Points of law and their sources that accompany the arguments that the attorney believes support the case or motion.

precedent A judicial decision that serves as a guide for future cases.

regulations Rules established by the executive branch of government to carry the law into effect.

reports, reporters Legal reference books reporting the history of the cases in federal, state, supreme, and appellate courts, detailing the names of the parties, the facts, the opinions of the court, and its decisions or judgments.

supplement An addition to law books that updates the original and is inserted in the back pocket of the hardbound book.

treatise An author's discussion on a particular subject of law.

Westlaw A computerized database for legal research that provides the ease of using key numbers.

World Wide Web A vast series of electronic documents called Web pages or Web documents that are linked together over the Internet.

STUDENT ASSESSMENT 1

Instructions: Circle T if the statement is true or F if the statement is false.

T F 1. A code is a compilation of laws that deals with a particular subject.

T F 2. Code books have been compiled only for laws at the state level.

T F 3. Form books are helpful to the attorney for the wording and style in the preparation of legal cases.

T F 4. Law books are updated regularly with all the changes in the law in the supplements or pocket supplements.

T F 5. An important aspect of the job of the legal support staff is to keep code and reference books current.

T F 6. Citations should not be abbreviated when they are used as an authority for a statement of law.

T F 7. A useful book for reference in typing citations is the *Harvard Blue Book*.

T F 8. Legal newspapers are used exclusively for the publication of legal notices.

T F 9. The United States Code contains federal statutes.

T F 10. Sets of law books are identified by their own abbreviations.

STUDENT ASSESSMENT 2

Instructions: Match the most correct letter to the number.

Section I

_____ 1. *Corpus Juris Secondum*

_____ 2. encyclopedias

_____ 3. Citator

_____ 4. digests

_____ 5. citation

Section I

A. a reference book used to find cases that provide similar citations for a topic of law

B. indexes to reported cases

C. *People v. Barry*, 94 Cal.481

D. encyclopedia

E. legal reference books that summarize law pertaining to a subject title

Section II

_____ 1. points and authorities

_____ 2. reports

_____ 3. annotated codes

_____ 4. *Harvard Blue Book*

_____ 5. form book

Section II

A. American Jurisprudence Pleading and Practice Forms

B. list of cases supporting attorney's case

C. decisions of federal and state supreme and appellate courts

D. compilation of laws on federal or state level with notations

E. rules for typing citations

Section III

_____ 1. National Reporter System

_____ 2. pocket part

_____ 3. WESTLAW

_____ 4. Martindale–Hubbell

_____ 5. treatise

Section III

A. legal directory

B. narrative on a subject of law

C. supplements to law book

D. published court decisions

E. computerized legal research

STUDENT ASSIGNMENTS

PROJECT 1: ACCESSING INTERNET WEBSITES PERTAINING TO LEGAL MATTERS

Instructions: Using the computer and your search tool, access these websites and find the information requested. Write down the information, and submit a copy of the written information to your instructor.

1. Access the website for the House of Representatives (http://www.house.gov/). Find and display the electronic mail address of the member of the House of Representatives from your district. If your representative is not listed, select the name of one that you recognize.

2. Access the website for Prentice Hall (http://www.prenhall.com/). Find and display the page that summarizes the information included in *Legal Office Procedures*, 7th Edition.

3. Access the website for the Indiana Law School (http://www.law.indiana.edu). Find and display the address for the law school and the name of the present dean.

4. Access the website for the National Federation of Paralegal Associations (http://www.paralegals.org/). Find and display the information on the requirements to become a member of the National Federation of Paralegal Associations, Inc.

Part 6

GETTING A JOB

Chapter 15
Getting a Job

15

GETTING A JOB

OBJECTIVES

Upon completion of this chapter, you should be able to:

1. List sources for employment
2. Prepare a list of your previous jobs and periods of employment
3. Describe the importance of doing a self-assessment in the job search
4. Prepare a self-assessment summary
5. Discuss the importance of a résumé
6. Explain the basic formats for creating a résumé
7. List the major categories of a résumé
8. Discuss the guidelines for preparing a résumé
9. Prepare a résumé
10. List the guidelines for preparing a cover letter
11. Prepare a cover letter
12. Describe how to prepare for an interview
13. Prepare a thank-you letter for the interview
14. Provide a checklist of basics for success on your first job

After you have acquired the necessary skills to perform the tasks required as a legal professional you are ready to begin your job-hunting campaign. You have mastered the necessary skills to be prepared for the job, you are familiar with the procedures and terminology used in law offices, and you are eager and willing to learn. You are also aware that legal procedures will vary from office to office depending on local court requirements and the preferences of your employer. You have learned enough about law offices to know that there are always changes in the law and procedures, and you recognize that this is what makes legal office work such an interesting and challenging career. You are willing to meet these challenges and grow both personally and professionally in your chosen field.

There is an increasing demand for qualified legal professionals. For people with the proper training and experience, the opportunities in the legal profession are unlimited. Whether you plan to work in the legal department of a large corporation or assist an attorney in a small general practice office, the more you develop your skills and knowledge of the law and legal procedures, the more valuable you will become to your employer and the more career opportunities and choices will be available to you.

SOURCES OF EMPLOYMENT

Many sources of employment are available to those prepared to work in a law office, and it is important that you know how to make good use of them. There is no one single method for finding a job, and it is important for you to expand your job search to contact the largest possible number of potential employers. This can be done through a variety of ways—by networking with family and friends in the legal profession, looking in the local newspapers, using resources available at your school or college, visiting regular and temporary employment agencies, and using the Internet.

Networking

Some of the best jobs in legal offices are never advertised, and it is important to let your friends and acquaintances in the legal community know that you are interested in employment. Sharing employment information with a network of others is an important method of obtaining employment. Attend career fairs and attend seminars where prospective employers and office administrators will be available to meet students. By volunteering to serve on committees or participating in professional organizations, you increase your opportunities to meet others and network by making yourself visible to others.

Build your information base by keeping current. Read the local daily newspapers and weekly magazines to keep abreast of the opportunities in the legal field and the opportunities in your particular community.

School Resources

Within your school, there are at least three sources of information about career opportunities: the college placement office, teachers, and counselors.

Placement Offices   Many colleges maintain placement offices for their students and graduates. Schools may also provide information on interviewing techniques and the preparation of résumés, and many provide a bulletin board listing job opportunities. These offices are a good source of information regarding positions available, salary ranges, and requirements for employment.

If your school provides these services, it is a good idea to check with the placement director about your career plans and advise them of when you will be available. Also, as a matter of courtesy, be sure to let your school placement office know when you have accepted a job.

Teachers   Especially while still in school, students can get job information from teachers. Many attorneys have come to depend on schools as their source for employees, and former students often call teachers to let them know about both part-time and full-time career opportunities.

Counselors   Almost every college has a counseling service. Often, employers interested in part-time or temporary office help call the school guidance office. Most counselors are familiar with job opportunities and can serve as a good source for employment information, as well as provide assistance in your career choices.

Professional Organizations and Friends

Your local legal support associations also may be a good source of information on employment opportunities. Get to know the members and participate in the activities of the organization. Participation also can be a source of personal and professional fulfillment.

Friends who are already employed in a law firm usually can give you some information as to the firm's personnel needs. Some firms encourage employees to recommend prospective employees. Friends may also be able to recommend you to attorneys or law firms with whom they have done business.

If you have worked part-time in a law firm, you may find the contacts you have made there invaluable. The attorneys and legal staff you have come to know personally may be able to recommend you for openings with other law firms.

Newspapers and Journals

Your local newspaper has a classified section listing employment opportunities, as do some legal publications and journals. It is good to check the classified section in the newspapers of the area where you want to work. The Sunday edition of metropolitan newspapers usually contains a large section of classified ads.

Private Employment Agencies

Private employment agencies differ from school placement offices because they usually involve a fee. If you accept a job from an agency, your prospective employer pays the fee or you must pay a certain percentage of your salary to the agency. If you plan to use a private employment agency in your job search, be sure you understand the financial arrangements before you accept any interviews or pay out any money.

Private employment agencies are usually listed in the classified section of the newspaper under the heading Employment Agencies. Some agencies serve all occupational areas, while others specialize in the occupational areas pertaining to the office environment.

The Internet

Another way to search for a job is through the Internet. Check the websites for law offices in your area to obtain information about the firms and any postings that may be listed for applicants. If you are interested in a particular firm, go to its website to obtain information about its practice of law, organization, and services.

As technology is advancing, companies are increasingly accepting letters of application and résumés on the Internet. A growing number of companies are using electronic scanning systems to scan, store, and track résumés and application letters. When recruiters are looking for a certain type of applicant, they can supply key words that are essential and scan the documents for those words—such as *bilingual*, *civil litigation*, *probate*, or *family law*. If confidentiality is a concern, you can list your skills and experiences without listing employer names, use a rented mailbox as your address, or set up a new e-mail address specifically for your job search.

You should create your cover letter, résumé, and thank you letter in a word processing program before you use the Internet for your job search. This allows you to prepare your materials in advance, to review the documents, and to use the spell check feature and grammar check so that your documents are professionally done. When you find a position of interest in your job search, you can customize these preformatted letters to suit the job opportunity.

The following are some employment-related websites:

Employment sites:
www.americasjobbank.com
www.careerbuilder.com
www.hotjobs.com

www.monster.com
www.occom.com

Federal government jobs:
www.fedworld.gov
www.usajobs.opm.gov

Occupational Outlook Handbook, U.S. Bureau of Labor Statistics:
www.stats.bls.gov/oco/home.htm

Salary information:
www.jobstar.org
www.salary.com

Be aware that new websites are posted on a regular basis, and these websites may change from time to time.

APPLYING FOR A JOB

The steps you take to find a job depend to a great extent on the circumstances involved. If you are responding to a newspaper ad, you should write a letter of application, enclosing a résumé with information on your background and training. If a friend, instructor or school placement officer has referred you to a prospective employer, you may need only to telephone to arrange for an interview. In either case, it is important that you prepare a résumé for the initial interview (Figure 15-1).

Self-Assessment

The purpose of self-assessment is to help you to focus on your qualifications, skills, and achievements so that you can best present them in a résumé. In order to do this, however, you must review all the jobs that you have held (part-time, full-time, and volunteer) and the activities in which you have participated.

The *Work Chronology* and *Skills Assessment* forms at the end of this chapter will assist you in determining the type of work you have done and the kind of work you like to do. You may find that you like to work alone, or you may be the happiest when you work with people. You may like to take directions, or you may prefer to solve problems and be the organizer or person in charge.

Common threads may not at first be apparent, and you may find it easier to discuss these forms with a spouse or friend who can help you to recognize your special qualities. While skills required for a job may be more valued than those used for a hobby, homemaking, or volunteer work, they may be the same skill. Anything from organizing a car pool to managing an office requires a special skill.

The manner in which you state your accomplishments is no less important than the details themselves. Active, energetic phrases attract more of the reader's attention than do dull or passive words. *Created,* for example, sounds more interesting than *began; promoted, instituted,* and *produced* are much more attention getting than *worked on, became,* or *finished.*

Focus on accomplishments that had a noticeable or measurable effect on some part of the place where you worked. The entries in Table 15-1 serve as models for work achievement, and the use of action words and specific details helps to demonstrate how the accomplishment was achieved.

TABLE 15-1   Examples of Job Skills and Accomplishments

Job Experience (paid or unpaid)	Accomplishments
Alumni Committee Member	• Created and organized parent-student orientation program for incoming and transfer students • Coordinated annual phone-athon for alumni contributions • Wrote alumni news column in quarterly newsletter
Executive Secretary to President	• Edited annual company report • Supervised office of 15 staff members • Created marketing brochures describing product and support services • Produced program and organized annual convention for 300 participants
Assistant Food Manager for Produce Outlet	• Purchased foods • Determined price lists • Interviewed and employed 6 salespeople • Kept monthly books • Produced monthly reports for management

Preparing a Résumé

Preparing your résumé is one of the most important aspects of your job hunt. A résumé is a word portrait that you will show your prospective employer, and it includes the highlights of the background, training, and experience that you wish to emphasize. The résumé is your professional introduction, and while it cannot get you a job, it can help get you an interview—and that is the purpose of the résumé. Your self-assessment will help you to recognize the skills and accomplishments you have to offer an employer. You want to demonstrate that you are the person to be called in for the interview because you are the best-qualified person for the job.

FIGURE 15-1 *Give thoughtful answers to the interviewer's questions.*

Everything on your résumé must be verifiable. If fraud is detected, you will be eliminated from the applicant list or, if you have the job, it is most likely that you will be fired. On the other hand, it is far more likely that you will not give yourself credit for what you have achieved.

Format   There are three basic formats for creating a résumé: chronological, functional, and combination. Each has advantages and disadvantages, and you need to decide which one is most appropriate for your use.

The *chronological résumé* lists education and work experience in chronological form from the present to the past.

The *functional* or *skills résumé* emphasizes experiences that relate to the job the candidate is seeking. This format stresses skills and achievements and does not focus on specific dates and places, although they are included.

The *combination format* blends the advantages of the chronological résumé with those of the functional résumé. Therefore, it can be the most general, specific, and complete.

Though the final order of your résumé will depend on the format that you choose, there are some major categories that you should use, as follows:

- Personal information
- Career objective
- Summary of skills and qualifications
- Education
- Work experience
- Professional activities
- Special awards and recognition
- Military experience
- Special interests and community activities
- References

Personal Information   The only personal information that you need to include in your résumé, as required by law, is your name, address, e-mail address, and telephone number. This information should appear at the top of your résumé. Do not list nicknames or formal titles. If a change of address is imminent, be sure to include the old and new address and the date that the new address becomes effective.

If you can be reached at more than one telephone number, include both numbers. Do not list a work phone unless you have permission to do so. If you are not able to answer your calls personally, it is acceptable to use an answering machine. Make sure that you have a clear, direct message on the machine, and indicate when you will return the calls. Personal items that reveal your age, health, or marital status are not required and may work to your disadvantage.

Career Objective   Employers are looking for people with specific skills, and a brief career objective can indicate that to a prospective employer. A statement of goals allows the employer to tell whether the applicant's objective and the employer's needs are compatible. A person who plans carefully will be a careful planner on the job, especially if the educational experience records provide evidence of progress toward these objectives. A career objective will focus on what you can and would like to do based on your skills and experience. Some examples of career objectives might be the following:

- A legal professional position offering increasing responsibilities and opportunities in the area of probate
- A challenging position in a legal environment that will enable me to use my interpersonal and computer application skills

Summary of Skills and Qualifications Although this section may be optional, it can serve a useful function by focusing on those qualifications that you have acquired. This section also can allow you to pull together the various types of experiences that you have acquired in different types of jobs. Review your strengths to determine your most marketable qualifications.

Education This area is essential, and an employer will want to see your education, background, and training. List your legal office training first, where and when you received it, and your specialty. Be sure to include the significant information that indicates your training and the specific courses or the hours of training. If you have not attended college, focus on your particular achievements in high school that indicate important qualifications. If you attended college, include the college, your major, minor, and your degree. If you received any academic honors or awards, be sure to include them.

Work Experience In this section, indicate where you worked, your title, what you did on the job, and the dates. Do not omit dates, as employers like to verify where you worked and when. Indicate your jobs, the skills you developed, and how these skills will be an asset to an organization. You may want to include internships and volunteer work if you have not had extensive job experience.

Special Honors and Awards If you have received special honors or awards, you may want to include them. This will indicate to your prospective employer that you are someone with special talents and achievement.

Military Service If you have served in the military, you may want to include that service and any special training, foreign languages, computer skills, and education that you may have received.

References It is not appropriate to include a list of your references, as you will be asked to include them on a job application. Be sure to ask your references for permission to use their names, and mention the fact that they may be contacted. At the bottom of your résumé you may include the following statement: "References available upon request."

Appearance of the Résumé

There are some important points to keep in mind as you create your résumé. Most employers prefer a one-page résumé. If it is done carefully and thoroughly, it will save you time later when you apply for a job. You should also send a résumé with your letters of application, if such letters are needed to arrange job interviews.

The résumé goes by various names—personal data sheet, summary, qualification sheet, or personal profile. Ordinarily, it is clipped to the back of the application letter. Therefore, the prospective employer reads the résumé after reading the application letter. Nevertheless, it should be written first. Preparing the résumé will force you to evaluate yourself and the job before writing the letter. This thinking and evaluating process serves as good mental preparation for writing the letter.

By arranging the résumé in a pleasing manner and presenting the information in the appropriate sequence, you will demonstrate to the prospective employer that you have organizational ability. A résumé makes a good impression if the space is used economically without giving a crowded appearance and if the headings provide easy reference to the information.

People who are just getting out of school may never have held a full-time job, though they may have worked part-time between school terms. If you have no work experience, however, you will probably not want to stress this fact on your résumé by saying, "Experience: None." Instead, mention any clubs or organizations in which you have held positions of responsibility, or make a definite selling point of the specialized courses you have taken in preparation for employment.

In preparing your résumé, try to apply the following guidelines:

1. *Choose the format most suitable for you.* Make the arrangement neat and uncrowded.

2. *Choose high-quality paper* (twenty-five pound rag content), either white, off-white, gray, or beige. Whatever you select, you should use the same shade and quality for the envelope.

3. *Choose standard-sized paper.* Standard paper size is 8½ by 11 inches. The envelope you select may be regular business size, or you may want to use a larger envelope to match your résumé. Wherever practical, use phrases rather than complete sentences. This practice will save space and provide for consistency in organization.

4. *Use high-quality output.* With the advances in technology and printers today, many professional processes are available to make your résumé look professional or even printed. You may wish to have your résumé typeset, and the price difference is so small that it is worth the additional investment. Laser printers have become commonplace, and the output from these printers is very high quality. Dot matrix printers are not acceptable for final résumés; handwritten résumés are never acceptable.

5. *Copy should be error free.* While you may choose high-quality paper and professional printing, it is still important that the copy be carefully proofread and error free. You are ultimately responsible for any misspellings, printer's errors, or typographic errors. If you are a poor speller, consult a dictionary for misspelled words, or ask a friend who is proficient in these matters to proofread your copy. Proofread the copy again before it is printed.

6. *Indicate name and address changes.* If the organizational or institutional name of a former employer has been changed, indicate the former as well as the current name. If a change of address is imminent, be sure to include the old and new address and the date the new address becomes effective. If you can be reached at more than one telephone number, include both numbers.

7. *Strive for easy reading and eye appeal.* Use white space for easy reading, and use ample, uniform margins. Don't try to cram a lot of information into your résumé. By having your résumé typeset, you will be able to include more information and use smaller type.

8. *Watch your language.* Avoid pompous or self-serving descriptions. Let your reader be the judge of your achievements and accomplishments.

9. *Keep your résumé current.* Do not send out a résumé that is incorrect or out of date.

10. *Limit your résumé to one page.* There is no rule against using two pages, but busy employers appreciate brevity.

11. *Keep your résumé factual.* Use your letter of application to interpret the facts with respect to specific job requirements.

12. *Let your résumé be a reflection of you.* Your résumé should reflect your education, work experiences, professional accomplishments, and style. Your selection of material for inclusion, as well as the formatting and layout, should reflect your personal style and be as unique as you are as an individual.

You may want to use the résumés in Figures 15-2, 15-3, and 15-4 as guides in preparing your own résumé. These examples employ the following specific features:

1. The heading identifies the applicant.

2. An objective or a statement of goals allows the employer to tell whether the applicant's objectives and the employer's needs are compatible. A person who plans objectives carefully will also be a careful planner on the job, especially if

FIGURE 15-2   *Résumé 1.*

ANNE L. STEVENSON
2148 Orangethorpe
Fullerton, CA 92634
(714) 555-3241
astevenson@aol.com

OBJECTIVE: A legal office position in a general practice firm that would utilize my strong computer training.

EDUCATION:	Certificate in Office Skills Fullerton Community College Fullerton, California	2006
	Associate of Arts Fullerton Community College Fullerton, California	2006

LEGAL HIGHLIGHTS: Word processed complaints, answers, interrogatories, summons, court briefs and memoranda. Completed courses in Business Law, Civil Litigation, and Introduction to the American Legal System.

PROFESSIONAL SKILLS:

Administrative

- Performed general administrative/clerical duties
- Handled petty cash, banking, payroll, accounts payable
- Prepared and filed tax forms
- Performed word process in data entry

Communication

- Inventoried, displayed, sold merchandise
- Managed sales department during peak periods
- Assisted with promotion campaign/designed brochure

Specialized Skills:

- Microsoft Office, WORD, WordPerfect, EXCEL, Powerpoint, Access, Keyboarding (65 wpm)

EMPLOYMENT:

2003–2006 Tri-Lab Products, Inc., Fullerton, CA
2001–2003 Office Depot, Fullerton, CA
2000–2002 Macy's Department Stores, Anaheim, CA

REFERENCES: Available upon request

the educational experience records provide evidence of progress toward these objectives.

3. The section on education emphasizes a connection between education and the requirements for the job. If a list of related courses is excessively long, the most closely related courses will not get the emphasis that they deserve.

4. The section on employment affords the applicant an opportunity to demonstrate the relationship between his or her background and the job requirements. To provide the employer with a complete picture, the applicant should state precisely what the duties were on previous jobs. This information can be included in the résumé.

After you are satisfied with the final version of your résumé, arrange to have copies made. The résumé represents you in both appearance and style. Be sure to have extra copies made up so that you can send them to prospective employers or leave them with those who interview you.

ROSE CRISP
136 Maple Street
Syracuse, New York 11530
(516) 555-3729
rcrisp@earthlink.com

CAREER OBJECTIVE: To find a challenging legal office position that would enable me
to use my intensive general office training, and my diverse
academic and employment background.

EDUCATION:

2006   Syracuse City College, Syracuse, New York
Legal Assistant Program
Office Technology

2005   Syracuse University, Syracuse, New York
Bachelor of Science in Education

Junior academic year: Madrid, Spain
Special studies in educational theory and practice

EMPLOYMENT:

2000 – 2006   Member, Planning Team for Curriculum Reorganization. Conducted
research for educational planning, implemented and evaluated pilot programs
for three-school system. Wrote daily reports and assisted teachers.

Board of Education of New York City, Brooklyn, New York

1994 - 1998   Various positions held to finance college education

1986 - 1988   Proof Operator. Bank of New York, Syracuse, New York
Encoded checks for all Worker's Compensation Fund accounts. Developed
debit/credit accuracy check system. Trained new operators to work on
specialized projects with time deadlines.

1984 - 1987   File Clerk. East Syracuse Memorial Hospital, Syracuse, New York
Reorganized and maintained comprehensive filing system of hospital outpatient
records. Developed medical terminology reference guide.

1982 - 1984   Library Assistant. Syracuse University Library, Syracuse, New York
Worked with collection and acquisition librarian. Processed and maintained
periodical files.

INTERESTS   Backpacking; Member, Conservationists Club
Volunteer, Drug and Alcohol Rehabilitation Center

FIGURE 15-3   *Résumé 2.*

BARBARA MACHES
2674 Indian Trails
Houston, Texas 60187
(713) 555-4674
bmaches@earthlink.com

PROFESSIONAL OBJECTIVE	A challenging position in an environment which will enable me to use my interpersonal skills and legal office training.

EDUCATION

2006	South Texas Vocational College Legal Office Studies Introduction to American Legal System Business Communications, Office Technology I & II Word Processing, Spreadsheets
2000	Sam Houston High School; graduated with honors

EXPERIENCE

COMMUNICATION SKILLS
- Worked with clientele from diverse backgrounds
- Provided customer assistance and information
- Contacted suppliers by telephone and letter

NEGOTIATION SKILLS
- Arranged for and executed purchasing of materials
- Coordinated deliveries

ORGANIZATIONAL SKILLS
- Assisted in planning presentation of stock
- Assisting in compiling inventory reports
- Implemented filing system to follow up orders

EMPLOYMENT

1998-2000	Child care and homemaker
1997-1998	Office Assistant, Houston Medical Group, Houston, Texas
1996-1997	Social Services Volunteer, Orangewood Childrens' Home, Houston, Texas

REFERENCES   Available upon request

FIGURE 15-4   *Résumé 3.*

THE COVER LETTER

Once you have completed your résumé, you are ready to contact potential employers. Sometimes, however, you may need to write a letter of application to the company before you can apply in person for the job. In nearly all such situations, write a brief letter of application that introduces you to the prospective employer. You should not duplicate the content of your résumé, since your résumé will be included with the letter. (See Figures 15-5 and 15-6.)

FIGURE 15-5 *Letter of application 1.*

2148 Orangethorpe
Fullerton, CA 92634
(714) 555–3241

October 1, 20--

Mr. Jim Anderson
Anderson & Tobler
348 Main Street
Fullerton, CA 92634

Dear Mr. Anderson:

In response to your advertisement in the <u>Times</u> of September 22, I would like to apply for the legal office assistant position listed by your firm.

Recently, I graduated with honors from the Office Technology Program at Fullerton College. In addition to intensive computer application courses, I completed courses in the legal and business areas.

My office experience over the last three years has also given me the opportunity to become familiar with office procedures. Combined with my undergraduate studies in legal and business courses, this experience and training should contribute to my effectiveness as a future law office assistant.

I would like to discuss employment opportunities at Anderson & Tobler, and how my skills and qualifications can meet your needs.

Thank you for your interest and consideration. I will call your office within the next week to request an appointment at a time convenient to you.

Sincerely yours,

Anne L. Stevenson

Here are some helpful guidelines to follow when an employer asks for a letter of application:

1. Keep the letter short. Type it neatly on 8½ by 11-inch bond paper. Proofread carefully to make sure that it is error free.

2. Whenever possible, address your letter to a specific person, by name and title, rather than just to "office manager" or "personnel director." You may need to phone ahead to get the correct name and address of the firm and the correct spelling of the name of the person responsible for taking applications.

3. Read the job ad *very carefully*. Be sure to tailor your qualifications to their needs. If they are looking for someone with specific skills, be sure to use the exact same language to describe what you have to offer them.

4. Indicate in the first paragraph your reason for writing, for example, "Please consider me as an applicant for the position of legal office assistant advertised in the Sunday edition of the *Times*," or "RE: Your Ad in the *Times*." If a mutual acquaintance referred you, be sure to include the name of that person. Also, include a sentence or two about how you feel you could be an asset to the company.

5. In the second and third paragraphs, point out the outstanding features detailed on your résumé and explain why you are especially qualified for the position as advertised. This part of your letter should distinguish you from the other applicants.

6. Demonstrate that you understand the requirements of the position and that you have credentials and qualifications to fulfill those requirements.

7. Be confident and positive about the qualities that you have, and avoid any negative or apologetic remarks concerning qualifications that you may not have.

FIGURE 15-6 *Letter of application 2.*

136 Maple Street
Syracuse, New York
(516) 555–3729

October 11, 20--

Ms. Lois Bridges
834 Norwood Avenue
Syracuse, New York 11539

Dear Ms. Bridges:

Rudy Baron of your Research Department has informed me of a legal office assistant opening in your corporation. He feels that my background and training qualify me for this position, and has suggested that I apply.

As a recent graduate of Syracuse City College Office Technology Program, with a specialty in Legal Procedures, I have strongly developed skills in this particular area. In addition, I have had practical experience in working with a small realty firm, performing a wide variety of duties. Such training and experience could make me an asset to your firm.

I will call your office within the next week to request an appointment to discuss this position.

Thank you for your interest and consideration, and I look forward to meeting you.

Sincerely yours,

Maria Gonzalez

8. In the fourth and final paragraph, briefly tell the reader how to contact you. This is the action part of the letter. It should encourage the employer to contact you for a personal interview. You may also want to include a statement in this section thanking the employer for considering your application.

PREPARING FOR THE INTERVIEW

The employment interview can be one of the most important events in your experience; the twenty or thirty minutes you spend with an interviewer could determine the course of your entire future. The following sections discuss how to get yourself ready for the interview.

The Time and Place

Find out the exact place and time of the interview. This may sound almost too basic, but it is an unfortunate applicant who assumes that the interview is to be held in a certain place and then discovers two minutes before the hour that the appointment is somewhere else. If your interview is in the city, allow time for traffic and parking. Write down the time of the appointment and the full name and address of the company, and keep the notation with you. Don't rely on your memory. Be certain you have your interviewer's full name and find out how to pronounce it if it looks difficult.

FIGURE 15-7 *Do some prior research on the firm interviewing you.*

Dress Appropriately

The first impression you make on your interviewer is very important, so be sure to dress appropriately. You should be well groomed and feel comfortable in what you are wearing. It is best to be a little on the conservative side rather than to dress too casually or in extreme styles. Recall how the staff in legal offices is groomed and dressed. This will give you an indication of the appropriate dress for the office.

Research

Do some research on the firm interviewing you. It will be helpful if you know the type of law practiced and the number of attorneys associated with the firm (Figure 15-7).

Think about the questions that you might wish to ask before you go to the interview. Bring a pen and pencil and a notebook. If you have some samples of legal work you have done, you may want to bring them along, too.

References

It is important that you decide whom to use for references before the interview. Be sure to select business and professional references who really know you and are interested in you and your career, rather than someone who only knows you casually. Instructors and former employers are good references, although you will probably not want to limit your list to them. Try to provide a balance to your list of references. You should list a minimum of three, but no more than five references. Be sure their names are spelled correctly and their job titles, addresses, and phone numbers are complete and accurate. It is a good idea to type all this information on a card or piece of paper that you can take with you to the interview.

You should contact each of your prospective references to explain that you are looking for a job and that you would like permission to use his or her name as a reference. This gesture serves a double purpose—it provides you with an opportunity to tell them about your plans and it gives you permission to use their names.

The Application Form

You may be required to complete an application form when you go for your interview. Complete the information on the application neatly and carefully. Write neatly and answer the questions accurately and completely. If some of the information does not apply, draw a line through the space provided for the answer. Here is where it will be handy to have prepared in advance your list of references and any other information that might be requested.

The Interview

After you have prepared your résumé and completed the application form, the next step is the actual job interview. In most situations, a receptionist or office assistant will have given the interviewer your completed application form as well as your personal résumé.

Some interviews can last for quite some time, perhaps as long as an hour or more. Others may last only a few minutes. The length of the interview depends on many things: the policy of the firm, the job for which you are applying, the time available on the part of the interviewer, and the information that the firm has already received about you.

Job interviews usually can be divided into four parts:

1. Opening the interview
2. Information gathering by the employer
3. Information gathering by the applicant
4. Closing the interview

Opening the Interview

When you arrive at the office, you will probably have to introduce yourself to the receptionist, who, in turn, will probably introduce you to the office manager or attorney (Figure 15-8). After you have been introduced, acknowledge the introduction graciously by simply saying, "How do you do?" or "Good morning." Look for an indication from the interviewer as to where you should sit. If no indication is given, look for a comfortable location facing the interviewer.

Information Gathering by the Employer

In most job interviews, the person doing the interviewing will take the lead and begin asking the questions. Some of the most frequently asked questions are:

- Why do you think you would like to work for our firm?
- What is important to you in a job?
- Why do you think you are qualified for this kind of work?
- Tell me something about yourself.
- How do you feel about working overtime and weekends?
- What type of boss do you prefer?
- How do you like to spend your spare time?
- What do you consider your major strengths? Your weaknesses?
- How would you describe yourself, if you were another person talking about you?
- What are your long-term career objectives?
- When can you begin work?
- What salary do you expect?

FIGURE 15-8 *The opportunities in the legal field are unlimited for the qualified applicant.*

It is usually best to provide short, thoughtful responses to the interviewer's questions. Most attorneys are very busy, and they do not have time for long, drawn-out answers. On the other hand, it is generally not enough to respond with only a yes or a no answer.

Throughout the interview, try to give straightforward and honest answers. Be enthusiastic and give the interviewer your full attention. Be pleasant and look at the person during the interview.

Information Gathering by the Applicant

You, too, have the right to ask questions during the interview. In fact, you have a responsibility to learn about the company so that you will know whether to accept the job if it is offered to you. Most interviewers want the applicant to ask questions.

When asking questions, try to ask only meaningful ones. Do not ask questions for the sake of asking questions, but carefully think out the things that you would like to know about the company. The following questions are some that you may want to consider asking during the interview.

- Is this a new position? If so, why is this position needed?
- What are the responsibilities of the job?
- To whom do I report?
- What are the hours of employment?
- What is the pay and how is it computed? What is the amount of pay for overtime? How are raises determined?
- Does your firm encourage continuing education and professional development?
- What major problems will I encounter on this job?
- When do you think you will be making your hiring decision?

You should feel free to ask any of these questions, as well as others that you can think of. It is perfectly acceptable to ask the interviewer to respond to these questions if they are sincerely and courteously asked.

FIGURE 15-9   *The interviewer will indicate when the interview is over.*

Close of the Interview

In most situations, the interviewer will indicate the close of the interview (see Figure 15-9). Such comments as "You should be hearing from us within ten days" or "I have thoroughly enjoyed talking with you" indicate that the interview is coming to a close. Thank the person for giving you the interview, stand and face the interviewer, and prepare to leave. If the interviewer has not indicated when you will hear about the job, it is perfectly acceptable to ask, "When may I expect to hear from you about the position with your firm?"

At the close of the interview, be sure to thank the interviewer for the interview. Also, on the way out, be sure to thank the receptionist.

Writing a Thank-You Letter

Immediately after the interview, you may want to write the interviewer a thank-you letter. This letter will serve two purposes: It will thank the interviewer for considering you for a position with the firm and it will show your interest in the position. This letter should be short and to the point. (See Figure 15-10 for an example of a thank-you letter.)

Expressing Regrets

If you have had several interviews and you find that you are definitely interested in one or more of the positions, let the person who interviewed you at each of the other firms know that you are not interested in working for them. The easiest way to do this is to phone the person who interviewed you and explain that you are not interested in the position—the reason may be that transportation is too difficult, the hours could not be arranged, or the salary is too low. If you do not wish to telephone a regret, simply send a short note saying that you are not interested in the position.

STARTING YOUR FIRST JOB

Congratulations! You passed the interview with flying colors. You have been offered a job and you have accepted. It is natural to feel some anxiety your first day on the

FIGURE 15-10   *Thank-you letter.*

> 2148 Orangethorpe
> Fullerton, CA 92634
>
> September 21, 20--
>
> Mr. Jim Anderson
> Anderson & Tobler
> 348 Main Street
> Fullerton, CA 92634
>
> Dear Mr. Anderson:
>
> It was a pleasure meeting you today to discuss the job opening in your firm.
>
> The position seems to be an opportunity for me to use my background and training in a stimulating environment. In reviewing the plans for your company's growth, I am even more enthusiastic about the contributions I can make as a Law Office Assistant.
>
> Again, I did appreciate the opportunity to talk with you, and hope that we will be working together in the future.
>
> Sincerely,
>
> Anne L. Stevenson

job, and you will need a little time to get used to the procedures and office routine. No two offices are the same, so it is important that you observe everything carefully. You will find that some things are done differently from the way you learned in school or on previous jobs. Remain flexible, but be willing to offer suggestions if you feel that they will improve the organization or operation of the office.

Try to learn as much on your own as you can. Check the files for legal style and to see how previous documents have been executed. Find someone in the office who is familiar with the procedures and willing to assist you as a resource person. Show appreciation when others take time from their busy schedule to help you. Respect the value of their time, and try not to interrupt them more than necessary.

Give attention to the human relations aspect of your job—it is important that you get along with the other members of the staff. See how they conduct themselves and try to adapt to the general routine of the office. Show consideration for your employer and note his or her preferences in the way that the work is to be accomplished and the procedures that are to be followed.

Your consideration for others and your willingness to grow and learn on the job will make you a positive addition to the office staff.

GROWING PROFESSIONALLY

As you grow professionally in your job, you will continue to acquire a great deal of knowledge and experience in the field of law. You will need to learn all that you can while you are in the office, but you can also make your out-of-office activities contribute to your growth. Participation in legal office support organizations, as well as attendance at legal seminars, will add to your professional growth.

SUCCESS ON YOUR FIRST JOB

Few employees fail because they lack the capabilities to handle the job. In most cases, failure can be traced to the inability to relate to people and the difficulty in adjusting to new surroundings and diverse personalities. Your success at your first job and your acceptance by the other employees in your office will be influenced by your attitudes and your approach to the job situation (Figure 15-11).

The following is a checklist of some basic do's and don'ts that you may find helpful as you begin your first job:

1. Be aware that first impressions are often crucial ones. When you report for work, give careful attention to your personal grooming and good manners. Avoid extremes in clothing and grooming, and quickly assess what types of dress and personal appearance are acceptable for your firm.

2. Learn as much as possible about the office or firm and its people during the very first weeks of employment. Study the office policies and procedures manuals. Find out how things are done, including whom you should consult when you have a problem or need information.

3. Recognize that you are an outsider coming into the organization. Resolve to "come on slow" with the other people, and try to earn their trust, confidence, and respect. Most people in an office situation will be willing to accept you if you demonstrate some humility and give them evidence that you are worthy of being accepted. Little is accomplished by trying to force yourself on people on the one extreme or being a loner on the other. Act as normal as possible, and do what you can to win friends among the majority of people.

4. Respect those who are more experienced than you, and don't stereotype mature employees as being rigid and inflexible just because of their age. Some young people are just as rigid and stubborn in their attitudes, values, and the way they do things. Try to keep an open mind and be flexible and positive in everything you do and say.

5. Recognize the formality of the office routines and begin on a somewhat formal basis unless you are told to do otherwise. Generally, it is better to address management on a more formal basis, such as Mr. Jones, Mrs. Smith, and so on,

FIGURE 15-11 *Make the most of your future and career.*

unless you are given permission to do otherwise. As you become more comfortable on the job, it is perfectly acceptable to ask those individuals how they would prefer to be addressed.

6. Try to develop a clear understanding of what your boss wants you to accomplish. Try to have periodic discussions with your boss and determine together what type of performance he or she expects of you on the job. If you feel that you need more training or job exposure in other areas, be sure to articulate these needs to your employer.

7. Learn to tolerate frustration. Solving problems, working with complex situations, and associating with fellow employees may be trying at times. Avoid emotional outbursts and shows of temper. Your employer will be impressed with the nature and forthright manner in which you solve problems and control frustrations.

8. If you are placed in a supervisory capacity, recognize that some employees may know a great deal more about the company than you do. Rely on them, and appeal to their sense of pride to help you to learn the job.

9. Most bosses are receptive to carefully conceived ideas. Before you make suggestions, however, research and analyze them well. Be sure you have laid the groundwork carefully for the implementation of these ideas with the other employees.

10. Despite what some people may say, there is still a premium in most organizations and offices for hard work, effort, and loyalty to employer or organization. Be careful that you do not fall into negative thinking patterns. Remain positive and optimistic and take pride in the work that you do.

Good luck! It's up to you to make the most of your job and the opportunities that will be made available to you in this challenging and changing field.

STUDENT ASSIGNMENTS

PROJECT 1: WORK CHRONOLOGY

Instructions: Using the Work Chronology Sheet (Sample 15-1), list all the jobs that you have held, the dates of employment, organization, titles, duties, and accomplishments. Describe your most significant contributions to that job in the accomplishments column. Begin with the most recent year and list backward.

PROJECT 2: SKILLS ASSESSMENT

Instructions: On the Skills Assessment (Sample 15-2), indicate the degree of competence that you feel you have achieved. This will help you to focus on these skills as you prepare your résumé.

PROJECT 3: PREPARE A PERSONAL LETTER TEMPLATE AND RÉSUMÉ

Instructions: Prepare a letterhead template that you will use for your own correspondence. Use a font and style that best suits you. Save this to disk as **ch015_TM**. Select an advertisement for a position in a legal office for which you would like to apply. Write a résumé for this position. You may actually use this résumé in your job search.
    Save your document as **ch15_RES**, and print one copy for your instructor.

PROJECT 4: PREPARE A COVER LETTER

Instructions: Using the letterhead template that you created in Project 3, prepare a cover letter to go with your résumé.
    Save your document as **ch15_COV**, and print one copy for your instructor.

(continued)

PROJECT 5: COMPLETE A JOB APPLICATION FORM

Instructions: Make a copy of the application for employment (Sample 15-3a and 15-3b) and fill in the appropriate information that relates to your application for employment. After you have filled in all the information, submit the completed form to your instructor.

PROJECT 6: PREPARE A THANK-YOU LETTER

Instructions: Using the letterhead template that you created in Project 3, prepare a thank-you letter for a hypothetical interview that you may have experienced.

Save your document as **ch15_THK**, and print one copy for your instructor.

WORK CHRONOLOGY				
Year	Organization	Title	Duties/Activities	Skills/Accomplishments

SAMPLE 15-1

SKILLS ASSESSMENT

Skill	Excellent	Very Good	Good	Fair	Skill	Excellent	Very Good	Good	Fair
Analyzing					Problem solving				
Budgeting					Persuading				
Building					Policy making				
Computer Skills					Promoting				
Specific Programs					Researching				
					Repairing				
					Selling				
Coordinating					Supervising				
Counseling					Speaking				
Creating					Teaching				
Decision making					Training				
Designing					Troubleshooting				
Directing					Writing				
Drafting									
Editing					Others:				
Inventing									
Keyboarding									
Languages (specify)									
Leading									
Listening									
Managing									
Meeting planning									
Motivating									
Negotiating									
Observing									
Organizing									
Performing									
Planning									
Presenting									

SAMPLE 15-2

EMPLOYMENT APPLICATION

PLEASE FILL OUT APPLICATION COMPLETELY

LAST NAME	FIRST	MIDDLE	DATE

STREET ADDRESS	CITY	STATE	ZIP	HOME PHONE

SOCIAL SECURITY NUMBER	DATE AVAILABLE	WORK DESIRED	BUSINESS PHONE

ARE YOU SEEKING FULL OR PART TIME?	TEMPORARY	TEMP TO PERM	PERMANENT	WAGE OR SALARY DESIRED

ARE YOU AVAILABLE FOR EVENINGS OR WEEKENDS?	HAVE YOU EVER BEEN CONVICTED OF A FELONY?	HOW DID YOU HEAR OF US?

IF EMPLOYED, YOU WILL BE REQUIRED TO SUBMIT DOCUMENTATION SHOWING YOU ARE LAWFULLY AUTHORIZED TO WORK IN THE USA

EDUCATION	NAME AND LOCATION OF SCHOOL	GRADUATE?(Y OR N)	DIPLOMA/DEGREES	GRADE AVERAGE	MAJOR
HIGH SCHOOL					
COLLEGE OR UNIVERSITY					
TECHNICAL OR TRADE SCHOOLS					

ON A SCALE OF 1 - 5 (5 BEING HIGH) HOW WOULD YOUR PREVIOUS EMPLOYERS RATE YOU IN THE FOLLOWING AREAS?

____ INITIATIVE	____ JOB SKILLS	____ TEAM WORK	____ FLEXIBILITY
____ ENERGY/ENTHUSIASM	____ SELF DISCIPLINE	____ ATTITUDE	____ PUNCTUALITY
____ COMMITMENT	____ ATTENDANCE	____ ATTENTION TO DETAILS	____ TAKING DIRECTION

PLEASE CHECK EACH CATAGORY FOR SKILL QUALIFICATIONS

TYPING / SECRETARIAL	TELEPHONES	CLERICAL	BOOKKEEPING
____ SPEED	____ MULTILINE EQUIPMENT	____ FILE	FC ____ A/R ____ FIN. ST.
____ CORRESPONDENCE	____ # of INC. ____ # of EXT.	____ DATA ENTRY	____ TRIAL BAL. ____ A/P
____ STATISTICAL	____ VOICE-MAIL ____ PAGING	____ MAIL ROOM	____ PAYROLL PROCESSING
____ DICTAPHONE	____ # CALLS DAILY ____ OTHER	____ FED EXPRESS	____ 10 KEY ____ GEN. LEDGER
____ SHORTHAND	____ NAME OF	____ FAXING	____ SIGHT ____ JOUR.ENTRS.
____ SPEEDWRITING	____ PHONE	____ CODING	____ TOUCH ____ BANK REC.
____ COURT REPORTING	____ SYSTEMS	____ DATE STAMPING	____ COMPUTERIZED ACCT.

COMPUTERS / WORDPROCESSORS

____ IBM ____ NBI	
____ MACINTOSH ____ VAX	
____ BANYAN ____ OTHER	
____ SYNTREX ____ OTHER	

LEGAL / SPECIAL TERMINOLOGY

____ BUS. LITIGATION	____ TRANS/RE	____ PROBATE	____ CIVIL. LIT.
____ CORPORATE	____ ENVIRONMENTAL	____ PI PLAINTIFF	____ TAX
____ WORKERS COMP	____ PI DEFENSE	____ PUBLIC LAW	____ ESTATE
____ BANKRUPTCY	____ LABOR LAW	____ AVIATION	____ MED MAL
____ MUNICIPAL	____ IMMIGRATION	____ HEALTH CARE	____ STATE/FED FILING
____ CONSTRUCTION	____ ARBITRATION	____ APPELLATE	____ NOTARY

SOFTWARE PROGRAMS

				NET WORK	DESK TOP PUBLISHING
____ WORDPERFECT	____ WP WINDOWS 6.0	____ TIME SLIPS	____ MS WORD	____ NOVEL	____ PAGEMAKER
____ WORD FOR WINDOW	____ QUICKEN	____ Q AND A	____ PARADOX	____ UNIX	____ QUARK EXP.
____ QUATRO PRO	____ LOTUS	____ LOTUS WINDOWS	____ ALL WAYS	____ APPLE TALK	____ VENTURA
____ WIZYWIG	____ EXCEL WINDOWS	____ AMIPRO	____ POWER POINT	____ VAX	____ COREL DRAW
____ JD EDWARDS	____ LEGAL SOLUTIONS	____ SOFT SOLUTIONS	____ OTHER	____ LAN TO LAN	____ OTHER
____ PRO FORMA	____ D BASE	____ HARVARD GRAPHICS	____ OTHER	____ OTHER	

SAMPLE 15-3a

EMPLOYMENT HISTORY (PLEASE FILL OUT COMPLETELY)

WE ARE AN EQUAL OPPORTUNITY EMPLOYER. PLEASE DO NOT INCLUDE ANY INFORMATION REVEALING YOUR RACE, RELIGION OR NATIONAL ORIGIN.

NAME AND ADDRESS OF YOUR PRESENT (OR MOST RECENT) EMPLOYER

TYPE OF BUSINESS

TELEPHONE ( )

IMMEDIATE SUPERVISOR'S NAME

TITLE

WHEN MAY WE CONTACT?

STARTING DATE | STARTING JOB TITLE | STARTING SALARY | ENDING DATE | ENDING JOB TITLE | ENDING SALARY

RESPONSIBILITIES INCLUDED (LEAVE BLANK)

WHAT DID YOU LIKE MOST ABOUT YOUR JOB?

WHAT DID YOU LIKE LEAST?

WHY ARE YOU CONSIDERING LEAVING (OR WHY DID YOU LEAVE) THIS ORGANIZATION?

NAME AND ADDRESS OF EMPLOYER

TYPE OF BUSINESS

TELEPHONE ( )

IMMEDIATE SUPERVISOR'S NAME

TITLE

WHEN MAY WE CONTACT?

STARTING DATE | STARTING JOB TITLE | STARTING SALARY | ENDING DATE | ENDING JOB TITLE | ENDING SALARY

RESPONSIBILITIES INCLUDED (LEAVE BLANK)

WHAT DID YOU LIKE MOST ABOUT YOUR JOB?

WHAT DID YOU LIKE LEAST?

WHY DID YOU LEAVE THIS ORGANIZATION?

AFFIDAVIT

I HEREBY AUTHORIZE ALL SCHOOLS, PERSONS AND EMPLOYERS TO FURNISH YOU MY RECORD, REASON FOR LEAVING, AND ALL INFORMATION THEY HAVE CONCERNING ME, AND I HEREBY RELEASE THEM AND YOU FROM ALL LIABILITY FOR ANY DAMAGE WHATSOEVER ARISING THEREFROM. I ALSO AUTHORIZE INVESTIGATION OF ALL STATEMENTS MADE IN THIS EMPLOYMENT APPLICATION. I AFFIRM THAT THE STATEMENTS ARE TRUE AND ACCURATE. I UNDERSTAND THAT IN THE EVENT OF MY EMPLOYMENT BY YOU, I SHALL BE SUBJECT TO DISMISSAL IF ANY OF THE INFORMATION I HAVE GIVEN IN THIS APPLICATION IS FALSE OR IF I HAVE FAILED TO GIVE ANY MATERIAL INFORMATION HEREIN REQUESTED. I UNDERSTAND ALL EMPLOYEES ARE "EMPLOYEES AT WILL" UNLESS THERE IS A SPECIFIC WRITTEN CONTRACT.

APPLICANT'S SIGNATURE

DATE

COMMENTS   (DO NOT WRITE BELOW THIS LINE - OFFICE USE ONLY)

SAMPLE 15-3b

Appendix 1

FORMS OF ADDRESS

Federal, State, and Local Government Officials

Addressee	Form of Address	Salutation
Cabinet officers:		
Secretary of State	The Honorable John Smith Secretary of State	Dear Mr. Smith:*
Attorney General	The Honorable John Smith Attorney General of the United States	
Chief Justice of the Supreme Court	The Chief Justice of the United States	Dear Mr. Chief Justice:*
Governor	The Honorable John Smith Governor of _____	Dear Governor Smith:
Judge, federal	The Honorable John Smith United States District Judge	Dear Judge Smith
Judge, state or local	The Honorable John Smith Chief Judge of the Court of Appeals	Dear Judge Smith:
Lieutenant Governor	The Honorable John Smith Lieutenant Governor of _____	Dear Mr. Smith:
Mayor	The Honorable John Smith Mayor of _____	Dear Mayor Smith:
President, U.S.	The President	Dear Mr. President:*
Representative, state (same format for assemblyman)	The Honorable John Smith House of Representatives State Capitol	Dear Mr. Smith:
Representative, U.S.	The Honorable John Smith The United States House of Representatives	Dear Mr. Smith:
Senator, U.S.	The Honorable John Smith United States Senate	Dear Senator Smith:
Speaker, U.S. House of Representatives	The Honorable John Smith Speaker of the House of Representatives	Dear Mr. Speaker:*
Vice-President, U.S.	The Vice-President United States Senate	Dear Mr. Vice-President:*

*Women in these positions can be addressed as Mrs., Ms., or Miss.

Clerical and Religious Orders

Addressee	Form of Address	Salutation
Archbishop	The Most Reverend Archbishop of _____ The Most Reverend John Smith Archbishop of _____	Your Excellency: Dear Archbishop Smith:
Bishop, Roman Catholic	The Most Reverend John Smith Bishop of _____	Your Excellency: Dear Bishop Smith:
Bishop, Episcopal	The Right Reverend John Smith Bishop of _____	Right Reverend Sir: Dear Bishop Smith:
Clergyman, Protestant	The Reverend John Smith The Reverend Dr. John Smith (with a doctor's degree)	Dear Mr. Smith:* Dear Dr. Smith:
Monsignor	The Right Reverend	Dear Monsignor Smith:
Patriarch (of an Eastern church)	His Beatitude the Patriarch of _____	Most Reverend Lord:
Pope	His Holiness Pope His Holiness the Pope	Your Holiness: Most Holy Father:
Priest	The Reverend Father Smith The Reverend John Smith	Dear Father Smith: Dear Father:
Rabbi	Rabbi John Smith Rabbi John Smith, D.D. (with a doctor's degree)	Dear Rabbi Smith: Dear Dr. Smith:
Sisterhood, member of	Sister Mary Angelica, S.C.	Dear Sister Mary Angelica: Dear Sister:
Sisterhood, superior of	The Reverend Mother Superior, S.C.	Reverend Mother: Dear Reverend Mother:

College and University Officials
Dean of a college or university	Dean John Smith	Dear Dean Smith:
President of a college or university	President John Smith	Dear President Smith:
Professor at a college or university	Professor John Smith	Dear Professor Smith:
Administrator at a college or university	Robert K. Wales, Ph.D.	Dear Dr. Wales:

Miscellaneous Professional Titles
Attorney	Mr. John Smith Attorney at Law	Dear Mr. Smith:
Dentist	John Smith, D.D.S. Dr. John Smith	Dear Dr. Smith:
Physician	John Smith, M.D. Dr. John Smith	Dear Dr. Smith

*Women in these positions can be addressed as Mrs., Ms., or Miss.

SAMPLE CAPTIONS OF COURT DOCUMENTS

The style for typing the captions for court papers differs from state to state, jurisdiction to jurisdiction, and sometimes even from court to court. Some samples of various acceptable captions are illustrated below. These illustrations are merely examples of the different styles that are used. Be sure to check with your instructor to be sure you are using the caption required in your situation and/or jurisdiction.

One-Line Centered Heading:

Alabama

```
        IN THE CIRCUIT COURT OF MONTGOMERY COUNTY, ALABAMA

                                )
                                )
SAMUEL SMITH,                    )
                                )
            PLAINTIFF            )
                                )
        VS.                     ) NO. _____
                                )
CROWN MANUFACTURING, INC.,       )
A CALIFORNIA CORPORATION,        )
AND DOE ONE AND DOE TWO,         )
                                )
        DEFENDANTS               )
                                )


                ANSWER
```

Arkansas

```
        IN THE CIRCUIT COURT OF PULASKI COUNTY, ARKANSAS

SAMUEL SMITH                              PLAINTIFF

VS.              NO. _____

CROWN MANUFACTURING, INC.
and DOE ONE and DOE TWO                   DEFENDANTS
```

Kansas

```
        IN THE DISTRICT COURT OF LEAVENWORTH COUNTY, KANSAS

SAMUEL SMITH,                            PLAINTIFF,

        vs.                              Case No. _____

CROWN MANUFACTURING, INC., a
California Corporation, and
DOE ONE and DOE TWO,                     DEFENDANTS.

                COMPLAINT
```

Mississippi

```
                        CIRCUIT COURT

SAMUEL SMITH,

            PLAINTIFF

V.                                          CASE NO. ____

CROWN MANUFACTURING, INC., a
California Corporation, and
DOE ONE and DOE TWO,

            DEFENDANTS
```

Mississippi

```
                        CIRCUIT COURT

SAMUEL SMITH                             PLAINTIFF

VS.                                      CAUSE NO.____

CROWN MANUFACTURING, INC., a
California Corporation, and
DOE ONE and DOE TWO,                     DEFENDANTS
```

Nebraska

```
        IN THE DISTRICT COURT OF LANCASTER COUNTY, NEBRASKA

SAMUEL SMITH,                ]        DOCKET ____    PG. ____
                            ]
        Plaintiff,          ]
                            ]
vs.                         ]        NOTICE OF APPEAL
                            ]
CROWN MANUFACTURING, INC., a ]
California Corporation, and  ]
DOE ONE and DOE TWO,         ]
                            ]
        Defendants.          ]
```

Tennessee

IN THE CIRCUIT COURT FOR KNOX COUNTY, TENNESSEE

SAMUEL SMITH,)
        Plaintiff,)
)   CIVIL ACTION
vs.)
)   NO._____
CROWN MANUFACTURING, INC.,)
a California Corporation, and)
DOE ONE AND DOE TWO,_____)
        Defendants.)

Washington

SUPERIOR COURT OF WASHINGTON FOR _____ COUNTY

Samuel Smith,)
        Plaintiff,)
)   No. _____
      vs.)
)   COMPLAINT
Crown Manufacturing, Inc., a)
foreign corporation, John Doe,)
and James Doe,)
        Defendants.)

Multiple-Line Centered Heading:

Colorado

IN THE DISTRICT COURT IN AND FOR

THE COUNTY OF CHAFFEE

STATE OF COLORADO

Civil Action No. 5895

SAMUEL SMITH,)
          Plaintiff,)
)
      vs.)   AMENDED ANSWER
)
CROWN MANUFACTURING, INC.,)
a California corporation and)
DOE ONE and DOE TWO,)
        Defendants.)

Hawaii

NO. 3995

IN THE SUPREME COURT OF THE STATE OF HAWAII

OCTOBER TERM 19--

SAMUEL SMITH,)   CIVIL NO. 46898
)
      Plaintiff-Appellee,)   APPEAL FROM JUDGMENT FILED
)   JUNE 3, 19--
      vs.)
)   FIRST CIRCUIT COURT
CROWN MANUFACTURING, INC.,)
a California corporation, and)   HONORABLE WILLIAM SMITH
DOE ONE and DOE TWO,)   JUDGE
        Defendants-Appellants.)

RECORD ON APPEAL

Delaware

IN THE SUPERIOR COURT OF THE STATE OF DELAWARE

IN AND FOR _____ COUNTY

SAMUEL SMITH,)
          Plaintiff,)
)
      v.)   No. _____
)
CROWN MANUFACTURING, INC., a)
California corporation, and DOE)
ONE and DOE TWO,)
        Defendants.)

Idaho

W. ANTHONY PARK
Attorney General
State of Idaho

JAMES G. REID
Deputy Attorney General
State of Idaho

WAYNE MEULEMAN
Assistant Attorney General
State of Idaho
Statehouse, Boise, Idaho 83720
Telephone: (208) 555-2400

IN THE DISTRICT COURT OF THE FOURTH JUDICIAL DISTRICT OF

THE STATE OF IDAHO, IN AND FOR THE COUNTY OF ADA

SAMUEL SMITH,)
)
          Plaintiff,)   Civil No._____
)
vs.)   COMPLAINT
)
CROWN MANUFACTURING, INC.,)
a California Corporation;)
DOE ONE and DOE TWO,)
Individuals,)
        Defendants.)

Georgia

IN THE SUPERIOR COURT FOR THE

COUNTY OF FULTON, STATE OF GEORGIA

SAMUEL SMITH, §
                §
         Plaintiff, §
                §
      v. §   CIVIL ACTION FILE NO. _____
                §
CROWN MANUFACTURING, INC., a §
California Corporation, and §
DOE ONE and DOE TWO, §
        Defendants. §

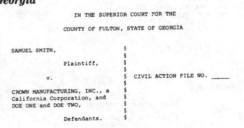

Nevada

```
Case No. _____                        Dept. No. ____


IN THE [SECOND] JUDICIAL DISTRICT COURT OF THE STATE OF NEVADA
                [EIGHTH]
               IN AND FOR THE COUNTY OF [WASHOE]
                                        [CLARK]


SAMUEL SMITH,                    )
                                 )
                  Plaintiff,     )
                                 )
         v.                      )
                                 )
CROWN MANUFACTURING, INC.,       )
a California corporation; DOE ONE )
and DOE TWO,                     )
                                 )
                  Defendants.    )
_____ )

                        PETITION
```

Nevada

```
IN THE _____ JUDICIAL DISTRICT COURT OF THE STATE OF NEVADA

         IN AND FOR THE COUNTY OF _____


SAMUEL SMITH,                    )  Case No. 216,000
                                 )
                  Plaintiff,     )
                                 )
         v.                      )
                                 )
CROWN MANUFACTURING, INC.,       )
a California corporation; DOE ONE )
and DOE TWO,                     )
                                 )
                  Defendants.    )
_____ )

                        ANSWER
```

New Hampshire

```
             UNITED STATES DISTRICT COURT
                     FOR THE
              DISTRICT OF NEW HAMPSHIRE

. . . . . . . . . . . . . . . . .
                               .
SAMUEL SMITH,                  .
                               .
               Plaintiff       .
                               .
         v.                    .          Civil No. _____
                               .
CROWN MANUFACTURING, INC.,     .
a California Corporation,      .
and DOE ONE AND DOE TWO,       .
                               .
               Defendants      .
. . . . . . . . . . . . . . . . .
```

Ohio

```
              COURT OF COMMON PLEAS
              FRANKLIN COUNTY, OHIO

SAMUEL SMITH                     )
Street Address                   )
City, State ZIP                  )
                                 )
         Plaintiff               )
                                 )  No. _____
         v.                      )
                                 )  SUMMONS
CROWN MANUFACTURING, INC., a     )
California Corporation           )
Street Address                   )
City, State ZIP                  )
and DOE ONE and DOE TWO          )
                                 )
         Defendants              )
```

Oklahoma

```
    IN THE DISTRICT COURT, _____ COUNTY

    COURTHOUSE, (or address of court),
         (city or town) , OKLAHOMA


Samuel Smith,                    )
                                 )
               Plaintiff,        )
                                 )
         vs.                     )          No. _____
                                 )
Crown Manufacturing, Inc., a     )
California Corporation, and Doe One and )
Doe Two,                         )
                                 )
         Defendants.             )
```

Oregon

```
      IN THE CIRCUIT COURT OF THE STATE OF OREGON

              FOR THE COUNTY OF _____

SAMUEL SMITH,                    )
                                 )
               Plaintiff,        )
                                 )  No. _____
         v.                      )
                                 )  COMPLAINT
CROWN MANUFACTURING, INC., a     )
California Corporation, and DOE  )
ONE and DOE TWO,                 )
                                 )
         Defendants.             )
```

Pennsylvania

```
IN THE COURT OF COMMON PLEAS OF BUCKS COUNTY, PENNSYLVANIA
                 CIVIL ACTION - LAW

SAMUEL SMITH                 :       NO. 73-1060-65-2

         VS.                 :       I.D. # 02056

CROWN MANUFACTURING, INC.,   :       IN ASSUMPSIT
a California Corporation,
and DOE ONE AND DOE TWO,     :

                   AMENDED ANSWER
```

With the Word *Scilicet:*

Indiana

```
STATE OF INDIANA  )              IN THE MARION CIRCUIT COURT
                  ) SS:
COUNTY OF MARION  )


SAMUEL SMITH,                )
                Plaintiff,   )
    -vs-                      )    CAUSE NO. C78-1069
                             )
CROWN MANUFACTURING, INC.,    )
a California Corporation, and )
DOE ONE and DOE TWO,          )
                             )
                Defendants.   )


                    ANSWER
```

New Hampshire

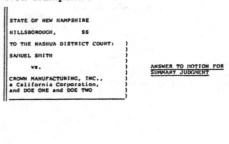

```
STATE OF NEW HAMPSHIRE

HILLSBOROUGH,        SS
TO THE NASHUA DISTRICT COURT:  )
SAMUEL SMITH                    )
    vs.                         )    ANSWER TO MOTION FOR
                               )    SUMMARY JUDGMENT
CROWN MANUFACTURING, INC.,      )
a California Corporation,       )
and DOE ONE and DOE TWO         )
```

Maine

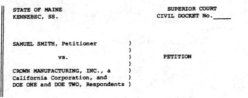

```
STATE OF MAINE                    SUPERIOR COURT
KENNEBEC, SS.                     CIVIL DOCKET No.____


SAMUEL SMITH, Petitioner    )
                           )
        vs.                )       PETITION
                           )
CROWN MANUFACTURING, INC., a )
California Corporation, and  )
DOE ONE and DOE TWO, Respondents )
```

Rhode Island

```
STATE OF RHODE ISLAND                   SUPERIOR COURT

NEWPORT, Sc. [or PROVIDENCE, Sc.]


Samuel Smith, Plaintiff    :
                           :
    v.                     :  C. A. No. 87-667
                           :
Crown Manufacturing, Inc., :
        Defendant


                M O T I O N
```

Massachusetts

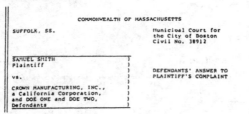

```
            COMMONWEALTH OF MASSACHUSETTS

SUFFOLK, SS.                 Municipal Court for
                             the City of Boston
                             Civil No. 38912

SAMUEL SMITH                )
Plaintiff                   )
                            )
vs.                         )     DEFENDANTS' ANSWER TO
                            )     PLAINTIFF'S COMPLAINT
CROWN MANUFACTURING, INC.,  )
a California Corporation,    )
and DOE ONE and DOE TWO,    )
Defendants                  )
```

Vermont

```
STATE OF VERMONT                      COUNTY COURT
CHITTENDEN COUNTY, SS

                        Civil Action, Docket Number____

SAMUEL SMITH, Plaintiff    )
    of (City)              )
    (County)               )
        v.                 )   (Title of Document)
CROWN MANUFACTURING, INC., )
    of (City)              )
    (County)               )
and DOE ONE and DOE TWO, Defendants )
```

New Hampshire

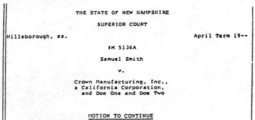

```
        THE STATE OF NEW HAMPSHIRE
            SUPERIOR COURT

Hillsborough, ss.                 April Term 19--

                #M 5136A
            Samuel Smith
                  v.
        Crown Manufacturing, Inc.,
          a California Corporation,
           and Doe One and Doe Two


            MOTION TO CONTINUE
```

Wyoming

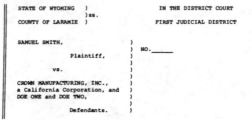

```
STATE OF WYOMING   )          IN THE DISTRICT COURT
                   )ss.
COUNTY OF LARAMIE  )          FIRST JUDICIAL DISTRICT


SAMUEL SMITH,                )
              Plaintiff,     )  NO.____
                            )
    vs.                     )
                            )
CROWN MANUFACTURING, INC.,   )
a California Corporation, and )
DOE ONE and DOE TWO,         )
                            )
              Defendants.    )
```

Miscellaneous

Florida

IN THE CIRCUIT COURT OF THE THIRTEENTH JUDICIAL CIRCUIT IN AND
FOR HILLSBOROUGH COUNTY, STATE OF FLORIDA.   CIVIL ACTION.

SAMUEL SMITH,

             Plaintiff,

vs.   CASE NO. 74-6789D

CROWN MANUFACTURING, INC.,   DIVISION "E"
a California Corporation,
and DOE ONE AND DOE TWO,

             Defendants.

New York

SUPERIOR COURT OF THE STATE OF NEW YORK
COUNTY OF NEW YORK

SAMUEL SMITH,   Index Number: 6843/--

             Plaintiff,

     -against-   ANSWER

CROWN MANUFACTURING, INC., and
"JOHN DOE,"

             Defendants.

Louisiana

ORDER ESTABLISHING PRIORITY CLAIMS
AND DIRECTING PAYMENT OF SAME

SAMUEL SMITH   NUMBER _____ , DIVISION _____

VERSUS   19TH JUDICIAL DISTRICT COURT

                       PARISH OF EAST BATON ROUGE

CROWN MANUFACTURING, INC.,   STATE OF LOUISIANA
AND DOE ONE AND DOE TWO

North Carolina

NORTH CAROLINA   IN THE GENERAL COURT OF JUSTICE

PASQUOTANK COUNTY   DISTRICT COURT DIVISION

                       File No._____
                       Film No._____

SAMUEL SMITH,

             Plaintiff

     Vs.   COMPLAINT

CROWN MANUFACTURING, INC.,
a California Corporation,
and DOE ONE AND DOE TWO

             Defendants

Maryland

SAMUEL SMITH
840 Elm Drive
Baltimore, Maryland 21220
         Plaintiff

        vs   IN THE CIRCUIT COURT
                       FOR
CROWN MANUFACTURING, INC.   _____COUNTY
a California Corporation,
and DOE ONE AND DOE TWO
840 Main Street
Timonium, Maryland 21093
        Defendant

             DECLARATION

North Dakota

STATE OF NORTH DAKOTA   IN ____DISTRICT____ COURT

COUNTY OF ___BURLEIGH___   FOURTH JUDICIAL DISTRICT

Samuel Smith,
            Plaintiff,

       vs.

Crown Manufacturing, Inc., a
California Corporation and
Doe One and Doe Two,
          Defendants.   SUMMONS

               CIVIL NO. _____

New Jersey

GEORGE F. KUGLER, JR.
Attorney General of New Jersey
Attorney for Defendants
State House Annex
Trenton, New Jersey 08625

By: Kenneth F. Olex
     Deputy Attorney General
     (609) 555-9999

                      MERCER COUNTY COURT
                      LAW DIVISION
                      DOCKET NO. 1973

SAMUEL SMITH,

             Plaintiff,   Civil Action

     v.   SUMMONS

CROWN MANUFACTURING, INC.,
a California Corporation
and DOE ONE and DOE TWO,

         Defendants.

South Carolina

STATE OF SOUTH CAROLINA)
                     IN THE COURT OF COMMON PLEAS
COUNTY OF   )

SAMUEL SMITH,   )

         Plaintiff,   )

     -vs-   )   COMPLAINT

CROWN MANUFACTURING,   )   CASE NO.
INC., a California   )
Corporation, and   )
DOE ONE AND DOE TWO   )

        Defendants   )

Virginia

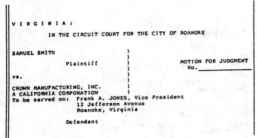

```
V I R G I N I A :

          IN THE CIRCUIT COURT FOR THE CITY OF ROANOKE

SAMUEL SMITH                    )
              Plaintiff         )          MOTION FOR JUDGMENT
                                )          No.
vs.                             )
                                )
CROWN MANUFACTURING, INC.       )
A CALIFORNIA CORPORATION        )
To be served on:  Frank A. JONES, Vice President
                  12 Jefferson Avenue
                  Roanoke, Virginia

              Defendant
```

West Virginia

```
IN THE CIRCUIT COURT OF KANAWHA COUNTY, WEST VIRGINIA

SAMUEL SMITH,
              Plaintiff

v.                                    Civil Action No. _____

DOE ONE, DOE TWO, and CROWN
MANUFACTURING, INC., a corporation,
              Defendants

              COMPLAINT
```

Wisconsin

```
STATE OF WISCONSIN        CIRCUIT COURT        DANE COUNTY

Samuel Smith,
              Plaintiff

       vs.                                     COMPLAINT

Crown Manufacturing, Inc.,
and Doe One and Doe Two,

              Defendants
```

INDEX